PEAK WITH BOOKS

An Early Childhood Resource for Balanced Literacy

THIRD EDITION

Marjorie R. Nelsen
Jan Nelsen-Parish

Illustrator
Nadine M. LaLonde

CORWIN PRESS, INC.
A Sage Publications Company
Thousand Oaks, California

For information address:

Corwin Press, Inc.
A Sage Publications Company
2455 Teller Road
Thousand Oaks, California 91320
E-mail: order@corwinpress.com

SAGE Publications Ltd.
6 Bonhill Street
London EC2A 4PU
United Kingdom

SAGE Publications India Pvt. Ltd.
M-32 Market
Greater Kailash I
New Delhi 110 048 India

Printed in the United States of America

Library of Congress Cataloging-in-Publication Data

Nelsen, Marjorie R.
    Peak with books: An early childhood resource for balanced literacy /
Marjorie R. Nelsen, Jan Nelsen-Parish. — 3rd ed.
        p. cm.
    Includes bibliographical references and index.
    ISBN 0-8039-6796-9 (alk. paper)
        1. Children — Books and reading — United States. 2. Children's stories
— Study and teaching — United States. 3. Reading — Parent participation
United States. I. Nelsen-Parish, Jan. II. Title.
    Z1037.A1 N347 1999
    011.62 — dc21
                                                                99-6080

This book is printed on acid-free paper.

99 00 01 02 03 04 05 10 9 8 7 6 5 4 3 2 1

Typesetter: Publisher's Studio
Cover Designer: Michelle Lee

Contents

Foreword

by Jim Trelease, Author of
<u>The New Read-Aloud Handbook</u>

Dr. Burton L. White, author of *The First Three Years* and one of America's leading child development experts, maintains that for more than half a century psychologists focused on "sick" people and wondered, "What went wrong in their lives?" It is only recently that we've begun to focus on "well" individuals and wonder, "What went right?"

The same thing could be said for child development. For years, Dr. White nötes, we studied children who behaved in a way that set them apart from their peers, children who were slower, less curious, less coordinated, and less prepared for school experiences. What went wrong, we wondered. But recently, experts like Dr. White have begun to focus on "well" children, to study their early childhood years to find out "what went right" in those formative years. With that knowledge in hand, the next step would be to help parents and educators put those "right" things into the lives of all children and not just some.

In numerous studies, certain things quickly became evident in the lives of children who achieved early school success with ease. These were children who had frequent conversations with adults. That is, they were talked to *and* listened to. Their opinions and feelings were solicited in conversations with their caregivers.

These successful children were the ones whose experiential background included more than just watching television adventures. Instead, they had their *own* adventures—bus rides, car trips, planes, visits to the zoo, museum, post office, fire station, and library. Through all of these experiences, language flowed between child and parent as the child built understanding with the blocks of experience.

Some of the most dramatic results were seen in studies of children whose parents or caregivers read to them on a regular basis. Indeed, when the national Commission on Reading issued its 1985 report, *Becoming a Nation of Readers,* reading aloud to children was singled out as the single most important activity to ensure future classroom success for the child.

In light of that finding, Marge Nelsen, a nationally acclaimed educator, has provided parents and teachers with a simple, hands-on guide to the experience of reading to young children. In *Peak With Books,* Marge and her coauthor, Jan Nelsen-Parish, outline dozens of the best books for reading aloud and provide follow-up activities that clarify or expand the child's understanding of the story.

It is these activities that separate this book from others in the marketplace. The authors' parent and classroom experiences convinced them of one thing above all others: The prime purpose of becoming a reader is to *enjoy* reading. With that in mind, their activities avoid the drill-and-skill approach some would impose on youngsters. The questions, conversations, and activities are failure free and fun-filled.

Here are the simple, easy-to-do things that every parent or teacher can share with children to make their literacy learning not only stress-free but a time of joy as well. Imagine the difference it makes when a child sits down to the learning table with all the tools a student needs: words for questions and answers, curiosity, attention span, confidence, and background knowledge. That difference, quite simply, is what *Peak With Books* is all about.

Preface

Honoring Diversity

If the classroom is to be a place where diversity is honored and respected, it must begin with us, the teachers. Multiculturalism needs to influence our selection of storybooks *all* year long, not just within a theme topic. Throughout *Peak With Books,* we have included our choices of storybooks with positive portrayals of the daily lives of children of many cultures. Not only do these books bring the finest quality literature and illustrations into your classroom, but they also bring a sense of pride and respect. That is the power of books, especially *Hush! A Thai Lullaby* by Minfong Ho, *Mama, Do You Love Me?* by Barbara M. Joosse, and *The Old Man & His Door* by Gary Soto.

New Chapters and Illustrations

Each of the six new chapters features an irresistible, recently published storybook. Written by well-known authors and illustrated with charm, the stories are rich with humor, rhythmic language, and predictable story lines. We have included photographs of the authentic responses of kindergarten and first grade children in multi-age classrooms. The children want you to see their celebrations of learning as they bring their own meaning to the stories through retellings, innovations, drama, charting, and story maps. Their beautiful art responses are a marvelous addition to the new text.

Learning Through Inquiry: Full-Color Insert of Children's Art

Inquiry is experiential learning, driven by questions generated by the students themselves and the answers they find through research. A full-color insert is devoted to two concept topics of study in kindergarten and first grade multi-age classrooms. The inquiry method of research and discovery, using both fiction and nonfiction literature, is presented through fascinating pictures of the children's responses and presentations of *The Grouchy Ladybug* by Eric Carle and *The Birth of a Whale* by John Archambault. The addition of full-color photographs truly enhances the new edition. The emphasis on inquiry adds strength to the underlying philosophy of each edition: Children must learn not only to read, but to *want* to read.

Story Structure and Graphics

Children develop a sense of story when they are able to see that all stories have a setting, characters, events, and an ending. A variety of strategies to help children understand story structure are presented through creative drama, discussions, sequencing the events of a story to a satisfying conclusion, and illustrating plot diagrams. Story structure matrices are appealing visual tools to help children organize story elements. We have given examples of circle story maps; beginning, middle, and ending charts; and child-illustrated summaries of the setting, characters, and events of a story. The graphics depicting story structure add a new look and a new appeal to the book.

ACKNOWLEDGMENTS

Many thanks to the reviewers of the third edition of *Peak With Books* for more than they possibly realize: Julia Beyeler, Ph.D., The University of Akron—Wayne College; Donna Goldammer, Ed.D., University of Sioux Falls; and Dr. Robert L. Doan, University of South Alabama.

We could not have written about children and their authentic responses to literature without teachers who were willing to open their classroom doors and let others look inside. Many teachers work diligently within the walls of one room, largely isolated from others. It is only the willingness of educators to collaborate and to share meaningful experiences that will break down that isolation. Consequently, we are grateful to a number of extraordinary early childhood educators and their students who let us see how they learn together. Their classrooms joyously reflect the mutuality of learning. For teaching us all, we thank:

Kim Bell and her kindergarten, Arbor Ridge Elementary, Orlando, Florida; Natalie Campbell and her kindergarten, Laurel Oak Elementary, Naples, Florida; Susan Conyers and her second grade, Pinellas Central Elementary School, Pinellas Park, Florida; Robyn DeCresie and her kindergarten, Shore Acres Elementary, St. Petersburg, Florida; Stephanie Elliot and her first grade, Keeth Elementary, Winter Springs, Florida; Mrs. Lewis and her Chapter I kindergarten, St. Petersburg, Florida; Pam McDonald and Sharon Rogier and their multi-age 1–2 class, Keeth Elementary, Winter Springs, Florida; Cindi Marshall and her kindergarten, Pinellas Central Elementary, Pinellas Park, Florida; Gwen Mugman and kindergarten, Union Park Elementary, Orlando, Florida; Mark and Graham Nelsen, multi-age K–2 students, Altamonte Springs Elementary, Altamonte Springs, Florida; Louise Stuart and her multi-age K–1 class, Country Hills Elementary, Coral Springs, Florida.

For their letters of encouragement, warm thanks to these revered authors—Aileen Fisher, Margaret Hillert, Bobbi Katz, and Charlotte Pomerantz.

We are thankful to three other colleagues and friends. Nancy Rolfs has nourished our writing with her years of experience as an early childhood educator. She has enriched the everyday learning activities with her suggestions and has been a loving cheerleader as well. Artie Almeida, an internationally known music clinician, has given generously of her time and knowledge. We appreciate her remarkably creative approach to integrated learning through music activities and selections. Mary Cornelius, storyteller and teacher extraordinaire, has contributed learning activities and six original finger rhymes to accompany our story selections.

We are grateful to editor Jay Whitney who has believed wholeheartedly in *Peak With Books* and has respected our voice as authors. It is because of his vision that the third edition came into being.

Michelle Derrow is a young writer wise and skillful beyond her years. We appreciate her gentle suggestions and honest feedback as she read the introduction and full-color inquiry insert.

Introduction

Peak With Books began in 1905. It was the year Bernice was born.

Alone at the age of five, Bernice stood behind the curtains of an empty parlor, waiting for her family to return. They never came. Although the older, childless couple who took her in learned to love the gentle, red-haired girl, eleven years passed before they adopted her. Even then, she did not call them mother and father.

Years later, when asked about childhood memories, a resilient Bernice quickly responded, "I remember Longfellow, James Whitcomb Riley, Sara Crewe, *Black Beauty* and *The Secret Garden.*" They were warm, familiar friends who mended the cracks of loneliness in an abandoned child's heart. Perhaps Bernice was comforted by a reflection of herself in *The Secret Garden,* the story of an orphan who discovers a healing friendship in a forbidden garden. Perhaps that is why my mother, Bernice, shared the story with me.

The delight of my childhood Christmases was a brown paper-wrapped package that traveled 900 miles to be placed, always on time, under our tree. It was purposely the last gift I opened. I read my new treasure from cover to cover before nighttime pulled down the shade on another Christmas. My adoptive grandmother, who cherished the classics, never forgot. From those impressions of childhood came the compelling desire to share the beauty of language and the warmth of sitting close and reading aloud to children. I wanted Bernice's literary heritage to become a standard of excellence for my own children and for those I taught. Happily, it did.

Through the years, there were always children who had not heard the rhythm and rhyme of Mother Goose, nor had they met the Little Red Hen or Peter Rabbit. They saw no magic in my treasure chest of brown paper-wrapped packages, introduced one by one at just the right moment of curiosity. I was consumed with the challenge of introducing these children to literary experiences. They were not going to fall in love with reading because of sterile workbooks and mindless dittos. They would fall in love with reading only if they were read to, like Bernice.

Convinced that meaningful reading and writing can take place all day in all subject areas, I first published *Peak With Books*. The goals were twofold—to re-create in early childhood classrooms the loving read-aloud bedtime experience that not all children had known, and to provide teachers with a guide to using familiar, beloved storybooks for early literacy experiences with text.

Later, my daughter Jan, a fourth-generation early childhood teacher, joined me in writing the revised, expanded *Peak With Books*. The intent of this second edition was to embrace first grade classrooms as well. Although research was embedded in the text, we chose to write in friendly, teacher language rather than a theorist's speech. We wrote from the inside—the teacher's and the child's views of learning.

The story-related strategies and responses in every chapter shared the common thread of sensory involvement, oral language, art and music, reading and writing, science and math, all woven into a literature-rich environment. The text married marvelous children's poetry, finger rhymes, and music to each storybook. We included an index to thematic units, bibliographies, and a challenging foreword by Jim Trelease, author of the million copy bestseller, *The New Read-Aloud Handbook*. We were gratified with the response. Teachers found they did not need to seek other resources because everything was complete in one volume.

So why a third edition? We respect the fact that some things *don't* change—a child's fundamental urge to make meaning of words, the joy of the breathtaking accomplishment of a child reading, the authentic learning responses that abound in a classroom rich in rhythmic literature and experiential, sensory learning. However, some things *do* change. As early childhood educators, *we* have changed. After observing and listening to countless teachers and children learning together and from each other, we are more informed and energized than ever before. We have thoroughly assessed each chapter of *Peak With Books* and made many compelling changes in this edition.

Dedication

The third edition, like the first and second, is dedicated to Bernice and the books that touched her heart and made something beautiful out of her life. So be it with the children we teach. May the brown paper packages keep coming, for the impressions of childhood go with us into maturity.

EXPANDED IN THE THIRD EDITION

* From birth, the wiring of millions of neurons in a child's brain creates a tapestry of lifelong learning connections. This knowledge of brain development compels us to focus on how and when a child best learns. To meet the challenge of brain-compatible instruction, in this edition we have expanded concrete involvement, repetition, and sensory exploration methods to assimilate a child's prior knowledge into meaningful learning.

* Because a child's brain is thirsty for the patterns of language and music, we have included more of the finest of children's poetry and musical activities. *Peak With Books* incorporates classical and traditional music, the infectious beat of eighty-four story-related music selections, eighty-four finger rhymes, and the wit and melody of eighty-two delightful poems written by best-loved children's poets. The new additions will bring energizing sounds and learning to your literature-based classroom.

* The 300 extraordinary storybooks highlighted in relevant chapters represent the absolute best in children's literature. You will find new nonfiction books that engage readers from the very first page; culturally rich stories; charming, contemporary storybooks; and time-honored classics. It is a treasure chest you will turn to again and again.

* It is the lively *talk* that surrounds literature experiences in a classroom that nurtures connections to children's lives. Consequently, the lessons overflow with opportunities for children's oral language. The conversations and questions that are the heart of shared reading have been carefully rewritten to ensure aesthetic responses and higher level thinking skills. The creative drama involvement that so naturally creates story meaning is a part of every chapter. Our renewed emphasis on oral language is reflective of the many early childhood educators who continue to help us change as teachers and learners today.

* The primary focus of every story, poem, drama, music, and art response is always on children enjoying and understanding the text. That enjoyment and understanding create a natural foundation for teaching strategies and skills. We have expanded ways to teach concepts of print, parts of speech, vocabulary development, and letter-sound relationships. We have paid particular attention to phonemic awareness and suggested specific ways to help children develop an understanding of phonemes and rhyming word families.

* Structure, model, guided, and content writing are essential to writing instruction and are included in every chapter. It is process writing that has captured our attention in this edition. Children write best when they write from their own experiences and for their own purposes. Choices are essential if children are going to see themselves as authors. We have given them readily.

ABOUT *PEAK WITH BOOKS*

To "peak with books" simply means to reach the highest point attainable in early literacy through the warmth and friendship of books. Each of the forty-two chapters is a self-contained literature-based study with its own distinct emphasis and appeal. Within each chapter, the interdisciplinary learning expressions have been carefully planned for early readers and writers. From prekindergarten to first grade, you will find a progression of authentic learning experiences in every chapter.

In our many years of teaching, we confess to a little resentment toward guides that told us what to say to children. That is not our intention in *Peak With Books*. Of course you will use your own words, ideas, and style of teaching because you know your children better than anyone. The purpose of the chatty, conversational style is to keep us all focused on our mutual objective—teaching children through the excitement and pleasure of shared stories and shared love.

Throughout *Peak With Books,* italics are used to denote emphasis on word meaning, such as story vocabulary. Italics also identify specific examples of children's text and responses, to be recorded in their original class books, murals, charts, and retellings. Quotation marks are used to identify direct quotes from storybooks. They also signify conversation within children's written text.

The use of the pronouns *he, she, him,* and *her* has been alternated and balanced throughout the book.

Illustrations

We can hear you now. "My children don't draw like that!" We know, and so does our talented graphic artist who is the mother of a kindergartener. We wanted you to smile and enjoy the charming illustrations of the ideas in the text as you motivate your children to be creative. You know the adage—a picture is worth a thousand words—or is it ten thousand?

Music

Children love the infectious beat, the patterns, and the joy of music. The songs suggested in this book are thematic springboards into learning. They are lively, singable, participatory, and often humorous. Self-expression and meaningful responses to music will create a rich learning environment in your classroom. Furthermore, the selections of classical music will stimulate creativity and the building of lifetime neural connections in children's brains. Don't plan your day without music!

Poetry

Children will always love the rhythm and repetition, the silliness and seriousness of poetry. The language of poetry invites children into the endless learning of attentive listening. When poems become familiar, children create their own word pictures and illustrations. We took great pleasure in finding both humorous and beautiful poems we could marry to the themes of the lessons.

Involvement

The first reading of a story is intended to capture children's interest and immerse them in the text and the illustrations. The interactive involvement that follows is a crucial link between the content of the story and the process of making meaning. Involvement also teaches children the beauty of story language and the difference between that story language and spoken language. The numerous choral reading, drama, and music responses will help children understand what they hear and read before skills, strategies, and vocabulary are emphasized.

Reproductions and Retellings

Reproductions and retellings are children's responses to literature through art, music, and drama, using their own language. In a reproduction, children make language come to life as they interact with the original text. A retelling is a summary of a story in the children's words. It is an effective tool for teaching children to recognize and organize story elements.

Innovations and Caption Books

Innovations follow reproductions. In an innovation, children create a new text by using the predictable, rhythmic pattern of a story. They may change the words, the characters, or the setting as they introduce new vocabulary in meaningful context. A caption book is an innovation with a repeated caption on each page, creating familiar, predictable text that is easily read.

When your children innovate a story or poem, *always* give credit to the original work on the cover or the title page of their adaptation.

The Writing Process

Early writing is a term that describes a child's developmental process in learning to write through explorations and approximations. The *process,* not the product, is paramount, as the young child writes from personal experience.

The constructive process of writing teaches children how to read unknown words. Children analyze phonemic sequences and use their knowledge of letter-sound relationships as they search for the probable letters to construct words. Journal writing, model writing, content writing, and process writing offer children the opportunity to discover the meaning of words as they make connections to their own lives.

A Print-Rich Environment

A literacy-rich environment offers repeated reading successes. Surround children with their own words written down—their class books, wall murals, journals, and language charts. Add print to your art activities and bulletin boards. Fill every learning center with independent reading activities. Create a poetry center; a pocket chart center; a listening center; an ABC center; a story sequencing center; a theme library; a nonfiction library; art, writing, math, and science centers filled with literacy props; a read-the-room center with back-scratchers and feathers and paint sticks as pointers. Surrounding children with print is a key to motivating readers.

Parent Involvement

No guide to early childhood learning is complete without family involvement. Because home and school must work together, the last page of every lesson offers creative suggestions for nurturing parenting and for everyday learning activities. The authentic, literature-based activites are correlated to classroom learning. The Everyday Learning Activities page in each chapter may be reproduced and sent home as a Parent/Caregiver letter. This page is a resource for classroom learning experiences as well.

About the Authors

Marjorie R. Nelsen

Marjorie Nelsen, an educator for more than thirty years, is a teacher of young children, their parents, and early childhood educators. The author received her B.A. degree in Elementary Education from Wheaton College, Illinois, and did postgraduate work in Early Childhood. Marjorie was a primary school teacher for nineteen years, and in 1987 was chosen Teacher of the Year in Seminole County, Florida from among 2400 teachers. That same year she was 1 of only 111 in the nation to receive a National Christa McAuliffe Fellowship Award for Educators. She was a recipient of the University of Central Florida Economics in Education Award, and was nominated for Who's Who in American Education. Marjorie is the founder and director of Partners In Learning, Inc., an educational organization providing seminars and literacy workshops to early childhood parents and teachers. In addition to *Peak With Books*, she is the author of *The Terrific No Tears Bedtime Book*, an interactive book for ages two to six; and *A Child's Book of Responsibilities*, an interactive book to develop self-reliance through guided tasks for three- to eight-year-olds. She is married, the mother of four and a devoted grandmother of eleven.

Jan Nelsen-Parish

Coauthor Jan Nelsen-Parish is a fourth generation kindergarten teacher and a National Early Childhood Consultant for primary teachers and administrators. Jan received her B.A. degree in Elementary Education from Wheaton College, Illinois, and an M.Ed. in Early Childhood from the University of Central Florida. Jan is a nationally recognized speaker and trainer in emergent literacy, presenting at numerous national and state education conferences. She is an instructor in university graduate-level Early Childhood education courses and a contributing author of early literacy training manuals. Jan is married and the mother of two young daughters.

A Theme-Centered Approach

ANIMAL HABITATS
Birth of a Whale, The (See insert)
Blueberries for Sal
Brown Bear, Brown Bear, What Do You See?
Have You Seen My Duckling?
Hush! A Thai Lullaby
Make Way for Ducklings
Mama, Do You Love Me?
Rosie's Walk
Very Hungry Caterpillar, The

BEAR HUGS
Ask Mr. Bear
Bedtime for Frances
Blueberries for Sal
Brown Bear, Brown Bear, What Do You See?
Each Peach Pear Plum
Little Mouse, the Red Ripe Strawberry,
    and the Big Hungry Bear, The

BUGS
Grouchy Ladybug, The
Have You Seen My Duckling?
Very Hungry Caterpillar, The

CAPS AND HATS
Caps for Sale
Whistle for Willie
Who Took the Farmer's Hat?

CHICKS, DUCKS, AND BUNNIES
Good Morning, Chick
Have You Seen My Duckling?
Make Way for Ducklings
Mr. Rabbit and the Lovely Present
Pig in the Pond, The
Rosie's Walk
Runaway Bunny, The
Tale of Peter Rabbit, The
To Market, To Market

CIRCLE STORIES
Chicka Chicka Boom Boom
Grouchy Ladybug, The
Hush! A Thai Lullaby
If You Give a Mouse a Cookie
Pig in the Pond, The
Rosie's Walk
Runaway Bunny, The
Skip to My Lou
Tough Boris
Where the Wild Things Are

DAYTIME AND NIGHTTIME
Bedtime for Frances
Freight Train
Goodnight Moon
Grouchy Ladybug, The
Hush! A Thai Lullaby
Little Mouse, the Red Ripe Strawberry,
    and the Big Hungry Bear, The

Napping House, The
Noah's Ark
Peter Spier's Rain
Snowy Day, The
Ten, Nine, Eight
Where the Wild Things Are

DIVERSITY
Bedtime for Frances
Chicka Chicka Boom Boom
Each Peach Pear Plum
Hush! A Thai Lullaby
If You Give a Mouse a Cookie
Little Red Hen, The
Mama, Do You Love Me?
May I Bring a Friend?
Mr. Rabbit and the Lovely Present
Old Man and His Door, The
Peter Spier's Rain
Rosie's Walk
Snowy Day, The
To Market, To Market
Whistle for Willie
Who Took the Farmer's Hat?

FAMILY AND FRIENDS
Ask Mr. Bear
Bedtime for Frances
Blueberries for Sal
Good Morning, Chick
Hush! A Thai Lullaby
Mama, Do You Love Me?
May I Bring a Friend?
Mr. Rabbit and the Lovely Present
Old Man and His Door, The
Peter's Chair
Runaway Bunny, The
Tale of Peter Rabbit, The
Ten, Nine, Eight
Tough Boris
Whistle for Willie

FARMYARD
Good Morning, Chick
Little Red Hen, The
Pig in the Pond, The
Rosie's Walk
Skip to My Lou
Who Took the Farmer's Hat?

FOLKLORE AND FAIRY TALES
Each Peach Pear Plum
Gingerbread Boy, The
Hush! A Thai Lullaby
Little Red Hen, The
Mama, Do You Love Me?
Oh, A-Hunting We Will Go
Skip to My Lou
Three Billy Goats Gruff, The

GIVING AND SHARING
Ask Mr. Bear
If You Give a Mouse a Cookie
Little Mouse, the Red Ripe Strawberry,
    and the Big Hungry Bear, The
Mama, Do You Love Me?
Mr. Rabbit and the Lovely Present
Peter's Chair
Tough Boris

MANNERS
Grouchy Ladybug, The
If You Give a Mouse a Cookie
Little Red Hen, The
Mama, Do You Love Me?
May I Bring a Friend?
Mr. Rabbit and the Lovely Present
Where the Wild Things Are

PUDDLES, PONDS, AND OCEANS
Birth of a Whale, The (See insert)
Have You Seen My Duckling?
Make Way for Ducklings
Noah's Ark
Peter Spier's Rain
Pig in the Pond, The
Three Billy Goats Gruff, The
Tough Boris

TIME
Bedtime for Frances
Caps for Sale
Grouchy Ladybug, The
May I Bring a Friend?
Skip to My Lou
Very Hungry Caterpillar, The
Where the Wild Things Are

WALKING
Ask Mr. Bear
Blueberries for Sal
Brown Bear, Brown Bear, What Do You See?
Caps for Sale
Mr. Rabbit and the Lovely Present
Old Man and His Door, The
On Market Street
Peter Spier's Rain
Rosie's Walk
Snowy Day, The
Three Billy Goats Gruff, The
To Market, To Market

WIND AND WEATHER
Bedtime for Frances
Blueberries for Sal
Mama, Do You Love Me?
Napping House, The
Noah's Ark
Peter Spier's Rain
Snowy Day, The
Who Took the Farmer's Hat?

REINFORCING SKILLS

Title	Cultural Diversity	Letter-Sound Relationships	Phonemic Awareness	Concepts of Print	Class and Story Alphabet Books	Creative Drama	Music Expressions	Story Structure	Writing Expressions	Language Structures/Vocabulary	Parts of Speech	Math/Science Concepts	Inquiry Strategies	Theme Topics	Feelings/Emotions	Simulations/Celebrations	Higher-Order Thinking Skills
Ask Mr. Bear			•	•		•	•	•	•	•	•	•		•	•		•
Bedtime for Frances	•	•		•	•		•		•			•		•	•		•
Blueberries for Sal		•		•		•	•	•	•	•		•	•	•			•
Brown Bear, Brown Bear, What Do You See?				•		•	•		•			•		•			•
Caps for Sale		•		•	•	•		•	•	•	•	•					•
Chicka Chicka Boom Boom	•	•	•	•					•	•				•		•	•
Each Peach Pear Plum	•	•	•	•			•		•			•					•
Freight Train			•		•	•	•	•	•	•		•					•
Gingerbread Boy, The		•	•		•	•		•	•			•				•	•
Good Morning, Chick		•	•	•			•	•	•	•	•	•		•	•		•
Goodnight Moon			•	•			•		•	•		•					•
Grouchy Ladybug, The		•		•		•			•	•	•	•	•	•	•		•
Have You Seen My Duckling?		•		•		•	•	•						•			•
Hush! A Thai Lullaby	•	•	•	•		•	•	•	•	•	•	•		•			•
If You Give a Mouse a Cookie	•			•			•	•	•			•					•
Little Mouse, the Red Ripe Strawberry . . .				•			•	•	•			•			•		•
Little Red Hen, The	•			•				•	•	•				•			•
Make Way for Ducklings		•	•	•				•	•			•		•			•
Mama, Do You Love Me?	•		•	•			•	•	•	•	•	•		•	•		•
May I Bring a Friend?	•		•						•			•			•	•	•
Mr. Rabbit and the Lovely Present	•								•			•		•		•	•
Napping House, The			•	•			•		•	•	•	•					•
Noah's Ark		•		•	•		•		•		•	•					•
Oh, A-Hunting We Will Go		•	•	•		•	•		•	•		•					•
Old Man & His Door, The	•							•	•	•	•	•					•
On Market Street		•			•				•	•		•		•		•	•
Peter Spier's Rain	•			•			•	•	•		•	•					•
Peter's Chair			•	•					•		•	•			•	•	•
Pig in the Pond, The			•					•	•	•	•					•	•
Rosie's Walk	•							•	•	•			•	•			•
Runaway Bunny, The						•	•	•	•			•		•	•		•
Skip to My Lou			•	•		•	•	•	•	•		•					•
Snowy Day, The	•		•				•		•	•		•					•
Tale of Peter Rabbit, The		•				•	•	•	•	•		•		•		•	•
Ten, Nine, Eight			•	•			•		•	•	•	•			•		•
Three Billy Goats Gruff, The		•		•		•		•	•	•	•	•					•
To Market, To Market	•		•			•	•	•	•	•	•	•		•			•
Tough Boris		•		•			•	•	•	•		•	•		•		•
Very Hungry Caterpillar, The		•						•	•	•		•	•	•			•
Where the Wild Things Are		•	•	•		•		•	•	•	•				•		•
Whistle for Willie	•	•	•	•			•		•	•		•					•
Who Took the Farmer's Hat?	•			•			•		•		•	•		•		•	•

Ask Mr. Bear

by Marjorie Flack

* Concept of giving
* Story structure
* Phonemic awareness
* Animals and their products

* Structure writing/Guided writing
* Parts of speech
* Math/science concepts
* A family activity

SETTING THE STAGE

Instantly singable songs and the appealing rhyme and rhythm of finger plays will encourage children to be involved in story time.

"On the Move" by Greg and Steve, *On the Move*
(An excellent musical game about motor skills)

"Shoo Fly" by Greg and Steve, *On the Move*
(A calypso version of the original with movement activities)

LITTLE COW
One little cow, all brown and saying "moo,"   *(lift fingers as rhyme*
Sat beside another one. Then there were two.   *indicates)*
Two little cows, happy as can be,
Another came to join them. Then there were three.
Along came another cow. Then there were four.
Four little cows, glad to be alive,
Found a lonely friend. Then there were five.
Five little cows, just happy as can be,
Five little cows, friends for you and me.

CAN YOU WALK ON TIPTOE
Can you walk on tiptoe   *(follow actions as*
   As softly as a cat?   *rhyme indicates)*
Can you stamp along the road
   Stamp, stamp, just like that?
Can you take some great big strides
   Just like a giant can?
Or walk along so slowly,
   Like a bent old man?

FIRST READING

When you have a question about something, whom do you usually ask? In our story today a little boy named Danny had a question, but he couldn't ask his mother because the question was about her. Who do you think he asked? Can you tell from the cover of the story? Danny asked some of his animal friends and one of them had just the right answer. The name of the story is *Ask Mr. Bear.* It was written by Marjorie Flack; she also drew the pictures.
    Encourage the children to join in the predictable pattern of Danny's question and the animals' answers as anticipation builds to the surprise ending.

GETTING INVOLVED

Ask Mr. Bear is full of words that describe how Danny and the animals moved. What words do you remember? Let's act out the meaning of the words together. First, Danny and the Hen *skipped* along. Show me how they moved. Do you remember what they did next when the Goose joined them? Yes, try *hopping* on one foot and then change to the other foot. When the Goat came along, Danny and the animals all *galloped.* Tell me what you think that word means. Did they need space to *gallop?* Show me how the Hen and the Goose and the Goat all galloped. And last of all, what do you think the word *trotted* means?
    It is always fun to move to music, so listen to the words I say *and* to the music as you move around the room like Danny and the animals. I'll tell you whether to skip or hop or gallop, and the music will tell you when to keep your feet soft and light and when to let them bounce with great big steps. When the music is over, sit down and give yourself a big bear hug.

A CLOSER LOOK

With each rereading of a story, children gain new understanding. Pause often for a spontaneous flow of oral language as the children share their feelings and observations. Extend the learning process with your own questions in repeated readings of the story.

* I wonder what Danny is thinking in the little round picture after the title page. *(reflecting)*

* Every time I come to the words "until they met," tell me the next animal before I turn the page. *(predicting)*

* Why was a pillow a good gift for the goose to give? *(association)*

* How can a goat give a gift of cheese? *(association)*

* How can a sheep give a blanket for a gift? *(association)*

* What would happen if we changed the order of the animals? *(application)*

* Why didn't the animals want to go with Danny to find Mr. Bear? *(reasoning)*

* Would you have gone into the woods with Danny? *(reflecting)*

* What did the bear whisper in Danny's ear? *(interpretation)*

* Did Danny's present for his mother cost him any money? *(reasoning)*

* Do we have to wait for birthdays to give special gifts? *(reasoning)*

* Would you agree that *Ask Mr. Bear* has a good ending? *(evaluating)*

* I wonder if Danny ever saw Mr. Bear again. *(reflecting)*

STORY TIME EXTENSIONS

The Bear's Toothache by David McPhail

How Do Bears Sleep? by E. J. Bird

Flower Garden by Eve Bunting

The Wednesday Surprise by Eve Bunting

We're Making Breakfast for Mother by Shirley Neitzel

BALANCED LITERACY ACTIVITIES

POETRY

ON OUR WAY
What kind of walk shall we take today?
Leap like a frog? Creep like a snail?
Scamper like a squirrel with a furry tail?

Flutter like a butterfly? Chicken peck?
Stretch like a turtle with a poking-out neck?

Trot like a pony, clip clop clop?
Swing like a monkey in a treetop?

Scuttle like a crab? Kangaroo jump?
Plod like a camel with an up-and-down hump?

We could even try a brand-new way—
Walking down the street
On our own two feet.
Eve Merriam

INVOLVEMENT

CREATIVE DRAMA

Creative drama is a natural beginning to children's discovery of story structure. Ask them how they think the author created the setting of *Ask Mr. Bear*. Talk about the story characters, the sequence of events, and the satisfying turning point that solved Danny's problem. Encourage the children to make connections to their own lives because that is what gives birth to a story's meaning.

Discuss with the children how they would like to present the story. Fill your art center with a variety of materials and encourage the children to make literacy props, perhaps animal headbands with ears or beaks, paper plate stick puppets, or tagboard cards with pictures and names. Look around the room for a step Danny can sit on, a circle path to walk on, a hill to climb, and some woods for Mr. Bear to hide in. Then let the repetitious language draw the children into the story.

As you narrate the story, Danny can walk around inside a circle of children, stopping in front of the Hen to ask, "Good morning, Mrs. Hen. Can you give me something for my mother's birthday?" After the Hen replies, the two children can join hands and skip around the circle. Continue dramatizing the story with pairs of children moving around the circle as each of the animals moves. The special Big Birthday Bear Hug will be a perfect ending. Keep copies of *Ask Mr. Bear,* the literacy props, and a tape of the children's drama in your listening center for an ongoing literacy activity.

INTEGRATION

THE BIG BIRTHDAY BEAR HUG

Pencil in the outline of a simple, outdoor scene on a large piece of bulletin board paper. Using small paint sponges or colored chalk for a subdued background effect, have the children illustrate the house, the path, the hill, and the woods where Danny walked. Then have them paint the story characters on strong doubled paper. After they have cut out and stuffed the characters, staple them to the bulletin board for a colorful, three-dimensional effect. Ask the children how they can make Danny into a stick puppet to move through the story.

Together, write short sentences such as *The Hen skipped. The Goose hopped. The Goat galloped.* As you write, ask the children to listen for the sounds that make up the words. Have the children place the sentences under the right animals. Print the story title, *Ask Mr. Bear* by Marjorie Flack, across the top of the mural. On the bottom, print the words, *Danny gave his mother a Big Birthday Bear Hug!* The mural will become an inviting reading experience as the children *walk* Danny through the story they have told.

ASK MR. OWL

Involve the children in a discussion of an animal they would like to substitute for Mr. Bear in an innovation of the story. Then brainstorm about the chosen animal's environment, such as Mr. Owl in the forest. Talk about other animals that also live there and what they each could give Danny for his mother. Encourage the children to think of words to describe the gifts, such as a smooth skin from the snake, pointed antlers from the deer, bright feathers from the parrot, and tiny acorns from the squirrel. Decide on Mr. Owl's gift, which will be the surprise ending, such as *"I can give you a wink and a hoot, I love yoooooo!"*

When every child has an idea to draw, give each one a large piece of paper with the following words printed on the bottom, *"I can give you my _____ _____ ," said the _____ .* Guide individual students to hear and see the sound-letter connections in the words they dictate to you. Encourage independent writers to write their own captions using developmental spelling. Children pay conscious attention to phonemes when they identify sounds in words, both as they write and later as you edit. You also will be teaching adjectives and the purpose for quotation marks, in meaningful context.

Choose pairs of children to illustrate the cover and the title page, which will give credit to the author and the original story, *Ask Mr. Bear*. Bind the illustrated pages together in a class book titled *Ask Mr. Owl*. It will be a favorite in your reading center. Children return again and again to the books they have authored.

"I can give you my smooth skin."

"I can give you my bright feathers."

"I can give you my tiny acorns."

"I can give you a wink and a hoot, I love yoooo."

PRESENTS FOR DANNY'S MOTHER

Encourage the children to respond to *Ask Mr. Bear* with memories from their own experiences. Have they ever tried to find the perfect present for someone? Ask them to bring from home something they would have offered to Danny. Each morning, have a child hide his present inside a gift-wrapped box. The other children have a total of twenty questions to guess what is inside the box. The questions must be answered by "yes" or "no." Have a child tally the questions asked in sets of five. Point out to the children how effective concept-type questions are in directing their thinking, such as, "Is it round?" or "Is it made out of wood?" The children will see how the information learned from all the "yes" answers helps them to reason and deduct what is inside the box.

Every time they are able to guess an object before the twenty questions are used up, list that gift on a class chart, Presents for Danny's Mother. Have the children illustrate the chart, sign all their names, and think of ways to deliver their *perfect* presents to Danny's mother. If you involve your children in theme cycle choices, you may find your next emphasis will be on writing letters to Danny or planning a trip to the post office.

ON OUR WAY

The rich language of poetry opens the door to children's imaginations. With each rereading of the delightful "On Our Way," keep the focus on enjoying and understanding the poem. Give opportunities for the children to respond, surrounding the text with their oral language. Encourage them to think about the exciting words the author used to help them see the animals in their minds. After printing the poem on chart paper, ask the children to make those words come to life in their illustrations. Read the marvelous *Peck Slither and Slide* by Suse MacDonald and discuss the power of verbs in talking and in writing. It is oral language in a classroom that nurtures connections between the text and children's experiences.

EVERYDAY LEARNING ACTIVITIES

Positive parenting; developmental learning activities; and a warm, nurturing environment are major factors in a child's academic success and lifetime learning.

Ask Mr. Bear by Marjorie Flack is the story of a little boy who went for a walk, looking for a present for his mother. His walk turned into an adventure with a very happy ending. Years ago, families had an advantage. They walked everywhere together. While they were walking, they probably talked about all the little things that parents and caregivers and children like to share. You can do the same. Even a short walk in your own neighborhood can be an adventure and a real learning experience for a child. Talk about traffic and things that move. Compare what goes fast with what moves slowly. Look at houses and buildings; compare their sizes and their structures. Teach a child to look up and tell you everything she sees, or to look down and do the same. Walk backward and sideways and notice if things look different. Count dogs or bicycles, smiling faces or crying children. You are not only spending time together but also teaching a child to look around and notice her world. Her vocabulary will increase continually. A child loves big words. If she hears them often enough, the words will become a natural part of her vocabulary. At bedtime ask a child to name everything she remembers from your walk, a great memory builder. A child will never have a better teacher than a caring, attentive adult.

✳ New words are all around us. One short pleasure walk in your own neighborhood could teach a child the meaning of concrete, curb, gutter, property, hedge, and foliage. Make a book with the same words on the bottom of each page: *I went for a walk and I saw* _____. Fill in one word on each page with a simple illustration for a successful reading experience. *(vocabulary)*

✳ Walking together is a great time to practice the motor skills of hopping and skipping as the animals did in *Ask Mr. Bear*. Ask a child to hop to the next driveway on one foot, then change to the other. When she has mastered that with good balance, suggest alternate hopping, changing her feet with every hop. Skipping is one of the hardest motor skills to master. The easiest way to teach a child to skip is to take her hand and say, "Right foot, step and hop, left foot, step and hop," over and over again. When she can do it fast, she will be skipping. *(motor skills)*

✳ If a child is not ready for jumping rope the traditional way, have two people hold a rope close to the ground. Make it wiggle like a snake. Have her jump over. Raise it a little for the child to "jump the river." *(eye-foot coordination)*

✳ Suspend a child's plastic inner tube or a hula hoop (remember them?) from a porch ceiling or a tree limb. Give a child a beanbag to throw underhanded through the bull's-eye. As her skill increases, move her farther away from the target. Add to the learning by teaching addition. A bull's-eye is two points. Take turns throwing and catching. Children love catching beanbags because their fingers always manage to grab a corner. How about two more points for a catch? *(motor skills, math)*

Bedtime for Frances

by Russell Hoban

* Cultural diversity
* Letter-sound relationships
* Model writing/Process writing
* Recognizing fears
* Theme topics: wind and quilts
* Sequencing
* Nonfiction
* A family activity

SETTING THE STAGE

Instantly singable songs and the appealing rhyme and rhythm of finger plays will encourage children to be involved in story time.

"Sleep, Sleep" by Rosenshontz, *Share It*
(A hilarious song about children's excuses for not going to bed)

"A, You're Adorable" by Sharon, Lois & Bram, *Smorgasbord*

THIS LITTLE GIRL

This little girl is ready for bed,	*(finger in other palm)*
Down on the pillow she lays her head;	*(thumb as a pillow)*
Wraps herself in covers so tight,	*(wrap fingers around)*
And this is the way she sleeps all night.	*(close eyes)*
Morning comes, she opens her eyes;	*(open eyes)*
Back with a toss the cover flies;	*(open fingers)*
Up she jumps, is dressed and away,	*(index finger up)*
Ready for frolic and play all day.	*(hops away)*

TEDDY BEAR

Teddy Bear, Teddy Bear, turn around.	*(follow actions as rhyme*
Teddy Bear, Teddy Bear, touch the ground.	*indicates)*
Teddy Bear, Teddy Bear, show your shoe.	
Teddy Bear, Teddy Bear, that will do.	

Teddy Bear, Teddy Bear, run upstairs.
Teddy Bear, Teddy Bear, say your prayers.
Teddy Bear, Teddy Bear, turn off the light.
Teddy Bear, Teddy Bear, say good night.

FIRST READING

Do you know what kind of animal is on the cover of our book? It *looks* like a little bear, but it's really a badger and it belongs to the weasel family. Badgers get their name from the badges or markings on their faces. Can you see one on this little badger's face? Her name is Frances. The man who wrote the story, Russell Hoban, likes Frances so much he has written seven stories about her.

What do you think would be a good title for this story? Mr. Hoban has called it *Bedtime for Frances*. Let's find the words on the cover. Can you find them again on the title page? Do you think Frances wants us to come into her house? I'll just turn the pages and let you tell the story before we read the words.

GETTING INVOLVED

When Frances couldn't fall asleep, she made up an alphabet song. Tell me what you do when you can't fall asleep. Does music help? We can turn Frances' song into a game, but let's be careful not to wake her up. Stand up in your place and say the words with me.

A is for apple pie.	*(pretend to smell the delicious pie)*
B is for bear.	*(hunch over and shake your tail)*
C is for crocodile combing his hair.	*(pretend to comb hair)*
D is for dumplings.	*(rub your tummy and smile)*
S is for sailboat.	*(move your hands through space)*
T is for tiger.	*(make a low, growling sound)*
U is for underwear, down in the drier.	*(make spinning motion)*

Why did Frances stop singing? Do you ever see things in your room in the dark? Now let's finish the alphabet song for Frances and think of something for the letters *V, W, X, Y,* and *Z.* After all those good ideas, we are ready to read *Bedtime for Frances* again.

A CLOSER LOOK

With each rereading of a story, children gain new understanding. Pause often for a spontaneous flow of oral language as the children share their feelings and observations. Extend the learning process with your own questions in repeated readings of the story.

* What were you thinking when you listened to the story? *(reflecting)*

* What did Frances want to do before she said "good night"? *(memory)*

* Why did Frances start to sing? *(comprehension)*

* Why did the letter *T* make Frances afraid? Do you remember why Frances' father thought it was a friendly tiger? *(interpretation)*

* What did Father say was the wind's job? Father's job? Frances' job? *(comprehension)*

* Did the teddy bear also have a job? *(reasoning)*

* In your opinion, were Mother and Father patient with Frances? *(evaluating)*

* Why did Frances finally decide to go to sleep? *(interpretation)*

* Imagine you were Frances. What would you do? *(reflecting)*

* Where in the story did you think, "Oh, I just love that part"?

* Did *Bedtime for Frances* make you think of another story? *(reflecting)*

STORY TIME EXTENSIONS

Can't You Sleep, Little Bear? by Martin Waddell

The Sleepytime Book by Jan Wahl

Night Noises by Mem Fox

An Edward Lear Alphabet by Edward Lear

A You're Adorable by Martha Alexander

BALANCED LITERACY ACTIVITIES

POETRY

NIGHT COMES . . .

Night comes
leaking
out of the sky.

Stars come
peeking.

Moon comes
sneaking,
silvery-sly.

Who is
shaking,
shivery-
quaking?

Who is afraid
of the night?

Not I.

Beatrice Schenk de Regniers

IN THE NIGHT
by Marchette Chute
from *The Merry-Go-Round Book*
by Nancy Larrick

CRICK! CRACK!
by Eve Merriam
from *Blackberry Ink*
by Eve Merriam

INVOLVEMENT

AN ALPHABET SONG

In the story *Bedtime for Frances* the little badger sang an alphabet song to put herself to sleep. Pretend you are singing to Frances and introduce your boys and girls to "A, You're Adorable," an alphabet song with a cheery melody that children love to sing (see p. 8). With the music playing and the children sitting in a circle, tap one child to stand for each letter of the alphabet. Continue around the circle until all the children are standing. Play the song again and this time tap each child to sit down. Just wait for the giggles when you get to "*K*, You're so kiss-able"! It won't be many sing-alongs before the children have the words memorized.

Extension: Make alphabet cards by giving each child a letter of the alphabet to illustrate, with the words of the song printed under the letter. Keep a pointer, the alphabet cards, and a tape of the children singing "A, You're Adorable" in a learning center. Later, bind the alphabet cards into a class book for independent reading.

UNPACK YOUR PILLOWCASE

Review with the children all the things Frances wanted before she could go to sleep: a glass of milk, a piggyback ride, kisses, her teddy bear, a doll, and an open door. Because children are fascinated with little incidents from a teacher's own life, sit on the floor with a brightly colored pillowcase on your lap. As you pull out one object at a time, tell the children a story about all the little things *you* do to get yourself ready for sleep. Then every day pull a child's name out of your pillowcase. That child will come to school the next day with her own pillowcase full of little things that will describe her bedtime routine as she plays "Unpack Your Pillowcase." The oral language will easily lead to a writing experience as each child draws, writes with developmental spelling, or dictates a story about bedtime at her house.

Extension: The children could bring old, white pillowcases to decorate with permanent markers in your art center. The pillowcases will be nightly reminders of their little friend, Frances, whom they met in a story.

INTEGRATION

GO TO SLEEP, FRANCES

The wooden bed, bench, and window in Frances' bedroom are all made of simple shapes. Help the children cut out large rectangles to create a bed for Frances on a bulletin board. Small groups of children can put smaller shapes together to add a pillow, a window and curtains, and the bench. Have a child draw Frances to tuck into bed. After brainstorming together, have each child draw and cut out something to put in Frances' bed to help her go to sleep.

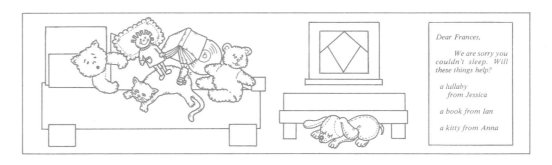

Together, write a letter to Frances telling her what the class has done. Print the children's words on chart paper, modeling the writing process for them as you think out loud about letters and sounds, spacing and capitalization. The children will want to illustrate the letter and sign their names. They will read it again and again.

A QUILT FOR FRANCES

Just as lullabies and bedtime go together, so do quilts, memories, and cultures. Bring a quilt to class and tell the children why it is special to you. Suggest that the children write letters home to see if any members of their families have quilts to bring to class and share. That is authentic writing at its best because it is writing for a purpose.

Introduce stories about quilts, including the charming books *The Quilt* by Ann Jonas and *The Quilt Story* by Tony Johnston. Talk about the ways a quilt wrapped itself around a loving African-American family in *The Patchwork Quilt* by Valerie Flournoy. Ask how *The Keeping Quilt* by Patricia Polacco "was like having the family in backhome Russia dance around us."

After you have read the stories, ask the children to tell you everything they discovered about the patterns, colors, and pictures in the quilts. Print a list of their observations on a chart.

Involve the children in a discussion of what kind of quilt Frances might have enjoyed having on her bed. Then give the children an endless supply of brightly colored, precut shapes to create their own quilt designs on large white squares. Mount their quilt pieces on vivid background squares and paste them on a large piece of colored bulletin board paper. Your quilters will be proud of their color-splashed quilt for Frances.

THE WIND'S JOB

When the wind blew the curtains and frightened Frances, her daddy told her that the wind was just doing its job. What a springboard for learning about the many ways air, water, and wind work for us. Read the appealing nonfiction book *Feel the Wind* by Arthur Dorros.

Have fun with the rhyme and cumulative text of *The Wind Blew* by Pat Hutchins and *Mike's Kite* by Elizabeth MacDonald. Read the rich language of *The Windy Day* by G. Brian Karas as the wind "leaps tickles brushes stirs rushes gusts and scolds" its way into a tiny town. Discuss the dramatic language of *Storm* by W. Nikola-Lisa as a whipping wind sweeps over a farm, and the visual images of a mischievous wind that turns things upside down in *The Turnaround Wind* by Arnold Lobel. It is the talk that surrounds literature that leads to meaningful reading and writing.

EVERYDAY LEARNING ACTIVITIES

Positive parenting; developmental learning activities; and a warm, nurturing environment are major factors in a child's academic success and lifetime learning.

Children easily identify with the little badger who just couldn't go to sleep in *Bedtime for Frances* by Russell Hoban. At some time or another, bedtime becomes a scary time for almost every child. Fears and anxieties often intensify in the dark when a child is separated from his family. Respect those feelings. A child needs to know you understand. Let him have the comfort of a night-light, a stuffed animal, or soft music. Leave the door open and tell him exactly where you will be. A frightened child usually needs a response from you, and only *you* can decide just how much reassurance he needs. Remember that putting himself to sleep is a skill every child must learn. Being able to deal with separation is one of many steps toward independence and self-sufficiency.

✳ Help a child talk through his fears at bedtime. Make a very simple book by just folding some plain paper. On the bottom of each page, write the same sentence: *I'll talk to a _____ and I'll say, "_____."* Have the child tell you the word for whatever might frighten him—a monster, a robber, and so on. End the little book with *I'll talk to my teddy bear and I'll say, "Good night."* Let the child read his book to you at bedtime. *(words in print, identifying fears)*

✳ When Frances couldn't sleep in the story *Bedtime for Frances,* she made up an alphabet song. Make a simple bedtime alphabet book with a child. Put one letter in the top left corner of each page to direct a child's eyes to begin on the left. Then have the child think of a word that begins with that letter. Write complete sentences such as *A is for alligator.* Use the book as a part of your bedtime routine every night. The last page could say, *Good night, Frances! (letter-sound association, words in print)*

✳ Understanding the concepts of before and after; yesterday and tomorrow; and morning, afternoon, and evening is part of a child's grasp of time. Refer often to the hours on a clock. They will begin to have meaning when they are connected to the activities of a child's day. *(concept of time)*

✳ It is helpful to have a quieting down activity at bedtime rather than a loud or busy activity that will *rev* a child's motor. Puzzles are an excellent activity and also are wonderful skill builders. The eyes and hands must work together. Often when a puzzle has been mastered, it can be made more challenging by mixing the pieces of two or three puzzles together and completing all three at the same time. Another variation is to do the puzzle upside down. Puzzles can be easily made by gluing a magazine picture to a piece of cardboard and cutting it up. *(visual discrimination)*

✳ Plan a library visit specifically for a child to get his own library card. Look for calming, comforting bedtime stories such as *Guess How Much I Love You* by Sam McBratney and *Time for Bed* by Mem Fox. They are two authors you will want to look for again and again. *(bedtime routine)*

Blueberries for Sal

by Robert McCloskey

* Comparing/Contrasting
* Concepts of print
* Story structure
* Model writing/Process writing
* Graphing
* Sequencing
* Theme topic: bears
* Nonfiction

SETTING THE STAGE

Instantly singable songs and the appealing rhyme and rhythm of finger plays will encourage children to be involved in story time.

"Peanut Butter and Jelly" by Sharon, Lois & Bram, *Smorgasbord*
(Digging peanuts and picking berries)

"Paw Paw Patch" by Hap Palmer, *Simplified Folk Songs*
(A game song about "picking")

MY FACE

Two little eyes to look around,	*(point to body parts as rhyme*
Two little ears to hear each sound,	*indicates)*
One little nose to smell what's sweet,	
One little mouth that likes to eat!	

THE BEAR WENT OVER THE MOUNTAIN

The bear went over the mountain,	*(walk in place, then fingertips*
The bear went over the mountain,	*together)*
The bear went over the mountain,	
To see what he could see!	*(hand over eyes)*
To see what he could see!	
To see what he could see!	
The other side of the mountain,	*(walk in place, then fingertips*
The other side of the mountain,	*together)*
The other side of the mountain,	
Was all that he could see!	*(hands out, palms up)*

FIRST READING

Look at the picture on the cover of our book today. Where do you think the little girl is? What do you think she is picking? Let me give you some clues. They are small and blue. They are round and smooth. They grow in clusters on bushes and are simply delicious. The name of our book is *Blueberries for Sal.* Now do you know the child's name and what she is picking?

The round medal you noticed on the cover is called the Caldecott Honor Medal. It is an award given for books with beautiful, detailed illustrations. Mr. Robert McCloskey is the author *and* the illustrator of *Blueberries for Sal,* and his book was one of the books chosen for the award many years ago in 1948. Look at his first picture, even before the title page. What do you think Sal and her mother are doing with the blueberries? Tell me all the things you see in their kitchen that are different from the things in your kitchen. What do you predict will happen in the story?

GETTING INVOLVED

Let's go blueberry picking together. Tell me what kind of pail you would take to Blueberry Hill. Have you ever seen a *tin* bucket like this one? Does it look like Little Sal's tin pail? I'm going to drop three blueberries into the bucket. What words would you use for the sounds they just made? Now listen while I drop three blueberries into this plastic pail. What words would you use for those sounds? Were the sounds of the berries hitting the pails alike or different? Decide which pail you'd like to take with you.

Stretch your arm out straight to the side; now curl it into your body to make a pail. You can pick blueberries with your other hand while you're tramping along behind your mother. "Kuplink, kuplank, kuplunk!" Reach for the blueberries to the right of you, now to the left, and down by your feet. Be careful not to squish any berries on the bushes. Now walk like Little Bear walked and hustle along to catch up with your mother. When you find her, give her a big hug and sit down to rest right in the middle of the blueberries.

A CLOSER LOOK

With each rereading of a story, children gain new understanding. Pause often for a spontaneous flow of oral language as the children share their feelings and observations. Extend the learning process with your own questions in repeated readings of the story.

* How was Little Sal's mother getting ready for winter? *(comprehension)*

* How was Little Bear's mother getting ready for winter? *(comprehension)*

* Why is Little Sal smiling as she picks berries? *(inferential)*

* I wonder why the blueberries didn't sound "kuplink" in mother's pail. *(interpretation)*

* Why were there more blueberries in mother's pail than in Little Sal's pail? *(reasoning)*

* Tell me all the reasons you can think of why Little Sal and Little Bear got lost. *(reasoning)*

* Have you ever been lost? *(reflecting)*

* What made Little Sal's mother turn around? Little Bear's mother? *(interpretation)*

* I wonder what Little Bear and his mother did when they got home. What did Little Sal and her mother do? *(reflecting)*

* Do you think Little Sal and Little Bear ever went to Blueberry Hill again? *(reflecting)*

STORY TIME EXTENSIONS

Gotcha! by Gail Jorgensen

It's the Bear! by Jez Alborough

Jamberry by Bruce Degen

Lost! by David McPhail

Let's Go Home, Little Bear by Martin Waddell

BALANCED LITERACY ACTIVITIES

POETRY

BERRIES ON THE BUSHES
Berries on the bushes
In the summer sun.
Bring along a bucket
And pluck every one.

Look at my teeth,
They're raspberry red.
Look at my fingers,
They're strawberry pink.
Look at my mouth,
It's huckleberry purple.
Look at my tongue,
It's blackberry ink.
     Eve Merriam

GOOSEBERRY, JUICE BERRY
   by Eve Merriam
   from *Blackberry Ink*
   by Eve Merriam

YELLOW BUTTER
   by Mary Ann Hoberman
   from *Read-Aloud Rhymes for the Very Young*
   by Jack Prelutsky

INVOLVEMENT

ON BLUEBERRY HILL

Because there is action in almost every sentence in *Blueberries for Sal,* the story is an easy one for creative dramatics. Using drama helps children understand story structure. Talk about Robert McCloskey's setting, the story characters, and the series of events in the adventure. Ask the children to identify the problem in the story and how it was solved. Record their responses on a story structure matrix with the following headings: Setting, Characters, Events, and Climax. Children make sense out of what they are learning when they talk about it.

Set up your room for a dramatization of the story by deciding on an area for Blueberry Hill, a clump of bushes on one side for Little Sal, and a clump (children will love the word!) of bushes on the other side for Little Bear. Find a place for the rock from which Little Sal heard a noise.

In your art center, help the children create two pails; two sets of headband bear ears; and signs to label Blueberry Hill, the rock, and the bushes. Because children often feel more confident dramatizing a story when they act in pairs, print two sets of name cards for Little Sal, Little Sal's mother, Little Bear, and Little Bear's mother. As you narrate the story, the children will listen intently for cues as they role-play the characters. Have the other children join in on "kuplink, kuplank, kuplunk."

INTEGRATION

THE BEAR WENT OVER THE MOUNTAIN

As with many traditional favorites, "The Bear Went Over the Mountain" has a simple, singable melody that children enjoy. It will not be long before they have the text memorized. Write the words on chart paper, modeling the writing process for the children as you think out loud about letters and sounds and spacing. Print with the same color the words that are repeated, such as *The bear went* in brown, the word *over* in blue, and the phrase *the mountain* in green. Write the sentence *To see what he could see* in black. Repeat a color pattern in the last verse also. The children will want to illustrate the chart with bears and mountains for colorful reading.

Extension: Using the same colors, print the text on sentence strips for children to arrange in sequence or match to the song chart. For an additional reading activity, print one sentence on each page of a book for the children to illustrate. Bind the mounted pages into a class big book to add to your listening center, along with a tape of the children singing.

A RETELLING

In a retelling, children reproduce a story by using their own language. Begin by brainstorming the key vocabulary in *Blueberries for Sal*. As you are charting the vocabulary, ask the children to listen for the sounds that make up the words. When the word web is complete, direct the children's attention to story structure. Ask them to identify the beginning, the end, and the middle of the story plot, adding one or two events between the beginning and the middle and one or two events between the middle and the end. Use the children's language and the charted vocabulary words as you print their retelling. Return often to the word web and to their story for individual, paired, or group reading. You will be guiding children's attention to print and to story structure.

A LETTER TO LITTLE BEAR

Little Sal and Little Bear didn't even meet each other when they were picking berries. Have Little Sal write a letter to Little Bear, inviting him to come to her house to play and eat blueberries. As the children dictate the sentences, write the letter on a chart to which they will surely want to add some pictures and sign their names. Some children may choose spontaneously to write to one of the story characters or Mr. McCloskey himself. Writing is a natural way to learn language.

BLUEBERRIES, BLUEBERRIES

After talking about all the ways we enjoy eating blueberries, give each child a long, narrow piece of paper with the words *Blueberries, Blueberries* printed on the left. On the folded flap on the right, print the words *I like them. . . .* Under the flap have each child draw and write his favorite way to eat blueberries, such as *on my pancakes, in my muffins,* and so on. Bind the illustrated pages into a new reading book for your reading center. Predictable text helps children learn to read.

MY BERRY, YOUR BERRY

Author Bruce Degen has written a special message on the last page of his visually delightful book *Jamberry*. His message is a wonderful introduction to the rhyming, rollicking adventure of a bear and a little boy on a berry hunt. List on a four-column wall graph the kinds of berries the child and the bear found. Have each child draw a picture of his favorite berry to paste to the graph. Write a summary of the graph results. Which berry was the least favorite? The most? How many more? How many less?

LET'S LOOK AT BEARS

What kind of bear was Little Bear? How do bears stay warm in the winter? Write the children's questions on a chart titled What Do We Want to Know about Bears? Read extraordinary nonfiction books such as the magnificent *Every Autumn Comes the Bear* by Jim Arnosky and *Bears Out There,* a beautiful book by Joanne Ryder with rich, lyrical language and detailed drawings. Include *Alaska's Three Bears* by Shannon Cartwright, a storyteller's look at grizzly, polar, and black bears; the factual and appealing *Let's Look at Bears* by Malcolm Penny; and *Animals in Winter* by Susanne Riha. Have each child draw a picture and write a sentence about one thing she has learned. Allow time to share because children need to talk about what they are learning. Then, as a class, write a second chart, What We Have Learned about Bears.

EVERYDAY LEARNING ACTIVITIES

Positive parenting; developmental learning activities; and a warm, nurturing environment are major factors in a child's academic success and lifetime learning.

A young child is already developing eating habits and food likes and dislikes that he will probably carry with him for the rest of his life. If a child craves sugar and sweets now, he will most likely crave them twenty years from now. Don't give sweets as a source of comfort and don't withhold them as a punishment. That makes them twice as desirable. When sweets are used as snacks, they rob a child of his appetite at mealtime. Most children are happy with fruit, raw vegetables, cheese, or peanut butter, which make far more nutritious snacks. Offer new foods at the meal that a child eats best. Be relaxed and nonchalant about the amount of food a child eats. Power plays result when a child gets too much negative reinforcement about eating. An uptight adult sets the stage. We also influence a child's eating habits by our casual conversation, often talking to others about a reluctant eater in his presence. Every time he hears that he doesn't eat well, he will prove you are right. The principle that a child will repeat the behavior for which he gets attention can work *for* you in encouraging good eating habits.

✳ Is it blueberry season? Find a pick-your-own commercial blueberry patch and pick blueberries for a wonderful hands-on learning experience guaranteed to fill the tummy! Look for blueberries at the grocery store. Since there are no blueberry bushes in the store, how did the blueberries get there? Study the packaging. Decide if the berries are the same as the ones in *Blueberries for Sal* by Robert McCloskey. *(sensory experience)*

✳ Count your blueberries. Make piles of ten. Then group your blueberries into piles of dark and light blue, or big and small, or stem and no stem. Let the children think of new ways to group. *(counting and grouping)*

✳ Have the children make up their own recipe for blueberry jam. Write the ingredients and the steps for cooking exactly as they dictate. Tape the recipe inside *Blueberries for Sal* and read it together often. *(language)*

✳ Read about rollicking berry picking with a rhyme-spouting bear in *Jamberry* by Bruce Degen. Ask the children to name all the real berries they can think of. Make a list. Then have fun writing a list of fanciful berries (hayberries, pinkberries, and so on). Paint a picture for each list. *(language)*

✳ Using blocks or Legos, make a pattern on the floor by simply repeating two colors: red, blue, red, blue, and so on. Ask a child what color will come next in the pattern. When he can extend a two-color pattern, add a third color, then a fourth. Vary the object sizes as well. Tell the child to think up the hardest pattern he can possibly think of for you to complete. Make a pattern with Cheerios, raisins, grapes, and so on, and end the game with a party. *(visual skills)*

Brown Bear, Brown Bear, What Do You See?

by Bill Martin, Jr.

* Choral reading
* Predicting
* Directionality
* Classifying
* Sequencing

* Structure writing/Content writing
* Nonfiction
* Theme topic: animal habitats

SETTING THE STAGE

Instantly singable songs and the appealing rhyme and rhythm of finger plays will encourage children to be involved in story time.

"Mary Wore Her Red Dress" by Raffi, *Everything Grows*
(A musical "fashion show" using colors)

"Brown Bear, Brown Bear, What Do You See?" by Greg and Steve, *Playing Favorites*

COLORS	
Colors, colors, what do I see?	*(hand shade eyes)*
I see colors all around me!	*(look all around)*
I see the blue sky	*(point up)*
Where the birds go.	
I see the green grass	*(point down)*
Tickle my toe.	
Colors, colors, what do I see?	*(hand shade eyes)*
I see colors all around me.	*(look all around)*
I see flowers just for you,	*(pick flowers)*
Red and yellow and purple, too!	
Colors, colors, what do I see?	*(hand shade eyes)*
I see colors all around me!	*(look all around)*

Mary Cornelius

SPECKLED RED	
Chook, chook, chook, chook, chook,	*(curtsy or bow)*
Good morning, Mrs. Hen.	
How many chickens have you got?	
Madam, I've got ten.	*(hold up ten fingers)*
Four of them are yellow,	*(close all but four)*
And four of them are brown,	*(four on other hand)*
And two of them are speckled red,	*(wiggle two thumbs)*
The nicest in the town.	

FIRST READING

What do you see on the cover? What is that bear doing? The title of the book tells us the bear is looking at something—*Brown Bear, Brown Bear, What Do You See?* The book was written by Bill Martin, and the colorful pictures were done by Eric Carle, the man who wrote *The Very Hungry Caterpillar.*

Are you ready for a look inside the cover? Why are all those pretty colors there? Let's read the words on the title page together. Now I will just quietly turn the pages. You tell me everything you see.

Do we know the story yet? Sometimes the whole story isn't found in the beautiful illustrations. We must also hear the words printed on each page. Some stories such as *Brown Bear, Brown Bear, What Do You See?* are meant to be read aloud. This book is especially fun because of the pattern of words. See if you can hear what the pattern is. You can help me read.

GETTING INVOLVED

Do you think Brown Bear was sitting down when he saw the animals? How does a bear move? Tell me the other animals in the story that move on all four legs. How about the animal that flies? Can you name the two animals that move through water? And how about the one that hops wherever it goes? I'm wondering if there were any animals in *Brown Bear, Brown Bear, What Do You See?* that moved on two legs instead of four. Do you think people can be called animals?

There is a name for what we just did. It is called classifying. Tell me your ideas about what that word means. Now listen while I call out the names of the animals and you can show me how you think each one was moving when Brown Bear saw it.

Did you know that the words of the story can be sung to the tune of "Twinkle, Twinkle, Little Star"? It's beautiful. Two musicians named Greg and Steve recorded the song for us. First, let's sing "Twinkle, Twinkle, Little Star" so we hear the melody in our heads. Now I'll turn the pages of the book and we'll sing *Brown Bear, Brown Bear, What Do You See?* to the same melody.

A CLOSER LOOK

With each rereading of a story, children gain new understanding. Pause often for a spontaneous flow of oral language as the children share their feelings and observations. Extend the learning process with your own questions in repeated readings of the story.

✳ I wonder how Mr. Martin got the idea for writing *Brown Bear, Brown Bear. (reflecting)*

✳ Tell me the name of a color. What animal was that color in the story? *(association)*

✳ Of the eight colors you usually find in your crayon box, which color did Brown Bear not see? What color did he see instead? *(analyzing)*

✳ This time when we read the story, tell me what Brown Bear will see next *before* I turn the page. *(predicting)*

✳ Which two animals did the illustrator color with fanciful colors, just for fun? *(interpretation)*

✳ Look at the feet of all the animals. Can we group the animals by their different kinds of feet? *(classifying)*

✳ Which animals live in water? In the air? On land? How else can we group the animals? *(classifying)*

✳ Count the children and the animals. Which set has more? Less? *(math concepts)*

✳ If you could have one animal for a pet, which one would you choose? *(opinion)*

STORY TIME EXTENSIONS

What Neat Feet by Hana Machotka

Color by Ruth Heller

Mouse Paint by Ellen Stoll Walsh

There's a COW in the Road! by Reeve Lindbergh

Polar Bear, Polar Bear, What Do You Hear? by Bill Martin, Jr.

BALANCED LITERACY ACTIVITIES

POETRY

IN THE SUMMER WE EAT
In the summer we eat,
in the winter we don't;
In the summer we'll play,
in the winter we won't.
All winter we sleep, each curled in a ball
As soon as the snowflakes start to fall.
But in spring we each come out of our den
And start to eat all over again.
Zhenya Gay

GRANDPA BEAR'S LULLABY
by Jane Yolen
from *Sing a Song of Popcorn*
selected by Beatrice Schenk de Regniers

INVOLVEMENT

CREATIVE DRAMA

The repetitive chant and bright, appealing characters of *Brown Bear, Brown Bear, What Do You See?* lend themselves beautifully to expression through drama. Have each child choose a favorite character to draw and color. Be sure someone draws the teacher and the group of children. Mount the children's drawings on paper plates to make face masks or on tagboard to hang around the children's necks. The children may prefer to add popsicle sticks to create stick puppets. Separate the children into groups of red birds, yellow ducks, and so on as they hold their props. Read *Brown Bear, Brown Bear* again with each group joining in on its character's part and then asking the next question.

INTEGRATION

BROWN BEAR'S WALK

Involve the children in a discussion about all the places Brown Bear must have walked to see his animal friends. Using small paint sponges or colored chalk, create a simple outdoor scene on a large piece of bulletin board paper. Label the path of Brown Bear's walk with directionality phrases such as *under a nest, around a pond, across a pasture, beside a farm, over a stream,* and *in front of a house.* Have the children paint and cut out the story characters to add to the appropriate places on the wall mural. The scene will become an independent or a paired reading experience as the children walk a Brown Bear puppet through the story.

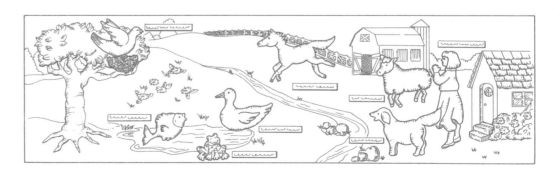

CHILDREN, CHILDREN, WHO DO YOU SEE?

Because authoring often begins with oral language, have fun with an oral innovation of the story by substituting the children's names in the repetitive pattern. *"Jeremy, Jeremy. Who do you see?"* and Jeremy answers, *"I see Nathan looking at me."* After every child has participated, decide on a sequence of names. Give each child a piece of paper with the words of the question, *"_____, _____, Who do you see?"* printed at the top and the answer printed at the bottom, *"I see _____ looking at me."* The children will probably think of copying name cards as they write names in the spaces on their pages. Bind the illustrated pages in a class book titled, *Children, Children, Who Do You See?* The purpose of structure writing is to create an easily read and appealing class book. Because children return to their own books again and again, this one will soon be a well-read favorite in your reading center.

Extension: Have each child bring an individual photo of himself to class. Use the same text as above, but print the question on the top left of each child's paper. A child's picture and the answer to the question will be hidden under a folded flap on the right side of each page. The children must lift the flaps to read the story. Be sure to include the teacher's picture and a class picture of all the children on the last two pages.

MY BROWN BEAR BOOK

The rhythm and predictability of *Brown Bear, Brown Bear* is a constant delight to children. It presents a wonderful opportunity for them to write independently as they practice writing in the context of a story. To help the children imagine Brown Bear in a different plot and setting, introduce them to the magnificent illustrations and rich vocabulary of *Imagine* by Alison Lester. This beautiful book really celebrates the imagination of children as it takes them into the jungle, under the sea, and even to Australia. Give each child a blank book to draw and tell his own Brown Bear adventure. You will need a sign-up sheet by the Author's Chair for children who will be eager to read their innovations to the class.

WHERE ARE YOU GOING NEXT, BROWN BEAR?

For a fascinating nonfiction unit that will probably take you into next month(!), build on the curiosity and language inspired by Alison Lester's *Imagine.* Fill your library corner with other extraordinary nonfiction books, including the clever, wordless *In the Pond* by Ermanno Cristini; the superbly illustrated *Junglewalk* by Nancy Tafuri; the appealing and informative *What Do You Do at a Petting Zoo?* by Hana Machotka; and the beautifully laid out *When We Went to the Zoo* by Jan Ormerod.

Ask the children to name different animal habitats (they will love the big word!) that Brown Bear might have visited. Print the habitats on a classroom chart. List the animals the children suggest for each category. Have them decide on a habitat and a sequence of animals and their colors, such as *"Red parrot, Red parrot, What do you see?"* Don't forget an all-important surprise ending as you plan a class adaptation of *Brown Bear, Brown Bear.*

EVERYDAY LEARNING ACTIVITIES

Positive parenting; developmental learning activities; and a warm, nurturing environment are major factors in a child's academic success and lifetime learning.

The appealing, repetitive text of *Brown Bear, Brown Bear, What Do You See?* by Bill Martin Jr. is simply the result of asking the same question to a group of endearing animals. A wise parent or caregiver stimulates a child's learning by asking skillful, open-ended questions. Effective questions require a child to organize his thoughts and process the information in his mind. *What does that mean? What would happen if. . . ? Which would you choose? Will it fit? Why won't it float?* Asking questions is a game that can be played anywhere, any time. Questioning leads to logical thinking and sequencing and problem solving. Your questions also say, "I am listening. Your thoughts are important. I really do want to know what you are thinking." Such approval adds something to a child's inner stature. Even more important than teaching a child's eager mind, you are building his confidence in himself. Your *voice* will always be your greatest teaching tool because you are conveying feelings as well as words. Ensuring the emotional well-being of a child is perhaps the single most important task of a loving caregiver.

* Have a child draw and color simple pictures of the animals from *Brown Bear* on large index cards. Line up the cards for an animal parade with Brown Bear leading the way and the other animals following in sequence. The same activity on a simple flannel board (just flannel or felt laid over cardboard) is fascinating to a child. You could lay thin paper over each animal on the last page of the book. Then lay the traced outline on a piece of felt and cut out the animals. Note: Allowing a child to trace can make him dissatisfied with his own artwork. *(sequencing)*

* *Concept* development is easy in the context of play. Using the same animal cutouts, arrange them in different ways to have fun with smaller and bigger, in the middle, on the left or right, above, under, next to, between, before, and after. On succeeding days, add the concepts of first, second, and third; few and many; more or less; every other one; adding or taking away; or grouping by sets. Be sure to let a child have fun being the teacher and giving *you* directions to follow. *(directionality, math concepts)*

* *Predict* how many candies, colored marshmallows, or pieces of cereal are in a handful. Then predict how many there will be of each color before you separate the colors. Which color has the most? The least? Make a simple graph. Then have a party and eat the graph! *(predicting, graphing)*

* Every child has favorite stories that are like warm, familiar friends he must meet again and again. In a story like *Brown Bear, Brown Bear, What Do You See?* let the child predict what is coming next. Pause and let him hear a rhyming word in his head. Point to the words on a page and show him how the words look alike. Recognizing that print has meaning is the beginning of reading. Look for the sequel, *Polar Bear, Polar Bear, What Do You Hear?* by Bill Martin Jr., and other books that have repetitious patterns of words. The brains of young children continually seek patterns as they make neural connections for learning. *(words in print)*

Caps for Sale

by Esphyr Slobodkina

TEACHING FOCUS

* Vocabulary
* Directionality
* Punctuation
* Graphing

* Structure writing/Guided writing
* Math/science concepts
* Parts of speech
* A class alphabet book

SETTING THE STAGE

Instantly singable songs and the appealing rhyme and rhythm of finger plays will encourage children to be involved in story time.

"Copycat" by Greg and Steve, *Kidding Around*

"Just Like Me" by Greg and Steve, *We All Live Together, Vol. 4*
(A mirror movement musical game)

MONKEY SEE, AND MONKEY DO

A little monkey likes to do	
Just the same as you and you.	*(point)*
When you sit up very tall.	*(straighten back)*
Monkey sits up very tall.	
When you pretend to throw a ball	*(stand)*
Monkey pretends to throw a ball.	*(act out)*
When you move your arms up and down	*(move arms)*
Monkey moves his arms up and down.	
When you sit down on the ground,	*(sit down)*
Monkey sits down on the ground.	

QUIET BE

Let your hands clap, clap, clap;	*(clap hands three times)*
Let your fingers tap, tap, tap,	*(tap fingers three times)*
Fold your arms and quiet be,	*(fold arms)*
Roll your hands so wide awake.	*(roll hands)*
Let your fingers shake, shake, shake.	*(shake fingers)*
Climb the ladder; do not fall,	*(climb hands up, up)*
Till we reach the steeple tall.	*(hands make steeple)*
Fold your hands and quiet be.	*(fold hands)*

FIRST READING

Tell me all the things on the cover of this book that make you smile. What do you think is happening? Is it strange to see a man in the tree and the monkeys on the ground?

The name of the story is *Caps for Sale, A Tale of a Peddler, Some Monkeys and Their Monkey Business*. Do you know what a peddler is? It is someone who sells things but does not have a store. Instead, a peddler brings what he is selling right to you. Can you find the peddler on the cover? What do you think the words *monkey business* mean? Let's read about the trouble a peddler had with some mischievous monkeys.

The children will naturally begin to speak along with the peddler and the monkeys. Their participation is part of the fun of the story.

GETTING INVOLVED

I'm curious about some of the new words we heard in *Caps for Sale*. The author said the peddler was not an *ordinary* peddler because he carried his *wares* on his head. Tell me your ideas about the word *ordinary*. What were the peddler's *wares?* The peddler walked slowly so as not to *upset* his caps. What does *upset* mean? Next he leaned against the tree so he wouldn't *disturb* the caps. I'm wondering what the word *disturb* means. And last, did the story tell you what the words *monkey business* mean?

Stand up tall in your very own space and we'll act out those new words. Reach up and stack your *wares* on your head, first your own checked cap, next the gray caps, then the brown, the blue, and last, the red ones. Walk slowly, slowly. Don't *upset* your caps! Now sit down ever so carefully. Don't *disturb* your caps while you take a nap. Oh, those silly monkeys are up to their *monkey business*. Stand up and shake your finger at them! Pretend to throw down your cap. It worked! Pile all the caps back on your head and walk ever so slowly back to your place.

A CLOSER LOOK

With each rereading of a story, children gain new understanding. Pause often for a spontaneous flow of oral language as the children share their feelings and observations. Extend the learning process with your own questions in repeated readings of the story.

＊ Look again at the cover. Now why do you think the peddler is in the tree? *(reflecting)*

＊ Where did the peddler sell his wares? *(comprehension)*

＊ Why did the peddler call out the words "Caps for Sale" as he walked? *(comprehension)*

＊ How could we count the number of all the caps on the peddler's head? *(reasoning)*

＊ Why do you think nobody wanted any caps one morning? *(reasoning)*

＊ I wonder if the story would have been different if the peddler had sneezed. *(reflecting)*

＊ Was it nighttime when the peddler went to sleep? *(comprehension)*

＊ What would you have said to the monkeys? *(reflecting)*

＊ Have you ever thrown something down when you were angry? *(reflecting)*

＊ In your opinion, was the peddler trying to get the monkeys to imitate him when he threw down his cap? *(evaluating)*

＊ Would you rather be the peddler or a monkey? *(evaluating)*

STORY TIME EXTENSIONS

Monkey Do! by Allan Ahlberg

Five Little Monkeys Sitting in a Tree by Eileen Christelow

The Monkey and the Crocodile by Paul Galdone

What do you do with a kangaroo? by Mercer Mayer

If You Walk Down This Road by Kate Duke

BALANCED LITERACY ACTIVITIES

POETRY

WHEN YOU TALK TO A MONKEY
When you talk to a monkey
  He seems very wise.
He scratches his head,
  And he blinks both his eyes;
But he won't say a word.
  He just swings on a rail
And makes a big question mark
  Out of his tail.

Rowena Bennett

BEFORE THE MONKEY'S CAGE
The monkey curled his tail about—
  It looked like so much fun
That as I stood and watched him there,
  I wished that I had one.

Edna Becker

INVOLVEMENT

DRAMATIZATION

Caps for Sale offers an ideal setting for creative dramatics. To make the language come to life, have the children freely pantomime the movement of all the story characters. Add a variety of colors of fabric, felt, and wallpaper to your art center and encourage the children to make the peddler's checked hat and a bunch of gray, brown, blue, and red caps. Just plain circles may stack best on the peddler's head. With one child role-playing the peddler and the other children acting as monkeys (and loving it!), the caps are the only literacy props you will need for a hilarious dramatization.

INTEGRATION

A MUSICAL PEDDLER

A musical version of *Caps for Sale* will make a fascinating rereading of the story. Sing the peddler's cry to this simple melody.

With the children in small groups, add a rhythm instrument sound for each color cap as it is mentioned, such as checked caps—jingle bells, gray caps—scrapers, brown caps—woodblocks, blue caps—tambourines, and red caps—triangles. For the monkeys' response, shake maracas on each "tsz, tsz" sound. The children will be actively listening as they wait for their part to come. Story participation allows children to make meaning in their minds. They get excited about learning because it makes sense to them.

A HAT ON MY HEAD

Have each child bring one hat of any size, shape, or color to school. Ask the children how the hats could be sorted, such as by colors, shapes, feathers, rims, sports, careers, or seasons. Make a multicolumn picture graph by having each child draw a picture of her favorite hat to place on the graph. As a group, tally the results and write summary sentences next to the graph. Which column of hats has the most? The least? How many more? How many less?

Extension: Introduce the clever, informative book *Whose Hat?* by Margaret Miller in Shared Reading. The colorful pictures identify hats associated with various careers and then depict a child role-playing the career and wearing the hat. Have each child draw a picture of herself wearing a hat. Let her draw on her knowledge of letters and sounds and make approximations in spelling as she writes a sentence about her picture. The children can take turns reading their sentences and talking about their pictures as they sit in the Author's Chair. Children make sense out of what they are learning when they talk about it.

THE PEDDLER LOOKED

With the story illustrations as a guide, brainstorm with the children about other places the peddler might have looked for his caps. Emphasize position words. Choose a small group of children to illustrate a cover, a title page, and a surprise ending for your story. Then give each child a piece of paper with the words *He looked* _____. written at the top and the phrase *No caps!* printed at the bottom.

After each child has illustrated a page, have her write or dictate the words she has chosen to finish the sentence. Point out sound-symbol relationships and conventions of print as you work one-on-one with each child. You are encouraging children to practice writing in the context of a story that has meaning. The resulting predictable text will help them learn to read. Bind the mounted pictures in a big book or hang them on the wall for paired or independent reading.

THE PEDDLER'S WARES

The idea of someone walking up and down the street selling something is a new concept to children. Discuss the word *wares* and brainstorm about other items that could be sold by a peddler. Talk about the prices he might charge. Give each child a blank book with the sentence *A _____ for _____ cents.* printed on each page. Each day have the children draw something new, decide on a price, and dictate the words to finish the sentence. Miss Slobodkina updated an old folktale when she wrote *Caps for Sale.* Your authors will be doing the same.

Extension: Make a class book, *The Peddler's Wares ABC Book,* by deciding on wares that begin with every letter of the alphabet.

MONKEY TAILS

The poem "When You Talk to a Monkey" gives us a word picture of monkeys turning their tails into question marks. Lead the children in a discussion of what questions monkeys would ask if they could talk. Have each child draw and cut out a monkey with a big question mark tail. For a classroom display, act as recorder and write the monkey's question on a sentence strip to tuck under his tail. You have taught questions and question marks in meaningful context, put print on the walls, and provided another fascinating reading experience.

A THREE HAT DAY

Laura Geringer's warm, comical story about a lonely man and his extraordinary collection of hats offers a wealth of language, drama, art, and writing possibilities. *A Three Hat Day,* with charming illustrations by Arnold Lobel, will be a favorite.

EVERYDAY LEARNING ACTIVITIES

Positive parenting; developmental learning activities; and a warm, nurturing environment are major factors in a child's academic success and lifetime learning.

There is nothing so appealing, at any age, as good manners. How often we wish our little ones would simply inhale good manners overnight! Being respectful is a composite of all good manners. Because children are imitators, parents and caregivers do their best teaching when they are modeling the right behaviors themselves. That means saying "please" and "thank you" to a child, not interrupting her, honoring her feelings, and so on. A child who has been treated with respect can be expected to treat others the same. Parents and children should be more polite to each other than they are to anyone else. Insist on manners and allow plenty of time for practice, over and over again. Praise is a better motivator than punishment. A child with good manners is welcome anywhere and a pleasure to have around.

✳ Listening for unusual sounds, like those the monkeys made in *Caps for Sale* by Esphyr Slobodkina, will help a child's auditory discrimination. Help her stay tuned to the sounds in her environment. Listen together for sounds and rhythms around you: your heart, a dripping faucet, rain, a tree branch scraping, popcorn popping. Listen for sounds outside and inside, and compare daytime and nighttime sounds. *(auditory perception)*

✳ Have some family fun with music, a wonderful mood changer. Teach a child some of the songs you learned as a child. Clap out rhythms and let the child echo you. Clap the rhythm of a familiar song for her to guess. Reverse roles, too. You are sharpening a child's listening skills. *(auditory perception)*

✳ Learning left and right is an ongoing process. Encourage learning the skill in relaxed everyday situations. Mimic the peddler's actions in *Caps for Sale.* He looked for his caps *to the right* and *to the left,* in *back* of him, and *behind* the tree. Reinforce the left/right concept by putting a drop of lotion or cologne on a child's right wrist every morning. Always identify each hand but only the right one gets the lotion. After several days in a row, a child will automatically hold out her right hand. Encourage the child to identify her right and left hand or foot as she dresses, washes, eats, or plays, but give reminders freely and don't expect mastery. It is a continuing learning process. *(laterality)*

✳ Recycling broken or stubby crayons will pique a child's interest in the colors of her world. As she identifies a crayon color, ask her to name all the things she can think of that match that color. Put the broken, mixed pieces of crayons in a lightly greased muffin tin. Heat them in a slow oven (250 degrees to 300 degrees) until the crayons are melted together. Don't stir. Allow them to harden away from little hands. When the recycled crayons are cool, encourage the child to describe what happened and then color a rainbow picture. *(color recognition)*

Chicka Chicka Boom Boom

by Bill Martin, Jr. and

John Archambault

* Cultural diversity
* Mini language skills
* Letter-sound relationships
* Choral reading

* Matching capitals and lowercase
* Phonemic awareness
* Model writing/Process writing
* A class alphabet book

SETTING THE STAGE

Instantly singable songs and the appealing rhyme and rhythm of finger plays will encourage children to be involved in story time.

"Alphabet Song/ABC Jig" by Sharon, Lois & Bram, *Sing A–Z*
(An appealing alphabet jig that includes nursery rhymes)

"L-O-L-L-I-P-O-P/S-M-I-L-E-/W-A-L-K/B-I-N-G-O" by Sharon, Lois & Bram, *Sing A–Z*
(A spelling medley)

CLAP, CLAP, CLAP YOUR HANDS

Clap, clap, clap your hands   *(follow actions as rhyme*
As slowly as you can.   *indicates)*
Clap, clap, clap your hands
As quickly as you can.

Shake, shake, shake your hands
As slowly as you can.
Shake, shake, shake your hands
As quickly as you can.

Repeat the verse with roll, rub, wiggle, and pound.

DID YOU EVER GO FISHING

Did you ever go fishing on a bright sunny day—   *(follow actions as rhyme*
Sit on a fence and have the fence give way?   *indicates)*
Slide off the fence and rip your pants,
And see the little fishes do the hootchy-kootchy dance.

FIRST READING

Can you tell from the cover what this story will be about? Let me read the title for you, *Chicka Chicka Boom Boom*. Do you know yet? Let's look inside the cover and see whether you have an idea. What do you think about the colors the artist has used for the alphabet letters?

Now look at the title page. Does it look like the cover of the book? Do you think you know what the brown circles are? Read the words with me. Look for the same words on the next page.

One of the authors, Bill Martin, Jr., wrote *Brown Bear, Brown Bear, What Do You See?* That rhyming story was about animals. This story is about the letters of the alphabet trying to climb a coconut tree. Now tell me what you think the brown circles are.

GETTING INVOLVED

Here are all the lowercase letters of the alphabet lined up so you can see them. When I tap you, pick out any letter you want and sit down with that letter.

Now let's look at the cards on the floor in the middle of the circle. They are the matching capital letters turned over so you can't see them. This time when I tap you, turn over two letters on the floor and see if you can find the capital letter that matches your letter. Watch closely because someone else may turn over the very letter you need and you will want to remember exactly where it is.

Whatever alphabet letter you are holding is the letter you will be in the story. This time as I read, listen for your letter. Stand up when you hear it. After the whole alphabet is up the tree, *Chicka Chicka Boom Boom*, everyone falls and we will start all over again.

A CLOSER LOOK

With each rereading of a story, children gain new understanding. Pause often for a spontaneous flow of oral language as the children share their feelings and observations. Extend the learning process with your own questions in repeated readings of the story.

✳ I wonder how the author thought of the words *Chicka Chicka Boom Boom. (reflecting)*

✳ Would the story have been different if the letters had climbed a banana tree? *(evaluating)*

✳ Did all the alphabet letters rhyme with the word "tree"? *(rhyming words)*

✳ Why was the letter *K* called "tag-along"? *(comprehension)*

✳ When did you notice the tree starting to bend? *(observation)*

✳ Why do you think the coconuts fell out of the tree? *(reasoning)*

✳ Why did the sun go down when *X, Y,* and *Z* joined the race? *(reasoning)*

✳ How do we know the letters *D, E,* and *F* were hurt in the fall from the tree? *(comprehension)*

✳ Why did the capital letters *Z, R, J,* and *N* wrap around the lowercase letters after they fell? *(comprehension)*

✳ What did you notice about *M, N,* and *O* after the fall? *(observation)*

✳ Which alphabet letter would you like to be? *(evaluating)*

STORY TIME EXTENSIONS

Old Black Fly by Jim Aylesworth

Tomorrow's Alphabet by George Shannon

Running the Road to ABC by Denizé Lauture

The Folks in the Valley: A Pennsylvania Dutch ABC by Jim Aylesworth

Alphabet Puzzle by Jill Downie

BALANCED LITERACY ACTIVITIES

POETRY

SO MANY MONKEYS
Monkey Monkey Moo!
Shall we buy a few?
Yellow monkeys,
Purple monkeys,
Monkeys red and blue.
Be a monkey, do!
Who's a monkey, who?
He's a monkey,
She's a monkey,
You're a monkey, too!
   Marion Edey and Dorothy Grider

TREE HOUSE
   by Shel Silverstein
   from *Sing a Song of Popcorn*
   selected by Beatrice Schenk de Regniers

OUR TREE
   by Marchette Chute
   from *Sing a Song of Popcorn*
   selected by Beatrice Schenk de Regniers

INVOLVEMENT

CHORAL READING

What a story for joining in! The lively rhythm, rhyme, and steady beat of *Chicka Chicka Boom Boom* are an instant invitation to children to join in the fun. Have them suggest a body movement or a rhythm instrument to accompany the phrases "chicka chicka boom boom" and "will there be enough room?" every time they appear in the story. Then have the children start a steady beat by tapping their knees. As the children keep the beat, begin reading the story again, adding the movements and sounds but always returning to the beat again . . . and again!

THE COCONUT TREE DRAMA

Choose a child to stand on a small chair with a sign around his neck that says "coconut tree." (Can't you see it now?) Give each of the children sitting in a circle a yarn-tied letter card with a single letter on it to put around his own neck. (*QRS* can be on one card and *XYZ* on another.) As you slowly read the story, have each child go to the coconut tree when his letter is called and put his letter card on the child on the chair. When you read, "Oh, no! Chicka Chicka . . . BOOM! BOOM!" the coconut tree sways and the letters fall, with the remaining children running to the tree to "hug their dears and dust their pants." As you continue reading, the letters get up one by one until letter *A* starts the Coconut Tree Drama all over again.

INTEGRATION

MEET YOU AT THE COCONUT TREE

Repeat the bold colors of *Chicka Chicka Boom Boom* on a bulletin board which will brighten your room for days. Draw a pencil outline of a large coconut tree. Have the children paint and stuff with newspaper the bending tree trunk, leaves, coconuts, and cheery sun. Give each child a square with a black letter in the middle. The children will surround the black letters with bright crayon colors and then *paint-wash* over the *crayon resist*. The colorful alphabet squares will climb up, hang from, and fall off the swaying tree. Add the book title and author's name to your appealing bulletin board.

A LETTER FROM A COCONUT

Involve the children in a discussion of the overloaded coconut tree. Did the coconuts like the alphabet letters racing to the top? Did the tree? How did that feel?

Using their responses, model the writing process as you write a letter on chart paper from the coconut tree to the alphabet letters. Will the letter be friendly? Scolding? Think out loud about the sounds that make up the words. Draw attention to directionality and one-to-one correspondence. Talk about punctuation. Underline the words you want children to be able to spell and add them to your word wall. Put out pointers for independent or paired reading. Through their writing, children learn to read.

Children see themselves as authors when they are able to make decisions for themselves about writing. Give daily opportunities for children to write from their own experiences and for their own purposes. A letter from a coconut, a wiggle-jiggle *UVW,* and a "dare double dare" could all be catalysts for individual writing.

MORE LEARNING WITH THE ALPHABET

An alphabet book too good to miss is *Old Black Fly* by Jim Aylesworth, a hilarious story of an old black fly driving everyone crazy on a hot summer day. Have the children decide how they will keep the beat throughout the story and what motion they will use to get rid of the pesty fly every time the text says, "Shoo fly, shoo fly, shoo!" They will be engaged in the story from the very first humorous page.

The storyteller who can sing the text will surely have the children joining in. Try singing the words of the first page to the folk tune "Buffalo Gals." Use those words and melody as a *sing-together* refrain after every fourth page of the story. You are guaranteed a very *good* day as the fly has a very busy *bad* day!

Alphabet books from other cultures offer meaningful learning because the cultures are so embedded in the marvelous illustrations. *The Folks in the Valley: A Pennsylvania Dutch ABC* by Jim Aylesworth is a lovely portrait of a Dutch settlement in a rural valley. The vibrant pictures of *Running the Road to ABC* by Denizé Lauture show Caribbean schoolchildren excitedly outracing the townsfolk as they rush barefoot to school. The *African Animals' ABC* by Philippa-Alys Browne is full of strong verbs and rich illustrations. Stephanie Feeney's *A Is for Aloha* is an accurate portrayal of Asian-American experiences that are universal to all children.

A WEB OF WORDS

To teach letter-sound association in meaningful context, choose a letter from the coconut tree to put in the center of a web. Ask the children for the name of the letter, then the sound the letter makes. Talk about any of their names that begin with that letter, adding the names to the web. Have the children look at the print around the room to find words that begin with that letter. Print the words on the web as you talk about the sound the letter makes. Add new words as children discover them in their reading, writing, and listening experiences.

Extension: For further development of sound awareness, introduce the same letter in the medial and final positions in words.

AWAY THEY SWAM TO THE BOTTOM OF THE SEA

Brainstorm ideas with the children about where else the alphabet letters could have met—at the zoo, in space, at the bottom of the sea. With the children clapping and with alphabet cards in view, create your own rhythmic chant, such as:

> *A chased B, B chased C, Away they swam to the bottom of the sea!*
> *C chased D, D chased E, Away they swam to the bottom of the sea!*

Keep chanting the letters. Every time you come to a letter that rhymes (*G, P, T, V,* and *Z*), chant the words, *Away they swam to the bottom of the sea!* Together, decide on a surprise ending.

Add to the fun by writing your chant. Give each child a Post-it showing the letters he will be writing. Mount the illustrations in an accordion book the children will return to often and exclaim, "That's my page!"

A CELEBRATION

Celebrate your ABC theme by having the children plan an alphabet day.

* Bring alphabet games to school to play in small groups.

* Make alphabet letters out of play dough or craft dough.

* Decorate cupcake treats with alphabet letters on the frosting.

* Dramatize *Chicka Chicka Boom Boom,* read alphabet books and the children's writing, and sing alphabet songs such as "A, You're Adorable" to invited guests.

EVERYDAY LEARNING ACTIVITIES

Positive parenting; developmental learning activities; and a warm, nurturing environment are major factors in a child's academic success and lifetime learning.

When asked in an interview how her family heritage had contributed to her success, a famous author answered that her father had given her the *habit of happiness*. What a gift! Although satisfying relationships probably have the most to do with a child's inner sense of well-being, we can guide a child into a *habit of happiness*. Encourage a child to be resourceful in creating play from what she has. Nurture her with your own laughter; with happy music; and with cheery, mood-setting stories like *Chicka Chicka Boom Boom* by Bill Martin Jr. and John Archambault. The infectious chant is irresistible. Who could read the story and not smile? Introduce a child to the authors and illustrators who are especially talented in creating fun with words and pictures. Always begin a story by pointing out the author's name and the illustrator's name. They will become real people to a child and soon she will be looking for more books by her favorite authors. A child who loves books will want to learn to read herself, an accomplishment that can bring many hours of happiness.

* Draw a simple coconut tree like the one in *Chicka Chicka Boom Boom*. Put it on your refrigerator or breakfast table. Every morning, hang a simple message on the tree for a child to find. She will be learning that the silly letters that raced up the coconut tree can be put together to make words. Children love to receive messages. They soon understand that learning to read means receiving a message. *(understanding words in print)*

* Letters are everywhere in a child's world: in alphabet books like *Chicka Chicka Boom Boom,* on stores and signs, on toys and games. Have fun pointing them out everywhere. Collect some colorful, familiar labels from cereal boxes, toothpaste, soup cans, and so on and put them in an attractive reading basket. Put the basket close to the child's books or blocks or dolls to use in her play. It doesn't matter if she points to the wrong word when she reads the label. What does matter is that words have meaning for her. *(word meaning)*

* Children are also learning about letters as they watch you write. Surround a child with words written down. Label things in her bedroom. Write names and words on photos in your family photo albums. Let the child dictate a simple story to you about anything she wants. As she watches, write one short sentence on the bottom of each page of a book you have made by stapling pieces of white paper together. Have the child draw a picture on each page. Read her book with her often until she has memorized the words. Reading from memory is a beginning step in reading. *(words in print)*

* Make an *alphabet basket* for a child by using any little basket she will enjoy carrying around. Put just one letter inside, both capital and lowercase. Walk through the house together, looking for little objects that begin with the sound of that letter, such as a marble, marshmallow, and marker for the letter *M*. Find that letter in *Chicka Chicka Boom Boom*. Have fun with the same letter for a week, adding objects and words to the basket. Encourage the child to take her *alphabet basket* with her in the car or to bed at night so she will feel that letters and words are very special. *(letter-sound association)*

Each Peach Pear Plum

by Janet and Allan Ahlberg

TEACHING FOCUS

* Cultural diversity
* Letter-sound association
* Phonemic awareness
* Graphing

* Classifying
* Comparing/Contrasting
* A family activity
* Theme topic: picnics

SETTING THE STAGE

Instantly singable songs and the appealing rhyme and rhythm of finger plays will encourage children to be involved in story time.

"Rhyme Time" by Greg and Steve, *Kidding Around*
(A game song in which children call out rhyming words)

"Goin' on a Picnic" by Raffi, *Corner Grocery Store*

LITTLE BO PEEP

Little Bo Peep has lost her sheep,	
And can't tell where to find them.	*(hands over eyes, looking)*
Leave them alone and they'll come home,	*(beckoning motion)*
Wagging their tails behind them.	*(hands behind back)*

JACK AND JILL

Jack and Jill went up the hill	*(thumbs "climb" hill)*
To fetch a pail of water.	*(grasp pail)*
Jack fell down,	*(one thumb falls to lap)*
And broke his crown	*(hands on head)*
And Jill came tumbling after.	*(roll hands)*

FIRST READING

Our story today is really a hide-and-seek book. There are many tiny things hidden all over the front and back covers. *(Open the book so children can see the front and back simultaneously.)* You must look ever so carefully to find them. Do you see any little animals that fly in the air? Swim in the water? Walk or crawl on land? Can you find any kinds of food? What else do you see? That's the way it is in the story, too. There are little animals and people hidden on every page so we can play a hide-and-seek game called "I spy with my eye." What do you think that means? The name of the book is *Each Peach Pear Plum*. It was written by Janet and Allan Ahlberg.

You read the title with me on the next page. What is the little mouse doing? I wonder if we will see that plum pie again in the story. Listen to the words of the poem. Now let's turn to the title page and you read the title with me one more time. Do you think this story takes place in the city or the country? Do you "spy" anything that was on the cover? Let's see what we can "spy" in the story.

Because finding the characters in the pictures is the fun part of this story, encourage the children to join in. Point out to them that the first time they spy a character they can see only part of him. All of the character is shown in the very next picture.

GETTING INVOLVED

Let's play our own hide-and-seek game. If you are chosen to hide, make sure that some tiny part of you is still showing so we can *spy* you. I'm looking for someone to be the first little person who was hidden in *Each Peach Pear Plum*. Who was that? *(Role-play the characters in sequence, giving the children quick glances at the story for reminders of who was spied next.)*

Another time have the children stay seated and use just their eyes to find colors, shapes, or objects in the room. Give at least two visual clues. Encourage the children to answer, "I spy with my eye," when they have located the object described. And be sure to give them the opportunity to choose the objects and give the clues.

CLOSER LOOK

With each rereading of a story, children gain new understanding. Pause often for a spontaneous flow of oral language as the children share their feelings and observations. Extend the learning process with your own questions in repeated readings of the story.

✳ In your opinion, is Tom Thumb a good name for the little boy? *(evaluating)*

✳ What is growing on the trees? *(observation)*

✳ Could Tom Thumb and Old Mother Hubbard be *inside* the same house we saw on the title page? *(interpretation)*

✳ What do the two pictures tell you about Tom Thumb? *(observation)*

✳ What do you spy in Mother Hubbard's cellar that you would not find anywhere in your house? *(association)*

✳ Is that the way you picture Cinderella in your head? *(reflecting)*

✳ What does the word *bunting* mean? Where is Baby Bunting? What happened to Little Bear's gun? *(comprehension)*

✳ Will the Three Bears be the baby's friends? *(predicting)*

✳ Tell me when you see pictures of the nursery rhymes we said together before we read our story. *(association)*

✳ Would you like to be inside Robin Hood's den? *(reflecting)*

✳ How did Baby Bunting get to the bridge? *(comprehension)*

✳ Do you spy any story characters hiding at the picnic? What will happen to the plum pie? *(observation, predicting)*

✳ Who would you like to sit next to at the picnic? *(reflecting)*

STORY TIME EXTENSIONS

One of Each by Mary Ann Hoberman
Positively Mother Goose by Diane Loomans
Babushka's Mother Goose by Patricia Polacco
The Completed Hickory Dickory Dock by Jim Aylesworth
Mother Goose and the Sly Fox by Chris Conover

BALANCED LITERACY ACTIVITIES

POETRY

TWO SAD
It's such a shock, I almost screech,
    When I find a worm inside my peach!
But then, what really makes me blue
    Is to find a worm who's bit in two!
William Cole

MUNCHING PEACHES
Munching peaches in the summer,
Munching peaches cool and sweet,
Munching peaches morn to midnight,
Munching peaches. Such a treat.
Munching peaches. Munching peaches.
What a way to spend the time.

While munching,
    munching,
       munching peaches,

I had time to write this rhyme.
Lee Bennett Hopkins

INVOLVEMENT

CHORAL READING

The simple text of *Each Peach Pear Plum* is ideal for a choral reading activity. Divide the children into two groups, with each group alternating phrases. Choose a child to direct the choral reading with a pointer.

RHYME TIME

An oral *cloze* activity will help the children identify the rhyming word pairs in the story. Pause as you read, giving the children time to fill in the rhyming words. When they are familiar with the word pairs, write the words on color-coded word cards. Pass out the word cards and let each child find her rhyming word partner. As you read *Each Peach Pear Plum* again, pause and let each child answer when you come to her word in the story. Keep the rhyming word pairs, a tape of the choral reading, and the storybook available for an independent or a paired reading activity.

READING GLASSES

Involve the children in a discussion of which story characters were from Mother Goose rhymes and which were from fairy tales or folklore. Make two lists to put up in your library corner. Start a collection of Mother Goose books in one basket and folktales in another. Perhaps the children will want to bring their own books from home. Compare the witty new verses written to the pattern of the old in Jim Aylesworth's *My Son John*. Then contrast that book with the unbelievable illustrations and word play in *Babushka's Mother Goose* from author Patricia Polacco's beloved Ukraine.

Keep an assortment of reading glasses (no lenses, of course!) nearby. A child's desire is to read like an adult. Have the children play their own version of "I spy" as they read the books and look for the characters from *Each Peach Pear Plum*.

INTEGRATION

THE LETTER *P*

As you write the words *Peach, Pear,* and *Plum* in the middle of a semantic web, ask the children how the words are similar. Ask them for the name of the letter *P*, then the sound that the *P* makes. Look around the room for other words that begin like *Peach* and write them on the web, each time asking the children what sound they hear at the beginning of each word. Add new words to the web as the children discover them in their reading, writing, and listening experiences.

Extension: For further development of sound awareness, look for the same letter and sound in the medial and final position in words, always in meaningful context.

I SPY

Write the poem that appears on the title page of *Each Peach Pear Plum* on the first page of a class retelling of the story. Write the words *I spy* _____ on the bottom of each child's page. Offer a choice of art materials and let every child choose a story character to hide somewhere in her drawing. Choose pairs of children to illustrate the cover, the title page (which will give credit to the author and the original story), and all the story characters on the last page. Bind the brightly mounted pages into a class big book for your reading center.

FAVORITE CHARACTERS

Write the names of the story characters on a wall graph. Give each child a small white square on which to draw his favorite character and a choice of background colors for mounting his square. As the children make observations about the graph, talk about sets, more and less, equal and zero. Write their summarizing sentences on a chart.

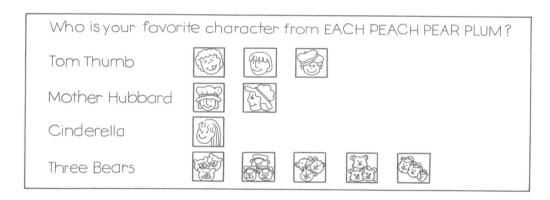

FOLKTALES

That children do not weary of classic folktales is shown by the multiple versions of the timeless stories that continue to satisfy children. Look for unusual retellings of folktales for your library corner. Compare *Deep in the Forest,* the story of *The Three Bears* from Goldilocks' viewpoint by Brinton Turkle, with the traditional story by Paul Galdone. Compare *Little Red Riding Hood* as told in verse by Trina Schart Hyman with the humorous retelling by James Marshall or the lovely traditional version by Beatrice Schenk de Regniers. The contrasting art styles are a study in themselves.

A PICNIC CELEBRATION

The charming scene at the end of *Each Peach Pear Plum* is an irresistible invitation to have a picnic. Bring a picnic basket to school full of wonderful stories about picnics, such as *Ernest and Celestine's Picnic* by Gabrielle Vincent, *The School Picnic* by Jan Steffy, *In the Forest* by Marie Hall Ets, and *We Had a Picnic This Sunday Past* by Jacqueline Woodson. Contrast the affectionate mouse family in *Picnic* by Emily Arnold McCully with the zany family that invites so many to their picnic that their boat sinks in *A Change of Plans* by Alan Benjamin and Steven Kellogg. Arrange the classroom for an indoor picnic story time. Complete the setting with a checkered cloth, food, and cheery music as you listen to "Teddy Bears' Picnic" recorded on *Greatest Hits* by Bill Shontz.

Plan a picnic for guests. Let the children decide the time, place, food, and invitations. Make charts for what is needed and what you will make. During the actual picnic, have someone jot down comments the children make as they enjoy the festivities. Read the comments to the children the next day. Then write them in a book, *A Picnic Celebration,* for the children to illustrate.

EVERYDAY LEARNING ACTIVITIES

Positive parenting; developmental learning activities; and a warm, nurturing environment are major factors in a child's academic success and lifetime learning.

Children who have been introduced to Mother Goose will enjoy *Each Peach Pear Plum* by Janet and Allan Ahlberg. They will recognize the characters from the nursery rhymes hidden on the pages. One of the reasons Mother Goose has been a favorite for so long is the rhythm and rhyme of the language, which is a constant delight to the ears of little children. They simply love the musical flow of the sounds and, in many homes, Mother Goose was one of their first listening experiences. Even though the rhymes were written years ago in another country, many of them still match a child's everyday activities today. You will build wonderful associations and happy memories if you begin repeating a specific rhyme for the same activity every day. A child will love to hear "One, Two, Buckle My Shoe" while he is getting dressed, "Little Jack Horner" while he is eating, "Rub-a-Dub-Dub" for bath time, and "Deedle, Deedle, Dumpling" for bedtime. Even better, sing the words. Music stimulates early learning in a child. Every child should have a well-illustrated Mother Goose book of his very own. He just won't tire of it!

✱ Play "fill in the missing word" with nursery rhymes that a child already knows. Leave out a rhyming word and wait for him to supply it. The child will love it when you switch roles, letting him say the rhyme and waiting for you to fill in the missing word. *(auditory memory)*

✱ Talk about the delightful picnic in the story *Each Peach Pear Plum*. Let children plan the menu and invite their stuffed animals to your own picnic. Write down the menu and the *guest* list. Hide each animal so only a tiny part is showing for your own game of "I spy with my eye." Encourage the children to describe where they found each hidden *guest—under* the tablecloth, *behind* the teapot, or *next to* the basket. *(directionality)*

✱ Play "I spy" in the kitchen, the backyard, driving in a car, shopping in a store, anywhere! Include clues that will help a child organize information in his mind, such as "I spy a fruit and it is red" or "I spy something with two wheels and it is smaller than a car." Be sure to let the child do the spying and give you clues. *(classifying)*

✱ Exercising together can be a great family time. Be sure to include balancing with one foot off the floor, eyes open and then closed; hopping on one foot and then alternating feet; jumping with two feet together as though they were tied with an imaginary rope; and walking backward, eyes open and then closed. *(gross motor skills)*

✱ Environmental print, that is, store and street signs, logos, advertising, even a stop sign, is often the first print children recognize. The words become familiar because of their distinctive colors and shapes. Point them out. Talk about letters, sounds, and words. You are teaching that written language has meaning. *(words in print)*

Freight Train

by Donald Crews

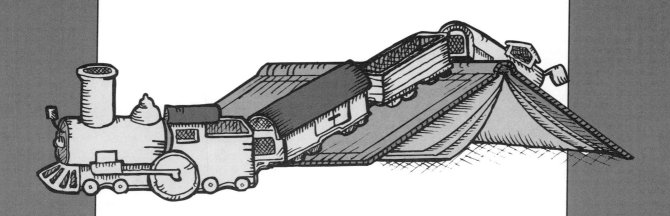

* Phonemic awareness
* Story structure
* Graphing
* Math story problems

* Theme topic: trains
* Nonfiction
* Sequencing
* A class counting book

SETTING THE STAGE

Instantly singable songs and the appealing rhyme and rhythm of finger plays will encourage children to be involved in story time.

"The Freight Train Boogie" by John Denver, *All Aboard*

"Clickety Clack" by Hap Palmer, *Witches' Brew*
(A super song about what a freight train carries)

THE TRAIN

I ride in the train	*(point to self)*
The whistle I blow	*(pull cord)*
I can do all the things	*(wheel motions with*
That will make the train go.	*hands)*
Whoo, whoo, goes the whistle,	*(hands to mouth)*
Clickety-clack go the wheels.	*(arms in wheel motions)*
I'm the chief engineer	*(pat chest)*
Til I'm called in for meals.	*(pretend to eat)*

TOOT! TOOT!

A peanut sat on a railroad track,	*(point to floor)*
His heart was all a-flutter;	*(hand over heart)*
The five-fifteen came rushing by—	*(point to wrist)*
Toot! toot! peanut butter!	*(pull cord)*

A second peanut sat on a railroad track,	*(same motions)*
His heart was all a-flutter;	
The five-fifteen came rushing by—	
Toot! toot! more peanut butter!	

FIRST READING

Flannel boards are like magic to young children. Without saying a word, put colored felt shapes on the flannel board until you have created a colorful train. Ask the following:

What did I make? Tell me where you think the train is going. Does it look like the train on the cover of our story? There are many different kinds of trains. This one is a freight train. I know, because that is the title of the book, *Freight Train*. It was written and illustrated by Donald Crews. He has his name on the cover, too, right under the title. *Freight Train* is an important Caldecott Honor Book because of the wonderful pictures. See if you can find out what the word *freight* means. We have a lot to learn about trains. All aboard. Here we go!

Variation: Magnetic boards also are fascinating. Place pieces of magnetic tape on the back of the story objects.

GETTING INVOLVED

What shapes would you use to make our own *Freight Train?* Here are eight differently colored rectangles *(felt or construction paper)* for the train cars. Tell me the color we need first. Let's put the *red* rectangle way over here on the *left* for the caboose. Keep telling me what color comes next until all the train cars are lined up. Why do we have two black rectangles?

Now we can be readers and match color words to the colors of the train cars. Look at the first letter. Listen to the beginning sound. What color do you think that is? Let's put the color word *red* right under the red caboose. *(Match all the color words to the train cars.)* Tell me where you think our freight train is going. Will it make any stops along the way?

The cars on our train need names. Let's begin on the *left* again. Right next to the word *red* we will add the word *caboose*. Read that with me, *red caboose*. Next to the word *orange*, let's add the words *tank car*. *(Add the remaining word cards and read all the phrases together.)*

A CLOSER LOOK

With each rereading of a story, children gain new understanding. Pause often for a spontaneous flow of oral language as the children share their feelings and observations. Extend the learning process with your own questions in repeated readings of the story.

* Have you ever been on a train? *(reflection)*

* Do passengers ride on *freight* trains? *(reasoning)*

* Where do the railroad tracks begin in the book? *(observation)*

* Tell me what you think each train car is carrying. *(association)*

* Why are the colors blurred? *(comprehension)*

* What did the train go through? Go by? Go across? *(comprehension)*

* Have you ever been in a tunnel? How did you feel? *(reflecting)*

* Tell me what you think the word *trestle* means. Does it look scary? *(evaluating)*

* How does a train travel in darkness? Is it safe? *(evaluating)*

* Would you rather travel in the daytime or nighttime? *(reasoning)*

* In your opinion, what is the most important car on the freight train in the book? *(evaluating)*

* What do you think the freight train will do tomorrow? *(evaluating)*

* What do you want to tell me about this book? *(reflecting)*

STORY TIME EXTENSIONS

Country Crossing by Jim Aylesworth

The Train by David McPhail

Hey! Get Off Our Train by John Burningham

I've Been Working on the Railroad by Nadine Bernard Westcott

I Spy a Freight Train: Transportation in Art selected by Lucy Micklethwait

BALANCED LITERACY ACTIVITIES

POETRY

A MODERN DRAGON
A train is a dragon that roars through the dark.
He wriggles his tail as he sends up a spark.
He pierces the night with his one yellow eye,
And all the earth trembles when he rushes by.
Rowena Bennett

TRAIN LEAVES THE STATION
by Eve Merriam
from *You Be Good & I'll Be Night*
by Eve Merriam

INVOLVEMENT

TRAIN SONG

The rhythm of the storybook *Train Song* by Diane Siebert fairly leaps from the pages. Children will be keeping tempo from the first reading. Use the first page, "out in back, railroad track, clickety clack, clickety clack," as a refrain for the children to repeat after each page of the book. They will say the chant two times, getting louder to the end. Then add a train whistle. The effect is dramatic. For an underlying accompaniment, have the children use sand blocks and jingle bells. Because the text is long, let the children decide what pages to read in each rereading, always ending with "hear the railroad lullaby."

TRAIN LEAVES THE STATION

The poem "Train Leaves the Station" by Eve Merriam also has a strong underlying rhythm that joyously pulls children into the text. They will want to keep the beat by tapping or clapping as you read. Have them chant with you the refrain, "Train leaves the station at one oh one." You can just feel the train moving—it is a wonderful experience.

MOVING RIGHT ALONG

Have the children identify things in the room that can become a train station, train tracks, a tunnel, a city, and trestles. Hang a sign around each child's neck showing the name and color of each train car. Choose an engineer to hook up the eight cars in sequence and direct the train to chug, speed up, slow down, or refuel as it goes over, under, through, and around objects in the room.

INTEGRATION

READING AND WRITING AT THE STATION

Create a simulation of a train station with a ticket window, chairs, appropriate train props, and signs in your dramatic play area. Keep literacy related materials visible, such as pencils and crayons, various colors and sizes of paper, and blank books to write in. Participate in the children's play as you guide them in literacy activities. For example, on a passenger train the children could write tickets and schedules, number the seats, make *No Smoking* and *Exit* signs, write messages for the passengers, and label the parts of the train. Have the children create their own costumes in the art center and dress up as the ticket taker, conductor, porter, engineer, and passengers. Write name cards to hang around their necks. Locate destinations on a map. Make a large clock to show departure and arrival times. You are setting the stage for children to make meaning from a literature experience.

GOING, GOING, CHUG, CHUG, GONE

Write a class innovation of *Freight Train*. On sentence strips or chart paper, print open-ended phrases about *moving* such as the phrase *Going through* _____. As the children suggest things a train could move through, such as the countryside, the snow, or a thunderstorm, record each of their answers on separate Post-its and add them to the end of the phrase. Draw attention to sounds of each word as you write the letters so children will hear and see the sound-letter connections. After taking dictation for four or five phrases, have the children decide which Post-it to keep for each phrase in their story. Print the words they have chosen in the blanks. Then have the children decide on an action for each phrase, similar to the familiar *We're Going on a Bear Hunt* story by Michael Rosen. Your new train story might look something like the following:

Going through a thunderstorm	*(slap thighs with alternating hands)*
Going by a highway	*(pretend to honk horn)*
Crossing a river	*(hands swish, swish)*
Moving in a fog	*(hands shading eyes)*
Going, going, chug, chug, gone!	*(circular wheel motions by sides)*

Extension: Using the text the class has written, print one sentence on each page of a class book for the children to illustrate.

LOADING THE CARS

Have the children choose the art mediums to create a colorful wall mural of eight large, labeled freight train cars. Involve them in a discussion of the purpose and the contents of each of the cars. Brainstorming gives children time to think and to prepare. Then have them create and cut out their ideas of what they can load onto one of the cars. Gather the children around the wall mural, and one by one have them add their freight or people to the appropriate train car.

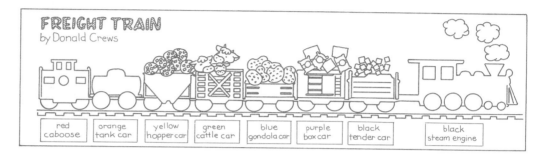

MATH ON THE TRAIN

✱ Discuss the results of their choices. How many objects are in each car? Which car has the most? The least? *Graph* the results on an eight-column graph with the name and color of each train car printed at the top. Have each child make a small picture of his freight or person to put in the appropriate column on the graph. As a group, write summary sentences to place beside the graph for more print to read in the room.

✱ Use the freight train cars to make addition and subtraction *story problems* meaningful. Model a few number stories such as "There were four windows in the caboose and two windows in the steam engine. How many windows in all?" Call on children to act out the story problem as the others write the number sentence, $4 + 2 = 6$, on paper or chalkboards. The children's observations of the freight cars will take on even more meaning as they create their own number stories.

✱ *big fat hen* by Keith Baker is a fascinating and beautiful *counting book* of a hen and her chicks playing out the rhyme "1, 2 . . . buckle my shoe." Another extraordinary, must-see counting book is Scott Gustafson's dynamic *Animal Orchestra*. With the text and large images of books such as these as models, plan a class *Freight Train Counting Book*—one red caboose, two orange tank cars, three yellow hopper cars, and so on. Perhaps the children can paste small flaps over some of their details for a fun lift-the-flap book with a surprise ending, of course!

ALL ABOARD

Use nonfiction books such as the well-illustrated *Trains* by Seymour Reit, the colorful *Trains* by Gail Gibbons, and the informative *All Aboard ABC* by Doug Magee and Robert Newman to expand your theme. Have each child draw a picture and write a sentence about something he has learned. Children pay conscious attention to phonemes when they identify sounds in words during invented spelling and the editing conferences that follow. Make a *train* on your wall of all the mounted illustrations or bind them in a class big book, *All Aboard!*

HEY! GET OFF OUR TRAIN

Consider the marvelous drama, art, and writing possibilities of *Hey! Get Off Our Train,* John Burningham's appealing story with a timely message.

EVERYDAY LEARNING ACTIVITIES

Positive parenting; developmental learning activities; and a warm, nurturing environment are major factors in a child's academic success and lifetime learning.

In the crucial early learning years, children master new words and meanings faster than at any other time of life. Children need to be surrounded with language, and that makes you the most important language teacher they will ever have. This is the perfect opportunity to build vocabulary. Don't be afraid to use unfamiliar words as you talk. Children love big words, such as *gondola* and *trestle* in *Freight Train* by Donald Crews. Try cutting a child's sandwich in a *diagonal,* or offering *privacy* in the bathroom, or giving her a *compliment* on good behavior. When she is learning to read and comes across a new word such as *garage,* she will remember the word if she has a mental picture in her head of what a garage is. So the more words a child understands, the more successful she will be in reading. Think of a new word and use it often, even in silly ways, and the child will love it.

✱ Teach a child the magic of color in the kitchen. Fill three large, clear glasses with water. Add red food coloring to one glass, blue to the second, and yellow to the third. Now set out three empty glasses. Pour some yellow water and some blue water into the same empty glass and talk about what is happening. The new color you have made, green, is the most dramatic mixture. Next pour some red and yellow into an empty glass to make orange. The last combination is red and blue to make purple. Purple is the hardest to see, so be sure to hold it up to the light. Line up all six glasses of colors. Label them and name them. *(color recognition)*

✱ Simple thinking games can be wonderful memory builders. Ask a child to tell you all the things she can remember that she saw today—at the store or in the yard or in a storybook. The more you praise her, the longer the list will grow. Ask her to remember things from yesterday such as what she was wearing or what she had to eat. Try *anticipating (she will love the big word)* what you will see tomorrow. Make a list so she can see her words in print. Don't be surprised if the child starts asking you to list what *you* remember. *(memory, categorizing)*

✱ Nonfiction books have become as appealing and colorful as fiction storybooks. Introduce children to the nonfiction section in your library. Build on their special interests, such as bugs, flowers, space, or trains. After reading the storybook *Freight Train* by Donald Crews, look for the nonfiction books *Trains* by Anne Rockwell and *Trains* by Gail Gibbons. *I've Been Working on the Railroad* is a funny, delightful book by Nadine Bernard Westcott. Children will be learning to go to books for information as well as pleasure. *(literature time)*

✱ Children need many opportunities for movement exploration. They will be gaining control of their bodies as they develop coordination. Think of objects for children to imitate with their bodies, such as a ball, a castle, a flower, a teapot, or a train. Challenge them to make their bodies crooked, straight, round, pointed, wide, or narrow. Stand in front of a mirror, add different tempos of music, and have fun! *(body coordination, creativity)*

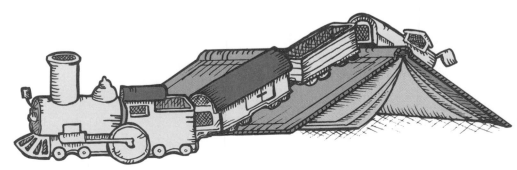

The Gingerbread Boy

by Paul Galdone

SETTING THE STAGE

Instantly singable songs and the appealing rhyme and rhythm of finger plays will encourage children to be involved in story time.

"Biscuits in the Oven" by Raffi, *Baby Beluga*
(Watch 'em rise!)

"Something in My Shoe" by Raffi, *Rise and Shine*
(A cumulative song about funny things a boy finds in his shoe)

RIGHT HAND, LEFT HAND

This is my right hand, I'll raise it way up high.	*(right hand up)*
This is my left hand, I'll touch the sky.	*(left hand up)*
Right hand, left hand	*(show palms)*
Whirl them round and round,	*(twirl hands)*
Right hand, left hand	*(show palms)*
Pound, pound, pound.	*(pound fists together)*

I SEE YOU

I have two eyes to see with,	*(touch eyes)*
I have two feet to run with,	*(tap feet)*
I have two hands to clap with,	*(clap hands)*
And nose I have but one,	*(touch nose)*
I have two ears to hear with,	*(touch ears)*
And a tongue to click each day,	*(click tongue)*
And two red cheeks for you to kiss,	*(touch cheek)*
And now I'll run away.	

FIRST READING

Our story today is one that has been around for a very long time. Your grandparents probably heard this story when they were little. Paul Galdone is a man who decided to draw the pictures and tell the story one more time, for children like you to enjoy.

Tell me about the little boy on the cover. What do you think he is made of? Have you ever tasted gingerbread? The title of our book is *The Gingerbread Boy,* and it is the story of a gingerbread cookie that popped right out of the oven and ran away.

Point out the gingerbread letters on the title page. Encourage the children to join you on the repetitive phrases.

GETTING INVOLVED

The Gingerbread Boy story doesn't tell us what the little old woman put in the dough. What does your mother put in dough when she is baking?

Let's pretend we are bakers like the old woman in the story. We are ready to make a whole batch of gingerbread boys. What ingredients do you think we will need? Let's list them on chart paper.

Now we're ready to mix. Put a big bowl right in front of you. Measure some shortening into your measuring cup and dump it in. Next comes the brown sugar and a little molasses and now some eggs. Better crack them first on the edge of your bowl. Now let's sift some flour and some ginger spice to make it smell good in the oven. Time to stir and stir. Now roll out your dough with your rolling pin. Next use your fingers to shape every part of his body. Looking good! Don't forget raisins for his eyes and mouth and buttons. How about a cinnamon drop for his nose? Now you are ready to slip your gingerbread boy into the oven and close the door very carefully. Sit down right in front of the oven so he doesn't run away.

A CLOSER LOOK

With each rereading of a story, children gain new understanding. Pause often for a spontaneous flow of oral language as the children share their feelings and observations. Extend the learning process with your own questions in repeated readings of the story.

✳ What did you think when you heard the words "Once upon a time?" *(evaluating)*

✳ Why did the little old woman make the Gingerbread Boy? *(comprehension)*

✳ I noticed how much the old woman's face changed in the story. What did you notice? *(observation)*

✳ What does *threshing* wheat mean? Why are the threshers holding sticks? *(comprehension)*

✳ Have you ever seen tools like the mowers used? *(reflecting)*

✳ What is your opinion of the thresher's statement, "Gingerbread boys are made to eat"? *(evaluating)*

✳ What does it mean to *run like the wind? (comprehension)*

✳ Could the people and animals chasing the gingerbread boy have come up with a *plan?* *(evaluating)*

✳ Did the fox have a *plan? (evaluating)*

✳ Why are the words "He was all gone!" in big letters? *(reasoning)*

✳ In your opinion, was the ending a good one? Would you like to change it? *(evaluating)*

✳ Do you think you could have caught the Gingerbread Boy? *(reflecting)*

STORY TIME EXTENSIONS

The Wolf Is Coming! by Elizabeth MacDonald

The Gingerbread Man by Jim Aylesworth

What's in Fox's Sack? by Paul Galdone

One Fine Day by Nonny Hogrogian

Donna O'Neeshuck Was Chased By Some Cows by Bill Grossman

BALANCED LITERACY ACTIVITIES

POETRY

JUST WATCH
Watch
  how high
  I'm jumping,
Watch
  how far
  I hop,
Watch
  how long
  I'm skipping,
  Watch
    how fast
    I stop!
Myra Cohn Livingston

SOMETIMES
  by Lilian Moore
  from *Talking Like the Rain*
  selected by X. J. Kennedy

THE GINGERBREAD MAN
  by Rowena Bennett
  from *Sing a Song of Popcorn*
  selected by Beatrice Schenk de Regniers

INVOLVEMENT

* The repetitive phrases and predictability of *The Gingerbread Boy* are an invitation to children to join in the story. They also offer an ideal setting for creative dramatics. Have the children create drama props in your art center or look in your dress-up box for hats or costumes. The tools for the threshers and mowers could be rulers or dowels with foil-covered cardboard blades. The children who are not playing the part of the characters can join in on the chant. Children will bring much to the drama from their own experiences.

* Draw simple pictures of the story characters on small pieces of paper. Give a picture to each of fourteen children. Give clues to the children, such as "I am thinking of a story character that had two legs and wore a bonnet." The child who is holding the picture of the little old woman would come sit by you. After the children have matched their pictures to your clues, have the child who was the Gingerbread Boy line them up in the order they ran after him in the story.

INTEGRATION

AN ABC COLLAGE OF GINGERBREAD BOYS

In collage art, every finished product is an expression of the child who created it. There are no losers, just as there are no two alike. To make collage art gingerbread boys, let each child choose any assortment of colors. Have every child tear out a head, body, arms, and legs for a gingerbread boy, gluing them down on a piece of white paper. Offer scraps of bright accent colors to tear for eyes, nose, mouth, and buttons.

Print an uppercase and a lowercase letter on the top left of each page. Write the words *"I ran away from a _____. Run! Run! Run! Catch me if you can!"* on the bottom. Each child will do a page for a letter of the alphabet, illustrated with her own gingerbread boy. Have all the children help with ideas for the difficult letters before you hand out the pages. Choose children to create a cover, a title page, and the last page of your ABC alphabet book—*"And I can run away from you, I can! I can!"* Structure writing allows children to read familiar, predictable text in an appealing class book.

CATCH ME IF YOU CAN

Tell the story of *The Gingerbread Boy* on a wall or bulletin board in your room. Have the children create large faces of the fourteen characters in the story. Offer a variety of art materials, such as tempera paint, watercolor paint, collage, tear art, construction paper, felt and fabric scraps, and water-based markers.

Put the face of the Gingerbread Boy on the far left with the faces of the other characters sequenced across the mural. Across the top of your scene, print the words *"Run! Run! Run! Catch me if you can!"* Under each face, put the sentence *"Stop," said the _____*. The familiar words of the story will offer one more opportunity for emergent reading.

HIGH-FREQUENCY WORDS

The mural is full of high-frequency words that children need to know for reading and writing. Talk about words like *stop, said, the, if, you, me, man,* and *woman.* Decide together what words to add to the word bank resource in your room.

AN EMPTY OVEN AND A MESSAGE

Children's ideas of recipe ingredients and proportions are often hilarious. Have the children name the ingredients you will need to make a gingerbread boy, the amount needed of each item, the directions for mixing and baking, and the oven temperature. Write their recipe on chart paper for the children to read and illustrate.

Show the children an actual gingerbread recipe you have written on separate paper. Have fun comparing the two recipes and deciding which one to follow. On a cookie sheet, shape the batter into a large gingerbread boy, add raisins for the features, and bake.

Return to the oven *after* someone has had a chance to hide the gingerbread boy. Have the children find a hot, empty oven with a note on the oven door saying, "You can't catch me! I'm the Gingerbread Boy, I am! Meet me in the office." When the children go to the office, they will find another note. The clues will send the children to various places in the school, such as the clinic, the custodian's room, and so on until the last clue directs them back to their own classroom, where the gingerbread boy is waiting.

THE CHASE IS ON

The marvelous *chase* through the pages of *The Gingerbread Boy* irresistibly draws children into the story. So it is with *Gotcha!,* Gail Jorgensen's hilarious story of "on and on they went" as determined bears chase a big, black, beastly fly. In Elizabeth MacDonald's *The Wolf Is Coming!,* a chaotic procession of panic-stricken animals race through a barnyard as a hungry wolf chases them. And in *Donna O'Neeshuck Was Chased By Some Cows* by Bill Grossman, a puzzled girl is chased by "mooses and gooses," cows and sows, and a parade of others who want her head-pats. The repetitive phrases and comical illustrations in all three books are priceless.

A TALE OF MY OWN

Children often get ideas for their own writing from a storybook that has been shared. Give them many opportunities to write independently because children write best when they make connections to their own experiences. Furthermore, their early writing efforts are the foundation of phonemic awareness as children focus on the sounds they hear in the words they are writing. *The Gingerbread Boy* could lead a child into writing a make-believe tale, a true story, a letter, a poem, a journal entry, or a chase through a place you never thought of.

THE KITCHEN

Create a simulation of a kitchen in your room. Arrange a collection of cookbooks in a basket to invite readers. Provide a supply of pencils, paper, and small blank books for children to write or copy recipes, including your own Gingerbread Boy recipe. Put out food coupons, a small message board, a calendar, a notepad, food cartons, mixing bowls, measuring cups, table settings, and whatever the children suggest for their imaginative role playing. Add a tub of colored dry rice with funnels, spoons, and a variety of containers. Keep individual chalkboards and chalk nearby. As the children work in pairs, they can estimate and tally the spoonsful of rice it will take to fill each container.

EVERYDAY LEARNING ACTIVITIES

Positive parenting; developmental learning activities; and a warm, nurturing environment are major factors in a child's academic success and lifetime learning.

The Gingerbread Boy by Paul Galdone is an example of a traditional tale that probably gave each of you a warm feeling when you heard the words again. Perhaps the story is a memory of your mother reading to you. When you think of your mother's voice, you are really thinking of her as a person because the voice and person are inseparable in your mind. That means you can use your own voice to create a wonderful association in a child's mind, just by reading to him often. Books and the memory of your voice can be an exciting part of a child's heritage. Some of the happiest memories we have of our own childhoods focus on the things our families did together, the things that gave continuity and a "oneness" to our family living. They were the experiences we could count on every year, the traditions that were expressions of love that kept on repeating themselves. By creating the tradition of reading in your home, you are giving a child a lifetime of memories.

✳ Baking is always a learning experience in measuring, sequencing, and following directions. Bake a gingerbread boy with a child, but let her find an empty oven when the timer goes off. Plan a trail of simple messages from the gingerbread boy, brief clues on little pieces of paper that will eventually lead a child to her hiding place. Party time! *(words in print)*

✳ Drawing, cutting, and pasting are all fine motor skills. Encourage a child to draw gingerbread boys of all shapes and sizes and then cut, paste, and decorate them with markers and buttons and bits of colored paper. Have the child paste the gingerbread people in a book and dictate a sentence for you to write on each page. *(fine motor)*

✳ Make Jell-O together. As you add a variety of tidbits (celery, nuts, apple and banana slices, mini marshmallows, and so on), ask your child to predict which will sink and which will float. Make a differently colored Jell-O every week. Encourage the child to identify that color wherever he sees it: inside, outside, shopping, in the car, in books, everywhere. *(predicting, colors)*

✳ Encourage a child to copy shapes the right way. Put big, bold dots on a piece of paper and show the child how to connect them to make a shape. Show him that circles begin at the top and are drawn counterclockwise. To make a triangle, also begin at the top and count out loud, 1, 2, 3, as you draw the three sides. Count 1, 2, 3, 4 as you draw a square from top left to top right. Praise all of a child's efforts and don't expect the end result to be perfect. *(copying shapes)*

✳ You can expand a child's vocabulary by teaching him the purpose or the function of many objects that he can already name. Make up "What Am I?" riddles for the child to guess such as "I am made of wood. I have an eraser on top. What am I?" You can make the game harder by asking, "I am a pencil. What do I do?" Use common household and classroom objects and, when the child is really good at solving the riddles, remember to reverse roles and let him make up some for you to solve. *(language)*

Good Morning, Chick

by Mirra Ginsburg

* Letter-sound association
* Phonemic awareness
* Mini language lessons
* Structure writing

* Sequencing
* Parts of speech
* Theme topic: egg-laying animals
* Nonfiction

SETTING THE STAGE

Instantly singable songs and the appealing rhyme and rhythm of finger plays will encourage children to be involved in story time.

"Rise and Shine" by Raffi, *Rise and Shine*

"Rockin' Round the Mulberry Bush" by Greg and Steve, *We All Live Together, Vol. 3*

THE FLUFFY CHICKENS

Five eggs and five eggs	*(hold up two hands)*
That makes ten.	
Sitting on the top is the Mother Hen.	*(one hand covers other fist)*
Crackle, crackle, crackle,	
What do I see?	*(move hand that was the fist)*
Ten fluffy chickens	
As yellow as can be!	*(hold up two hands again)*

BUSY MORNING

I am busy in the morning,	*(hand open, palm up)*
I have many things to do.	*(other hand same)*
I like to get all ready	
When the day is bright and new.	*(hands open, by face)*
I wash my face, I comb my hair,	*(imitate action)*
I eat my breakfast in my chair.	*(imitate action)*
And then it's time to go and play,	*(thumb over shoulder)*
And that is how I spend my day.	*(hands in lap)*
Mary Cornelius	

FIRST READING

Tell me a story about the picture on the cover of this book. How did you know the animals were on a farm? Can you see the animal that usually wakes up first on a farm? Look at the two little animals watching the mother hen from a distance. I wonder if we will see them again in the story.

What do you think the mother hen and the little chick are saying? Perhaps the mother hen has just said "good morning" to the baby chick. Those are the exact words of the title. Read the words on the cover with me, *Good Morning, Chick* by Mirra Ginsburg, pictures by Byron Barton.

The repetitive phrase "like this" invites the children to join in spontaneously.

GETTING INVOLVED

Did we see a farmer in the story *Good Morning, Chick?* Do you think there was one? Pretend to be the farmer waking up in the yellow farmhouse. Wake up *(stretch arms)*, get dressed *(act out)*, eat breakfast *(hand to mouth)*, and walk out the front door *(clap hands for the door closing)*.

Tell me the sounds the farmer heard in his barnyard that morning. Let's put those sounds in order. First, the farmer heard the chick breaking out of its shell, "tap-tap, crack." Next he heard Speckled Hen teaching the chick to eat, "peck-peck, peck-peck." Then the farmer heard the black cat "hissing" and the mother hen scolding him, "cluck-cluck-cluck." The rooster started crowing, "cock-a-doodle-do!" but the little chick could only say "peep-peep." Then the farmer heard the chick fall into the water, "plop," and the frog laughed, "qua-ha, qua-ha." The last sound the farmer heard was the mother hen and the happy chick looking for worms and seeds, "peck-peck, peck-peck."

Another time, let the children volunteer other animal sounds that a farmer might hear on a farm.

A CLOSER LOOK

With each rereading of a story, children gain new understanding. Pause often for a spontaneous flow of oral language as the children share their feelings and observations. Extend the learning process with your own questions in repeated readings of the story.

✱ Tell me what you noticed about the pictures in *Good Morning, Chick. (observation)*

✱ What do you think about the first sentence, "There was a little house white and smooth"? *(evaluating)*

✱ What did the hen's house look like? The chick's house? *(observation)*

✱ Tell me how you think the baby chick got out of his house. *(comprehension)*

✱ Why didn't the little chick look like his mother? *(reasoning)*

✱ Was Speckled Hen a good name for the mother? *(reasoning)*

✱ How did the chick learn to do things in the barnyard? *(interpretation)*

✱ Why do you think the black cat hissed at the chick? *(reasoning)*

✱ How did the Speckled Hen protect her chick? *(comprehension)*

✱ In your opinion, should the frog have laughed at the chick? *(evaluating)*

✱ Would you agree that Speckled Hen was a good mother? *(evaluating)*

✱ What do you want to say about the story? *(reflecting)*

STORY TIME EXTENSIONS

Here Comes Henny by Charlotte Pomerantz

Barnyard Banter by Denise Fleming

Farm Morning by David McPhail

Benjamin's Barn by Reeve Lindbergh

the day the goose got loose by Reeve Lindbergh

BALANCED LITERACY ACTIVITIES

POETRY

BABY BIRD
Watch the baby bird.
  He's hatching from his shell!
Out comes his head,
  And then comes his tail.
Now his legs he stretches,
  His wings he gives a flap.
Then he flies and flies and flies.
  Now what do you think of that?
Down, down, down, down, down, down, down, OUCH
                    Pamel Conn Beall

INVOLVEMENT

BABY BIRD

The poem "Baby Bird" is a scale song that can be sung easily with no accompaniment. With the children crouched low to the floor, begin singing the song on a low note on the scale. Sing all the words of the first phrase on that same note. Move up one note on the scale as you sing each phrase and have the children stand a little taller with each note. After singing "Now what do you think of that?" you are ready to come back down the scale again. Repeat the word "down" on each descending note. With the last word "OUCH!" the children will be laughing on the floor and asking to sing the song again.

CHICKENS CAN, CHICKENS CAN'T

Cut a large chick from doubled, sturdy paper. The children can paint and stuff it. Talk about all the parts of the chick's body. To encourage children to think in details, have them suggest words that describe each part of the chick. Print their descriptive phrases on word cards as you label the parts.

Talk about all the things the little chick could already do in the story *Good Morning, Chick*. He could split open his egg, look around, peck, eat worms, and so on. Write the action words on word cards. Then individually, in pairs, or in groups, have the children pantomime the sentence *Chickens can _____ like this!* Those watching must guess the missing action word, find it, and put it in the sentence.

Add to the fun by orally extending the sentence to *Chickens can _____ like this but can't _____ like this*. Ask the children to think of and pantomime both actions. For example, "Chickens can *peck* like this but can't *smile* like this." The children will enjoy the silly ones best!

INTEGRATION

LIKE THIS!

The predictable text of *Good Morning, Chick* makes it easy for children to write a simplified innovation of the story. Review the children's ideas about what chicks can do. Refer to the illustrations in the book until every child has an idea to draw. Give each child a piece of paper with the words *Chickens can _____* printed at the top. Print the phrase *like this* on the bottom.

Have each child finish his own sentence using developmental spelling. It is through writing that children pay attention to the sounds within words. Use individual conferences to edit the spelling before the pages go in the class book. Choose children to draw a cover and a title page. Mount the illustrated pages on colorful background paper and bind them in a class book to add to your library corner. The text will become so familiar that individuals or partners will be able to read it on their own. That is the purpose of structure writing. Children do learn to read through writing.

Variation: Make a caption book using the same sentence on every page, *Chickens can _____ like this but can't _____*. Give each child the opportunity to share his page with the class. The humor of this book will certainly make it a favorite.

A BARNYARD IN THE MORNING

The bold colors of *Good Morning, Chick* will create a beautiful story on the wall. Have the children create a simple background of grass and sky on a large piece of bulletin board paper. Talk about all the things Mirra Ginsburg put in her pictures to tell the story, such as the trees, house, barn, fence, and pond. Let the children decide on the characters and objects they want in their story. (This activity would adapt well to *tear art,* using brightly colored construction paper.) Staple or glue everything the children have made to the background. Add print. Label everything. Think of a descriptive word for every noun. Include the story title and the author's name. Perhaps your children will choose to add directionality phrases and *walk* the chick through their own barnyard story: *around the tree, next to the fence, into the puddle,* and *under Speckled Hen's feathers,* much like the pattern in *Rosie's Walk.* You are providing the text for another read-the-room experience.

Variation: A simpler activity would be to have each child draw and cut out a chick, hen, or rooster. Group the animals on the farm scene mural. Add a bright sun and smile at your "waking up" barnyard family.

MINI LANGUAGE LESSONS

To teach letter-sound association in meaningful context, ask the children for the name of the letter *g* in the word *good,* then the sound the letter makes. Have them find more words in the children's responses in the room that begin with that letter. Do the same for the letter *m* in the word *morning.* Brainstorm about a word family for *chick* by covering the consonant blend *ch* (the onset) and pointing to *ick* (the rime). Phonemic awareness develops when children hear the sound segments of a word. In other mini lessons, have the children identify the words *like* and *this* in your print by framing them with hands or slider frames, flashlights, or pointers. Add *like* and *this* to the word wall of high-frequency words in your room. Talk about the ending *ing* in the word *morning* and list other words the children know from their reading and writing that have the same ending.

WHEN I AM BIGGER!

Children create story meaning when they make connections to their own lives. Involve the children in a discussion about things older children and grownups can do that they can't. Talk about how they feel when they want to do something and are told to wait until they are bigger. After every child has had a chance to think of something, have him draw his idea on a large piece of paper. Act as recorder and write the sentence he dictates on his drawing. Then give everyone a second piece of paper with the words printed on the bottom, *Oh, well! I'll wait 'til I am bigger!* On those pages the wishes come true!

I want to mow the lawn.

Oh, well I'll wait til I am bigger.

I want to wear make up.

Oh, well I'll wait til I am bigger.

CHICKENS AREN'T THE ONLY ONES

The children's curiosity about the little chick pecking its way out of its shell can lead to an interest in other animals that lay eggs. *Chickens Aren't the Only Ones* by Ruth Heller is an outstanding nonfiction book with appealing, rhyming text and brilliant pictures. Just charting the remarkably diverse group of egg-laying animals is an opportunity for emergent reading and writing. *Chickens Aren't the Only Ones* will fascinate your beginning readers for a long time. Who knows what theme the book will lead to?

EVERYDAY LEARNING ACTIVITIES

Positive parenting; developmental learning activities; and a warm, nurturing environment are major factors in a child's academic success and lifetime learning.

In the story *Good Morning, Chick* by Mirra Ginsburg, the baby chick learned everything about the world around him by imitating his mother. Children are born imitators, too. They never stop learning by imitation. Children imitate friends and siblings, television and videos. And they imitate adults—your tone of voice, your language, your actions, the way you solve problems or spend your time. That means *who* you are, the person you are, speaks louder than what you say. Children are very likely to imitate in their own lives the values that you live out in front of them. That can be a very positive teaching tool. Children will spontaneously imitate the good behaviors you model day after day.

✱   Imitating can become a memory game. Tell a child to watch you as you make two different motions. Then slowly count to five before you ask her to repeat the two motions in sequence. When she is consistently successful, increase the number to three actions, then four. Change the activity to a listening skill by simply *saying* the directions. Watch to see how well she listens. It adds to the fun and the learning if you reverse roles, too. *(perceptual skills)*

✱   A child usually *matches* shapes before she identifies them by name. Read *Good Morning, Chick* again, looking for specific shapes such as *triangles* to match the hen's beak. Another time, look for *circles* to match the chick's eyes or *squares* to match the henhouse door. (Watch out for the perception change!) When a child has mastered those shapes, add *rectangles* like the fence posts or *ovals* to match the chick's egg. Activities that have meaning for a child provide far more effective learning than flash cards or workbooks. *(shape recognition)*

✱   Pretend to be the animals in *Good Morning, Chick* and act out the story. Another time, make up your own game by choosing one child to be Speckled Hen with everyone else pretending to be chicks. When Speckled Hen closes her eyes, the chicks find hiding places and make quiet peeping noises. Mother Hen must find her chicks by listening for the peeps and probably a few giggles as well! *(auditory skills)*

✱   Reading aloud is more beneficial to a child than any other single activity. When you read a favorite storybook again and again, point out concepts of print a child will need to know when she reads herself. Talk about the front and back and title page of a book. Discuss the author and illustrator as real people. Make them come alive. Talk about other books by the same writers and artists. Point out the directionality of print, from top to bottom, from left to right. When you come to the end of a line, make an exaggerated return sweep with your hand to the left again. You are training a child's eyes where to go on the page. However, nothing surpasses *meaning* as the most important part of a story. Let a child respond personally. Ask her what her feelings are, what she wondered about, what she liked best. A child's talk about the story is a meaningful conclusion to time well spent together. *(concepts of print)*

Goodnight Moon

by Margaret Wise Brown

TEACHING FOCUS

* Phonemic awareness
* Choral reading
* Concepts of print
* Matching word pairs

* Structure writing
* Categorizing
* Graphing
* A family activity

SETTING THE STAGE

Instantly singable songs and the appealing rhyme and rhythm of finger plays will encourage children to be involved in story time.

"Goodnight" by Hap Palmer, *Witches' Brew*
(Describes where all the creatures go to sleep)

"Starlight"/"Bye 'n Bye"/"Twinkle" by Sharon, Lois & Bram, *One Elephant, Deux Elephants*
(Three old favorites)

WEE WILLIE WINKIE

Wee Willie Winkie	
runs through the town,	*(run in place)*
Upstairs and downstairs	*(stepping motion)*
in his nightgown,	
Rapping at the window,	*(knocking motion)*
Crying through the lock,	*(hands to mouth)*
"Are the children in their beds?	
For now it's eight o'clock."	*(eight fingers up)*

HEY DIDDLE, DIDDLE

Hey diddle, diddle; The cat in the fiddle;	*(play fiddle under chin)*
The cow jumped over the moon.	*(hands make jumping motion)*
The little dog laughed to see such a sport;	*(hand to mouth, laughing)*
And the dish ran away with the spoon	*(two fingers run up arm)*

FIRST READING

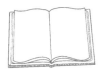

Does this storybook look familiar? It is probably the best-loved bedtime book ever written. Has anyone ever read this story to you? Tell me what you remember. If it is usually read at bedtime, why would we want to read the story now?

Let's do a picture walk through the book. You tell me everything you see. Be sure to look at the pictures on the bedroom wall and tell me when you see a bunny fishing. It is a picture from another story by Margaret Wise Brown called *The Runaway Bunny*. She put it in this book to be a little message to you from the author. Now I'll just turn the pages and you be the story-tellers.

I think Margaret Wise Brown would have loved your story. I know *I* did. In her story, the little bunny is already tucked into bed. Before he goes to sleep, he says good night to everything he can see in his room—good night to the clocks and his socks, good night to the mittens and the kittens, and even good night to the moon he can see through his bedroom window. And that's the name of the story, *Goodnight Moon*.

GETTING INVOLVED

When the little bunny said good night to everything in his room, he was relaxing before he went to sleep. I'm sure he would love to be here right now to do some relaxing exercises with us. Stand up and spread out your arms carefully so you have some space all your own. First, let's bend over and hang our arms down like a rag doll. Now pretend you are a puppet and there is a string on the top of your head. Pull the string to pull yourself up straight. Pretend you are a balloon and take three deep breaths to fill yourself up with air. Gently float around in a circle, moving your arms slowly up and down. Float down, down, down to the ground. Now pretend you are taking a trip on a magic carpet. You are flying right through the clouds, over the trees, into your own room, and right into your cozy bed. Before you go to sleep, let's say good night to the cow jumping over the moon. *(Say "Hey Diddle, Diddle" together.)*

A CLOSER LOOK

With each rereading of a story, children gain new understanding. Pause often for a spontaneous flow of oral language as the children share their feelings and observations. Extend the learning process with your own questions in repeated readings of the story.

* Tell me what you noticed about the pictures in *Goodnight Moon. (observation)*

* Why do you think the illustrator made some pictures black and white? *(reasoning)*

* Did you notice that one page has no picture at all? Why? *(reasoning)*

* Do you think this was a good beginning sentence, "In the great green room there was a telephone and a red balloon"? *(evaluating)*

* Would you like to sleep in a great green room? *(reflecting)*

* I wonder why there is a fireplace in the bunny's bedroom. *(reasoning)*

* Why do you think the socks and mittens are hanging from the rack in the bunny's room? *(comprehension)*

* Who is the quiet old lady? What is she doing? *(interpretation)*

* Tell me why you think the colors change in the bunny's room. *(reasoning)*

* Have you ever said good night to *mush*? What is it? *(comprehension)*

* I wonder why the quiet old lady is gone in the last picture. *(interpretation)*

* What do you wonder about the story? *(reflecting)*

STORY TIME EXTENSIONS

Time for Bed by Mem Fox

Papa, please get the moon for me by Eric Carle

Owl Moon by Jane Yolen

Wait Till the Moon Is Full by Margaret Wise Brown

Half a Moon and One Whole Star by Crescent Dragonwagon

BALANCED LITERACY ACTIVITIES

POETRY

MOON BOAT
Moon Boat, little, brave, and bright,
Tossed upon the seas of night,
One day when I'm free to roam,
I'll climb aboard and steer you home.
Charlotte Pomerantz

KEEP A POEM IN YOUR POCKET
by Beatrice Schenk de Regniers
from *The Random House Book of Poetry for Children* by Jack Prelutsky

SILVERLY
by Dennis Lee
from *Read-Aloud Rhymes for the Very Young* by Jack Prelutsky

INVOLVEMENT

CHORAL READING

✳ Encourage the children to read the illustrations for clues as you wait for them to add the rhyming words of the text in an oral cloze activity.

✳ Play quiet lullaby music as a background setting for an antiphonal reading of *Goodnight Moon*. You and the children alternate reading the phrases. Keep turning the volume of the music softer as the pictures of the bunny's room gradually darken.

✳ Make a cassette tape of the music and the choral reading for a listening center.

INTEGRATION

WHISPER GOODNIGHT

Guide the children in recalling the many things the bunny said good night to in the story. Have each child decide on one thing to draw on his square of white paper. Add the words *Goodnight* _____ under each child's drawing. (It won't matter if some objects from the story are duplicated or some are omitted.) Mount them on larger squares of green construction paper and group them later in a "great green room" collage.

Have the children bring their finished pictures to the circle as you play quiet music and turn off the lights. Be "the quiet old lady who whispered 'hush'" as each child whispers good night to whatever he has drawn. End the sharing by whispering, "Goodnight noises everywhere," as the children get ready for a quiet activity. The focus of any story participation is to make meaning out of the story.

MOON BOAT

The poem "Moon Boat" creates a wonderful word image of children steering moon boats across the sky. Create a night scene on your bulletin board by covering it with dark blue paper. Add some glittery stars and a moon. Let every child tear or cut from construction paper a moon boat and an oval. Have each child draw her face on the oval and paste it in the crescent moon to steer across the dark sky. Place the mounted chart poem "Moon Boat" on one side of your nighttime mural. Children will be drawn to their own artwork and the poetry as they "read the walls."

A POCKET CHART OF RHYMES

Goodnight Moon is a treasure chest of words with rhyming sounds. Perhaps that is why generations of children have loved the story. Read the text slowly, stopping just before a rhyming word so the children can say it. As they watch, write the rhyming word pair on a sentence strip. Continue that way through the story. Talk about the sounds the children hear and the spelling patterns they see as you write. Ask them if it is possible for words to rhyme and not have the same spelling pattern (like *bears* and *chairs*) or have a different number of syllables (like *air* and *everywhere*). Let the children illustrate the word pairs.

Search the story for more objects that the bunny could have said good night to, such as a fire, lamp, rug, book, stars, or bed. Ask the children to think of a rhyming word for each new object. Write the new rhyming word pairs on sentence strips for the children to illustrate. Then cut the rhyming word pairs in half and place all the separate words randomly in the pocket chart. The children will say the words and match the pairs in the pockets of the pocket chart. The more word pairs, the more learning. You have made an appealing pocket chart of rhymes for a learning center.

Extension: On subsequent days, choose one word from your chart such as *moon* and brainstorm *all* the words the children can think of that rhyme. List and illustrate the words. Keep the lists visible. Which word was the easiest to rhyme, the hardest, the most fun, the one Margaret Wise Brown might have used in another story?

OUR GOODNIGHT JOURNAL

When you initiate a project that involves families, you are building a bridge from home to school. You are also helping children create story meaning because they are making connections to their own lives. Make a class big book with a night scene drawn by the children on the cover and an illustrated first page that says, *The bunny in the bed closed his eyes and said, "Goodnight moon."* Include in the book a page for every child with these words printed on the bottom:

_____ *in the bed closed his eyes and said,*

"Goodnight _____ *and goodnight* _____ *."*

Provide a very special bookbag or canvas bag to hold the Goodnight Journal, crayons, pencils, markers, rulers, and a note explaining the project to parents. (Laminate both the journal and the note for durability.)

One at a time, let the children take the Goodnight Journal home to draw their bedrooms and the things they say good night to every night. Parents can help complete the sentences. Let every child read his sentences and talk about his picture when he brings the book back. Children need to talk about their writing. When your Goodnight Journal is complete, put it inside the canvas bag and keep it in your reading center for all to enjoy.

A GRAPHING TUB

From time to time add something to a graphing tub in your room, explaining to the children that when it is full you will all decide how to graph what is inside. Empty the contents on the floor in the middle of a circle with the children sitting around you. Have them name and talk about all the objects, such as a balloon, slipper, teddy bear, toothbrush, comb, soap, socks, and so on, until they have decided on two categories for grouping.

The categories might be objects that were in the bunny's great green room or not in the great green room, objects that are part of bedtime or not part of bedtime, objects found in a bathroom or found in a bedroom. Another day their choices might be the qualities of the objects, such as hard or soft, cloth or not cloth, or colors. Graph the actual objects on a two-column floor graph as you make conclusions about more than, less than, equal sets, and unequal sets.

EVERYDAY LEARNING ACTIVITIES

Positive parenting; developmental learning activities; and a warm, nurturing environment are major factors in a child's academic success and lifetime learning.

Goodnight Moon by Margaret Wise Brown is probably the best-loved bedtime book ever written. Children want to hear it over and over again because they don't tire of repetition as we do. Familiar stories become warm friends and are especially comforting at night. A predictable bedtime routine provides loving security to a child, both in repetition and in knowing limits. Allowing a child to make some choices in the sequencing of the routine is a great way to get her cooperation. Start early enough to allow time in the evening for yourself. Most children go to bed far too late, so remember the choice should not be theirs. Focus on quieting-down activities and be sure to include a bedtime book. Quiet music is soothing also, and children love the familiarity of the same bedtime music. When your routine is over, be quietly firm. Set limits and mean it when you say, "Our time is over. Good night and sweet dreams." Put a child to sleep every night with a good thought about herself—something she has said or done that day that has pleased you. Over the years, that adds up to a powerful package of what a child can believe about herself.

✳ The gradually darkening pictures and the stars and moon showing through the window are a perfect ending to this gentle story, *Goodnight Moon*. Plan a night for you and a child to stargaze. Allow her to stay up until the stars are visible. Take a large blanket and two pillows outside and lie side by side looking at the stars. Try to count twenty stars and encourage the child to choose a favorite. Say the nursery rhymes "Twinkle, Twinkle, Little Star" and "Star Light, Star Bright" together. Be sure to say good night to the stars and moon when you're ready to come in. *(night and day, Mother Goose)*

✳ Just before bedtime, sit in a chair together in a child's room. Let her name all her favorite things in the room. Suggest she add describing words, including colors. Then turn off the light, and see how many things she can remember. Encourage her to picture everything in her mind and say good night to each special thing, one by one. Because children are often afraid of the dark, it can be reassuring to remember all the familiar, friendly things in a room that don't change when the lights go off. *(visual memory)*

✳ Make up bedtime stories in which a child is the heroine, making all the right choices that you will want her to make some day in real life. She will feel more important and special with each new "chapter" you tell, and at the same time you will be subtly conveying all the values that you want her to learn. You'll probably surprise yourself with the stories you can create. *(self-esteem)*

✳ Have a child choose pictures of family, friends, or pets she would like to say good night to. Staple together some pages of colorful paper; glue one picture per page. Under each picture write, *Good night* _____. The child can read her own book every night as she says good night to the people and things that are special to her. *(words in print)*

The Grouchy Ladybug

by Eric Carle

* Concepts of print
* Identifying feelings
* Animal defenses
* Letter-sound association
* Mini language lessons
* Math/science concepts
* Structure writing/Model writing
* Process writing

SETTING THE STAGE

Instantly singable songs and the appealing rhyme and rhythm of finger plays will encourage children to be involved in story time.

"The Grump-a-Rump-a-Saurus" by Mr. Al, *Rock the Baby*

"The Rattlin' Bog" by Sharon, Lois & Bram, *In the Schoolyard*
(A fun, cumulative song)

BYE-BYE, BEE!

What do you suppose?	*(cock head to side)*
A bee sat on my nose!	*(put finger on nose)*
And what do you think?	*(cock head to side)*
She gave me a wink!	*(wink or blink)*
Then she said, "I beg your pardon,	
I thought you were the garden."	
Bye-bye, bee!	*(move finger through the air)*

CLAP YOUR HANDS

Clap your hands, clap your hands,	*(do each motion)*
Clap them just like me.	
Touch your shoulders, touch your shoulders,	
Touch them just like me.	
Tap your knees, tap your knees,	
Tap them just like me.	
Shake your head, shake your head,	
Shake it just like me.	
Clap your hands, clap your hands,	
Now let them quiet be.	*(fold hands in lap)*

FIRST READING

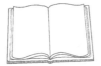

What kind of bug is on the cover of our story today? Would you want to hold one? Tell me what you know about ladybugs. Sometimes ladybugs are red and sometimes they are yellow, but they always have big dots on their backs. Those big dots are often black. Ladybugs are our good friends because they eat tiny insects called aphids that chew on leaves. Usually ladybugs are friendly, quiet little bugs. But look at the face on this ladybug. How do you think she is feeling? You are right—she is so very cross that the name of our story is *The Grouchy Ladybug.* It was written by Eric Carle. Perhaps you have seen his name before on *The Very Hungry Caterpillar.* Mr. Carle wrote us a special message about aphids and ladybugs right across from the title page. Let's read it together.

    Read The Grouchy Ladybug *through completely, remembering that the first reading is for enjoying the language and drama of the story. Discussion will come later. Begin with a soft, small voice for the yellow jacket and get a little louder with each page until the whale is the loudest of all.*

GETTING INVOLVED

Tell me why you think the author of *The Grouchy Ladybug* talked about the yellow jacket's stinger and the lobster's claws. Does every animal have a form of protection? Let's *pretend* our way through the ladybug's adventure. First the friendly ladybug "flew in from the left"; the grouchy one "flew from the right." Then she "flew off" and met the yellow jacket "showing its stinger." Where is the stinger? Show me the stag beetle "opening its jaws." Do you think it made a sound? How would a praying mantis "reach out with its long front legs"? Next the sparrow "opened its sharp beak." The lobster "stretched its claws." Why was it scary when the skunk started to "lift its tail"? Say the boa constrictor's words with me, "If you insis-s-s-t." Do you know how a boa protects itself? What does it mean when the hyena "laughed eerily and showed its teeth"? Show me how the gorilla "beat its chest" and next, the rhinoceros "lowered its horn." How did the elephant "raise its trunk and show its big tusks"?

Be ready now. When I say the word "slap," clap your hands with a huge clap. Remember the grouchy ladybug talked first to the whale's flippers, then its fin, and finally its tail. And the whale's tail gave the grouchy ladybug such a "slap" that it "flew across the sea and across the land" and *sat down* on the leaf with the aphids.

A CLOSER LOOK

With each rereading of a story, children gain new understanding. Pause often for a spontaneous flow of oral language as the children share their feelings and observations. Extend the learning process with your own questions in repeated readings of the story.

* Have you ever felt like the grouchy ladybug? *(reflecting)*

* Tell me what you noticed about the *sizes* of the animals? The pages? The words on the pages? *(observation)*

* Would you agree that the author was telling us to change our voices? *(evaluating)*

* What would happen if we changed the order of the animals in the story? *(application)*

* Why is the sun going *higher* on each page? When does it start going *lower*? *(analyzing)*

* Which animal would frighten you? *(reflecting)*

* Tell me why we can't see all of the whale on one page. *(analyzing)*

* I wonder if the whale heard the ladybug talking. *(reflecting)*

* Where in the story would you say, "Oh, I just love that part"? *(reflecting)*

* Why did the leaf say "thank you" when all the aphids were gone? *(comprehension)*

* I wonder if the grouchy ladybug and the friendly ladybug saw each other again. *(reflecting)*

STORY TIME EXTENSIONS

Fireflies, Fireflies, Light My Way by Jonathan London

When the Woods Hum by Joanne Ryder

Bee Tree by Patricia Polacco

Thomas' Snowsuit by Robert Munsch

Time To . . . by Bruce McMillan

BALANCED LITERACY ACTIVITIES

POETRY

BUT I WONDER
But I wonder . . .
The crickets in the thickets,
and the katydids in trees,
and ants on plants, and butterflies,
and ladybugs and bees
don't smell with little noses
but with *feelers,* if you please.
They get along quite nicely,
but I wonder how they *sneeze.*
Aileen Fisher

THE BIG CLOCK
Slowly ticks the big clock;
Tick-Tock, Tick-Tock!
But Cuckoo clock ticks double quick;
Tick-a-tock-a, tick-a-tock-a,
Tick-a-tock, -a, tick!
Author unknown

FIREFLY
by Elizabeth Madox Roberts
from *Read-Aloud Rhymes for
the Very Young*
by Jack Prelutsky

INVOLVEMENT

DRAMATIZATION

The dramatic words of the grouchy ladybug's encounters just beg children to join in the dialog of the story. Simple props add to the drama. Provide a variety of art materials in your art center and encourage the children to create headbands or stick puppets for the story characters. (The emphasis is on the creative process, not the product.) Be sure to include a friendly ladybug; the whale's flippers, fins, and tail; and some fireflies. Because children often feel more confident dramatizing a story when they act in pairs, make two sets of everything.

Have the children wear or carry the props as they sequence themselves in a line or a circle. The remaining children will be the chorus. Ask them what body movement they will use to add emphasis to the words, "Hey you, want to fight?"; a second movement for "If you insist"; and a third action for "Oh, you're not big enough." Talk about the way the words will sound. As you narrate the story, the children will role-play the animal characters and the chorus will join in on the marvelous repetitive phrases. The focus of dramatization is always to enjoy and understand the story. Shakespeare couldn't have asked for a better *in the round* drama!

Add to the fun with a large clock made from the side of an appliance box. Write large numbers on the face of the clock and attach the hands with big brads. Have two children stand beside the clock and rotate the hands for each time change in the story.

Keep the props available in a drama center for individual play. What child can resist the line, "Hey you, want to fight?"

INTEGRATION

BUT I WONDER

Poetry is the perfect beginning to any read-aloud experience. And the delightful poem "But I Wonder" is a perfect accompaniment to *The Grouchy Ladybug*. After the children have listened to the marvelous imagery of the poem, talk about all the phrases. Ask them to tell you about "crickets in thickets and katydids in trees." Then print the poem on chart paper with alternating lines of colors. Put pointers nearby. The text will be so familiar the children will read many of the words independently or in pairs. Divide the children into small groups to illustrate lines of the poem for an imaginative mural that will bring together the language of art and the language of words.

THE GROUCHY LADYBUG'S JOURNEY

To write an adaptation of the original story, brainstorm with the children about other animals the grouchy ladybug might have met on her journey. Talk about the size, habitat, and protection of each new animal. Sequence the animals according to size and create your own ladybug journey big book. (As with any innovation, give credit to the original story and author on the title page.) Cut the cover and all the pages of your book in the shape of a ladybug. At the top of the pages of text, print the words, *The grouchy ladybug saw a _____.* At the bottom of each page print, *It was too _____ to fight.* The text on the last page could be, *The grouchy ladybug saw a ladybug. Who wants to fight anyway?* After the children have illustrated the pages and written or dictated the words for the sentences, bind the pages into a class book for your library corner. Predictable text helps children learn to read.

WRITING AND THE LADYBUG

✳ Children bring meaning to stories through their prior experiences. The way each child constructs meaning is unique to him because of the connections he makes to his own life. Talk about feelings and the things that happen that make children grouchy. Ask the children how they can handle grouchy feelings without fighting. Responses might include "I will talk about my feelings," "I will stamp my feet," "I will jump up and down," or "I will go to Australia!" (like the child in Judith Viorst's story *Alexander and the Terrible, Horrible, No Good, Very Bad Day*).

As the children watch, write their responses on a chart, My Grouchy Days. Model the writing process by saying each word, emphasizing beginning, ending, or medial sounds. The children will hear and see the sound-letter connections. When you reread the chart, teach a mini language lesson on one-to-one correspondence or punctuation or verbs. Underline the most familiar words that children need to know in their reading and writing. Add them to the visible word wall resource in your room.

✳ Individual responses to storybooks are often expressed in children's writing. Children need daily opportunities to make choices about their own writing and to write freely without correction. Writing is a natural way to learn language. My Grouchy Days may very well nudge open the door of a child's imagination into a new grouchy ladybug adventure, a journal entry, a letter, or a contrasting response about My Happy Days.

✳ Write the old-time favorite Rice Krispie cookie recipe together, modeling the writing process as you think out loud about letters and sounds. Read one step of the recipe at a time and talk about measurements as you prepare the recipe together. Shape the no-bake, red-tinted ingredients into cookie ladybugs, adding raisins for spots and pretzels for legs and feelers. Where in the story rereading will the children choose to eat the ladybugs?

LADYBUG MATH

✳ *Estimate* the total number of insect feelers, legs, and wings on your poem mural. Write down each child's estimated number. Count by twos, then by fives, as you tally the actual number.

✳ Glue sets of black dots on tagboard ladybugs, one set for each numeral from one to ten. Make a plus sign and a minus sign. Use the tagboard ladybugs to make addition and subtraction *story problems* meaningful. Demonstrate a few number stories such as "Seven ladybugs flew into the thicket. Four flew out again. How many ladybugs were left in the thicket?" Call on children to choose the cards and the mathematical sign that will tell the story while the others write the number sentence, $7 - 4 = 3$, on paper or chalkboards. Ask the children to think of ladybug story problems and call on others to solve the equations.

A THEME TOPIC STUDY OF LADYBUGS

You will find a nonfiction inquiry research project on ladybugs in the full-color Inquiry insert.

EVERYDAY LEARNING ACTIVITIES

Positive parenting; developmental learning activities; and a warm, nurturing environment are major factors in a child's academic success and lifetime learning.

Sometimes children are just like the ladybug in *The Grouchy Ladybug* by Eric Carle, acting tough or in very inappropriate ways simply because they are children. They are just learning what behavior is acceptable in the adult world. The word *discipline* is really a very positive word. It means the process of teaching that goes on all the time as you quietly train children to use desirable behavior and avoid undesirable behavior. Remember the basic principle: children will repeat whatever behavior gets the *payoff* of your attention. You want to "catch them doin' good" and respond with attention and praise. Children are so desirous of your approval that they will repeat the behavior you noticed and responded to. In fact, if a child's choice is between the negative attention of a scolding or a spanking or no attention at all, he will choose the negative. If a child is being as stubborn as the grouchy ladybug, step in early. Take control and stop the undesirable behavior calmly and firmly. Have him sit on a chair until the timer goes off. Don't say, "Now the next time . . ." because that just challenges a child to misbehave again. Expect obedience. Never make a request that you don't intend to follow through on. The child will soon learn whether you are a person of empty words or of action. It is the overall atmosphere of quiet firmness that conveys the message, "You are safe. I won't let you go too far." That's what good discipline is all about.

✳ In the story *The Grouchy Ladybug,* every animal had its own form of protection. Read the story again and discuss why animals need protection. Talk about the skunk's defense, the yellow jacket's stinger, the lobster's claws, and so on. Go out in the yard and look for aphids on the underside of leaves. Decide if *they* have any form of protection. *(science concepts)*

✳ Teach a child to identify his feelings and work through them without hurting others. You may want to say, "The rule in our house is there will be no hitting" or "no unkind words." Sometimes a whole family needs to find ways to respect the feelings of others. *(identifying feelings)*

✳ Using old magazines and construction paper, let a child cut and paste an animal collage. Have him dictate a title and a sentence for you to write on his picture. *(classifying, print)*

✳ A child must understand the concept of morning, afternoon, and evening before he is able to tell time. Talk about what you do each part of the day. Point out the hands of the clock at different times during the day. When a child is ready for the skill of telling time, you will enjoy *The Grouchy Ladybug* all over again. It is a good example of a book that offers continuous learning as a child grows. *(concept of time)*

✳ Enjoy reading *Thomas' Snowsuit* by Robert Munsch, a hilarious tale of "no!" as a determined child refuses to put on his snowsuit. Read also *Donna O'Neeshuck Was Chased By Some Cows* by Bill Grossman, the story of a little girl being chased by animals and townspeople because they want her head pats.

Have You Seen My Duckling?

by Nancy Tafuri

TEACHING FOCUS

* A wordless book
* Concepts of print
* Letter-sound association
* Sequencing

* Model writing/Structure writing
* Process writing
* Theme topic: a pond habitat
* Nonfiction

SETTING THE STAGE

Instantly singable songs and the appealing rhyme and rhythm of finger plays will encourage children to be involved in story time.

"Five Little Ducks" by Raffi, *Rise and Shine*

"Six Little Ducks" by Raffi, *More Singable Songs for the Very Young*

FIVE LITTLE DUCKS
Five little ducks went in for a swim;
The first little duck put his head in.
The second little duck put his head back;
The third little duck said, "Quack, quack, quack."
The fourth little duck with his tiny brother,
Went for a walk with his father and mother.

(hold up hand, extend fingers)
(point to each finger in turn)

("walk" fingers up opposite arm)

I CAN
I can tie my shoe lace,
I can brush my hair,
I can wash my hands and face
And dry myself with care.

I can clean my teeth too,
And fasten up my frocks.
I can say "How do you do"
And pull up both my socks.

(lead the children through appropriate motions with each phrase)

FIRST READING

Wordless books have a valuable place in children's literature. The joyful process of reading pictures is the earliest stage of reading. Wordless books encourage children to notice the details of beautiful illustrations, make discoveries for themselves, and anticipate what is going to happen next. Because the plot is supplied through the illustrations, children concentrate on telling the story in their own words. You are just a skillful guide. The children are the real storytellers. They will feel a sense of accomplishment in their ability to read a complete book.

The title of this book, *Have You Seen My Duckling?*, is a question that a mother duck asks her friends who live nearby in the pond. Count the ducklings on the cover. What do you think will happen?

The silver medal on the cover lets us know this is a Caldecott Honor Book. That is an award given to the illustrator and author, Nancy Tafuri, for the lovely, detailed pictures. They make you feel you are right there on the pond with Mother Duck asking, "Have you seen my duckling?"

If you begin with the title page and then look carefully at every picture, you will be able to tell the story in your own words. Be sure to always count the ducklings. Watch the butterfly and see whether you can spot the wandering duckling in every picture.

GETTING INVOLVED

Play "Find the Missing Duckling" with a mama duck and her ducklings. While everyone's eyes are covered, select one duckling to wander away from the nest. First have the children identify which duckling is missing. Then act out the story with the hidden duckling quacking softly as his family searches for him. Celebrate with soft quacks when he is discovered.

Variation: Have the children name in sequence the pond animals that Mother Duck talked to as she swam around the pond. Write the names of Mother Duck, the eight ducklings, the butterfly, and the animals on name cards to hang around the children's necks. Mother Duck, with seven ducklings in line behind her, can approach each of the animals in turn to ask, "Have you seen my duckling?" It will be a new experience for the children to dramatize a story with a single line of text.

A CLOSER LOOK

With each rereading of a story, children gain new understanding. Pause often for a spontaneous flow of oral language as the children share their feelings and observations. Extend the learning process with your own questions in repeated readings of the story.

✱ Did the author start telling the story on the title page? *(observation)*

✱ Why did the duckling leave the nest? *(reasoning)*

✱ Who noticed the duckling leaving? What do you think they are saying to him? *(interpretation)*

✱ What do you suppose the ducklings are saying to Mother Duck? *(interpretation)*

✱ I wonder why ducklings swim in a line behind a mother duck. *(reflecting)*

✱ Do you think the animals that Mother Duck met were her friends? *(reasoning)*

✱ In your opinion, is a pond a good place for the animals to live? *(evaluating)*

✱ How can it be that the other duck and ducklings look so different from Mother Duck? *(reasoning)*

✱ Would you agree that the butterfly was an important part of the story? *(evaluating)*

✱ Who found the duckling? Was he ever very far away? *(comprehension)*

✱ Do you think the duckling ever felt frightened that he was lost? *(interpretation)*

✱ What do you imagine the little duckling is saying to the turtle and butterfly? *(reflecting)*

✱ Tell me all the words you can think of to describe the last picture. *(interpretation)*

✱ Where do you think the butterfly is in that picture? *(interpretation)*

✱ Does *Have You Seen My Duckling?* make you think of another story? *(application)*

STORY TIME EXTENSIONS

In the Small, Small Pond by Denise Fleming

Little Beaver and the Echo by Amy McDonald

Otters Under Water by Jim Arnosky

Fish Is Fish by Leo Lionni

The Story of Ping by Marjorie Flack

BALANCED LITERACY ACTIVITIES

POETRY

SALLY AND MANDA
  Sally and Manda are two little lizards
Who gobble up flies
  in their two little gizzards.
They live by a toadstool
  near two little hummocks
And crawl all around
  on their two little stomachs.
  Alice B. Campbell

DUCKS IN THE RAIN
Ducks are dabbling in the rain,
Dibbling, dabbling in the rain.
Drops of water from each back
Scatter as ducks flap and quack.

I can only stand and look
From my window at the brook,
For I cannot flap and quack
And scatter raindrops from my back.
  James S. Tippett

INVOLVEMENT

QUACK, QUACK, QUACK

Children enjoy singing the catchy melody of the song "Six Little Ducks" (see p. 74). Each time you sing, choose a child to hold a feather and sing the words, "Quack, quack, quack" all alone. After the children have memorized the words, ask them to suggest other actions to substitute for "quack, quack, quack" such as "He led the others with a waddle, waddle, waddle" or "a flap, flap, flap." The children won't need much encouragement to move as the ducks moved.

Extension: Print the words of "Six Little Ducks" on the pages of a book for the children to illustrate. Put the reproduction and a tape of the children singing in a listening center for independent or paired reading. Music is a language of patterns and reading is a language of patterns.

INTEGRATION

IN A POND

Compare the pond where the duckling lived in *Have You Seen My Duckling?* to a river, a lake, and an ocean. As the children read the pictures and retell the story, ask them to name the other animals that lived in the pond. List the animals on chart paper using alternating colors. Guide the children's attention to the print as you ask them to say the names of the letters and the sounds they make.

Another time, have the children look for characteristics of a pond habitat, such as cattails, reeds, lily pads, nests, dams, stones, and mud. Print the words on a second list, again focusing on letters and their corresponding sounds.

Gather a variety of nonfiction books for your reading center, such as the short and simple *Busy Beavers* by Lydia Dabcovich, the wordless *In the Pond* by Ermanno Cristini, and the imaginative yet scientifically correct *Lizard in the Sun* by Joanne Ryder. The children will keep turning the pages of the superbly illustrated *Chameleons* by Claudia Schneiper as well as John Schoenherr's *Rebel,* the story of a wild gosling that leaves the nest to explore the pond alone. Enjoy also the marvelous language and illustrations of the books suggested in Story Time Extensions on the previous page. As the children discover new animals and new characteristics of a pond habitat, add them to your lists. Allow time for children to share their discoveries because children must talk about what they are learning.

Create a pond habitat on a large piece of bulletin board paper. Decide on a daytime scene with butterflies or a nighttime scene with fireflies. Pencil in a simple background for the children to paint, encouraging them to add all the things unique to a pond setting that you have listed. Have each child draw, tear, or cut out something that lives in the pond, again referring to your list. Label everything and print the name and author of the story. Hopefully, you will have room to add Mother Duck and the eight ducklings swimming right through the middle of your pond.

H FOR HABITAT

Print the words *Have* (from the book title) and *Habitat* (from the pond charts). Ask the children to tell you everything they notice about the two words. When they observe that the words begin the same, ask for the name of the letter *H,* then the sound the *H* makes. Challenge them to find other words in the children's responses in the room that also begin with *H.* Print them on your chart. Letter-sound association has meaning for children when it is taught in the context of familiar words.

AUTHOR'S CHAIR

The simple plot and familiar setting of *Have You Seen My Duckling?* offer a perfect opportunity for independent writing. Provide an individual blank book for each child to retell the story or create an original story based on the book's pattern. It can be a wordless book or one written with developmental spelling or with the child's language dictated to the teacher. Then, sitting in the Author's Chair, let each child lead the children through her story. Children read their own language best.

NO, I HAVE BEEN BUSY!

The animals in the story did not respond when Mother Duck asked if they had seen her duckling. Involve the children in a discussion of what each animal might have said. Perhaps the beaver was too busy chewing, the frog was busy croaking, the salamander was busy laying eggs. Refer to your list of pond animals until every child has an animal to draw. Each child will have two pages to illustrate. The first page will have the words *Have you seen my duckling?* printed at the top. The second page will say, *No, I have been busy* _____. Mount and sequence the pages in a class book that your emergent readers will return to again and again.

HAVE YOU SEEN MY BABY BEAVER?

Every time children write an innovation they are giving meaning to a familiar story and making it their own. Create an original story based on *Have You Seen My Duckling?*'s format, pattern, and setting. As a group, decide on a different mother animal, where she will look for her missing baby, and who she will ask. For example, a mother beaver with seven little beavers behind her could swim under and above water, asking a fish, snake, frog, turtle, and so on, *Have you seen my baby beaver?* Have children illustrate the pages individually or in pairs with the same sentence repeated on each page. Of course the hidden baby beaver will reappear on the last page for a happy reunion.

Variation: This activity would adapt well to small group learning, with each group of three or four children deciding on a different animal for its story. Mount the illustrated pages and bind them in class books or display them on the walls. By now, your room will probably resemble a pond!

SALLY AND MANDA

Because of the funny words in "Sally and Manda," it will not be long before the children have memorized the poem. Model the writing process as you write the text on chart paper, thinking out loud about letters and sounds. The language will come to life when the children illustrate the words. Then write the lines on sentence strips for the children to sequence or match to the chart poem in your poetry corner.

EVERYDAY LEARNING ACTIVITIES

Positive parenting; developmental learning activities; and a warm, nurturing environment are major factors in a child's academic success and lifetime learning.

In the story *Have You Seen My Duckling?* by Nancy Tafuri, the little duckling was safe even though it was out of sight. Sadly, in today's world, children are no longer safe. It is the parents' and caregivers' responsibility to protect them. No longer can children be out of sight, even for a minute, in grocery stores, parking lots, malls, schoolyards, and playgrounds. Set boundaries and make consistent rules for a child. In her book *Your Baby and Child,* Dr. Penelope Leach (p. 427) encourages parents to establish the absolute rule that a child "must never go anywhere with anybody without coming to tell you, or whoever is looking after him, first." She states that the message is easy for this age to understand and to remember because it can be practiced every day. Rather than create fears, always assure a child that it is your job to keep him safe.

* Every child needs to be able to identify herself and where she lives. Sometimes we use a child's full name only when we are upset with her. Instead, we should make a child feel special when we use her first, middle, and last names. After all, she is probably the only person in the world with that exact name. Talk to her often about the day she was born and of everyone's happiness at her birth. Teach her her birthdate and also her full address. A child needs to know the name of her town or city, as well as the street she lives on. She can easily learn her phone number as well, for a child learns simply by repetition. Sing it to a familiar tune and she will remember. *(safety, self-esteem)*

* A fun way to practice gross motor skills, using the large muscles of arms and legs, is to pretend to be different animals. Running like a horse, hopping like a frog, and jumping like kangaroos are all ways to practice these skills outside. *(motor skills)*

* To increase visual memory skills, place four different items on a tabletop. Have a child close her eyes while you remove one item. When she guesses, switch roles. Gradually build up the number of items until she can spot one item removed from ten. *(visual memory)*

* Encourage a child to look, really look, at something the way a scientist would. Choose a different object to observe each day—a ray of sunshine on the floor, an animal, clouds, ants, insects. Be clever. Keep drawing out observations about how things look; move; make noise; have color, shape, legs, wings, and protection. *(visual discrimination, science)*

* Every time a child looks at a storybook, she should be able to see something new she has not seen before. Reading pictures is a beginning step in reading. *(visual discrimination)*

Hush! A Thai Lullaby

by Minfong Ho

* Cultural diversity
* Phonemic awareness
* Process writing
* Story structure

* Mini language lessons
* Math story problems
* Theme topic: lullabies
* A family activity

SETTING THE STAGE

Instantly singable songs and the appealing rhyme and rhythm of finger plays will encourage children to be involved in story time.

"Hush Little Baby"—*traditional song*

"Gartan Mother's Lullaby" by Walt Disney Recordings, *For Our Children*
(A haunting, beautiful melody sung by a loving mother to her child, sung by Meryl Streep)

OUR LITTLE BABY

One little baby	*(one finger up)*
Rocking in the tree.	*(rock clasped arms)*
Two little babies	*(two fingers up)*
Splashing in the sea.	*(arms splashing)*
Three little babies	*(three fingers up)*
Crawling on the floor.	*(crawl fingers up legs)*
Four little babies	*(four fingers up)*
Banging on the door.	*(one fist over other)*
Five little babies	*(five fingers up)*
Playing hide-and-seek.	*(cover face with hands)*
Keep your eyes closed tight, now,	
Until I say . . . PEEK!	*(uncover face)*

ROCK THE BABY

This is baby ready for a nap,	*(lift index finger)*
Lay baby down in a loving lap.	*(finger in other palm)*
Cover baby up so it won't peep.	*(close hand over finger)*
Rock the baby till it's fast asleep.	*(rocking motion)*

FIRST READING

Tell me everything you see on the cover of this book. Why do you think the mother has her finger up to her lips? Do you ever do that and say "Sh"? The mother is saying "Hush!" to a mosquito and that is exactly the name of the story. Does that give you a clue as to what the story is about?

The author of the story, Minfong Ho, grew up in a country far away called Thailand. I'll help you find it on our map. The cover of the book tells us that "in Thailand, Minfong Ho was lulled to sleep by evening sounds—the whine of mosquitoes, the call of bullfrogs and lizards, the soft swish of a water buffalo's tail." Do you hear sounds like that when you are falling to sleep? What sounds do you hear at night? Many years later, when Minfong Ho was singing her own baby to sleep, she remembered the sounds of the countryside and made up this lullaby. Tell me what you think a lullaby is. The title of the story is *Hush! A Thai Lullaby*.

The silver medallion on the book is the Caldecott Honor Medal. That is an award given to the illustrator, Holly Meade, for her beautiful pictures. Let's do a picture walk through the story. Tell me all the details you see in the illustrations and what you think is happening. Every page, even the title page, has something you would see in Thailand but rarely in our country *(reed fan or broom, hammock, woven mat, objects suspended from above, stilts, and so on)*. Be sure to look for the baby, too. After our picture walk, I'll read the words of the story.

GETTING INVOLVED

Did the animal noises in *Hush! A Thai Lullaby* sound different to you? Why do you think they were strange? Say the sounds with me so you can join in when we read the story again. The small mosquito came weeping "wee-wee, wee-wee." The long-tailed lizard was peeping "tuk-ghaa, tuk-ghaa." Here's one that's familiar! What did the lean black cat say when he came creeping? The fat gray mouse was squeaking "jeed-jeed, jeed-jeed." Then the green frog came leaping "op-op, op-op." Next the muddy fat pig was sniffling "uut-uut, uut-uut." The glossy white duck came beeping "ghap-ghap, ghap-ghap." Then the loose-limbed monkey came swinging "jiak-jiak, jiak-jiak."

Let me show you the words for the next animal sound. Why do you think the words are written in capital letters? That old water buffalo came sweeping with a loud voice "MAAAU, MAAAU." Look, the elephant's words are in capital letters, too. He came shrieking "HOOM-PRAAA! HOOM-PRAAA!" No wonder the mother said, "Hush!"

This time when I read the story, you join me. Put your finger up to your lips every time I read the word "Hush!" Move like the animals as you make their sounds with me. I can't wait to see the muddy fat pig sniffling! Remember to join in every time I read the words "Don't you cry, My baby's sleeping right nearby."

A CLOSER LOOK

With each rereading of a story, children gain new understanding. Pause often for a spontaneous flow of oral language as the children share their feelings and observations. Extend the learning process with your own questions in repeated readings of the story.

* I wonder how the author thought of the words, "Who's that weeping in the wind?" *(reflecting)*

* Do you think that was a good beginning sentence? *(evaluating)*

* Would you call that a broom or a fan in the first picture? A lamp or a lantern? *(reasoning)*

* In your opinion, is a hammock a good bed for a baby? *(evaluating)*

* What do you see hanging from the ceiling? Why? *(comprehension)*

* Why were the house and rice barn on stilts? Why the ladders? *(reasoning)*

* Do you think the mother knew the baby was awake and wandering about? *(evaluating)*

* Tell me what you know about the words *sty*, *well*, *thatched*, and *water pot*. *(vocabulary)*

* What would happen if we changed the order of animals? *(application)*

* Are all the animals in the nighttime mountain picture? The baby? *(observation)*

* How does the nighttime mountain picture make you feel? *(reflecting)*

* Would you like to be there? *(reflecting)*

STORY TIME EXTENSIONS

Hush Little Baby—A Folk Lullaby by Aliki

Hush! A Gaelic Lullaby by Carole Gerber

Grandfather's Journey by Allen Say

Fishing Sunday by Tony Johnston

Grandfather's Dream by Holly Keller

BALANCED LITERACY ACTIVITIES

POETRY

COME TO THE WINDOW
Come to the window,
　My baby, with me,
And look at the stars
　That shine on the sea.
There are two little stars
　That play at bo-peep
With two little fish
　Far down in the deep;
And two little frogs
　Cry neap, neap, neap;
I see a dear baby
　That should be asleep.

Traditional

SLEEP, BABY, SLEEP!
　Sleep, baby, sleep!
Thy father watches the sheep.
Thy mother is shaking the dreamland tree,
And down falls a little dream on thee.
　Sleep, baby, sleep!

　Sleep, baby, sleep!
The large stars are the sheep.
The little stars are the lambs, I guess.
The big round moon is the shepherdess.
　Sleep, baby sleep!

Traditional

(Teaching point: thy *and* thee, *words from another generation)*

INVOLVEMENT

LULLABY MUSIC

Would you believe you can sing this lullaby to another lullaby tune? It's beautiful. Sing the words the mother spoke to each creature to the melody of the traditional "Hush Little Baby, A Folk Lullaby."

　　On another day, add the sound of a wind chime or rain stick every time mother repeats the words to the pattern, "Hush! Who's that weeping in the wind?"

　　In another rereading, give each animal's voice a sound with a rhythm instrument, such as a triangle, drum, scraper, maraca, woodblock, or jingle tap. Let the children decide which sound best represents the "wee-wee, wee-wee" of the mosquito, the "jiak-jiak, jiak-jiak" of the swinging loose-limbed monkey, or the shrieking "HOOM-PRAAA! HOOM-PRAAA!" of the great big elephant.

　　Not only does music allow children to feel the *voice* of a story, but also the patterns in music and the patterns of repetitive language stimulate learning connections in the brain.

DRAMATIZATION

Drama, art, animal characters, and repetitious language are a powerful combination that exclaims, "This story *must* be performed!" Provide a basic outline for a mask and a variety of paints that children can mix together. Encourage them to paint or add features to their masks that are unique to the animals they have chosen.

Talk about and chart on a story structure matrix the setting, characters, and sequence of events in the story. Drama is a powerful teaching tool in helping children understand the plot structure of a story. Write a list of props as the children decide what they need. Then assign speaking parts to the animals with the others joining in on the repetitive chant.

Put a tape of the drama, the masks, and the props in the drama center for the children to revisit spontaneously. Perform both the play and the musical story reading as a celebration at the conclusion of your learning with the storybook *Hush!* This thespian art needs an audience!

INTEGRATION

ANIMAL MATH

Use the animal character masks to make addition and subtraction story problems meaningful. Demonstrate a few number stories such as "There were two animals behind the rice barn. Three animals joined them. How many animals in all?" Have the children who are holding animal masks act out the story problem as the others write the number sentence, $2 + 3 = 5$, on paper or chalkboards. Your children will be "squeaking" and "shrieking" to take over and create their own stories.

WORD STUDY

Write the repetitive chant and the animal names on sentence strips. Encourage the children to manipulate the text and change the animal name sentence strips as they read. Have the children draw illustrations for the chart.

Make a second chart to include the verb phrase for each creature, such as *Mosquito, mosquito, don't come weeping; Lizard, lizard, don't come peeping;* and so on. The question *Can't you see that baby's sleeping?* will stay at the bottom of the pocket chart to be read after every animal's verb phrase.

MINI LANGUAGE LESSONS

Mini language lessons and demonstrations of reading skills and strategies will flow naturally out of the charts you and the children have made. Depending on the language skills of your children, consider demonstrating left-to-right progression, beginning and ending sounds, sequencing, contractions, question marks, quotation marks, and the word ending *ing*. Modeling, experimenting, and working together are vital parts of the learning process.

Hush!
Elephant, elephant,
don't you cry.
My baby's sleeping
right nearby.
Mosquito, mosquito.
Monkey, monkey,
Buffalo, buffalo,
Black cat, Black cat,
Green frog, green frog,

PHONEMIC AWARENESS

Using the story's *eep* word family, help children discover each word's onset and rime by dividing the base words into first sounds and final sounds. For example, ask them to say "weep" without the *w* and then say weep without the *eep*. Do the same with each *eep* word in the story.

As the children watch, write each word on a word card, adding the *ing* ending to each base word. Have the children actually cut apart each word card into onset, rime, and ending. Put the word parts in a pocket chart. Let the children manipulate the word parts, creating the word family once again. Some children may choose to reproduce the words on a chalkboard or with rubber ABC stamps. Some may copy the words from the chart by writing the onset in one color, the rime in another, and the ending in a third. Word recognition is easier for children when they focus on chunks of sounds.

THE FASTEST WAY TO GET BABY TO SLEEP

Children comprehend the meaning of a story when they make connections to their own lives. The dilemma of the mother who couldn't get her baby to sleep is something most children can respond to from their own experiences. Ask them for their ideas on the fastest way to get a baby to sleep. Children are eager for opportunities to talk about their experiences. Encourage them to give you the beginning, middle, and ending sounds of the words as you write their answers on a chart. After each child has a phrase to illustrate, mount their pictures and add their wisdom and humor to the reading responses in your room.

IN ANOTHER LAND AFAR

In Floella Benjamin's lovely and reflective *Skip Across the Ocean: Nursery Rhymes from Around the World,* the author says a treasure chest of lullabies is opened every time a child is born. With lullaby music playing, read aloud her collection of lullabies and poems from many lands. Read also the more familiar traditional rhymes and gentle lullabies of Michael Hague's *Sleep, Baby, Sleep: Lullabies and Night Poems.* Listen to the bilingual language of *Grandmother's Nursery Rhymes Las Nanas de Abuelita* by Nelly P. Jaramillo. Compare the ways mothers from seven continents croon their infants to sleep, each in her own language, in

Nancy Van Laan's peaceful *Sleep, Sleep, Sleep: A Lullaby for Little Ones Around the World*. It is a well-crafted book that begs to be chanted aloud as each culture says, "Good night, go to sleep, little one."

WRITING A TREASURE CHEST OF LULLABIES

Encourage children to talk about the lullabies of other lands. Challenge them to comparative thinking. Is the language for bedtime the same around the world? Were the children soothed and comforted by words from other countries? How did the illustrations make the words come to life?

Decide together how to create your own *Treasure Chest of Lullabies*. Storybooks often give birth to children's own ideas in writing. Some may choose to retell or innovate a favorite lullaby from a book you have read. Some may write an original rhyme for a baby brother or sister or ask mom and dad to sing a remembered lullaby. Children's writing has meaning for them when they can write from experience without corrections or constraint. Play lullaby music while the children are writing, as well as every time you read together from your class *Treasure Chest of Lullabies*. Music stimulates learning and creativity. "Barcarolle" by Offenbach, "Cradle Song" by Schubert, "Lullaby" by Brahms, and the folk songs "Hush Little Baby" and "All the Pretty Little Horses" are beautiful.

ALL AROUND THE ANIMAL WORLD

Children delight in listening to and talking about animal stories. Do animal mothers lull their babies to sleep? The masterful illustrations of *Sleep, Sleep, Sleep* are a natural springboard into the world of mother animals as they soothe their babies to sleep. Your children will be fascinated with the rich language and illustrations of Denise Fleming's delightful *Time to Sleep* as the animals see, smell, hear, and taste the signs of their impending winter naps. And from their nighttime habitats, the animals of Africa will call to them in the rhythmic language and stunning pictures of Daniel Alderman's *Africa Calling Nighttime Falling* and Rachel Isadora's extraordinary *A South African Night*. The powerful word pictures of all the books are lessons in themselves.

A CELEBRATION

Create a simulation of the thatched cottage, pig sty, and rice barn in your room. Use large cardboard cartons, building blocks, and branches, or put the children's bulletin-board-paper illustrations on the walls. Suspend a hammock made of a sheet from the ceiling and weave a mat for the floor. Add sandals, flour sacks of crumpled paper, jugs, a plastic pool for the pond, a huge lid for the well cover, a ladder made from broomsticks and paper towel tubing, stuffed animals, and puppets. Ask the children for ideas on how to make and decorate a treasure chest for your lullabies.

Write lists and choose committees to plan a program, design invitations, and welcome the guests. On the big day, have the children perform the music-enriched drama of *Hush!* and share their many responses to another culture through their poetry, art expressions, and original lullabies. You are celebrating literature as the common ground for children's learning.

EVERYDAY LEARNING ACTIVITIES

Positive parenting; developmental learning activities; and a warm, nurturing environment are major factors in a child's academic success and lifetime learning.

The storybook *Hush! A Thai Lullaby* by Minfong Ho is an endearing story of a mother in Thailand soothing her baby to sleep with a lullaby. The language of bedtime is the same around the world. Music is not only a comfort and a source of joy to children but also, surprisingly, it is food for the brain. Music is made up of patterns, and the trillions of neurons waiting to be wired in a child's brain are hungrily seeking patterns. Music feeds the brain by building synapses between eagerly receptive neurons that are making connections for lifetime learning. Furthermore, the pathways of learning created in the early years are the identical connections a child will use later in life for logic, math, and science skills. Start now! Immerse your children in the beats, rhythms, and melodies of music from the moment of birth. Enjoy finger plays and chants, sing nursery rhymes, surround a child's play with classical music, dance and move to music, and sing along in the car. Give your child a rich musical environment that not only provides happy experiences now but also paves the way for trigonometry!

✳ Music and memory go together. Children retain much more of what they learn if it is put to music. Using a familiar tune, make up a rhyme about a child's address and phone number. She will not forget. *(memory)*

✳ Fill a small tub with soft, silky scarves, streamers, and ribbons. Help a child cut crepe paper, ribbon, or yarn streamers and staple them to popsicle sticks. Turn on the music and move, sway, and march together, swirling the scarves or streamers with wide, sweeping motions. Dance with happy abandonment to all kinds of music. Children must experience rhythm and patterns in their bodies. Add drums, wooden sticks, bells, clackers, and film canisters full of dry objects, such as macaroni, to the tub. The best instrument of all is a child's body. *(movement exploration)*

✳ The baby in the storybook *Hush!* slept in a hammock. Create a hammock for doll/baby play by tying the ends of a sheet and attaching both ends to something sturdy. Together, look for stuffed animals and a doll to be the characters of the story. Play lullaby music as you act it out. The beautiful words of the story will come to life. Stories have so much more meaning for children when they are involved. Later, use the same sheet to make a fort, a tent, or a parachute for more creative play. *(dramatization)*

✳ Prepare a party for the story characters in *Hush!* Spread rice cakes with peanut butter and make raisin triangles for eyes, circle banana slices for noses, apple slices for mouths. Better still, put out a variety of choices—marshmallows, cheese shavings, chocolate chips, pretzels, dry cereal—and let the children create the animal faces. The elephant and buffalo will be a challenge. *(self-expression)*

If You Give a Mouse a Cookie

by Laura Joffe Numeroff

TEACHING FOCUS

* Concepts of print
* Story structure
* Estimating
* Categorizing

* Cultural diversity
* Structure writing
* Sequencing
* A family activity

SETTING THE STAGE

Instantly singable songs and the appealing rhyme and rhythm of finger plays will encourage children to be involved in story time.

"Thank You for Being a Friend" by Billboard Presents, *Family Friendship Classics*

"What's Mine Is Yours" by Billboard Presents, *Family Friendship Classics*

THE BABY MICE

Where are the baby mice? Squeak, squeak, squeak.	*(one hand behind back)*
I cannot see them. Peek, peek, peek.	*(one hand over eyes)*
Here they come from the hole in the wall.	*(bring one hand around)*
One, two, three, four, five—that's all!	*(count fingers)*

I RAISED A GREAT HULLABALOO

I raised a great hullabaloo	*(arms waving over head)*
When I found a large mouse in my stew,	*(hold up mouse)*
Said the waiter, "Don't shout	*(finger to lips)*
And wave it about,	*(waving motion)*
Or the rest will be wanting one, too!"	*(pointing all around)*

FIRST READING

Why does the picture on the cover of this book make you smile? Tell me what you think is happening. Have you ever shared a cookie with a mouse? The name of the story is *If You Give a Mouse a Cookie*. It was written by Laura Joffe Numeroff and the pictures were drawn by Felicia Bond. She must really like little mice. You are going to smile when you see her wonderful pictures. Look for the mouse on every page. Sometimes he is very tiny, but he is there.

Turn to the half-title page. Where do you think the little mouse is walking? Tell me what you think he has on his back. Can you read the words on the page?

Where do you think the little boy is on the title page? Do you see the mouse? We have already seen the words "If You Give a Mouse a Cookie" three times. Read them with me. I'll turn the pages and you tell me the story.

GETTING INVOLVED

What did you like about the story *If You Give a Mouse a Cookie?* Tell me everything you know about mice. Now show me how they move. You are right—they move without a sound. Move about like mice until you hear me clap. That means danger, someone is coming, so be very still. When I clap three times, scurry back to your mouse hole for safety.

In the story it looks like the mouse and the boy told each other what they wanted without talking. Let's divide into two groups and you can tell me the story with your bodies and your faces. This group right here will be for everyone who would like to be the mouse. You will act out whatever the mouse does. If you would like to be the boy, stand in this group. Every time the boy does something, you will show us what he did. Let's practice. The story begins, "If you give a mouse a cookie," so the boys will pretend to hold out a cookie. Then the story says, "he's going to ask for a glass of milk," so the mice will pretend to hold a glass of milk. Good acting. I think Laura Joffe Numeroff would love to see you tell her story. *(Continue through the story, pausing for the two groups to pantomime each action.)*

Let me show you the last page of the story. Mice, you are sitting down with a cookie in your hands. Boys, you are sitting down with your eyes closed. You are probably thinking, "Oh no, not again!"

A CLOSER LOOK

With each rereading of a story, children gain new understanding. Pause often for a spontaneous flow of oral language as the children share their feelings and observations. Extend the learning process with your own questions in repeated readings of the story.

* Tell me what you liked about the mouse in the story. *(reflecting)*
* Would it be a lot of work to have a mouse for a pet? *(evaluating)*
* Would you agree that the boy was a good friend to the mouse? *(evaluating)*
* What do you think a "milk mustache" is? *(comprehension)*
* Why did the boy get nail scissors instead of regular scissors? *(reasoning)*
* What does it mean to get "carried away"? *(comprehension)*
* Have you ever gotten "carried away" with something? *(reflecting)*
* Tell me what the boy used to make a bed for the mouse. *(observation)*
* I wonder what the words are on the crayons. *(comprehension)*
* Tell me about the picture the mouse drew. Is he in the picture? *(comprehension)*
* What will happen if the boy gives the mouse another glass of milk? *(application)*
* Tell me your favorite part of the story. *(reflecting)*

STORY TIME EXTENSIONS

Mouse Mess by Linnea Riley

Shrinking Mouse by Pat Hutchins

Livingstone Mouse by Pamela Duncan Edwards

Who Sank the Boat? by Pamela Allen

Young Mouse and Elephant—An East African Folktale by Pamela J. Farris

BALANCED LITERACY ACTIVITIES

POETRY

MICE
I think mice
Are rather nice.

Their tails are long,
Their faces small,
They haven't any
Chins at all.
Their ears are pink,
Their teeth are white,
They run about
The house at night.
They nibble things
They shouldn't touch
And no one seems
To like them much.

But I think mice
Are nice.
Rose Fyleman

THE OLD WOMAN
by Beatrix Potter
from *Read-Aloud Rhymes for the Very Young*
by Jack Prelutsky

GOOD NEIGHBORS
by May Justus
from *Read-Aloud Rhymes for the Very Young*
by Jack Prelutsky

INVOLVEMENT

COOKIES AND MICE

What an irresistible combination—a charming mouse and a child's favorite cookie. No wonder children never tire of listening to *If You Give a Mouse a Cookie.* Add to the fun with a mouse puppet turning the pages as the children listen and share cookies (see Cookie Math). Pause often for a cloze activity with familiar nouns in the story such as "When he's finished giving himself a trim, he'll want a _____ to sweep up."

Another time, have the children sit in a circle with all the objects from the story (a cookie, a glass of milk, a straw, a napkin, a mirror, and so on) in the middle. As you read, ask the children to sequence the objects in a circular pattern. They will discover the story begins and ends with the cookie.

INTEGRATION

A CIRCLE STORY MAP

Create a circle story map by drawing a large circle on chart paper and dividing it into twelve equal sections. Place a cookie above the circle to identify the beginning and ending point of the story. Moving clockwise, with the circle story map on the floor, have the children add one object to each section of the circle as you read the story.

Replace the objects with child-drawn pictures. Paste them on the story map and hang it up in the room. Create a mouse corner with the chart, some stuffed animals, and a rocking chair. The predictable sequence will invite the children to become the storytellers.

Extension: Print the names of the objects on word cards for children to match to the pictures. Keep the word cards, the mouse puppet, and *If You Give a Mouse a Cookie* available in a reading basket. Smiles and reading guaranteed.

A MOUSE ACCORDION BOOK

✳ Make a class accordion book of the twelve objects in the story. The children can work individually or in pairs as they draw or paint a cover, a title page, one page for each object with the word printed under the picture, and a last page that says, "And chances are . . ." Mount the pages on poster board, tape them together with clear tape, and your colorful accordion book will tell its own story.

✱ The children may choose to write an innovation of *If You Give a Mouse a Cookie* by dictating new content to the familiar pattern. As a class, begin with the cookie and milk and brainstorm what the mouse might want next, for example, "When you give him milk, he'll probably ask you for some cereal." Continue innovating, using the children's ideas. Create a circle story of the innovation to make the new story structure visible. Then print one segment of the new story on each page of a class book for the children to illustrate. Tape the pages together for an accordion book story to put in your reading center. If you give children a new story to read, they will probably ask you for. . . !

MOUSE BEDS

Have the children bring in very small boxes of varying sizes and shapes. Let each child decorate a box to create a mouse bed for the little mouse he has made out of modeling clay. Provide fabric, tissue paper, and cotton to add pillows and blankets to each labeled mouse bed. To display the mouse beds, have the children group them into families of mice.

Alana's mouse bed

MICE ARE NICE

Enjoy the sound and feel of the rhythmic language in the delightful poem "Mice." Have the children listen with their eyes closed; another time, play music as you read. Let the children respond with their thoughts about the poem. Every reading should be for the purpose of enjoying the marvelous word pictures.

Print the poem on chart paper with lines of alternating colors. Read it together often, one finger point per word. Let the children each choose a phrase to illustrate. The bright pictures surrounding the poem will show all the characteristics of "the mice that are nice."

COOKIE MATH

✱ As the children look at a large chocolate chip cookie, have each child *estimate* the number of chocolate chips in the cookie. Record their estimates on a chart. Then break apart the cookie, count the chocolate chips, and compare that number with their estimates. How many children estimated too few chocolate chips? Too many?

✱ Tell your children something special about your favorite chocolate chip cookie recipe. As the children watch, print on a chart the list of ingredients needed for your recipe. Print the directions for making the cookies on a second chart. Plan when you can make the cookies together, an interactive experience at its best.

✱ After baking the cookies, *sort* them by appearance. Talk about all the differences you have discovered. Then make a list of all the ways the children can think of to eat the cookies, such as alone, with others, one chip at a time, by nibbling, and with eyes closed. At last, it's time to invite the mice and have a party.

EVERYDAY LEARNING ACTIVITIES

Positive parenting; developmental learning activities; and a warm, nurturing environment are major factors in a child's academic success and lifetime learning.

In the safety of play, a child can be the boss, make up the rules, and try on any role for size. He can experiment with the power of words as he says, "I am the mother and you must drink your milk." Play is a safe place for a child to express his feelings as he learns that it is the adults in his life who set up the rules for acceptable behavior. It is adults who must quietly insist on a child taking responsibility for his own actions. And it is adults who must show a child that all his little ploys and promises won't change the rules for acceptable behavior. A child who is a crier must learn that tears won't make you change your mind. A child who is a manipulator must learn that it simply will not work to promise, "I won't do it again if you let me play just this once." The pouting child must learn that you won't change your mind when he is giving you the message, "See, I'm not having any fun and it's all your fault." The child who blames someone else when he was the one who misbehaved must learn it's simply unacceptable to say, "George did it!" The retaliator, who "accidentally" knocks down someone else's blocks must learn the rules of fair play. You simply won't accept unacceptable behavior. That's all a part of preparing a child to live life skillfully.

* Make a tape of a family member reading *If You Give a Mouse a Cookie* by Laura Joffe Numeroff. Begin with the title, author, and illustrator. A child can point to the words as he listens for a particular sound that tells him when to turn the pages. *(recognizing print)*

* Have a child draw or paint his own mouse family picture to hang on your refrigerator. Add yarn or pipe cleaner whiskers and tails. Write each mouse's name under his picture and make up a story about the little mouse sharing his cookie with his family. Read together *The Doorbell Rang* by Pat Hutchins and *One of Each* by Mary Ann Hoberman, two delightful books about sharing. *(language)*

* Read the words of a cookie recipe together. There are so many skills to learn about measuring ingredients (he will love the big word!) and following directions. After the cookies are baked, encourage the child to divide them onto two plates, teaching full, empty, more, less, equal, and sets. Be sure to end your fun by sharing with a friend. *(math concepts)*

* In the story *If You Give a Mouse a Cookie,* we see the mouse only in the daytime. Encourage a child to think about where the mouse might be at night. Where do other animals sleep at night? Do they like the dark? Are they protected? Talk about people at night and the jobs that some people do while others sleep. Compare nighttime sounds with daytime sounds. Night and day are a good introduction to the concept of opposites. *(comparisons)*

The Little Mouse, The Red Ripe Strawberry, and THE BIG HUNGRY BEAR

by Don and Audrey Wood

* Story structure
* Concepts of print
* Math/science concepts
* Process writing

* Concept of sharing
* Categorizing
* Sequencing
* Family activities

SETTING THE STAGE

Instantly singable songs and the appealing rhyme and rhythm of finger plays will encourage children to be involved in story time.

"Share It" by Rosenshontz, *Share It*
(Share with a friend and feel good about yourself)

"The Sharing Song" by Raffi, *Singable Songs for the Very Young*

ME

This is my nose,	*(point to body parts)*
These are my ears,	
These are my eyes	
That make the tears.	
This is my mouth,	
It smiles when I say	*(big smile)*
I think I like myself	*(pat on the back)*
Just this way!	

ONE LITTLE BODY

Two little hands go clap, clap, clap.	*(follow actions as rhyme indicates)*
Two little feet go tap, tap, tap.	
Two little hands go thump, thump, thump.	
Two little feet go jump, jump, jump.	
One little body turns around.	
One little body sits quietly down.	

FIRST READING

I love the cover of this book. It makes me want to start reading right away to find out what will happen. Tell me what you think the story will be about. What do you predict will happen?

The name of our story is one of the longest book titles I have ever read. It's *The Little Mouse, The Red Ripe Strawberry, and THE BIG HUNGRY BEAR*. I can see a little mouse and that enormous, red, ripe strawberry, but can you find a big hungry bear on the cover? Do you think the mouse has his finger up to his mouth because the bear is close by? Is that why he is on a ladder? I wonder where that big, hungry bear is.

Perhaps he will appear on the title page. No, he is not there either. Why do you think the letters of his name, "THE BIG HUNGRY BEAR," are larger than the other letters in the title? Why is that little door open with a ladder sticking out? Let's read and find out.

GETTING INVOLVED

Now let's have some fun with *The Little Mouse, The Red Ripe Strawberry, and THE BIG HUN-GRY BEAR*. Stand up and stretch out your arms so you have some space of your own. Pretend you are the little mouse. Watch me and I will show you everything the little mouse did:

First walk in place with the ladder under your arm.
Now stand the ladder against the bush and start climbing.
Pull hard on the strawberry until it falls to the ground.
Carry it to your little house and cover it with dirt.
Get a heavy chain and wrap it around the strawberry.
Time to disguise the strawberry with some glasses and a funny nose and a mustache.
Uh, oh! You can hear the big, hungry bear!
Better get a knife fast and cut the strawberry in half.
Will you share half with me? Thank you for sharing.
Now settle down into your little hammock and close your eyes.

A CLOSER LOOK

With each rereading of a story, children gain new understanding. Pause often for a spontaneous flow of oral language as the children share their feelings and observations. Extend the learning process with your own questions in repeated readings of the story.

* Do you think the author wanted us to decide if there really was a hungry bear nearby? *(reflecting)*

* Was "Hello, little Mouse. What are you doing?" a good beginning to the story? *(evaluating)*

* Where do you think the little mouse lives? *(interpretation)*

* Why does the mouse need a ladder? *(reasoning)*

* When did you notice the hammock? *(observation)*

* Does the little mouse's face tell you what he is thinking? *(analyzing)*

* I wonder why the vine, the strawberry, and the mouse are all shaking. *(comprehension)*

* Why do you think the mouse and the strawberry ended up on the ground? *(comprehension)*

* What does it mean to *romp?* To *guard?* To *disguise? (comprehension)*

* In your opinion, did the little mouse think of good hiding places? *(evaluating)*

* Where in the story could you say, "Oh, I just love that part"? *(reflecting)*

* What was the mouse's problem? Do you like the way he solved it? *(evaluating)*

* In the last illustration, tell me about the mouse's face, his front paw, and his *hat. (interpretation)*

* Was that picture a good ending to the story? *(evaluating)*

* What would you say to the little mouse? *(reflecting)*

STORY TIME EXTENSIONS

One of Each by Mary Ann Hoberman

Watch Out! Big Bro's Coming! by Jez Alborough

A Mouse's Tale by Pamela Johnson

Chrysanthemum by Kevin Henkes

The Doorbell Rang by Pat Hutchins

BALANCED LITERACY ACTIVITIES

POETRY

WANTED
I'm looking for a house
Said the little brown mouse,
      with
One room for breakfast,
One room for tea,
One room for supper,
And that makes three.
One room to dance in,
When I give a ball,
A kitchen and a bedroom,
Six rooms in all.
     Rose Fyleman

THE HOUSE OF THE MOUSE
by Lucy Sprague Mitchell
from *A New Treasury of Children's Poetry*
by Joanna Cole

NIGHT-LIGHT
by Eve Merriam
from *Blackberry Ink*
by Eve Merriam

INVOLVEMENT

THE MOUSE'S FACE

The Little Mouse, The Red Ripe Strawberry, and THE BIG HUNGRY BEAR has all the qualities that make a children's story endearing: it teaches, entertains, has a simple text, and is beautifully illustrated. Oh, the face of that dear little mouse! In your next rereading, focus the children's attention on the changing expressions of the mouse. Has the artist told the story on the mouse's face?

A MESSAGE

With the lights off in your room, give each child a strawberry to hold (or a red felt one if it isn't strawberry season). Pretend a bear is stalking the room, waiting to have a feast. Brainstorm ways the children can save the strawberries they are holding from the hungry bear. The children may think of reasons why their own ideas will not save the berries. Continue the discussion until a child comes up with the idea that the only way to outsmart the bear is to eat the strawberries—now! Then turn the lights on and have the children find paw prints and a message from the bear, "Oh how I wanted those strawberries!"

INTEGRATION

SIX ROOMS IN ALL

The charming poem "Wanted" is full of imagery. The children will visualize something new each time they hear the words, whether listening with their eyes closed or with music playing. Give the children opportunities to respond. They will be surrounding the text with oral language as they describe the word pictures in their heads. How do they picture the rooms? Do they imagine a whole family of mice living there? Would the rooms look like the mouse's home in *THE BIG HUNGRY BEAR?* Who came to the ball?

Using six large pieces of paper with phrases of the poem printed on the bottom, have the children illustrate the story of the *house for the brown mouse* in a wall story format for all to read.

Extension: Have the children decide on a room in their own homes to draw. Encourage them to visualize everything in the room. Read the poem "Night-light" by Eve Merriam, which describes all the things a night-light (a clever idea!) can see at night such as "a sleepy picture nodding on the wall." After labeling everything they have drawn, the children could create frames and roofs for the houses with straws, toothpicks, yarn, pipe cleaners, crinkly cookie paper, fabric scraps, painted popsicle sticks, or something you never thought of!

THE LITTLE MOUSE AND THE RED RIPE STRAWBERRY

A retelling is a summary of story events in the children's words. It is an effective tool for comprehending and organizing story elements. Lead a large group retelling by asking the children to tell you just the beginning of the story. Combine and condense their answers into one sentence and write the words in the first segment of a simple story matrix. Follow the same pattern in deciding the ending and the middle of the story. Then give the children individual pieces of paper folded into thirds. They will label each section *B, M,* and *E* and copy from your model the summarizing sentences. Adding illustrations to the simple retelling will help children develop their understanding of literary elements.

The Little Mouse, The Red Ripe Strawberry, and THE BIG HUNGRY BEAR

B	M	E
The little mouse picked a red, ripe strawberry.	The little mouse hid the red, ripe strawberry.	The little mouse cut the red, ripe strawberry and shared half of it.

WHERE ARE YOU, BEAR?

The children will have their own ideas of why the bear never appeared in the story. Was he nearby? Was he hiding? Have fun hunting for the big hungry bear by acting out the chant "We're Going on a Bear Hunt," now beautifully illustrated in a book by Michael Rosen. The language is exceptional as a father and his four children splash, splosh, and stumble through a field, a deep river, swampy mud, a dark forest, a whirling snowstorm, and a gloomy cave, looking for a bear.

JOURNAL OF A TRAVELING MOUSE

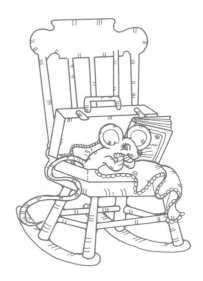

There is probably no animal more appealing to children than a little mouse. Think of ways to include a lovable, stuffed mouse or a soft mouse puppet in your daily teaching until the children consider it to be a part of your class. When they arrive one morning, have a little suitcase waiting in your chair. Explain that each child will have a turn to take the suitcase home. Have the children guess what is inside before you open the suitcase and show them the little mouse, a blanket, a small journal, and a note to parents asking them to write a few sentences about what the lovable mouse did with their child before it came back to school. At the end of the year, you will have a marvelous story to share about each of your children and a traveling mouse.

A TASTING PARTY

Prepare four small containers with the hidden tastes of *sweet, sour, salty,* and *spicy.* Working with small groups of children on a number of successive days, have each child dip a popsicle stick or coffee stirrer into the four containers. Guide them into categorizing and labeling the tastes. Print the headings *sweet, sour, salty,* and *spicy* on a four-column wall graph.

Have the children each bring something from home, talk about its taste, and then draw a small square picture to add to the right column on the chart.

Write sentences about what the children bring in your daily class news or encourage the children to write in their journals.

EVERYDAY LEARNING ACTIVITIES

Positive parenting; developmental learning activities; and a warm, nurturing environment are major factors in a child's academic success and lifetime learning.

In the story *THE BIG HUNGRY BEAR* by Don and Audrey Wood, the little mouse had several plans to protect the strawberry. Being able to think of a plan of action and to solve problems are skills that even a young child can learn. They will encourage a child to organize her thoughts and build her verbal skills. Ask her often for suggestions. For example, if her pants get torn, ask her, "What can we do about it?" She might suggest sewing them or buying a new pair of pants or wearing them torn. By repeating the child's choices, you are telling her you like her thinking. "Good, we have three choices. We can sew your pants, or buy new ones, or let you wear them torn. Which plan should we use? You decide." The more opportunities a child has to think, to plan, to make choices, and to follow through, the more confident and self-directed she will become.

✱ If sharing always means giving up something that is very special, it isn't appealing to a child. We make it so hard on a child at birthday parties and holidays when we want her to be excited about a gift we have chosen just for her and then, in the next breath, expect her to share it with someone else. Help her make up a "sharing basket" of games and toys she feels good about sharing with anyone, and let her keep a few treasures of her own in a special place. Sometimes it works to set the timer on the stove. When the buzzer goes off, it's time to share, and no one gets cross with mommy. *(social development)*

✱ Enjoy ripe, red strawberries (or any fruit) with a child. Using a dull table knife, let the child slice the strawberry in half. Talk about how two halves make a whole. Next, put two strawberries on a plate and let the child decide how to divide them. If she figures that out easily, try four strawberries on a plate to be shared. Suggest "One for you and one for me." Everyday activities are rich learning experiences because a child learns best by doing. *(concept of half)*

✱ Tiny animals and animal homes fascinate children. That is why the character of the little mouse in *THE BIG HUNGRY BEAR* is so appealing. Start observing insects and little animals in your yard and in the child's storybooks. How do they travel? Do they make noise? Where do they sleep? How do they protect themselves? What do they eat? Add to the learning by creating a shoe-box *home* for little animals. Every day put in a new set of written or picture clues for a child to guess the name of the imaginary little critter inside. Estimate how many tiny animals could fit in the shoe-box *home. (science, observation)*

✱ Pouring rice involves the eyes and hands working together as well as the ability to make judgments. To make pouring more challenging, place rubber bands around clear plastic containers, perhaps at the halfway mark. Tell a child to pour to the rubber band. Add scoops, funnels, and measuring cups. Ask her to estimate how many scoops of rice it will take to fill each cup. Add some small plastic animals and little people to the tub for creative fun. *(coordination, math concepts)*

The Little Red Hen

by Paul Galdone

* Teaching responsibility
* Mini language lessons
* Story structure
* Cultural diversity

* Vocabulary
* Concepts of print
* Structure writing
* A family activity

SETTING THE STAGE

Instantly singable songs and the appealing rhyme and rhythm of finger plays will encourage children to be involved in story time.

"In My Garden" by Raffi, *One Light, One Sun*

"Oats, Peas, Beans" by Raffi, *Baby Beluga*

DIG A LITTLE HOLE

Dig a little hole,	*(dig)*
Plant a little seed,	*(drop seed)*
Pour a little water,	*(pour)*
Pull a little weed.	*(pull up and throw away)*
Chase a little bug,	*(chasing motions with hands)*
Heigh-ho, there he goes!	*(shade eyes)*
Give a little sunshine,	*(cup hands, lift to the sun)*
Grow a little rose.	*(smell flower, eyes closed, smiling)*

MAKING BISCUITS

I am making biscuit dough,	
Round and round the beaters go.	*(follow actions as rhyme*
Add some flour from a cup,	*indicates)*
Stir and stir the batter up.	
Roll them, cut them nice and neat.	
Put them on a cookie sheet.	
Bake them, count them: one, two, three,	
Serve them to my friends and me.	

FIRST READING

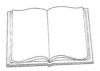

Tell me about the hen on the cover of our book today. Do you think she has a job to do? Does she have any tools to work with? I wonder if she will need help with her job. The name of the story is *The Little Red Hen*. It was illustrated by Paul Galdone, a man who loves to draw animal pictures. I know they will make you smile.

Let's turn to Mr. Galdone's first picture on the half-title page. Tell me what you see. The next page, the title page, shows something that grows and I'm wondering if you know what it is called. The kernels of wheat are what we use to make bread and cakes.

In the story, the little red hen asked three animal friends to help her make a cake. I'm going to ask *you* to help me tell the story. Every time the cat, the dog, and the mouse say "Not I," you say the words with me. And at the end of the story, you can join me when the animals say "I will."

GETTING INVOLVED

Let's talk about some of the new words in *The Little Red Hen*. The story said the little red hen's house was *cozy*. What does *cozy* mean? Show me what the little mouse did when she *snoozed* all day. The little red hen also *tended* the wheat. Was that important? How did she *hoe* the garden? The story said the wheat was *ripe*. What does that mean? Show me how the cat moved when she *strolled*. How did the mouse move when she *scampered?*

Now let's have some fun with this story. I'll pretend to be the little red hen and you pretend to be her helpers, not lazy at all like the cat and dog and mouse in the story. Ready? Who will help me plant this wheat? *(Lead the children through the actions as they pretend to plant the wheat in the ground.)* Now the wheat is tall and yellow. Who will help me cut this wheat? *(Lead the children through the cutting motions.)* At last it's all cut! Who will help me take this wheat to the mill? *(Pretend to sling the wheat over your shoulder and walk in place to the mill.)* And now my last question, Who will help me make this wheat into a cake? You deserve to eat the cake! We didn't have a lazy cat or dog or mouse in the room.

A CLOSER LOOK

With each rereading of a story, children gain new understanding. Pause often for a spontaneous flow of oral language as the children share their feelings and observations. Extend the learning process with your own questions in repeated readings of the story.

✳ What did you think when you heard the beginning words "Once upon a time"? *(application)*

✳ Tell me what you noticed about the four mailboxes by the cozy house. *(observation)*

✳ What is the cat dreaming of? The dog? The mouse? *(comprehension)*

✳ What chores did the little red hen do inside the house? How did she get water in her kitchen? *(interpretation)*

✳ Tell me about the chores the little red hen did outside. *(memory)*

✳ What tool did the hen use to cut the wheat? Do you remember seeing that tool in *The Gingerbread Boy? (application)*

✳ Why did the hen take the wheat to the mill? *(comprehension)*

✳ In your opinion, did the little red hen do the right thing when she ate the cake all by herself? *(evaluating)*

✳ I wonder if the hen had baby chicks. Do you think she would have shared with them? *(evaluating)*

✳ Imagine you were the little red hen. What would you have done? *(reflecting)*

✳ Do you suppose the mouse, the cat, and the dog helped the hen the next day? *(reflecting)*

STORY TIME EXTENSIONS

Farmer Duck by Martin Waddell

Tops and Bottoms by Janet Stevens

Mole's Hill by Lois Ehlert

Just Plain Fancy by Patricia Polacco

Mrs. Huggins and Her Hen Hannah by Lydia Dabcovich

BALANCED LITERACY ACTIVITIES

POETRY

THE NOTHING-DOINGS
Meet the lazy Nothing-Doings,
all they do is stand around,
when it's time for doing nothing,
Nothing-Doings can be found,
when it's time for doing something,
you won't find a single one,
for the Nothing-Doings vanish
when there's work that must be done.
Jack Prelutsky

I WENT UPSTAIRS
I went upstairs to make my bed.
I made a mistake and bumped my head.
I went downstairs to milk my cow.
I made a mistake and milked the sow.
I went in the kitchen to bake a pie.
I made a mistake and baked a fly.
Traditional

INVOLVEMENT

✳ The predictable pattern of the words "Not I" and "Then I will" encourages children to enter into the story with the very first reading of *The Little Red Hen.* To vary their participation and to keep them listening intently, divide the children into four groups. As you narrate the story, have one group join you on the little red hen's words and the other groups join in for the dog, the cat, and the mouse.

✳ Help the children create drama props in your art center, making hats, headbands, or ears for each animal. Paper bags also make good props. Cut large holes in the fronts of the bags for the children's faces and slit the sides to fit over the children's shoulders. They can draw feathers, fur, ears, or whiskers around the holes to create their story characters.

✳ Add to the fun by making word cards to hang around the necks of the children who are playing the parts of the dogs, cats, and mice. On one side print, "Not I," and on the other side print, "I will!" Have the children turn the cards at just the right moment in the drama.

✳ Read and dramatize other versions of *The Little Red Hen.* Have the children decide which drama they would like to perform (with props, of course) for their parents or another class.

INTEGRATION

"NOT I!"

A favorite read-it-again story, photos of your smiling children, and authentic language lessons—what a splendid scaffold on which to build a meaningful literature time in a learner-centered classroom. First, let the children's oral responses surround the text for that is how they make meaning. Then, connect their oral language to reading and writing by leading the children through a simple retelling of the story.

Print a sentence at the top of each of five wall charts, pointing out beginning and ending sounds as you write. On the first chart, for example, write, "Who will help me plant the wheat?" On the next three lines, using alternating colors, write "Not I," said *Dishenda;* "Not I," said *Adonis;* and "Not I," said *Carlos.* (Of course you will substitute the names of your children.) Place a color photo of the child next to the child's name. Do the remaining four charts the same way, ending with the words "I will" on the last three lines, with individual photos of the three children speaking. In independent reading time, they will be drawn to their own pictures and the easily read repetitive text.

A WALL STORY

Have the children imagine that the little red hen asked other animals for help and they all said, "Not I." But the dog, the cat, and the mouse answered "I will." Tell the story of the lesson they learned on a wall mural in your room for all to read.

MINI LANGUAGE LESSONS

On subsequent days, as you read the wall charts together, there will be many opportunities for mini language lessons. Have the children frame the high-frequency words *not, I,* and *said.* Demonstrate one-to-one correspondence and left-to-right progression. Teach about capital letters, quotation marks, commas, and question marks. Another time, encourage the children to point out *anything* they know about the text; then read it together. When children are engaged in a happy reading experience, they will learn.

THE NOTHING-DOINGS

Ask the children if they think Jack Prelutsky had the story of *The Little Red Hen* in mind when he wrote the poem "The Nothing-Doings." As you read the story again, have the children listen for the *other* jobs the little red hen had to do by herself. There's quite a list. Could the dog and cat and mouse be called Nothing-Doings?

Read *Mrs. Huggins and Her Hen Hannah* by Lydia Dabcovich. (What alphabet letter would you enjoy teaching with that title?) It is a warmly satisfying story about an old lady and her beloved hen who are inseparable as they do chores together. Could they be called Nothing-Doings? Compare the stories orally because children need to talk about what they are learning. Make charts of the chores the two hens did or let the children create a Venn diagram to record their responses. Print will be everywhere in your classroom, as will be the theme of responsible helpers.

RESPONSIBLE HELPERS

✳ Brainstorm with the children about all the jobs around your room that need to be done every day. Make a Responsible Helpers chart for the classroom. Try to have a task for every child.

✳ Talk about ways the children can be responsible helpers at home as well. Have every child decide on something she can do to help at home. Each child can draw her idea and write or dictate a sentence on her page in your class book *Responsible Helpers.* When each child has a turn taking the book home, parents can write encouraging words on her page.

✳ Take a walk around school—down the halls, in the cafeteria, on the sidewalks, and out on the playground. Decide on ways to be responsible helpers for your school. Could your plan include recycling?

✳ As a large group experience, write a letter of apology from the mouse, the dog, and the cat to the little red hen. What do they want to say? Have they learned a lesson? Perhaps the children will choose to make individual pages in a class book, *I Am Sorry, Little Red Hen.* Each child will draw a picture and finish the caption on her page, *I am sorry, little red hen. I was busy* _____. The last page could say, *But now we are responsible helpers!* Have the children illustrate the ending with smiling faces and sign their names. Let them take turns checking out the class book to share at home.

✳ Read also *Farmer Duck,* Martin Waddell's delightful story of an uncomplaining duck who does all the work for a lazy farmer. Contrast the hard-working hare and the lazy bear in the clever *Tops and Bottoms* by Janet Stevens. Read about a dear mole who digs furiously to save her cozy burrow in *Mole's Hill,* another gem by Lois Ehlert. Enjoy the rhyming names and words in Jim Aylesworth's *Mr. McGill Goes to Town,* the cheery story of four friends who agree to help each other finish their chores. And don't miss a story from the heart, *Just Plain Fancy* by Patricia Polacco, about an endearing Amish child who is responsible for the chickens on the family farm. Oh, the lessons to be learned from the best of children's literature.

EVERYDAY LEARNING ACTIVITIES

Positive parenting; developmental learning activities; and a warm, nurturing environment are major factors in a child's academic success and lifetime learning.

The Little Red Hen by Paul Galdone teaches a meaningful lesson in a delightful way. One of the biggest tasks adults have is to teach a child to be responsible for his own actions. A child who blames others or makes excuses or can't follow through on a job he has been given is not ready for success in school. Begin by giving a child at least one job to do every day. Insist it be done before play or television begins. He needs to know that he has no choice in whether or not he must do his chores. Teach him to be responsible in other ways like picking up toys and putting his clothes in the hamper. Work on one thing at a time, beginning with whatever responsibility is most lacking in the child. Be clever and creative and come up with a way to make it his concern and not yours. Make a simple star chart and let him put up a star or a sticker every time he follows through on his responsibility. Let him put a penny in a jar or stay up ten minutes longer at bedtime. You are rewarding the very behavior you want repeated. That's teaching responsibility.

✳ Watch the miracle of the growth of a seed. Fill a clear plastic cup with wet paper towels. Gently slide three or four fast growing seeds, such as lima bean seeds, down the inside of the cup, between the cup and the paper towel. Keep the towels moist each day, a good responsibility for a child. Soon you will see the seed, roots, stems, and leaves through the cup. It is especially fun to plant more of the same seeds in dirt outside so you know what's happening under the ground before you see a plant growing. *(science concept)*

✳ Children's art is beautiful. Yet to a child, it is the process of creating that is more important than the end result. Never show a child a model of what something should look like. Give him total freedom. The important question when he is finished is not do *you* like it, but does *he* like it. Ask him! *(creativity, self-esteem)*

✳ Soft balls of all sizes are wonderful for developing motor skills. Have fun creating your own bowling alley, especially on a rainy day. Gather up some nonbreakable containers, such as plastic water jugs, empty milk cartons, oatmeal boxes, or soda bottles. Line them up across a hallway. From the other end of the "bowling alley," see how many "pins" a child can knock down by rolling a soft ball. Make it even more fun by putting the number *1* or *2* or *3* on each "pin" and show a child how to add up his score. Try to guard against winners and losers in games. *(gross motor skills, math)*

✳ Cutting with scissors is an often-forgotten skill that requires a lot of practice. It helps develop a child's fine motor coordination. However, scissors can be dangerous and destructive, so always supervise. Children like to "fringe" paper by snipping all around the edges. They enjoy cutting pictures from junk mail or catalogs. This skill can be frustrating and a child may want to give up before he has mastered it. Give short periods of practice with lots of praise and encouragement. You'll be glad *you* didn't give up. *(fine motor skills)*

Make Way for Ducklings

by Robert McCloskey

SETTING THE STAGE

Instantly singable songs and the appealing rhyme and rhythm of finger plays will encourage children to be involved in story time.

"Safety Break" by Greg and Steve, *Kidding Around*
(An upbeat song about crossing the street safely)

"Little White Duck" by Raffi, *Ever Grows*

SIX LITTLE DUCKS

Six little ducks that I once knew	*(six fingers up)*
Short ones, fat ones, skinny ones, too	
But the one little duck	*(one finger up)*
With the feather on his back	*(finger feathers on back)*
He ruled the others	
With his quack, quack, quack.	*(hands hinged, open, shut)*
Down to the river they would go,	
Wibble, wobble, wibble wobble to and fro	*(hands on hips)*
But the one little duck	*(one finger up)*
With the feather on his back	*(finger feathers on back)*
He ruled the others	
With his quack, quack, quack.	*(hands hinged, open, shut)*

TEN LITTLE DUCKLINGS

Ten little ducklings; dash, dash, dash!
Jumped in the duck pond; splash, splash, splash!
When the mother called them; quack, quack, quack!
Ten little ducklings came swimming right back.

FIRST READING

Tell me what you see on the cover of our story. Where do you think the ducklings are? Are there any clues on the cover to help you predict what might happen in the story? Sometimes we don't have any ideas until we turn the pages. The name of the story is *Make Way for Ducklings.* What do you suppose the words "make way" mean?

The gold circle on the cover is called the Caldecott Medal. Only one Caldecott Medal is awarded each year for the children's storybook with the very best illustrations. Mr. Robert McCloskey, who wrote the story *and* drew the pictures, was given the award many years ago in 1941. A few years later, Mr. McCloskey wrote the storybook *Blueberries for Sal,* and he won a Caldecott Honor award for the illustrations in that book.

When Mr. McCloskey was writing *Make Way for Ducklings,* he visited a family of eight ducklings on a pond near his home. Day after day, Mr. McCloskey watched the ducklings on the pond. He enjoyed watching them so much he decided to tell children like you all about the ducklings' adventures. When Mr. McCloskey was ready to draw the pictures for his story, he actually brought some of the ducklings right into his house and let them waddle around. He wanted to draw them just right. If you visited the Public Garden in Boston today, for it is a real place, you would see little statues of Mrs. Mallard and her ducklings. Let's do a picture walk through the book and enjoy Mr. McCloskey's wonderful illustrations of Mr. and Mrs. Mallard and their eight ducklings in the big city.

GETTING INVOLVED

When Mr. and Mrs. Mallard wanted to move from place to place in *Make Way for Ducklings*, there were three different ways they could travel. What were the three ways they moved about? Let's pretend we are Mr. and Mrs. Mallard flying over the city. Swoop down to the little pond in the Public Garden. Now fish for some breakfast at the bottom of the pond and eat the peanuts from the swan boat. Let's get up on land and look for a place on the island to build a nest. Oh dear—watch out for those bicycles. We better start flying again, up over the city. Tell me when you see the little island in the Charles River. Find a safe place there to land and make a nest for the eggs. Show me how Mrs. Mallard protected the eggs. Listen—already the ducklings are hatching. Count them with me as they hatch.

You be the ducklings and get in line behind me. I'll show you how to swim in a line. Now you must walk in a line and we'll find our way to the Public Garden to meet Mr. Mallard. Watch out! Make the screeching sounds of the cars coming to a quick stop! Quack at those cars and let them know you want to cross the street. Here comes Michael to stop the traffic for us to cross over. We'll swim right to the little island and to Mr. Mallard who is waiting for us, just like he promised.

A CLOSER LOOK

With each rereading of a story, children gain new understanding. Pause often for a spontaneous flow of oral language as the children share their feelings and observations. Extend the learning process with your own questions in repeated readings of the story.

✳ Tell me what you thought of Mr. McCloskey's brown and white illustrations. *(observation)*

✳ I wonder how he got the idea of drawing the duckling coming out of the egg on the inside of the cover. *(reflecting)*

✳ What were Mr. and Mrs. Mallard looking for? *(analyzing)*

✳ Tell me some of the dangers they faced as they tried to find a safe place for their ducklings. *(comprehension)*

✳ Did you know it could be so dangerous for animals in the city? *(reflecting)*

✳ Do Mr. and Mrs. Mallard look the same? *(observation)*

✳ What does it mean to *molt*? Why couldn't the ducks fly when they were molting? *(analyzing)*

✳ I wonder how Mr. McCloskey thought of the names for the ducklings. *(reflecting)*

✳ Do you suppose Mrs. Mallard ever got them mixed up? *(reflecting)*

✳ Do you have a favorite name? *(reflecting)*

✳ In your opinion, was Mrs. Mallard a good mother? What did she teach her ducklings? *(evaluating)*

✳ Would the ducks have been safe in the city without Michael? *(analyzing)*

✳ If you could talk to Mr. McCloskey about *Make Way for Ducklings*, what would you say to him? *(reflecting)*

STORY TIME EXTENSIONS

One Duck Stuck by Phyllis Root

Secret Place by Eve Bunting

The Little Wood Duck by Brian Wildsmith

A House for Hermit Crab by Eric Carle

Moving Day by Robert Kalan

BALANCED LITERACY ACTIVITIES

POETRY

PETER AND WENDY

My ducks are so funny, I think.
    They peck at the bugs in the ground,
And always wherever they go
    They follow each other around.

They like to play Follow the Leader.
    Just watch them awhile and you'll find
There's one of them always in front,
    The other one always behind.
                    Wymond Garthwaite

INVOLVEMENT

CREATIVE DRAMA

The illustrations in *Make Way for Ducklings* are so detailed and visually rich that the children will enjoy just talking about them in rereadings of the story. Creative drama will also help them to develop story comprehension. Set up your room for a dramatization by deciding on an area for the Public Garden, the Charles River and the island, the buildings, and the highway. Identify the places with signs. Make name cards for Mr. and Mrs. Mallard and the eight ducklings. See if the children can use the alphabetical order of the ducklings' names to decide how they should line up for "follow the leader" in the story. That will be the fun part as the children pantomime the drama.

INTEGRATION

A SAFE PLACE IN THE CITY

Review with the children the many hazards that faced the ducks as they tried to nest and live in the city. Then see if they can think of at least eight reasons why the island was an ideal, safe place—no foxes, turtles, bikes, or cars, but a quiet place to swim, dive, catch fish, and eat peanuts, with Michael nearby. List their answers on a chart for another reading experience in your room.

Have the children create their own colorful wall mural, A Safe Place in the City. Pencil sketch a simple outline of the river and island for the children to paint, leaving plenty of room for Mr. and Mrs. Mallard and the eight ducklings. Have some fun orally matching the phrases on the chart to the ducklings, imagining what each one might have said. Then have the children print the phrases as though they were words coming from the ducklings' beaks. They will be telling their own story as they swim across the mural, which combines the language of art and the language of words.

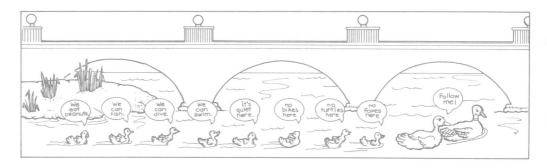

Extension: Involve the children in a discussion of all the things Mrs. Mallard had to teach the ducklings to keep them safe. Compare that list with the many things children must learn to be safe in and around home and school.

A LETTER TO MICHAEL

Undoubtedly the children listed Michael, the policeman, as one of the reasons why Mr. and Mrs. Mallard found the perfect spot to raise their family. Ask the children to think of all the things the ducks would thank Michael for. Write a class letter on chart paper from the ducklings to Michael. As the children dictate the sentences, draw their attention to the sounds within the words that you are writing. Talk about capital letters and punctuation. Let the children decide how to illustrate the letter and sign the ducklings' names.

Ask them also how to spell the ducklings' names and you will be setting the stage for a meaningful lesson on phonemic awareness. Begin by writing the name Jack. Show the children that you can remove the *J* (the onset) and keep *ack* (the rime). One at a time, add a new onset to the rhyme until you have listed all the ducklings' names. The children are now ready to write the names on the letter. Return often to the letter for a repeated reading experience, emphasizing one-to-one correspondence and left-to-right progression. Now friend Michael is helping a whole new group of learners.

THE SWAN BOAT

The beautiful swan boat in the story would capture any child's (or any duckling's) imagination. Have the children create a boat out of blocks or boxes with rows of small chairs for the passengers. Add literacy props to the center. Encourage children to think of things to write for the swan boat, such as numbers on the seats, tickets to sell, a name card for the tour guide, signs for feeding the ducks, and a list of departure times. Be sure to include a sign-up sheet for tourists in the Public Garden.

BUILDING THE SETTING

Because children of all ages learn best by *doing,* give them the hands-on experience of creating the story setting for *Make Way for Ducklings.* Cover a large rectangular table with white bulletin board paper, taped down at the corners. Draw a simple outline of the river banks, island, and city roads. Small groups of children can complete the details on the tabletop setting with markers or crayons. Let the children decide what to add next, perhaps a bridge, buildings, and cars all made with Legos, or ducks, police officers, and a swan boat made from clay. Keep a copy of the book nearby as children manipulate the characters and retell the story.

ALIKE BUT DIFFERENT

Even in the book's lithographed drawings, it is evident that Mr. Mallard was more vividly marked than Mrs. Mallard. Using books such as *The Wildlife 1-2-3: A Nature Counting Book* by Jan Thornhill, have the children find other animals whose male is larger or more colorful than the female. Make a list of the children's discoveries and conclude whether that is usual or unusual in the animal kingdom.

COMPARING ADVENTURES

Ducks Fly is the engaging story of a young duck's first flight, with simple text and lively illustrations by Lydia Dabcovich. In *Follow the River* by the same author, a duck family swims from the mountains to the sea. Let the children compare the adventures of the duck families in the joyful stories.

Secret Place by Eve Bunting is a not-to-be-missed, touching story about a little boy and his friends who know of a secret place in the heart of the concrete city. The watercolor paintings are absolutely beautiful and the parallels to *Make Way for Ducklings,* beginning with the book cover, are amazing. Have the children draw a Venn diagram to compare the setting, characters, and events of the two unforgettable stories.

EVERYDAY LEARNING ACTIVITIES

Positive parenting; developmental learning activities; and a warm, nurturing environment are major factors in a child's academic success and lifetime learning.

Make Way for Ducklings by Robert McCloskey is a delightful story of family members taking care of each other and keeping the little ones safe. Because a child's world is rather small, she loves the "familiar" and finds security in everything staying the same. That means changes, moves, new experiences, and even going to school can be scary to a child because they are all unknown. The family is the safety zone for a child, who continually moves in and out of new developmental stages and new experiences. She will never be loved or protected by the world as she is by her family. Be sure to create a sense of family in your home—that your family is special, and your family is a team with everyone working together to take care of each other. Some children are so busy vying for acceptance and approval that they can't feel love for a brother or a sister. Start a family box, which is simply a little box containing the name of every member of your family, including mom and dad. Each person draws a name from the box and finds all the ways he can take care of that person: being kind, helping, looking out for him, doing things without being asked. You might have more fun keeping the names secret. Draw new names every week until everyone has had a chance to take care of all the others.

✳ Protecting a child will always be your responsibility, so teaching safety outside the home is essential. Teach a child relentlessly about looking before crossing the street and watching traffic lights. If the child will be walking to school, walk the route with her many times. Point out landmarks and hazards along the way. Insist that she walk or play with other children and be sure she knows exactly what to do if she ever needs help. *(safety)*

✳ Write one of the ducklings' rhyming names on each page of a little book. Point out that the names sound alike because they end the same. Talk about each beginning letter and the sound it makes. Have the child illustrate her book and read it to you. *(rhyming words)*

✳ A child loves to make up nonsense words to rhyme with her own name. Be ready for the sillies! *(rhyming words)*

✳ Look around the house for sets of eight objects, such as colored toothpicks, paper clips, plastic spoons, and bits of colored paper. The hunting, collecting, and counting are part of the learning. Staple together pages of colored construction paper and have the child glue and label a set of eight objects on each page. *(counting sets)*

✳ The beautiful lithographed illustrations in *Make Way for Ducklings* are only one form of art. To help children understand the many forms of art, take them to a concert and to an art gallery. Let them hear an orchestra and see a ballet. The conversations that follow the real-life experiences will be meaningful teaching moments. *(experiential learning)*

Mama, Do You Love Me?

by Barbara M. Joosse

* Cultural diversity
* Phonemic awareness
* Story structure
* Mini language lessons

* Identifying feelings
* Parts of speech
* Math/science concepts
* Nonfiction

SETTING THE STAGE

Instantly singable songs and the appealing rhyme and rhythm of finger plays will encourage children to be involved in story time.

"Child of Mine" by Walt Disney Recordings, *For Our Children*
(A lovely melody with very special lyrics, sung by Carole King)

"You're a Wonderful One" by Art Garfunkel, *Songs from a Parent to a Child*
(A sweet song reassuring children of their parents' love)

LITTLE OWL, COMING
A Chippewa poem

Who is this? Who is this?	*(arms extended, questioning)*
Giving light	*(arms circle over head)*
On the top of my lodge.	*(hands over head)*
It is I—the Little Owl coming,	*(hands sweep toward chest)*
It is I—the Little Owl coming,	*(hands sweep toward chest)*
Down! Down!	*(hands stair-step downward)*

INUIT LULLABY
from the Inuit people of the Arctic

Do not cry, little one,	*(cradling motion)*
Your father will fetch you,	*(palms together, cupped)*
He is coming	*(arm extended, sweep inward)*
As soon as he has made	
His new harpoon head.	*(fingers pointed, touching)*
Do not cry, little one.	*(cradling motion)*
Do not weep. He is coming.	*(arms sweep inward, hug)*

FIRST READING

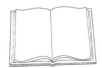

Perhaps the mother and child on the cover of this book have sung the words of the very same lullaby that we just said together. Who do you think they are? Tell me what you notice about their clothing. Where do you think they might live? Tell me about the very different sun in the sky.

Barbara Joosse has written a story about a mother and child all bundled up in warm clothing in a little boat. We might call them Eskimos, but they call themselves Inuit [IN-oo-eet]. The Inuit nations are among the Native Americans who live in the Arctic, one of the coldest places on earth. The Inuit mother and child in this story lived in the northern part of Alaska long, long ago. We can find their home on our world map.

Let's take a picture walk through the story. It is called *Mama, Do You Love Me?* What is the artist telling you on the title page? Now *you* tell me everything you see in the very beautiful pictures. Look for clues that show what is happening in the story. *(A picture walk is a time for pointing out the story illustrations and asking open-ended questions to give children a sense of story before the first reading. Use the glossary in the back of the book to explain vocabulary throughout your picture walk.)*

GETTING INVOLVED

Let's talk about some of the new words in the story that tell us all about life in the Arctic. First Mama spoke of a *raven*. How would you describe a *raven*? What was the *umiak* Mama and Dear One traveled in? Tell me about the *puffin* that howled at the moon. Does our story tell us if a *ptarmigan* is a bird? When Dear One wanted to put a *salmon* in Mama's *parka,* show me where she would have put it. Then she wanted to put a short-tailed weasel called an *ermine* in Mama's mittens and *lemmings* in Mama's *mukluks*. Tell me what *lemmings* and *mukluks* are.

Think about the exciting animals Dear One pretended to be. How would you move if you turned into a *musk-ox?* Where would your hands and feet be? Show me how you would move if you were a *walrus.* Watch out for your long tusks! Now crawl inside the *hide* of a polar bear. Be gentle as you chase Mama into her tent. Throw off your polar bear hide and sit down and smile because Mama loves you.

A CLOSER LOOK

With each rereading of a story, children gain new understanding. Pause often for a spontaneous flow of oral language as the children share their feelings and observations. Extend the learning process with your own questions in repeated readings of the story.

* What did you think about the way the artist illustrated the story? *(evaluating)*
* In what ways do Mama and Dear One and the doll look alike? *(observation)*
* What do you think the raven's treasure was? *(interpretation)*
* Tell me why a whale would love his spout. *(reasoning)*
* I wonder how the author thought of the words, "until the umiak flies into the darkness." *(reflection)*
* Why would breaking ptarmigan eggs be a disaster? *(analyzing)*
* Why would throwing water on the lamp be naughty? *(analyzing)*
* What did you notice each time a mask and an animal were shown on the same page? *(interpretation)*
* Tell me what you thought of when the wolves sang in the cave. *(reflecting)*
* What were you feeling when I read about the polar bear chasing Mama? *(reflecting)*
* In your opinion, would Mama ever stop loving Dear One? *(evaluating)*
* Did you ever feel like the little girl? *(reflecting)*
* What do you want to say about the story? *(reflecting)*

STORY TIME EXTENSIONS

Giving Thanks: A Native American Good Morning Message by Chief Jake Swamp

Knots on a Counting Rope by Bill Martin, Jr. and John Archambault

Songs Are Thoughts: Poems of the Inuit by Neil Philip

The Seasons and Someone by Virginia Kroll

The Legend of the Indian Paintbrush by Tomie dePaola

BALANCED LITERACY ACTIVITIES

POETRY

AMONG THEM I WALK
My great corn plants,
Among them I walk.
I speak to them;
They hold out their hands to me.

My great squash vines,
Among them I walk.
I speak to them;
They hold out their hands to me.
A Navajo Prayer

THE PTARMIGAN
The ptarmigan is strange,
As strange as he can be;
Never sits on ptelephone poles
Or roosts upon a ptree.
And the way he ptakes pto spelling
Is the strangest thing pto me.
Author unknown

INVOLVEMENT

DRAMATIZATION

The rich, poignant language of *Mama, Do You Love Me?* will come to life as the children create the setting and freely pantomime the movement of the story characters. The preparation is as exciting as the drama itself.

Together, make lists of the setting, story props, and characters you will need. Then let the children decide how to create in your art center ptarmigan eggs, the raven's treasure, long black braids, feathers, salmon, ermine, and lemmings. To make big animal faces or headbands, let them choose tagboard or any other medium. Suggest the children find something in your room to be the umiak, the lamp, a cave, Mama's tent and mukluks, and so on. Label the setting and the props. If the children want character name cards to hang around their necks, remember they gain confidence by being paired with another child.

As narrator, read the lyrical text slowly, pausing often for the children to interpret the words through their movement and voices. The children's fundamental urge to make connections to their own lives will become the real purpose of the drama.

INTEGRATION

WORDS FROM THE INUIT

Each rereading of a story is a new experience. Children refine and clarify their ideas as they figure out meaning for themselves. That is the power of words. As you first did a *picture* walk through *Mama, Do You Love Me?*, now do a *word* walk. Children's growing comprehension of the text will help them identify the words that are significant to Dear One's way of life.

As you repeat each word, ask the children to identify the syllables in the words by clapping, snapping fingers, or tapping feet. After the children have divided a word into syllables, have them blend the syllables to form the whole word again.

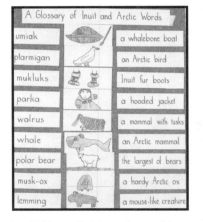

A Glossary of Inuit and Arctic Words		
umiak		a whalebone boat
ptarmigan		an Arctic bird
mukluks		Inuit fur boots
parka		a hooded jacket
walrus		a mammal with tusks
whale		an Arctic mammal
polar bear		the largest of bears
musk-ox		a hardy Arctic ox
lemming		a mouse-like creature

As you write on sentence strips the words selected, have the children divide each word into its component sounds to help them identify and isolate sounds within words. Discuss and decide on a definition for each word. The children's colorful illustrations will complete your meaningful pocket chart.

In small-group mini language lessons, focus on letter-sound associations for the initial consonants *p, m,* and *w.* Have children use their knowledge of one word's beginning or ending to form other words such as rhyming word families for *whale* and *bear.* Identify the phoneme *ar* in *ptarmigan, parka, largest, hardy,* and *Arctic.*

DANCING MASKS

Illustrator Barbara Lavallee has modeled the masks in *Mama, Do You Love Me?* after the ceremonial masks worn by Inuit medicine men in their traditional dances. The concentric rings within the mask represent heaven and earth. The objects attached to the rings are symbols of prayers to the spirits for abundant game and good hunting. In many ceremonies, Inuit dancers wore animal masks and imitated animal movements as they danced.

In pairs or small cooperative groups, have the children create original animal masks from tagboard, feathers, pipe cleaners, yarn, tissue and construction paper, markers, paints, or any medium of choice. Gather facts from resource books such as *They Put on Masks* by Byrd Baylor. Have each group create an imaginative dance that tells a story of its animal, such as a musk-

THE INQUIRY APPROACH TO LEARNING

There was not a single entry in Calvin's journal. The child did not want to be in school.

After two years in first grade, Calvin had been assigned rather than promoted to second grade. He languished in a system of workbooks and dittos and testing that kept him in the lowest-achieving group. Calvin had not yet caught the dream that he could learn to read.

One day I noticed Calvin drawing airplanes with unbelievably minute details and from every conceivable viewpoint — looking down from above, under the wings, even inside the cockpit. Since we began every morning with sharing time, I asked an unsuspecting Calvin the next day to share his airplane pictures with the class. The child spoke hesitantly, yet he told a splendid story about control sticks and navigation lights and instrument landings. The children were fascinated.

The next morning I asked Calvin to label his pictures so he could teach me, the teacher, about airplanes. Struggling to put the sounds of his words on paper, he wrote enough letters to spell turbojet engine, piston-driven propellers, and combustion chambers. Calvin read the words, amazed at what he had done. The next time the children wrote in their journals, I suggested Calvin choose a favorite picture and write a caption under it so I could learn about his airplane. He wrote, "Tha nstrmnz mzur wnd vlst." *(The instruments measure wind velocity.)* Later, when Calvin showed his picture and read the words to the class, it was the first sentence he had ever read. When the children clapped, Calvin smiled a rare smile.

The following day, Calvin found a pile of library books on his desk. For hours "and in and out of weeks and through a day," as Maurice Sendak would say, Calvin pored over his airplane books, sometimes copying words, sometimes drawing magnificent airplanes, sometimes writing sentences under his pictures. Calvin was learning to read through writing. Now the words had meaning.

It was Friday and today was Calvin's turn. Every week one child invited his father or mother to come to our room to talk about family and interests and career. Calvin's father walked into the room, smiling and handsome in the full-dress uniform of a Navy pilot. Under one arm he carried rolled-up charts and maps, under the other, a globe. The soft-spoken father explained how important reading was for him. Without that skill, he could not read his government assignments or find locations on his maps or read the letters he received every week from his son. Quietly, Calvin's father pulled a pile of letters from his pocket. The children and I moved in close to get a better look. How had this child, who had just begun to read and write, been able to compose letters? His father slowly unfolded the first letter — a detailed picture of an airplane, then another and another. Through his pictures, Calvin was saying, "I'm right there with you, Daddy. I know airplanes, too. I'm part of your life, Daddy. Stay close!"

Now Calvin was learning to read because he wanted to know. He had a purpose. The child brought his prior knowledge with him as he immersed himself in the library books, looking for answers to his own questions. When he wrote in his journal and shared with the class, Calvin was interacting with text because, finally, the words had meaning. That is the inquiry approach to learning.

Inquiry is a recursive, ever-evolving process driven by the learner's ideas, questions and purposes, for learning begins with personal connections. Inquiry is experiential learning. It involves immersing children in a topic with time to explore, wonder, investigate and research. The answers children find through research lead them to even more questions and more learning.

In the inquiry classroom, teachers and children are co-learners. They fill the room with invitations to ask questions and solve problems around individual and group topics. Even when a topic is mandated by curriculum, children are encouraged to pose their own questions, concentrate on their own research, and share information that is important to them. The curiosity aroused by their questions will propel them into learning.

INQUIRY AND *THE GROUCHY LADYBUG*

"Hey you, want to fight?" What child, chanting those words from *The Grouchy Ladybug,* would not want to know more about the feisty, tiny creature? Noticing that Eric Carle dedicated his book to all ladybugs everywhere, a kindergarten class decided their favorite author must really love the little bugs. They viewed the dedication he wrote as a personal letter just to them. They had to know more, thus beginning the process of inquiry in their room.

GATHERING RESOURCES

The learning began with the enthusiastic gathering of resources about ladybugs. Together, teacher and students filled book baskets with informational books, poetry books, nature magazines, pictures, tapes and objects. The children brought in newspaper clippings, computer printouts, real ladybugs — even interested parents! They interviewed anyone they considered to be knowledgeable about insects and brought the experts to class, as well. The children free explored with interest the illustrations and text in their abundant resources. All of the strategies for

gathering information created excitement in the room. They accessed the students' prior knowledge and sparked conversations that revealed what they knew. The children shared and collaborated, as all learners do. Then they recorded collectively, and with satisfaction, what they thought they knew about ladybugs.

ASKING QUESTIONS and FORMING RESEARCH TOPICS

Next came brainstorming with the children about what they wanted to study. Their explorations had inspired eager inquiries. Do ladybugs have enemies? Do their spots change color? How do ladybugs fly? The students' questions were recorded on a chart titled, "What do we want to study about ladybugs?" Then, using their categorizing skills, the children grouped the inquiries into general research topics.

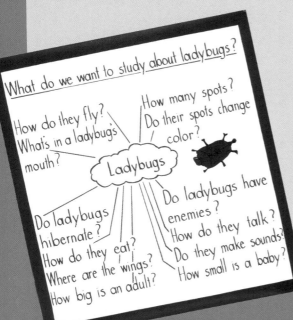

UNDERSTANDING THE HOW-TO OF RESEARCH

Eager to begin researching, the students brainstormed how they would investigate the topics. Their answers to the question, "How can we find out about ladybugs?" were recorded and illustrated on a colorful chart. Still spilling over with ideas, the children listed on a second chart all the ways they pictured themselves researching — by reading, discussing, drawing, storytelling, moving to music, writing and comparing. The energy in the room could not be confined to paper!

The teacher modeled research strategies in daily shared reading, using both informational fiction and nonfiction literature. She paused often to encourage the children to surround the text with their oral language and thereby construct meaning. It is oral language in a classroom that nurtures connections to children's prior experiences. During each read-aloud and discussion, the teacher modeled for the children how to read for information. She demonstrated the skill of note taking by recording on chart paper the phrases the children thought important. In subsequent shared readings, the children practiced the how-to's of reading for information and recording the facts in their notes.

ORGANIZING THE RESEARCH

Each child decided on his own research topic from the list the class had generated — predators, hibernation, male and female, and so on. It is individual interest that provokes questions. Those who shared a common interest were paired or

As in all inquiry, learning cannot be limited to one approach or a single set of tools. Choice is a powerful motivator! Consequently, some children chose to work in small groups and organize their findings in a different format, using topic charts rather than file folders. Each group had the opportunity to book browse and sit around tables of material relevant to their chosen topic. The small groups recorded what they had learned by

grouped for study. Next came research folders containing the questions significant to each learner. The students illustrated their folders, took notes, and wrote observations as they found information on their topics.

drawing and writing on a large sheet of paper headed by their particular topic.

Everyone in the classroom was earnestly engaged in learning. And because the classroom is a learning community, the students shared their ideas and insights from the folders and charts. A teacher could not ask for more!

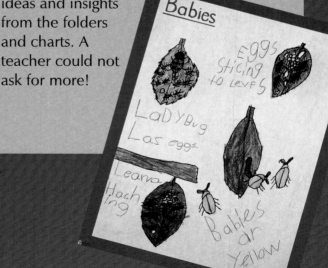

The teacher facilitated research with ongoing lessons on language and writing skills. She presented concepts of print and parts of speech through the characters in *The Grouchy Ladybug*.

Children who are learning to be researchers need to work for extended periods of time in a room where the hum of learning is appreciated. Learning through inquiry demands both listening and participation. Interacting with one another and the teacher is an important part of discovery.

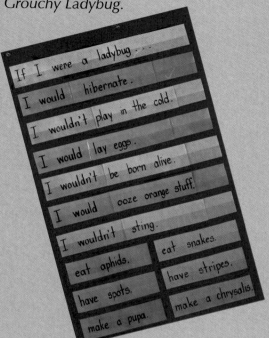

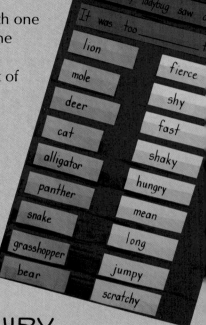

CELEBRATING INQUIRY

With the inquiry projects completed, the children communicated their personalized knowledge in a variety of ways. They celebrated their explorations with music, drama, storytelling, art responses and charting. The research from the children's file folders and topic sheets was recorded on two illustrated charts, "Discoveries" and "More Discoveries," for all to read.

A colorful mural, "But I Wonder," expressed the images the rich language of the poem had created in the children's imaginations. Their art expression was a perfect conclusion to their study of "ladybugs and bees don't smell with little noses but with feelers, if you please."

Another small group made an extraordinary mural of their study of the life cycle of the ladybug. The children's pride in their new knowledge was reflected in the careful, accurate drawings.

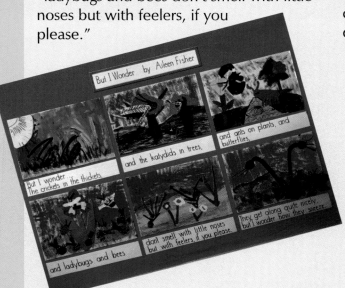

Two children presented a creative drama on how a ladybug learns to fly to demonstrate a fact that fascinated them — that a second pair of wings comes out from under the protective outside shell. Eager to have everyone understand the concept, they directed the children to pair off. With a lighter-weight student draped on the shoulders and back of a stronger student, the two leaders tried to demonstrate the two pairs of wings working together. The momentary chaos delighted the leaders who yelled, "Yesssss! You got it!"

Two students, with pointer in hand, explained their large, detailed diagram of the parts of a ladybird beetle, using the newly discovered scientific terms. They had labeled the claws and jaws, antennae and body parts, and had then drawn an upside-down ladybird beetle to show its defense position when attacked. "Anyway, that shows you how the legs are attached," they explained. Another small group of researchers presented their lovely watercolor mural of the different colors and spot patterns of ladybugs.

With the celebrations of learning shared and made visible, confident students were ready to think and to ask again. The children had both choice and ownership in their journey with *The Grouchy Ladybug*.

INQUIRY AND *THE BIRTH OF A WHALE*

Just as children are drawn to the irresistible chant of a ladybug, so too are they captivated by John Archambault's lyrical, exquisitely illustrated *The Birth of a Whale*. Reading that the whale is "fifteen feet long, weighing three tons, its blue eyes open in the deep water dark," children are hungry to learn more about the great creatures. The book is a masterpiece, rich in language, cadence and accurate detail. Children fall in love with the absolute beauty of the words and illustrations.

A shared experience, a captured lizard, an enchanting storybook — all can give birth to learning through inquiry. Magnificent pictures of whales are what caught the attention of the kindergarten children. They were eager to know more about the gentle giants of the sea.

Children's prior knowledge is a powerful determinant of what they will learn in an inquiry study, so time was given to browsing through books, listening to tapes, and talking to friends about whales. The kindergartners then created their first chart, "What do we think we know?," from a model for guiding student research. (The model is called KWHL, which is an acronym for What do you already know? What would you like to know? How will you find out? and What did you learn? (See Ogle, 1995.)

The children were immersed in the literature experiences of reading aloud and shared reading. That led to exciting, original discoveries. Their questions tumbled out onto a second chart, "What do we want to know?"

Leading children to research, the *how* of the KWHL model, included exploring the topic from many perspectives. Guest speakers, interviews, library visits, field trips and discussions allowed children to share observations and ask new questions. Shared reading, the study of text illustrations for information, and involvement through art and music presented multiple ways of knowing. Inquiry always integrates subject areas.

The deep water dark,
the deep water dark,
singing, dancing
in the deep water dark.

The melodious lyrics of *The Birth of a Whale* — "Singing, dancing in the deep water dark" brought music into the classroom in a meaningful way.

The children listened to an orchestral recording of *La Mer (The Sea)* by Claude Debussy and *The Aquarium* from *Carnival of the Animals* by Camille Saint-Saëns. They moved to the beautiful classical music with colorful ribbon streamers, pretending to be swaying seaweed on the ocean floor. As the teacher moved throughout the room, cutting the seaweed free, they floated around and up and down, matching the movement of the water.

Later, the somewhat haunting *Sounds and Songs of the Humpback Whales* became the background to rereadings of *The Birth of a Whale*.

Lastly, the children learned to sing the repetitive, poetic text of a father whale's song to a minor version of the melody of *The Farmer in the Dell*.

A literature-centered classroom and child-centered learning go together like a whale and its spout. The children delighted in *Dear Mr. Blueberry,* James Simon's engaging story of a girl who exchanged letters with her teacher about an imaginary whale in her pond. They enjoyed *My Friend Whale* by the same author, a touching story about a special friendship between a boy and a whale. They returned again and again to the striking photo-illustrations in Bruce McMillan's *Going on a Whale Watch*, a story that needed few words. The dramatic pictures of *The Whales' Song* by Dyland Sheldon so conveyed the feelings of the words that the children wanted to touch the graceful whales and hear their mysterious songs as well. Simple, fascinating facts about whales and their fragile environment were embedded in all the stories.

The Birth of a Whale remained their favorite, followed by Cynthia Rylant's masterful nonfiction book, *The Whales.* With a perfect choice of words, she describes the wonder and quiet dignity of the huge creatures — what they look like, how they behave, and where they live "as they swim past delicately, floating like feathers, carrying secrets between them."

The children enthusiastically chose topics, divided into research groups, and wrote and shared their questions. They studied the classroom resources and helped each other excitedly when they found an answer to someone else's question. As a class, the children completed their fourth KWHL chart, *"What have we learned?"*

The diversity of the finished research projects reflected the freedom the children had to pursue their own questions. One group created from blocks and boxes a whale watch boat for dramatic play, modeled after Bruce McMillan's photo essay, *Going on a Whale Watch.* With blue bulletin board paper "water" surrounding their boat, the children used binoculars to spot pictures of whales around the room. Another group discovered writing letters to be a marvelous way to convey the information they were learning about whales, just like *Dear Mr. Blueberry.*

What have we learned?

- Narwhals like to use their tusks as swords. Chris V.
- Some whales live in a pod. Samantha
- Beluga whales like to spy-hop. Ashley
- Whales are mammals. Ariel
- Whales have blubber. Willie
- Only male humpbacks can sing. Emily
- Killer whales have 50 teeth. Cory
- Whales can sleep in the water. Matthias
- There are 2 groups of whales, baleen and toothed. Keegan
- Sperm whales have spermaceti in their head. Chris H.
- Belugas are called sea canaries. Kiana
- Blue whales are the biggest whales. Chris G.
- Some whales eat krill. Stormy
- Blue whales hearts are as big as a car. Derrick
- Baleen whales have 2 blow holes. Keith
- Sperm whales eat giant squid. Dominique

A small group of researchers conducted an experiment about blubber, simulating the effect with vegetable shortening. They timed and recorded how long children could hold a hand protected by "blubber" (vegetable shortening) in ice water compared to how long they could keep an unprotected hand in the water. The children concluded that a whale's thick layer of blubber keeps it warm and helps it survive in cold water. The charted results were a visible example of how learning through inquiry erases the boundaries of subject areas in curriculum.

Another group that had researched the weight and length of whales unrolled cash register tapes outside until they equaled the actual length of a mother and a baby humpback whale. With paper and pencil in hand, they asked each classmate to estimate how many times he would have to lie down, head to toe, to reach the end of the tapes. Together, teacher and children charted the children's names and estimates — new vocabulary, new math skills, new accomplishment!

A colorful large-group response was a Venn diagram, completed after many class discussions about the similarities and differences of whales and fish.

A small group of researchers created a fact book, one statement and illustration per page, modeled after the factual storybook, *My Friend Whale*.

Humpbacks sing to communicate.

Humpbacks breach to scratch themselves.

Humpbacks bubble-net to catch krill.

Some students concluded their research on the life cycle of a whale by adding their carefully and accurately drawn whales to individual life-cycle maps.

Other children chose to present their information in a clever and colorful question-and-answer format in a class book.

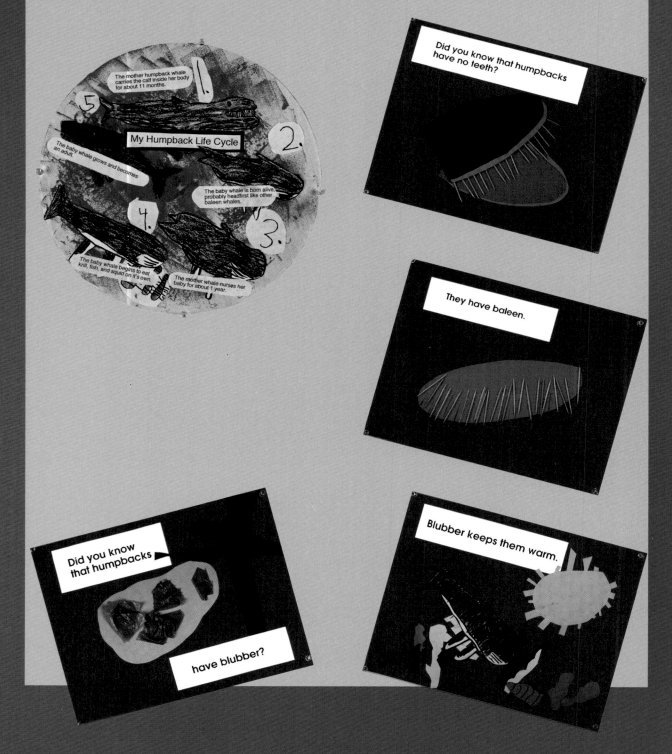

The children culminated their research by painting a mural of a swirling ocean with life-like whales and sea creatures. They added their individual statements from the class chart, "What do we know about whales?" The sections of their magnificent mural stretched across an entire wall and brought others to the classroom just to see what the kindergarten children had created. (See one section of the mural reproduced below).

When inquiry flows across curriculum, not defined by content areas or time schedules, it allows the motivation and persistence of the students to fuel and sustain the learning process. Inquiry gives children the freedom to explore the disciplines of science, music, art, math, and social studies, all of which offer different perspectives on learning. Even young children are engaged and challenged by multiple ways of knowing, gaining the important thinking skills they will need for a lifetime. Concludes educator and researcher Jerry Harste, "Since the only thing we can guarantee the next generation is problems which will have to be solved collectively, then all instruction should be inquiry-based" (Harste, 1995).

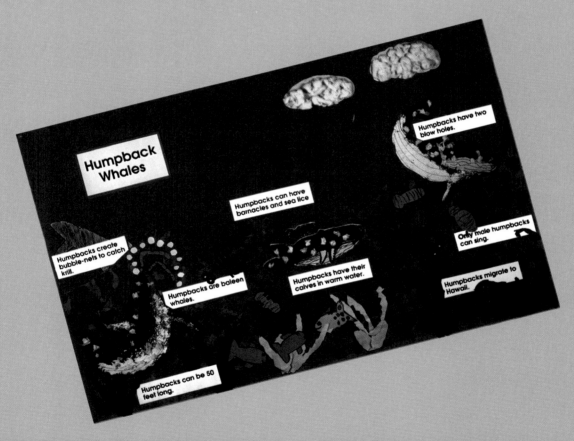

MORE CELEBRATIONS EXPERIENCING THE BEST OF CHILDREN'S LITERATURE

INDIVIDUAL RESEARCH PRESENTATIONS OF AMAZING EGG-LAYING ANIMALS

A literature response to the memorable nonfiction book, *Chickens Aren't the Only Ones,* by Ruth Heller (see p. 59).

AN ART EXPRESSION

A response to the vivid informational storybook, *Growing Vegetable Soup,* by Lois Ehlert, and the kindred poem, *Little Seeds,* by Else Holmelund Minarik (see pp. 211, 228, and 230).

LITTLE SEEDS

Little seeds we sow in spring,
growing while the robins sing,

by: Nancy K, Hayley, Jessica

give us carrots, peas and beans,
tomatoes, pumpkins, squash and
greens

by: Stacey, Michael, Beccca

And we pick them,
one and all,
through the summer,
through the fall.

Winter comes, then spring, and then
little seeds we sow again.

Else Holmelund Minarik

by: Andrew, Julie

A Character Web Using Describing Words

A literature response to a poignant storybook, *Tough Boris,* by Mem Fox (see p. 237).

A BASKET OF SHOPPING CHOICES

A literature response through innovation to the hilarious storybook, *To Market, To Market,* by Anne Miranda (see p. 231).

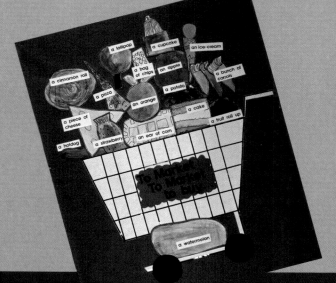

Harste, J. C. (Winter, 1995). Introducing the Center for Inquiry: Where learners are welcome and come in all sizes. *Talking Points,* p. 6.

Ogle, D. (1995). K-W-L: A teaching model that develops active reading of expository text. *The Reading*

ox grazing and sensing danger or shedding its winter underfur. Perhaps some children will add music to their performances; others may write facts or stories to present to the class from the Author's Chair.

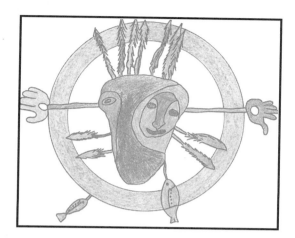

A DIVERSITY OF CULTURES

Just as Inuit tribes differed in their languages and traditions, so do all Native American tribes throughout North America. Expand your study. Read to your children from books that depict tribal cultures, looking for differences in clothing, shelter, food, art, and way of life. Locate the tribes on a map of North America.

Divide the children into groups. Each group can choose a nation and research from your resource books important facts about the customs and ingenuity that enabled the tribe to survive.

A CHORAL READING

Native American poems and prayers were written to be sung and meant to be shared. Composed in long hours of solitude and stillness, they are a window into the Native Americans' reverence for the natural world.

"Among Them I Walk" reflects a strong belief that plants respond to prayers and affection. After the children read the prayer aloud with you, give them time to share orally and connect to their own experiences. Say the words together in a slow, chanting rhythm; then a little louder; and finally soft again. Some children may want to sing the words, others may move as Native Americans did, and others may choose to respond in pictures or in writing.

LEFT: AMONG THEM I WALK
My great corn plants.
Among them I walk.
I speak to them.
They hold out their hands to me.

RIGHT: AMONG THEM I WALK
My great squash vines.
Among them I walk.
I speak to them.
They hold out their hands to me.

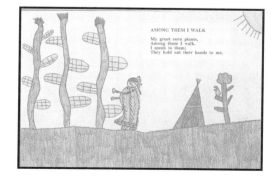

WEBS AND PYRAMIDS

The dramatic language of the storybook *The Seasons and Someone* by Virginia Kroll speaks of the remarkable ingenuity of the Inuit people, like Mama and Dear One, which enabled them to survive bitter climate and changing seasons.

Other tribes also continually moved, adapting food and dwellings to the seasons. Make a web for each tribe, showing the seasonal facts learned. For example, the web for the Ojibwa tribe would show that the Ojibwa moved to Lake Superior in summer to plant gardens, to swamps in the fall to plant wild rice, and to forests in winter to hunt and to gather maple sap in the spring.

Using facts from the webs, have the children write sentences about their chosen tribes. After editing and illustrating their text, the children can present their writing to the class in the form of books, dioramas, charts, or mobiles. That is authentic writing for a real purpose and a real audience.

MINI LANGUAGE LESSONS

* Even contractions can reflect the life of Native Americans. Drawing from the facts, art forms, charts, and stories throughout your room, have your children write sentences about Indian life. Fold a horizontal 8½-by-11-inch piece of paper by bringing the two outside edges to meet in the middle. Crease them. The folded paper will resemble a door. On the left side of the opening, write the word *can* and on the right side, write the word *not*. When the two flaps are opened, the child's sentence using the contraction, such as *The buffalo can't see the hunter,* will be visible.

* Have the children locate capital letters in their own writing and in the literature, maps, and children's responses around the room. Write their discoveries on a chart that probably won't be big enough to contain all their words. Discuss with them the reasons for all the capital letters they found—book titles, naming words such as Inuit and Arctic, the first word of a sentence, and so on.

* Action words abound in *Mama, Do You Love Me?* and the stories of Native Americans. As the children identify verbs such as *move, plant,* or *hunt,* print them in the first column of a class chart titled Action Words and Word Endings. The other columns will be headed *s* or *es* or *ies, ed,* and *ing.* Begin with a sentence such as, *The Ojibwa Indians move every season.* Have the children tell you sentences using *moves, moved,* and *moving* as you write the new words on the chart. Individuals or small groups can talk about or write four sentences for each of the other verbs on the list. The stories, poems, songs, and charts in your room will all be resources for teaching word endings in context.

WEAVING

As shown in the lovely text and illustrations of *Giving Thanks: A Native American Good Morning Message,* young Indians were taught to thank and revere Mother Earth for all gifts of life. They learned to decorate everything they made with objects and dyes from nature. Enjoy a walk outside with your children, gathering leaves and acorns and looking for gifts of life to celebrate. Then let the children count, measure, and cut their own colored paper strips to weave into brown construction-paper mats. Demonstrate the over-and-under pattern of weaving, alternating rows. Finally, have them arrange and glue the leaves and acorns on their weaving. Because literature weaves its own web throughout the curriculum, it creates a natural springboard to art responses.

A LANGUAGE OF SYMBOLS

Native Americans recorded their animal hunts, possessions, and wars through a language of picture symbols. Using brown butcher-paper vests or rectangles with crinkled edges to resemble animal skins, let the children compose messages or stories with Indian picture writing. Some may want to accompany their art language with a written message or story. Be available to listen as children talk about their writing and to help edit for publication. Writing is a natural way to learn language in every culture.

SAND PAINTING AND SYMBOLS

Brainstorm with your children about things the Native Americans were thankful for. Your list will be an ever-growing one. Give each child a word to illustrate, looking through your resources for ancient Indian picture symbols. Read about the native ceremonial art form of sand painting. Working on individual pieces of sandpaper, have each child draw his picture symbol lightly with pencil, then trace the outline with glue. Quickly sprinkle the glue outline with builder's sand that has been brightly colored with food coloring.

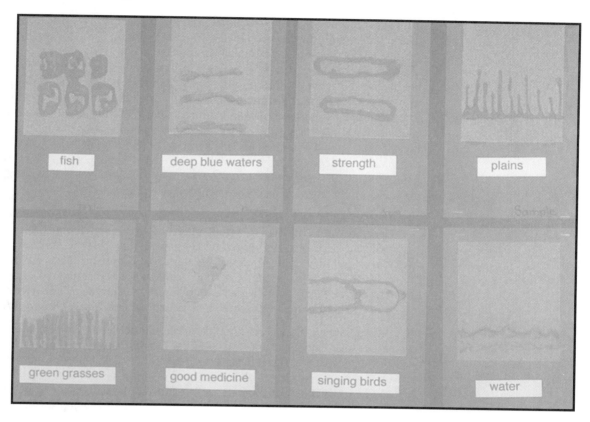

CINDERELLA FOLKTALES

The folklore of most tribal nations included a native adaptation of the age-old Cinderella tale. *Sootface: An Ojibwa Cinderella Story* was written by Robert D. San Souci and superbly illustrated by Daniel San Souci. The magical Algonquin interpretation *The Rough-Face Girl* by Rafe Martin is another dramatic read-aloud as goodness wins. Furthermore, the detailed illustrations reflect much of Indian life. Children will construct story meaning and deepen their understanding by organizing their ideas and information in a story matrix. Although the study of fairy tales is often best reserved for older children, enthusiasm for these Native American tales may lead to a theme on selected folklore.

Native American Cinderella Folktales

Title	Sootface: An Ojibwa Cinderella Story	The Rough-Face Girl An Algonquin Tale
Setting		
Characters		
Events		
Ending		

EVERYDAY LEARNING ACTIVITIES

Positive parenting; developmental learning activities; and a warm, nurturing environment are major factors in a child's academic success and lifetime learning.

Mama, Do You Love Me? by Barbara M. Joosse is a tender story of a child testing the limits of her independence. Dear One was really asking her mother, "No matter how naughty I am, will you still love me?" And Mama's reassuring responses first expressed her own true emotion of anger or fear before she spoke the awaited words, "But still, I would love you." A child cannot hear often enough the words, "I love you." Furthermore, if you physically touch a child when you are saying the words, you double the impact.

We sometimes overlook the easiest way to guide children into acceptable behavior: to simply tell them what *to* do. Children's brains work much more efficiently with positive information. They are programmed that way. Saying to a child "Don't sit on that chair" requires her mind to process negative information and transform it into something positive. A young child can't do that. Unlike adults, she does not yet have inner speech to suggest alternatives and tell herself what *to* do. So, instead of "Don't run in the parking lot," say "Take my hand and walk by my side." Replace the negative "Don't be rough with the baby" with "The baby will like it if you gently touch her toes." The child will know exactly what *to* do to gain your approval. Good discipline not only directs a child's behavior but also motivates it.

❋ Another delightful read-aloud about family love is *Mama, If You Had a Wish* by Jeanne Modesitt. Your child will turn to it again and again. For siblings who often wonder who is loved the best, read the warm and eloquent *I Love You the Purplest,* also by Barbara M. Joosse, and the lovable *Koala Lou* by Mem Fox. Adopted children will respond to the joyful story of love in *How I Was Adopted* by Joanna Cole. Remember every read-aloud should be followed by talk time. When a child talks about a storybook, she makes sense out of what she has heard by making connections to her own life. *(family relationships)*

❋ Incorporate cleanup as an integral part of play activities, training a child to put away one set of toys before getting out another. Playing together is more fun without endless clutter. Provide a specific place for specific toys. Label tubs. Mark places on shelves. Use book baskets for books. Identify parking places in the garage for outside toys. A child will learn to classify, cooperate, and organize. She will gain respect for toys as well as a sense of responsibility; the family runs more smoothly when she does her part. *(learning responsibility)*

❋ Have your child stand with you in front of a full-length mirror. Ask her to name things that make her special, such as "I have curly hair," or "I have dimples and a great smile," or "I can tell when my mama needs a hug." Record her sentences on individual pieces of paper. Then while sitting or standing in front of the mirror, help her draw a self-portrait. Add the sentences to her "I Am Special" drawing and read it together often. *(self-esteem)*

❋ Collect scraps of material, especially those that might be used in colder climates (quilted, corduroy, felt, wool, and so on). Cut the fabric into shapes. Let a child glue the collage pieces randomly onto sturdy paper, totally covering the paper. Using a marker, draw the outlines of parkas for Mama, Dear One, and the doll for a child to cut out and hold the next time you read *Mama, Do You Love Me? (story meaning)*

May I Bring a Friend?

by Beatrice Schenk de Regniers

SETTING THE STAGE

Instantly singable songs and the appealing rhyme and rhythm of finger plays will encourage children to be involved in story time.

"Friends Forever" by Walt Disney Recordings
(Sung by the characters in *Winnie the Pooh*)

"Friendship" by Billboard Presents, *Family Friendship Classics*

THE ELEPHANT

The elephant has a trunk for a nose,	*(arms out, hands clasped)*
And up and down is the way it goes;	*(move arms up, down)*
He has such a saggy, baggy hide!	*(flop arms and shoulders)*
Do you think two elephants would fit inside?	*(hold up two fingers)*

HERE'S A CUP OF TEA

Here's a cup, and here's a cup,	*(make two fists)*
And here's a pot of tea;	*("pop" thumb out of fists)*
Pour a cup and pour a cup	*(pour into left, then right)*
And have a cup with me!	*(extend cup to neighbor and pretend to drink)*

FIRST READING

Tell me all the things you see on the cover of our story. How are the king and queen dressed? Where do you think they are? What do you think the small boy is saying? I will just turn the pages without saying a word. You be the storytellers. Tell me everything you see and what you imagine is happening.

Beatrice Schenk de Regniers would have loved your story. I know I did! In her story, the little boy received a very special invitation to have tea in the king and queen's castle. The child asked one question, "May I bring a friend?" That is the title of our story. The illustrator, Beni Montresor, was given a very important award, the Caldecott Medal, for his beautiful pictures.

As I read, listen for the words, "So I brought my friend. . . ." You tell me who the friend is before I turn the page.

GETTING INVOLVED

Here are word cards for the days of the week and here are picture cards with the names of all the animal guests who came to the castle. What would you like to do with them? Where shall we begin? I like your ideas. Sunday is the first day of the week, so put that word card on the left. Now find the word card that says Monday. One by one, line up all the days of the week. Count them—we should have seven.

Now let's have some fun matching the picture cards to the days of the week. Show me the animal that was a guest for tea and put that picture next to the word Sunday. Pick out the picture of the friend who ate dinner on Monday. Next, find the playful friends who came to lunch on Tuesday. Who did the king and queen sit on for Wednesday's breakfast? Which friends wore masks on Thursday? Who played the horn on Friday? Tell me how we can show *all* the friends who enjoyed tea at the zoo on Saturday.

The king and queen entertained themselves waiting for the boy and his friends to arrive. I'll name the things they did *very slowly* so you can move about as they did. Show me how the king and queen sat on their royal thrones . . . picked flowers . . . danced together . . . went fishing . . . caught butterflies . . . and went swinging. Last of all, sit down and show me how they wound yarn into a ball for the queen's knitting.

A CLOSER LOOK

With each rereading of a story, children gain new understanding. Pause often for a spontaneous flow of oral language as the children share their feelings and observations. Extend the learning process with your own questions in repeated readings of the story.

*   Do you think the first sentence of *May I Bring a Friend?* was a good story starter? *(evaluating)*

*   Did the king and queen always send their invitations in a letter? *(comprehension)*

*   Tell me which animal guest surprised you the most. *(reflecting)*

*   How did the king and queen solve the problem when the elephant arrived? *(comprehension)*

*   Why did the lions wear masks? Why did they roar? *(comprehension)*

*   What would happen in the story if we changed the order of the guests' arrival? *(application)*

*   Do you agree that the king and queen and boy had good manners? Did the guests? *(evaluating)*

*   In your opinion, were the king and queen good friends to the boy? *(evaluating)*

*   Why did the king and queen have tea at the City Zoo? *(comprehension)*

*   Tell me what the banners say over the zoo. *(language)*

*   What was your favorite part of the story? *(reflecting)*

*   Imagine you were the boy. Who would you invite to see the king and queen? *(reflecting)*

STORY TIME EXTENSIONS

Nora's Surprise by Satomi Ichikawa

Don't Fidget a Feather by Erica Silverman

Mrs. Katz and Tush by Patricia Polacco

Amos and Boris by William Steig

Cookie's Week by Cindy Ward

BALANCED LITERACY ACTIVITIES

POETRY

POEM
I loved my friend.
He went away from me.
There's nothing more to say.
The poem ends,
Soft as it began—
I loved my friend.
Langston Hughes

TABLE MANNERS
by Gelett Burgess
from *The Random House Book
of Poetry*
by Jack Prelutsky

INVOLVEMENT

MAY I BRING A FRIEND?

A king, a queen, an invitation to the castle, and animal friends that just won't sit still—what a setting for creative dramatics. Have the children find a place in your room for the throne and a table for tea. Provide gold and glitter in the art center for crowns, a scepter, and a horn. Look in the dress-up box for royal robes. Hang a yarn-tied picture name card around each child's neck, showing the king, the queen, the child, and the animal guests. Group the monkeys and the lions. With you as narrator, have the children freely pantomime the movement of the story characters. Perhaps you can precede the drama with a discussion about manners in the castle.

INTEGRATION

RHYME TIME

The rhyming words that add so much to the listening pleasure of *May I Bring a Friend?* are simple, familiar words for which children can easily create rhyming word families. Each day write one rhyming word from the story, such as *boy,* in the center of your chart paper and make a web of rhyming words. As the children discover words that rhyme with the key word in their reading, writing, and listening experiences, add them to the web. Continue choosing new words from the story, such as *king, queen, tea, may,* or *bring,* to create new webs. Recognizing word families helps children learn the phonemes that make up language.

Graph the results on a multicolumn wall graph with the semantic web key words at the top of each column. Graph the words the children have discovered. Which word family is the largest? The smallest? The favorite?

A NEW CHAPTER

I wonder what happened on Saturday at half-past two after tea at the City Zoo. I wonder if the boy ever visited the king and queen again. Ask the children what they wonder about. It is the oral language surrounding literature that leads to meaningful writing. Then let the children choose what they want to write about because they see themselves as authors when they make their own decisions. Let the children draw on their knowledge of letters and sounds as they write developmentally. It is phoneme awareness that makes invented spelling possible. Give each child the opportunity to share in the Author's Chair (now we're rhyming, too!).

SUNDAY, MONDAY

Review with the children the guests that came on each day of the week. Choose a pair of children to illustrate a page for each day. At the top left of each page print the day of the week and the phrase, *I brought my friend(s), the. . . .* On the right, under a flap, have the children draw the animals guest(s) that came that day. Change the print on the last page to read, *On Saturday, we had tea at the zoo.* Under that flap, the children will draw all the animals having tea at the zoo. Your pages will tell a colorful story on the wall, out in the hall, or bound into a class big book. Predictable text helps children learn to read.

MORE FRIENDS FOR TEA

The world of children's literature is full of marvelous stories of friendship. Imagine what *May I Bring a Friend?* would have been like if the boy had invited friends from other stories. Read *Ernest and Celestine,* Gabrielle Vincent's masterpiece of charm about inseparable Mouse and Bear. Enjoy *Don't Fidget a Feather!,* a must-see, beautiful story about the friendship of champions gander and duck. Talk about the lovely choice of expressive words in *Amos and Boris,* a tender and comical story of devoted friends mouse and whale. Look for the friendships of other cultures in Patricia Polacco's *Mrs. Katz and Tush,* the poignant story of a lonely, Jewish widow and an African-American boy brought together by a scrawny kitten. Enjoy the rich folk art and characters from the author's beloved Ukraine in *Chicken Sunday,* another gem by Polacco.

YOU ARE INVITED TO A TEA PARTY

Plan a tea party in your room. Will you invite stuffed animals? Moms, dads, grandmas, grandpas? Another class? Make lists of things you need to do to prepare and what you want to do for your guests. Your lists might include the following:

* Write and decorate invitations shaped like teacups.

* Make place mats and paste paper doilies where the teacups will go.

* Mix lemonade tea.

* Cut out tea sandwiches with cookie cutters.

* Make streamers for the room and a welcome banner for the door.

* Decorate the pages of a guest book for guests to sign.

* Invite someone special from your school to be the king and queen and read *May I Bring a Friend?* to the guests.

* Sing the songs "Friends Forever" and "Friendship" (p. 120).

* Share the class stories you have written before you say good-bye.

EVERYDAY LEARNING ACTIVITIES

Positive parenting; developmental learning activities; and a warm, nurturing environment are major factors in a child's academic success and lifetime learning.

Much of the appeal of *May I Bring a Friend?* by Beatrice Schenk de Regniers is the poetry of the rhyming words. Children and poetry go together. A child's first poetry was the rhythmic heartbeat he heard in the womb. His next poetic experience was probably the delightful rhythm of nursery rhymes and folk songs. Because of the repetition, the child memorized the patterns of the sounds without even trying. Poems are good memory builders. They fit easily into the shared moments of busy days. A child loves poetry that relates to all the little things he experiences each day—smiles and tears, friends and animals, rain and sunshine. The nonsense and appeal of silly rhymes nudges open the door of imagination in a child's mind. Poems are also the perfect beginning to the read-aloud habit and a marvelous addition to any child's bedtime routine. A child will be captivated by the poetry and charming illustrations of *Read-Aloud Rhymes for the Very Young* by Jack Prelutsky or *The Random House Book of Mother Goose* by Arnold Lobel. No child should be without his very own treasured book of poetry.

✳ Create a calendar by dividing a large strip of paper into seven blocks. Write each day of the week across the top and read the words with a child. Every morning, ask the child to invite a guest for tea—a real or an imaginary friend, a stuffed animal, or a character from *May I Bring a Friend?* Together, set the table for a special tea party. Use a cookie cutter to cut bread or cheese or meat for tea sandwiches. Talk about how the food looks, tastes, and feels. Have fun role-playing good and bad manners. At the end of the week, decide which guest had manners fit for a king and queen. *(days of week, social skills)*

✳ Write colorful little invitations or messages such as "Time to read a story" or "You are invited to a tea party" or "You have just earned three hugs and a big kiss!" Hide the messages in obvious places during the day. When a child finds one, have him describe where he found it, such as under his plate or beside his teddy bear or on the car seat. Then read the message. Surrounding a child with print, or words written down, is one of the first steps of reading. *(language)*

✳ A ladder can provide endless practice in gross motor skills. A child will have twice the fun if he can invite a friend to join the activity. Begin with a simple skill like walking between the rungs of a ladder that is lying flat on the ground. Next have him crawl between the rungs of a ladder held on its side or climb up an inclined ladder. Make the skills progressively more difficult. Lay the ladder flat on the ground and hold the child's hand as he walks on top of the rungs of the ladder or jumps over the rungs one at a time. Another time, have the child walk sideways along a side beam, walk on his hands and feet between the rungs, or walk with one foot on a rung and one foot on a side beam. Laughter and silliness guaranteed! *(gross motor skills)*

✳ Think of rhyming word families for some of the words in *May I Bring a Friend?* (e.g., boy, king, queen, tea, may, and bring). Write them down. Which list is longest, shortest? *(rhyming, words in print, counting sets)*

Mr. Rabbit
and the
Lovely
Present

by Charlotte Zolotow

* Cultural diversity
* Concept of giving
* Classifying
* Comparing/Contrasting

* Math/science concepts
* Vocabulary
* Structure writing
* A family activity

SETTING THE STAGE

Instantly singable songs and the appealing rhyme and rhythm of finger plays will encourage children to be involved in story time.

"Apples and Bananas" by Raffi, *One Light, One Sun*
(A hilarious game song with vowels)

"Jenny Jenkins" by Sharon, Lois & Bram, *Smorgasbord*
(Rhyming song using colors)

THE VERY NICEST HOUSE
The fish lives in a brook,   *(hands wiggle)*
The bird lives in a tree,   *(hands fly)*
But home's the very nicest place   *(hands make roof)*
For a little child like me.   *(arms hug self)*

WHAT COLORS DO I SEE?
See, see, see
What colors do I see?
Purple plums   *(point to thumb)*
Red tomatoes   *(point to first finger)*
Yellow corn   *(point to second finger)*
Brown potatoes   *(point to third finger)*
Green lettuce   *(point to fourth finger)*
Yum, yum, yum, good!
I learn so many colors
When I eat my food!

FIRST READING

Look at the cover of this book and tell me what you see. Where do you think the little girl and the rabbit are? What do you think their conversation is about? Would you like to predict what will happen? Let's write down your predictions and see if they happen in the story.

The name of the story is *Mr. Rabbit and the Lovely Present*. It was written by Charlotte Zolotow and the pictures were drawn by Maurice Sendak. He also illustrated the book *Where the Wild Things Are*. I'm going to show you the pictures in both books. You tell me if you think they are alike or different.

When we were talking about the cover of *Mr. Rabbit and the Lovely Present*, you noticed the silver circle in the corner. That means the book was chosen to be a Caldecott Honor Book and Mr. Sendak was given an award for the beautiful illustrations. There is another very special award called the Caldecott Medal, which is given to only one picture book each year. Mr. Sendak received that gold medal award for his marvelous illustrations in *Where the Wild Things Are*. Not many illustrators have won both awards.

GETTING INVOLVED

What were you thinking of as I read *Mr. Rabbit and the Lovely Present?* What do you want to tell me about the story? Let me tell you what I was thinking. I loved the rabbit. I liked the pictures of him sitting down, crossing his legs, and sitting on the fence scratching his head. I wished I could be there listening to him talk. What did you love about the pictures?

Tell me the four colors the little girl's mother liked. Let's list them one at a time and name all the gifts that Mr. Rabbit suggested. We'll circle the gift the little girl chose for each color.

Now look at these little drawings of the presents Mr. Rabbit suggested for the color red. Name them as I spread them out: red underwear, red roofs, red cardinals, red fire engines, and red apples. Help me *match* the pictures to the words we have listed under red on our color chart. *(Do the same for each color group.)*

Colored markers and three-by-five-inch cards are a fast way to prepare this activity. A small piece of Velcro on the back of each card will hold it up on a flannel board for an eye-catching way to classify. Another time, ask the children to name new categories you could use for grouping, such as jewels, birds, things you can eat, things that have engines, and things you cannot give away.

A CLOSER LOOK

With each rereading of a story, children gain new understanding. Pause often for a spontaneous flow of oral language as the children share their feelings and observations. Extend the learning process with your own questions in repeated readings of the story.

* Do you think "Mr. Rabbit," said the little girl, "I want help" was a good story starter? *(evaluating)*

* Where are Mr. Rabbit and the little girl having their conversation? *(interpretation)*

* What time of day is it at the beginning of the story? The end? *(observation)*

* Why did the little girl need help? *(reasoning)*

* Do you agree with Mr. Rabbit that you can't give away colors? *(evaluating)*

* Why do you think the little girl's mother likes the birds to be in trees? *(reasoning)*

* What are emeralds and sapphires? Why couldn't the little girl afford them? *(reasoning)*

* Where do you think the rabbit went when he said good-bye? *(reflecting)*

* If the little girl's mother had liked the color orange, what do you think Mr. Rabbit would have suggested? *(association)*

* In your opinion, was the little girl's present a nice one? Would your mother have liked it? *(evaluating)*

* Did *Mr. Rabbit and the Lovely Present* make you think of another story? *(reflecting)*

STORY TIME EXTENSIONS

Somebody Loves You, Mr. Hatch by Eileen Spinelli

The Gardener by Sarah Stewart

Chicken Sunday by Patricia Polacco

Miss Rumphius by Barbara Cooney

Feathers for Lunch by Lois Ehlert

BALANCED LITERACY ACTIVITIES

POETRY

YELLOW
Green is go,
and red is stop,
and yellow is peaches
with cream on top.

Earth is brown,
and blue is sky;
yellow looks well
on a butterfly.

Clouds are white,
black, pink, or mocha;
yellow's a dish of
tapioca.
                David McCord

A TASTE OF PURPLE
    by Leland B. Jacobs
    from *The Random House Book
        of Poetry*
    by Jack Prelutsky

WHAT IS PINK?
    by Christina Rossetti
    from *The Random House Book
        of Poetry*
    by Jack Prelutsky

INVOLVEMENT

A LOVELY PRESENT

To help your children appreciate the gentle warmth of *Mr. Rabbit and the Lovely Present*, choose a new focus each time you read the story. First, listen for the phrase, "She likes," as the little girl identifies the colors her mother likes. Next, listen for the phrases that relate to birds, and finally, to the lovely present of fruit.

Using sentence strips backed with felt or Velcro, write a sentence for each color and each fruit the mother likes. Have the children draw a tree; a basket; and small, labeled pictures of the four birds and four fruits. Display all the sentences and pictures in front of the children. As you read the story again, pause every time a child should put a sentence on the felt board or put a bird in the tree. The fruit pictures will go in the basket at the end of the story. Keep the pictures, sentences, and a tape of the story in their own pretty little basket for an independent or a paired reading experience.

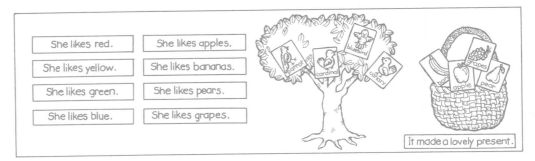

INTEGRATION

OBSERVATIONS, PLEASE

Put all kinds and colors of fruit on a table in your science center. Provide a magnifying glass, a balance scale, a measuring tape, and a ruler for children to independently explore, make observations, and compare. Add literacy props to your table for children to draw or write their observations.

OUR BOOK OF COLORS

To make a class book of a rainbow of colors, give every child a page with the sentence *What is* _____*?* printed at the top. Let each child choose a color word as well as the objects she will draw and label on her page, such as a fire truck, a stoplight, and a rose for the color red. Mount each child's picture on a background that matches the color she has chosen. Bind the pages into a colorful, easily read class book.

Variation: With one line printed on the top of each page, the illustrated phrases of the poem "Yellow" would make a beautiful wall display or class big book.

PRESENTS ARE EVERYWHERE

Discuss with the children the idea that presents are everywhere in our world. Let them unwrap three gift-wrapped boxes in which you have put an acorn, a picture of a rainbow, and a picture of a smiling baby. Brainstorm together about the source of the little presents until the children conclude that the acorn is a present from a tree, the rainbow is a present from the rain, and the smile is a present from a baby. When every child has an idea to illustrate, give him a page with the sentence *A* _____ *is a present from a* _____. printed on the bottom. Record the words the children dictate to finish their sentences, brightly mount the pages, and display them so children can "read the walls."

A BASKET IS A PRESENT FROM A FRIEND

Have each child bring from home a piece of fruit and the name of one person she feels should receive a gift basket from the children. Using a floor graph, have the children suggest different ways to sort the fruit. Record your observations on a chart for another emergent reading and writing experience. Then line several baskets with pretty tissue paper and fill them with the fruit. As a group, decide who will receive your *lovely presents.*

A CELEBRATION OF PRESENTS

Presents can be a delightful theme celebration with mommies, daddies, and caregivers as guests. Create the invitations in the shape of little presents. Make decorations for a bright, festive room and decide on refreshments the children can serve. Plan a program for the guests, perhaps incorporating the following activities:

* Sing "Apples and Bananas" and "Jenny Jenkins," perfect choices for guests to join in the fun.

* With you as narrator, have the children dramatize the story of *Mr. Rabbit and the Lovely Present.*

* Display the colorful fruit baskets. Have the children explain how they decided who will receive their lovely presents.

* Have each child read her illustrated page from *Presents Are Everywhere* and give it as a present to her guest.

EVERYDAY LEARNING ACTIVITIES

Positive parenting; developmental learning activities; and a warm, nurturing environment are major factors in a child's academic success and lifetime learning.

The softness and warmth of the story *Mr. Rabbit and the Lovely Present* by Charlotte Zolotow make you think the little girl must have had a very special relationship with her mother. It is during the all-important early years that a child learns to think of himself as a special person. Usually the way a child feels about himself when he enters kindergarten is the way he will feel about himself as an adult. Self-esteem is determined so early. A child has to believe what adults say about him, for he has no other basis on which to form a concept of who he is. If you label a child lazy or dumb, he will live up to that label because he believes you. If you label a child friendly or happy or helpful, he will see himself as all of those things. Usually a child becomes exactly what adults tell him he is. Give a child a wonderful image to live up to. Let him overhear you praising him as you talk to friends. The mistakes or problems need not be mentioned again. Remember praise is a great motivator. There isn't a human being alive who doesn't need more affirmation than criticism.

✱ Children love to feel generous and to give gifts to those who are special to them. Put a little box or tiny basket in a corner of a child's drawer. Give him special jobs to do and a weekly allowance of nickels and dimes. Then when it is time to buy a birthday or holiday present for someone in the family, the child will have his own supply of money to use. The size or cost of the gift doesn't matter. Learning to give is a wonderful lesson, along with the fun of shopping and making a choice. *(social skill)*

✱ Children can experience the feeling of generosity without any money being spent. The best kind of present is the one the child makes himself. Give him a little box of odds and ends like yarn bits, cookie crinkly paper, straws, buttons, fabric pieces, colored paper, and crayons. Encourage a child to create his own gifts and cards. The praise and attention he will get for his creations will be a wonderful esteem builder. *(creativity, self-esteem)*

✱ Have a child go through a catalog and cut out gifts he would give to Grandma or some other special person. Have him paste his choices on a piece of paper and label them. Write down the child's words as he dictates a simple letter of love to give or mail to Grandma. Words have a purpose! *(words in print)*

✱ Create a color basket. First, put in pairs of color cards for a child to match. Next, add *color words* to match to the colors. Last, play "Concentration" with pairs of color words for a child to turn over and match. *(color and word recognition)*

✱ Make a coupon book for a child to give a loved one. Each page will have one gift that the child decides to give. Have the child draw a picture and dictate a sentence for each coupon, such as *I will give you a hug* or *I will sing you a song* or *I will tell you a story* or *I will bring you the newspaper. (giving, print)*

The Napping House

by Audrey Wood

TEACHING FOCUS

* Parts of speech
* Vocabulary
* Comparing/Contrasting
* Phonemic awareness

* Concepts of print
* Sequencing
* Structure writing
* A family activity

SETTING THE STAGE

Instantly singable songs and the appealing rhyme and rhythm of finger plays will encourage children to be involved in story time.

"Rhyme Time" by Greg and Steve, *Kidding Around*

"Rain, Rain Go Away" by Greg and Steve, *Playing Favorites*
(A medley of familiar favorites)

GRANNY'S SPECTACLES

Here are Granny's spectacles	*(fingers around eyes)*
Here is Granny's hat	*(hands on head)*
Here's the way she folds her arms	*(arms folded)*
And sits like that!	
Here are Grandpa's spectacles	*(bigger glasses)*
Here is Grandpa's hat	*(bigger hat)*
Here's the way he folds his arms	*(arms folded)*
And sits like that!	

FIVE LITTLE MONKEYS

Five little monkeys	*(five fingers up)*
Jumping on the bed,	*(jump to other hand)*
One fell off	*(one finger up)*
And bumped his head.	*(hold head)*
Momma called the doctor	*(phone to ear)*
And the doctor said,	
"No more monkeys jumping on the bed!"	*(shake finger)*

*Repeat with four monkeys and so on
until no more monkeys remain.*

FIRST READING

Why does the cover of this book make you smile? You be the storytellers and tell me what you think is happening. The name of the story is *The Napping House.* It was written by Audrey Wood, and her husband, Don Wood, added the beautiful illustrations.

What is happening on the title page? Tell me why you think the fence and lovely flowers are there. Look! There they are again on the dedication page. How did the artist tell you it's raining? Do you see something else in the picture? Tell me what words you think are on the mailbox. I wonder if the gate is open for a reason. *(Turn the page.)* Oh, now we know. The fence and flowers and mailbox and gate are all inviting us into *The Napping House.*

The charming, cumulative text will have the children joining in long before the delightful surprise ending.

GETTING INVOLVED

The Napping House would not have been nearly as much fun to read if the words had said "a flea on a house on a cat on a dog." Let's act out all the wonderful words the author used to describe the characters in the story: *snoring* granny, *dreaming* child, *dozing* dog, *snoozing* cat, *slumbering* mouse, and *wakeful* flea.

Pretend you are a dreaming child on a snoring granny on your own cozy bed. Pile on the dog, next the snoozing cat, then the slumbering mouse and last . . . oh-oh! Here comes the wakeful flea. Look out! Crash! No one now is sleeping.

A CLOSER LOOK

With each rereading of a story, children gain new understanding. Pause often for a spontaneous flow of oral language as the children share their feelings and observations. Extend the learning process with your own questions in repeated readings of the story.

* Tell me how the illustrations in *The Napping House* made you feel. *(reflecting)*

* Do you suppose the author was inviting you to join in the words of the story? *(reflecting)*

* How did you know when it started raining? When did it stop? *(observation)*

* Tell me where the artist hid the dog before it climbed on the bed. The cat? The mouse? *(observation)*

* How did the artist make the flea easy to find in every picture? *(observation)*

* Did it surprise you that one little flea bite caused such a commotion? *(reasoning)*

* What would happen if we changed the order of things in the story? *(analyzing)*

* Why do you think the colors in the pictures changed? The bed? The pitcher and basin? *(comprehension)*

* Which house would you rather go in—the one at the beginning or the ending of the story? *(evaluating)*

* I wonder where in the story you were thinking, "Oh! I just love that part!" *(reflecting)*

* Which illustration is your favorite? Which character? *(evaluating)*

* I wonder if something like that ever happened to you. *(reflecting)*

STORY TIME EXTENSIONS

Time to Sleep by Denise Fleming

A Flea in the Ear by Stephen Wyllie

Peace at Last by Jill Murphy

A Mouse Told His Mother by Bethany Roberts

The Midnight Farm by Reeve Lindbergh

BALANCED LITERACY ACTIVITIES

POETRY

THE NIGHT
The night
  creeps in
  around my head
  and snuggles down
  upon the bed,
  and makes lace pictures
  on the wall
  but doesn't say a word at all.
      Myra Cohn Livingston

A FROG AND A FLEA
A frog and a flea
And a kangaroo
Once jumped for a prize
In a pot of glue:
The kangaroo stuck
And so did the flea,
And the frog limped home
With a fractured knee.
      Cynthia Mitchell

INVOLVEMENT

IT'S RAINING, IT'S POURING

Using the melody of the nursery rhyme song "It's Raining, It's Pouring," change the characters to match those in *The Napping House*.

It's rain-ing, it's pour-ing, the gran-ny is snor-ing, she

went to bed and bumped her head and could-n't get up in the morn-ing!

In subsequent verses, sing about the characters in the order they appear in the story. Sing the first verse with considerable volume because it is Granny who is snoring (can't you hear it now?), and become increasingly softer until the last verse, the flea, is almost a whisper: "It's raining, it's pouring, the flea is snoring. It went to bed and bumped its head and couldn't get up in the morning!" The joy and patterns of music are an integral part of learning.

A SLUMBER PARTY

Have each child bring a teddy bear or stuffed animal to school for story time. Before each child leaves for the day, have him place his teddy bear somewhere in the room to spend the night at a slumber party in *The Napping House*. After the children have gone, rearrange and group the teddy bears in play centers in the room. In the morning, have each child look for his teddy bear and describe where he found it and what he imagined his animal friend did during the slumber party in *The Napping House*.

INTEGRATION

A FLANNEL BOARD NAPPING HOUSE STORY

Print the story title and the following eight phrases—*a cozy bed, a snoring granny, a dreaming child, a dozing dog, a snoozing cat, a slumbering mouse, a wakeful flea,* and *the napping house where no one now is sleeping*—on felt-backed sentence strips.

Have the children draw small pictures for each phrase. As you read *The Napping House*, encourage the children to read each phrase as you place it on the flannel board, building the sequence from the bottom up. Ask a child to add each matching picture. After the flea causes everything to tumble, read the last phrase together: "in the napping house where no one now is sleeping." Keep the phrases and pictures available for paired or individual sequencing and reading during center time.

Variation: Write on chart paper or put sentence strips in a pocket chart.

INDIVIDUAL ACCORDION BOOKS

As a class, discuss new characters for an innovation of *The Napping House*. Talk about all the important words that will describe each character. Then orally sequence the characters by size, saving the tiniest one for last. To make individual accordion books, cut a twelve-by-fourteen-inch piece of paper in half lengthwise. Put the two pieces together to make one long rectangle, now six by twenty-eight inches. Fold the rectangle into eight pages, accordion style. (Make one as a sample. It really is *not* complicated!) Print the title, then the new phrases on the bottom of each page for the children to illustrate. The purpose of structure writing is to create an inviting, easily read class book.

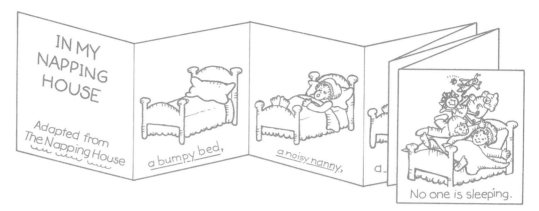

Variation: Have each child make an individual innovation at home with his family joining in the fun. Together, they could decide on a book format, the characters, descriptive adjectives, a sequence, and illustrations. Now that's truly *In My Napping House!* The children will have interesting stories to share when they bring their family projects back to class. Reading and writing have meaning when children make connections to their own lives.

THE NAPPING CLASSROOM

Lead the children in a discussion of the colorful descriptive words Audrey Wood has used so skillfully in *The Napping House.* For emphasis, read the story again, deleting all the adjectives. What a difference! Then brainstorm with the children about words that could describe each of them as they are napping, ideally using words that begin with the initial sounds of their names. (Extend your teaching by reading *Many Luscious Lollipops: A Book About Adjectives,* a delightful book by Ruth Heller that makes language come to life.)

Choose a small group of children to illustrate the cover and title page of your class book, *The Napping Classroom.* These three pages would come next:

Page One:
There is a classroom
A napping classroom
Where everyone is sleeping

Page Two:
And in that classroom
There is a rug,
A cozy rug in a napping classroom
Where everyone is sleeping

Page Three:
And on that rug
There is a . . .

Then give each child his own page to illustrate, adding a cozy rug cut from fabric, felt, or wallpaper before he draws himself napping. The last page could read, *In a napping classroom where everyone is snoring!* Children love to select their own reading material. They will return to this book again and again.

dozing David ,

snoozing Susan ,

cheerful Chad ,

in a napping classroom where everyone is snoring!

EVERYDAY LEARNING ACTIVITIES

Positive parenting; developmental learning activities; and a warm, nurturing environment are major factors in a child's academic success and lifetime learning.

In the first few years of life, a child learns more and at a faster rate than any other time. That means you are the most important teacher a child will ever have. You can do nothing better for a child than to introduce her at an early age to the joy and excitement of books. Reading together will create a loving, close bond between you and the child. It will plant within her the desire to learn to read herself. She will be hooked on the pleasure and delight of books long before she meets vowel sounds and dittos and tests in school. In a fun, natural way, you will be teaching your child the skills she will need for school success. Books will train her ears to listen to the sounds of letters and rhyming words, to pay attention, and to stay on task. Books will train a child's eyes to follow from left to right and to recognize colors and shapes, letters and numbers. Books will stretch both her imagination and her vocabulary. A child who loves books will want to read! She will be ready and you will have made it happen. Remember, a child learns most from the people she loves.

✳ A child's own *Napping House* bedtime routine will be a delightful ending to her day. What will she choose to pile on top of herself on her cozy bed? What tiny thing will start everything falling? Be sure to add interesting describing words and action words. (Don't hesitate to call them *adjectives* and *verbs* . . . The words will fascinate!) Tell the whole story together every night in your own napping house. Bedtime and laughter should go together. *(vocabulary, sequencing)*

✳ The story *The Napping House* by Audrey Wood ends with the phrase, "Where no one now is sleeping." What an ideal way to introduce the *concept of zero.* Not even one snoring granny means zero snoring grannies, and so on through the characters of the story. Another time, because children love a touch of the ridiculous, ask them how many wakeful animals are eating at their table. Zero fleas, elephants, or baboons are sure to bring giggles. Find new ways to teach zero while driving in the car or after snacks are gone. Have fun! *(math concepts)*

✳ A child's mastery of *gross motor skills* precedes her mastery of *fine motor skills.* Practice is essential. Show a child how to jump forward, then backward over an object, her feet tied together with an imaginary rope. Have her practice rhythmic jumping by swinging her arms, first a quarter turn, then a half turn, then a full turn around, smiles guaranteed. Have her hold a beanbag between her knees and jump, tumbles guaranteed. Jump into a tire or circle and out again, fun guaranteed! *(motor skills)*

✳ The characters in *The Napping House*—the flea, mouse, dog, and cat—are easy words to rhyme. Create rhyming word *families* as the children learn to hear the final sound in each word. *Predict* (children will love the word) how many words you will think of for each *family* before you begin. *(auditory discrimination)*

Noah's Ark

by Peter Spier

* Concepts of print
* A class alphabet book
* Letter-sound relationships
* Classifying

* Parts of speech
* Wordless book
* Structure writing/Model writing
* Nonfiction

SETTING THE STAGE

Instantly singable songs and the appealing rhyme and rhythm of finger plays will encourage children to be involved in story time.

"Noah's Old Ark" by Sharon, Lois & Bram, *Elephant Show Record*

"Who Built the Ark" by Raffi, *More Singable Songs*

PITTER PATTER

Pitter patter, pitter patter, Rain is coming down	*(fingers raining down)*
Pitter patter, pitter patter, Wind is blowing round.	*(hands side to side)*
Pitter patter, pitter patter, Rain is here and there	*(fingers left and right)*
Pitter patter, pitter patter, Rain is everywhere!	*(fingers in wide circles)*

TWO MOTHER PIGS

Two mother pigs lived in a pen,	*(show thumbs)*
Each had four babies and that made ten.	*(fingers up)*
These four babies were black as night,	*(one hand up, thumb bent)*
These four babies were black and white.	*(other hand, thumb bent)*
But all eight babies loved to play,	
And they rolled and rolled in the pen all day,	*(roll hands)*
At night, with their mothers, they curled up in a heap	*(make fists)*
And squealed and squealed till they went to sleep.	

FIRST READING

Wordless books have a valuable place in children's literature. The joyful process of reading pictures is the earliest stage of reading. Wordless books encourage children to notice the details of beautiful illustrations, make discoveries for themselves, and anticipate what is going to happen next. Because the plot is supplied through the illustrations, children concentrate on telling the story in their own words. You are just a skillful guide. The children are the real storytellers. They will feel a sense of accomplishment in their ability to read a complete book.

Most of the stories we have read have been make-believe stories. The authors used their imaginations as they wrote. But today's story comes from the Bible. It is the story of Noah and the flood and it is called *Noah's Ark*. Peter Spier, the man who painted the pictures, received a very special award for this book called the Caldecott Medal. Every time you look at the pictures you will see something new you didn't see before.

Look at the cover of *Noah's Ark*. What do you see? What do you think is happening? The story begins just inside the cover. Can you find Noah in the grape vineyard? Tell me what else you see. The half-title page shows Noah building a huge boat called an ark because he knows a flood is coming. Why would he be safe in the ark? Who do you suppose Noah's helpers are? Tell me about the camels and donkeys. Now let's turn to the title page. Is Noah finished building the ark? Does that mean his work is done? Tell me why you think there are so many baskets and bundles of grain and jugs and pots. The author of *Noah's Ark*, Peter Spier, wants you to tell the story as you read the pictures.

GETTING INVOLVED

Tell me what you think it was like on the ark. Would you have liked to have been there with Noah? I wonder how many animals you can remember that had two legs. Let me show you a picture again. Now tell me all the animals you can remember that had four legs. Were there any animals that had no legs at all? *(List the answers on a chart for another experience with words in print.)*

I'll choose a child to pretend to be Noah and make up a riddle about an animal on the ark. Whoever solves the riddle will be the next Noah. I'll do the first few riddles to get us started. "My name is Noah. I am looking at five baby animals on the ark. They have four legs and they are all sitting on their mother's back in the hay. What are they?" Yes, you remembered the picture of the possums in the loft. Here's another one. "My name is Noah. I am watching an animal with two short legs and many feathers. It is sleeping with one eye open and one eye closed. What is it?" I love that picture of the owls and the one who is winking at me. Here is my last riddle: "My name is Noah. I have a rope around the neck of an animal with four legs and I am trying to pull it up the ramp. What animal am I pulling?" Now it's your turn. You may look at the pictures in *Noah's Ark* to get an idea for your riddle. I know the next time we read the story you will be thinking of some tricky riddles for us to solve.

A CLOSER LOOK

With each rereading of a story, children gain new understanding. Pause often for a spontaneous flow of oral language as the children share their feelings and observations. Extend the learning process with your own questions in repeated readings of the story.

✳ In your opinion, was Noah a hard worker? *(evaluating)*

✳ What jobs did Noah have to do before he moved the animals into the ark? *(comprehension)*

✳ I wonder what Noah is saying to the different animals as they move up the ramp into the ark. *(reflecting)*

✳ Why do you think Noah closed the door? *(reasoning)*

✳ How did it sound inside the ark? How did it smell? *(reasoning)*

✳ Do you know what the word *conversation* means? Is Noah having a conversation with the lions? Are the mice having a conversation with the elephant? *(interpretation)*

✳ Why didn't Noah put the fish and dolphins and turtles inside the ark? *(reasoning)*

✳ Tell me how you think Noah is feeling when he is sitting by the candle in the dark. *(comprehension)*

✳ How did the ark rise high enough to get stuck on a mountain? *(comprehension)*

✳ Would you agree it was a happy day when the dove returned with an olive leaf? *(evaluating)*

✳ Why is there a rainbow in the sky? *(analyzing)*

✳ Tell me what you think happened to the ark. *(reflecting)*

STORY TIME EXTENSIONS

After the Flood by Arthur Geisert

Why Noah Chose the Dove by Isaac Bashevis Singer

Mr. Gumpy's Outing by John Burningham

Pretend You're a Cat by Jean Marzollo

Come a Tide by George Ella Lyon

BALANCED LITERACY ACTIVITIES

POETRY

SUN AFTER RAIN
Rain, rain,
went away.
Sun came out
with pipe of clay,
blew a bubble
whole-world-wide,
stuck a rainbow
on one side.
　　　Norma Farber

ANCHORED
　　by Shel Silverstein
　　from *The Light in the Attic*
　　by Shel Silverstein

OLD NOAH'S ARK
　　Folk rhyme from *Side by Side*
　　by Lee Bennett Hopkins

INVOLVEMENT

A MUSICAL INTERPRETATION

Music and movement create story meaning in the minds of children. Play an orchestral recording of "La Mer" ("The Sea") by Claude Debussy or "The Aquarium" from *Carnival of the Animals* by Camille Saint-Saëns. The music is soothingly beautiful and creates the feeling of being on water. Give the children colorful ribbon streamers. Have them pretend to be arks anchored to the ocean floor, gently swaying in the current. As you move about the room cutting the arks free, they will float around and up and down to match the rhythm of the melody.

PICTURE WALKS

Because Peter Spier's detailed illustrations are so visually rich and humorous, the children will delight in repeated picture walks through *Noah's Ark*. To help them make new discoveries, choose a new focus each time you "read the pictures," such as the variety of birds, the number of water animals, things that make you smile, and the tiniest animals on board the ark. It is oral language in a classroom that nurtures connections to children's lives.

MICE IN THE CORNER

Lead the children in a discussion of the dangers of being a very small animal on the crowded ark. Look for the little mice that are shown in every picture inside the ark. The children will surely have a story to tell about the elephant standing on the mouse's tail!

Pretend the children are all mice on *Noah's Ark*. Designate four corners of your room as safe places to hide from the larger animals on the boat. Hang the numbers *1, 2, 3,* and *4* above the corners. Choose a child to be Noah who closes his eyes and says, "Mice in the corner." As he slowly counts to ten, all the other children quietly tiptoe to the four corners of the room. Noah then calls out the number of one corner before he opens his eyes. The mice hiding in that corner must go back to their seats. Noah closes his eyes again and says, "Mice in the corner." All the remaining mice scatter to any of the four corners. Noah calls out another number and the mice in that corner must sit down, and so on. Anytime Noah calls the number of an empty corner, a new Noah is chosen. The suspense builds as the number of mice gets fewer and fewer until none is left.

INTEGRATION

OLD NOAH SAID, "COME ON IN!"

Enjoy another picture walk through the ark, listing on chart paper the names of all the animals the children find. As you write, ask the children to listen for and tell you the sounds that make up the words. From the list, print two name cards for each animal and add little picture clues next to the words. Give each child an animal name card to hold.

Find a place in the room for the ark, perhaps a boat the children have made from blocks or cardboard boxes, or your reading center now full of pillows and stuffed animals. With the children sitting in a circle, have them start a steady beat of clapping. Begin the chant, "Old Noah said, 'Come on in!' So the _____ went in, two by two." Call out the name of an animal. The two children holding the cards for that animal will march up the ramp and into the ark where Noah is waiting. The children will chant and keep the beat throughout as you call all the animals, two by two, into the ark. As a conclusion, let each child match his animal name to the list on the chart before placing it in Noah's Basket. You are ready for independent reading on the ark.

TWO BY TWO BY TWO

Structure writing not only provides children practice in writing the conventions of print but also creates predictable text that is easily read. Make a class book using the caption, *Old Noah said, "Come on in." So the* _____ *went in, two by two.* Let each child decide what pair of animals he will draw on his paper. He can copy the name of his animal from the class chart to finish the caption already printed on his page. Spread the finished pages on the floor and ask the children how they could classify the animals—those that fly, that swim, that walk on two legs, four legs, or no legs? Sequence the pictures according to the groups the children have suggested and make a class book of Noah's friends.

AN ARK FULL OF ANIMALS

Turn your bulletin board or a wall into a huge ark. Draw a simple outline of the ark for a small group of children to paint. Have each child draw a pair of animals or someone from Noah's family to cut out and add to the scene. Because music strengthens creativity and pathways of learning, play the musical selections noted (see p. 140) as your children work on their ark full of animals. Print the book title and author's name on your colorful mural. It will look like an original book cover even Peter Spier would be proud of.

NOAH'S ABC BOOK OF ANIMALS

Make an ABC book for the alphabet center in your room. Print the uppercase and lowercase letters on pages cut in the shape of an ark. Then decide on an animal that lived on the ark for every letter of the alphabet. For the more challenging letters, look at *Aardvarks, Disembark!*, an alphabet book by Ann Jonas about unusual animals on the ark. Bind the cover, title page, and illustrated pages in your ark-shaped book.

THERE'S WORK TO BE DONE

Ask the children if Noah's work was done when he finished the huge job of building the ark. In another picture walk through the story, find all the other jobs Noah had to do, from milking the cows to planting a vineyard. Print the children's sentences on a chart. Have the children find and highlight with yellow marker the action word in each sentence. Then cut the impressive list apart, giving each sentence to a pair of children to illustrate and paste on a page cut in the shape of the ark. Choose children to create a cover, a title page, and an ending to your story (chances are it will be a rainbow). The book will be a clever retelling of the story and surely a favorite in your library corner.

SUN AFTER RAIN

Children make sense of a poem out of what they know. After having been immersed for days in the rainy pages of *Noah's Ark,* the sunny images of "Sun After Rain" will be a joy for them to respond to. I wonder if Norma Farber had the story of Noah in mind when she wrote the poem. With four large pictures illustrating the four phrases of the poem, the language of "Sun After Rain" will come to life and brighten your room. Art expressions allow children to explore and respond to the voice of a poem.

EVERYDAY LEARNING ACTIVITIES

Positive parenting; developmental learning activities; and a warm, nurturing environment are major factors in a child's academic success and lifetime learning.

Imagine the variety of sounds on *Noah's Ark,* from the driving rain to the relentless animal noises, each carrying its own message to Noah's ears. Training a child's ears to listen to sounds everywhere will prepare her to hear the differences in letter sounds and rhyming words. This week, focus on all that a child can learn through her sense of hearing. The experiences are endless if she has been encouraged to listen, really listen, to the sounds around her—wind, birds, water, sirens, animals, insects, cooking, bells, laughter, music. Compare sounds that are high and low, loud and soft, pleasant and unpleasant. Compare daytime and nighttime sounds. Lie down in the grass outside, on a child's bed or anywhere, and just listen! Have the child close her eyes while you make sounds for her to guess, like bouncing a ball, tearing a paper, tapping your finger, or clicking your tongue. Soon the child will be pointing out sounds for *you* to hear!

✳ Give a child something specific to listen for. When she is watching television, ask her to listen for a person's name and to tell you when she hears it. When she is listening to a record or tape, direct her attention to something specific such as, "I wonder if you will hear an animal sound." *(auditory perception)*

✳ Give a child the opportunity to follow two-step directions in sequence, an important auditory skill. "Put your pajamas in the hamper, then find your teddy." "Touch your toes and then sit on the kitchen floor." The actions must be done in sequence, first action first, second action second. Build up to three actions. Have fun, laugh often, and praise continually. Be sure to turn the tables and let the child give you a set of directions to follow. Watch out! *(sequencing)*

✳ Wordless books give children the opportunity to be storytellers. They will be immersed in the details of the illustrations as they look for meaning. Encourage a child to tell you the story she sees in the pictures in *Noah's Ark,* illustrated by Peter Spier. Look for other wordless books, such as *The Snowman* by Raymond Briggs, *Have You Seen My Duckling?* by Nancy Tafuri, and *School* by Emily Arnold McCully.

✳ Repeating words in sequence is another readiness skill that can be learned anywhere: in the car, waiting in line, or while you are fixing dinner and a child is finding it impossible to wait. Repeat silly words in sequence, like MacDuff, Pouf-pouf, and Lilac. Try sentence building, always beginning with a complete sentence but making it increasingly longer each time the child can successfully repeat it. "The kangaroo is playing." "The kangaroo is playing outside." "The kangaroo is playing outside in the rain." "The kangaroo is playing outside in the rain at the zoo." *(sequencing)*

✳ Balloons are good skill builders. Blow up a balloon and gently toss it back and forth to a child. Chant a nursery rhyme together as you are tossing. *(gross motor skills)*

Oh, A-Hunting We Will Go

by John Langstaff

* Phonemic awareness
* Mini language lessons
* Concepts of print
* Letter-sound relationships

* Choral reading
* Graphing
* Math/science concepts
* Structure writing/Model writing

SETTING THE STAGE

Instantly singable songs and the appealing rhyme and rhythm of finger plays will encourage children to be involved in story time.

"Fooba Wooba John" by Nancy Cassidy, *KidsSongs 2*
(A rhyming folksong with easily singable nonsense verses)

"Peter and the Wolf"—*any orchestral recording of the musical story*
(French horns represent the hunters and timpani represent the hunters' guns booming)

LITTLE RABBIT

Little rabbit in the wood,	*(two fingers up for ears)*
Little man by the window stood,	*(hands like glasses over*
Saw a rabbit hopping by,	*eyes)*
Knocking at his door.	*(knocking motion)*
Help me! Help me!	*(arms up and down, fast)*
Or the hunter will shoot me dead!	*(gun motion)*
Little rabbit, come inside.	*(beckoning motion)*
Safe with me abide.	*(stroking rabbit ears)*

HANDS ON SHOULDERS

Hands on shoulders, hands on knees,   *(follow actions as rhyme*
Hands behind you, if you please.   *indicates)*
Touch your shoulders, now your nose,
Now your chin and now your toes.
Hands up high in the air,
Down at your sides; then touch your hair.
Hands up high as before,
Now clap your hands,
One, two, three, four.

FIRST READING

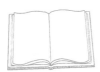

"Oh, a-hunting we will go, a-hunting we will go; we'll catch a fox and put him in a box, and then we'll let him go!" *(Softly sing or say the words as you hold up the opened book so both the front and back covers are visible to the children.)* The title of our story says, *Oh, A-Hunting We Will Go,* but I don't see any guns or bows and arrows. What do you see? Do the animals and people on the cover look like they are friends? This must be a different kind of hunting. Let's join them and go a-hunting, too!

This book is a marvelous example of all that we want children's books to be. It entertains, delights the ear, and teaches, all at the same time. Don't move too quickly through the pages. The wonderful illustrations catch all the humor and absurdity of the words. Ask your children to join in on the repetitive phrase "And then we'll let him go."

GETTING INVOLVED

Sometimes a storybook is both a song and a story. That is true of this book. The author, Mr. Langstaff, is a well-known folksinger. He sang the song "Oh, A-Hunting We Will Go" for many years before he decided to put the words in a book for children. Mr. Langstaff also put the music in his storybook so we could sing the words just like he does. *(The traditional melody is printed on the last page of the book.)*

Let's sing every verse of the song together as I turn the pages of the book. I'll stop every few pages and let you predict what's coming next. You'll know because of the rhyming words.

Variation: Another activity could focus on the rhyming word pairs. Name an animal in the story and ask the children to say the rhyming word. Extend the learning by asking them to think of an animal not included in the story and pair it with a rhyming word. Make-believe animals or nonsense words will add to the fun and creativity.

A CLOSER LOOK

With each rereading of a story, children gain new understanding. Pause often for a spontaneous flow of oral language as the children share their feelings and observations. Extend the learning process with your own questions in repeated readings of the story.

* Tell me why you think the author named this book *Oh, A-Hunting We Will Go. (reasoning)*

* What tools do the children have to hunt for a fox? How are they dressed? *(observation)*

* What surprised you about the picture of the fox? *(reflecting)*

* Why did the children change tools to catch a lamb? *(analyzing)*

* What is a *pram?* I wonder what the lamb is saying to the baby. *(reflecting)*

* Tell me what the children needed for mountain climbing. For hunting a bear? A whale? *(analyzing)*

* Who is the birthday cake for? I wonder if she will like a snake in her cake. *(reflecting)*

* Have you ever tried to catch a mouse? *(reflecting)*

* Tell me about the food the children used to catch the different animals. *(observation)*

* I love the picture of the skunk on the top bunk. Which picture did you like? *(reflecting)*

* How did the children dress to hunt an armadillo? A brontosaurus? *(observation)*

* What did the friends do with all the animals? Would you change the ending of the story? *(reflecting)*

STORY TIME EXTENSIONS

The Hunter and the Animals by Tomie dePaola

Hunter and His Dog by Brian Wildsmith

in a cabin in a wood adapted by Darcie McNally

Three Jovial Huntsmen adapted by Susan Jeffers

Wolf Plays Alone by Dominic Catalano

BALANCED LITERACY ACTIVITIES

POETRY

THE HUNTSMEN
Three jolly gentlemen,
  In coats of red,
Rode their horses
  Up to bed.

Three jolly gentlemen
  Snored till morn,
Their horses chomping
  The golden corn.

Three jolly gentlemen,
  At break of day,
Came clitter-clatter down the stairs
  And galloped away.
            Walter de la Mare

SINGING-TIME
  by Rose Fyleman
  from *Read-Aloud Rhymes for
    the Very Young*
  by Jack Prelutsky

SINGING IN THE SPRING
  by Ivy O. Eastwick
  from *Read-Aloud Rhymes for
    the Very Young*
  by Jack Prelutsky

INVOLVEMENT

* The strong rhythm and predictable pattern of *Oh, A-Hunting We Will Go* invites children to join in and read with you. If ever a book was written for the pleasure of participation, it is this one. After reading the story together a few times, divide the children into two groups. The groups can alternate reading the pages, with both groups joining in on the last page. The playful words are also fun to sing, and the melody is printed on the last page of the book.

* To dramatize the story, make name cards for each of the twelve animals and the four hunters. Hang the yarn-tied cards around the children's necks. As everyone sings the words, have the hunters find each animal and pretend to put the animal in its *cage* as the child mimes the part. The goat could jump into the boat and steady his sea legs. The snake could slither into a cake. The pig could flip his head to show off his extraordinary wig, and so on. The children will know what to do, especially when it is the skunk's turn!

INTEGRATION

RHYME TIME

It is the rhyming word pairs in the story that create the fun. See how many word pairs the children can name from memory. Print each animal's name on a card. Print the *cage* the animal was put into on another card. Draw small pictures clues (or have the children draw them) on both the animal and *cage* cards. Display all the words in front of the story. As you read the story again, call on children to find the right rhyming word pairs and place them in a pocket chart or on the chalkboard with magnets. (This activity could also be adapted to a felt board or a magnetic board.)

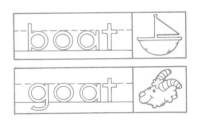

In another session, choose a single word such as *pig*. Say the sound of *p* (the onset) and the sound of *ig* (the rime). Write *ig* on a chart and have the children make a list of words that rhyme with *pig*. Hearing and writing words that rhyme help children learn phonemes, the small segments of sound that make up language.

Extension: Put each rhyming word pair, such as fox and box, on a sentence strip. Cut a jagged line between the words fox and box, making two puzzle pieces that will fit together when a child finds the right match. (For an additional self-checking cue, make the jagged line with a colored marker.) Keep the puzzle word pairs, a copy of *Oh, A-Hunting We Will Go,* and a tape of the children singing the song in a listening center for an independent reading activity.

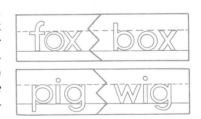

WHICH IS YOUR FAVORITE?

Make a large horizontal wall graph with the heading, *What was your favorite animal in* Oh, A-Hunting We Will Go? List the names of the animals across the top of the graph. Give each child a square of white paper on which to draw and write the name of her favorite animal.

Mount the squares on colored paper and place them on the graph. As the children make conclusions, write their sentences on chart paper next to the graph. Which animal had the most pictures? The least? How many more chose the brontosaurus than the armadillo?

OH, A-HUNTING WE WILL GO, TOO

John Langstaff dedicated his book to "all the children who helped me make up extra verses for this folk song." Even today as he travels, he inspires children to make up verses of their own. Brainstorm with your children about what it would be like to have John Langstaff in your room. What verses would the children write? What equipment would the four hunters need? Make a list of the animals and the clever rhyming places where the children would put them.

Print the verse of the folk song on every child's page, leaving a blank for the name of his new animal. Under a folded flap on the right, print the refrain with a blank for his new rhyming word. Print the last verse of the song on the last page, with a picture under the flap showing all the animals running away. Bind the pages into a class big book titled *Oh, A-Hunting We Will Go, Too* for your reading center. Lifting the flap will be part of the fun as the children read their book.

IT'S GETTING CROWDED IN HERE!

In the charming story *The Mitten,* adapted by Jan Brett, woodland animals wiggle into a child's mitten they find in the snow. The warm, cozy mitten becomes very crowded as each new animal squeezes in. After reading the story, have the children decide which one of their *cages* from *Oh, A-Hunting We Will Go, Too* could hold *all* their animals. Write the children's story on a chart, It's Getting Crowded in Here! Model the writing process by thinking out loud about letters, sounds, and concepts of print. After every third animal moves into the *cage,* repeat the phrase, *It's getting crowded in here.* For example, *A snail rolled in. A frog hopped in. A hippo sloshed in. It's getting crowded in here!* Your illustrated innovation will become an independent reading experience.

MINI LANGUAGE LESSONS

In subsequent readings of *It's Getting Crowded in Here!,* the teaching of skills develops naturally. Have the children identify words by framing them with hands or slider frames, flashlights or pointers. Draw attention to directionality and one-to-one correspondence. Look for contractions (*it's*) and word endings (*ed* and *ing*). Brainstorm word families for words like *snail* or *frog,* pointing out onset and rime. Together with the children, choose high-frequency words to add to the visible word wall resource in your room. When skills are taught in context, they have meaning.

EVERYDAY LEARNING ACTIVITIES

Positive parenting; developmental learning activities; and a warm, nurturing environment are major factors in a child's academic success and lifetime learning.

It is parents and caregivers who can best introduce a young child to the pleasures of books. Reading aloud to a child is the best way to plant within him the desire to learn to read himself, long before he meets vowel sounds and dittos and tests in school. The special attention and loving bond of an adult and a child reading together can result in a child's lifelong enthusiasm for reading. The rewards are too great to pass up, even in the hectic pace of everyday living. The best way to teach a child the value of books is to be sure he has many of his very own. Buy him book plates to identify his own. Books are wonderful to touch. They are warm friends, not cold and impersonal like television. Books can be a private world or they can be shared, but they are always friends.

✳ In the story *Oh, A-Hunting We Will Go* by John Langstaff, each animal was caught and put into a make-believe *house*. Talk about all the kinds of houses animals really live in, whether they are in your yard or in the park or just in your imagination. For example, a tree is a house for a woodpecker, dirt is a house for ants, a hole is a house for a squirrel, a log is a house for a worm. The book *A House Is a House for Me* by Mary Ann Hoberman is a delightful learning experience. *(creative thinking)*

✳ Plan your own hunting trip around the house and hunt for something different each time. Let the children decide what's fair game, such as a certain shape, a color, anything that is breakable, things that grow, or objects that begin with the same sound as the first letter in a child's name. You will be surprised at the endless possibilities. *(classifying)*

✳ Make up your own hunting game with a box of animal crackers. Whatever animal a child pulls out of the box, he must think of a word to rhyme with it before he can eat the evidence. *(auditory discrimination)*

✳ Music and memory go together. A child's brain makes valuable learning connections when he sings. Look for more storybooks that are also songs, such as the familiar favorites *Miss Mary Mack* adapted by Mary Ann Hoberman, *Frog Went A-Courting* illustrated by Chris Conover, and *The Itsy Bitsy Spider* adapted by Iza Trapani. The illustrations are beautiful and the fun is contagious. *(music, literature)*

✳ You will have instant attention if you begin with a child's own name when you talk about rhyming words. Make up silly words to rhyme with her name. She will soon hear that rhymes simply end with the same sound. Make up nonsense words to rhyme with spaghetti or pizza. Careful, the giggles are contagious. *(auditory discrimination)*

✳ Make texture rubbings by putting paper over textured surfaces and rubbing a peeled crayon over the paper. Like magic, the texture will show through. With a marker, have children create animals or animal houses from the drawings. *(texture art)*

The Old Man & His Door

by Gary Soto

* Cultural diversity
* Bilingual vocabulary
* Story structure
* Process writing

* Author study
* Math/science concepts
* Character web
* Parts of speech

SETTING THE STAGE

Instantly singable songs and the appealing rhyme and rhythm of finger plays will encourage children to be involved in story time.

"The Days of the Week" by Greg and Steve, *We All Live Together, Vol. 4,* and "Months of the Year," *Vol. 2*
(Upbeat songs sung in English and Spanish)

"Cada Niño, Every Child" by Tish Hinojosa, *Cada Niño, Every Child*
(Award-winning recording of eleven bilingual songs about heritage and traditions)

STORY TIME

Sometimes my hands are at my side	*(hold hands at side)*
Then behind my back they hide.	*(hands behind back)*
Sometimes I wiggle my fingers so	*(wiggle fingers)*
Shake them fast, shake them slow.	*(shake fingers)*
Sometimes my hands go clap, clap, clap.	
Then I rest them in my lap.	*(hands in lap)*
Now they're quiet as can be	*(to lips, say "sh")*
Because it's story time you see.	*(hands in lap, nod head)*

LA PUERTA

La puerta. [lah PWEHR-tah]	*(draw a door in the air)*
El puerco. [el PWEHR-koh]	*(draw a pig in the air)*
There's no difference	*(shrug shoulders)*
to el viejo. [el vee-EH-hoh]	*(make beard on own face)*
A Mexican jingle	

FIRST READING

I am interested in your observations about the cover of our new storybook. What are the people in the picture doing? Where might they be going? Tell me what you think the story will be about.

The old man on the cover knows how to speak two languages—Spanish and English. We call that bilingual. Do you know someone who speaks Spanish? In the story, the old man got his words mixed up one day when he did not listen to his wife. Have you ever been in trouble for not listening?

The name of the story is *The Old Man & His Door* by Gary Soto. Tell me what is happening on the title page. As we read, see if you can figure out what the old man's problem was and how he solved it.

GETTING INVOLVED

El viejo, the old man, must have been very strong to carry a heavy door so far. Let's see if we can help him. Get out your screwdriver and undo the screws. Tie a strong rope around the corner of the door and *heeeeave* it up onto your shoulders. Wait! Here comes the little girl and her baby sister. Very, very carefully, slide the door off your shoulders. Get behind it so you can play peekaboo with the baby sister. Good job—you made her laugh! Now heave that big door right up on your shoulders once again. Oh no, you bumped a beehive. Quick! Get down under the door to protect yourself from the angry bees. Better haul that door on your shoulders again so the ragged goose can hitch a ride. Oh no, hurry! Throw the door into the water and rescue the boy who can't swim. Now prop your door against a wagon and push the heavy piano up the ramp. One more time, heave the door back onto your shoulders just in time for the man to put watermelons on top. Finally, here we are at the barbecue. We need your door right in the middle to make a perfect table for all the food. Now sit down and tuck your feet under the table. You deserve a rest!

A CLOSER LOOK

With each rereading of a story, children gain new understanding. Pause often for a spontaneous flow of oral language as the children share their feelings and observations. Extend the learning process with your own questions in repeated readings of the story.

* Why was the old man's wife dressed in her best clothes? *(analyzing)*

* What was the old man *good* at doing? *(comprehension)*

* I wonder how the author thought of the words "pigs as plump as water balloons." *(reflecting)*

* What was the old man *not good* at doing? *(comprehension)*

* Why did the man get mixed up and take a door to the barbecue? *(interpretation)*

* Do you think the pig was the old man's pet? Would he have wanted to take it to the barbecue? *(reasoning)*

* What does the word *stampeding* mean? *Shabby? Scruffy? Piñata? (vocabulary)*

* How could the old man tell that the bees were gone? *(comprehension)*

* How did the goose say "thank you" to the old man? The swimmer? The piano mover? *(analyzing)*

* I noticed the pig was always smiling. Why do you think it was happy? *(analyzing)*

* What did *you* notice about the people sitting around the table at the barbecue? *(observation)*

* Do you know someone like the old man? *(application)*

STORY TIME EXTENSIONS

Moon Rope Un lazo a la luna by Lois Ehlert

Abuela by Arthur Dorros

Subway Sparrow by Leyla Torres

How My Family Lives in America by Susan Kuklin

In My Family/En Mi Familia by Carmen Lomas Garza

BALANCED LITERACY ACTIVITIES

POETRY

COME ALONG AND SEE
In one door
and out the other!
Ring around the tree!
Every minute
something doing . . .
come along and see.
Aileen Fisher

RICE AND BEANS—ARROZ Y HABICHUELAS
I like arroz y habichuelas.
I'm not at all fond of beans and rice.
Grandma isn't like other abuelas.
She gives me arroz y habichuelas.
Other abuelas, not half so nice,
Are always giving me beans and rice.
Charlotte Pomerantz

INVOLVEMENT

DRAMATIZATION

The make-believe that is so natural to children allows them to experience cultures and people unlike themselves. It is through drama that children will understand the character and actions of a confused old man who speaks two languages.

* Prepare for a vocabulary-oriented drama activity by printing the Spanish words on word cards. Say them together until the children can roll the words off their tongues! Narrate *The Old Man & His Door,* pausing at every Spanish word. Let the children repeat the new word and explain to the old man what it means before you read on. Mental imaging will let the children feel *they* understand; it is the old man *who doesn't get it!*

* Make name cards to hang around the children's necks, using the Spanish words for the old man, old woman, the neighbor, the pig, and the poor little girl. Write English words for the other characters. Find in your room something that will serve as a washtub, a dog, a hat, and a piano. Paint a large piece of cardboard for the door with the hole, and create in the art center a beehive, honey, an egg, fish, and watermelon. Remember, the preparation is as full of meaning to children as the performance.

* Arrange the room, hand out the props and name cards (with children paired for confidence), and let the words come to life as the drama begins. Although you are narrator, it is the children who take on the role of storyteller. The drama is a teaching tool for emergent literacy. Through linguistic diversity, it will enrich the language learning of all the students.

INTEGRATION

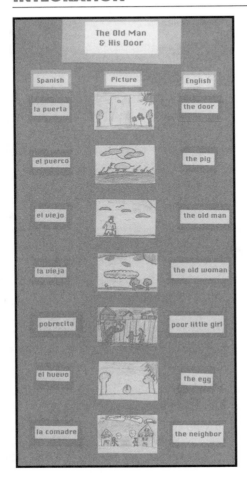

LANGUAGE DIVERSITY

Increasingly, new children's picture books reflect the importance of introducing in a positive way the languages and cultures of others. *The Old Man & His Door* is an example of authentic codeswitching or alternating the use of two languages. Spanish words are woven intermittently into the English text. It is reflective of real life because the practice of codeswitching is a distinctive characteristic of bilingual communities. A glossary of the Spanish terms found in the text includes a phonemic transcription in English to help with pronunciation.

Because the children have already experienced word meanings in the dramatization, make a chart of what they have learned. Write the Spanish words and the English translation for the children to illustrate and read. You are utilizing language diversity to enrich language arts instruction.

Variation: Make a class book of colorful sentence strips, printing the Spanish and English text on the left and adding the children's illustrations on the right. Bind the illustrated cover and sentence strips into a narrow book for the children to check out and take home to read to their families.

A CHARACTER WEB

The old man in the story is so lovable that children want to hug him and tell him it is all right to make a mistake. Let them draw the old man as big as life with his charming white mustache and beard. Mount the character on brightly colored paper. Then have the children tell you all the words they can think of that describe him. Surround the illustration of the old man with the mounted printed words. Put it on a bulletin board or suspend it for a mobile. Together, the art and the written language make a cheery character portrayal that is an invitation to read the story one more time.

A STORY STRUCTURE MATRIX

In their dramatization, the children have already discovered that *The Old Man & His Door* has a setting, characters, a series of events, a problem, and an ending that resolves the problem. Plotting those key elements on a story structure matrix will organize the story into a simple, visible framework. As a group, determine the headings for your matrix. Then, in the discussions that follow, help the children summarize their thoughts into short phrases or sentences, a skill in itself. As children talk, they will clarify their thinking about the story. That is why oral language that surrounds story text creates meaning in the minds of children.

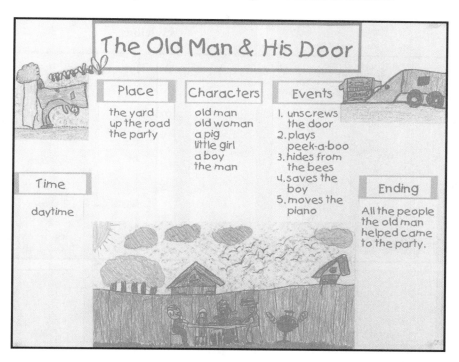

FIVE GOOSE HONKS—A COUNTING BIG BOOK

Make an original counting book that, in itself, is also a summary of the story plot. Brainstorm together about nouns and numbers that are embedded in the sequence of events, such as one brown door, two sloppy kisses, three buzzing bees, four globs of honey, five goose honks, six calls for help, seven scaly fish, eight grunts and pushes, nine watermelon stripes, and ten gulps of food. Children may choose to make individual counting books or a class big book. For the class book, assign children to illustrate the cover, the title page, the counting pages, and a surprise ending.

Variation: Let the children browse *Uno, Dos, Tres: One, Two, Three* by Pat Mora, a story about two sisters shopping in a busy Mexican market. The colorful bilingual presentation of the numbers one to ten may lead to a Spanish counting book featuring *uno el viejo!*

AN AUTHOR STUDY

Charlotte Pomerantz is a master of playful and rhythmic language. She would be a fascinating choice for an author study because of her linguistically diverse poems and storybooks. The author's award-winning *If I Had a Paka* is a book of poems in eleven languages. The poetry in her book *The Tamarindo Puppy* is written in two languages, English and Spanish. You will find more references to Ms. Pomerantz's delightful poems and stories in the following chapters: *Good Morning, Chick; Goodnight Moon;* and *The Pig in the Pond.*

OUR STORY OF THE OLD MAN

A retelling is a summary of a story in the children's words. It is an effective tool for helping children comprehend and organize story events. In a large group setting, guide the retelling by asking the children to identify the beginning of the story. Let them modify each other's answers until they agree on a summarizing sentence or two. Repeat the process, identifying the end and the middle. Write and number each segment of the story on chart paper. Then ask for an event or two between the beginning and the middle, and an event or two between the middle and the end. Reread, edit, and hopefully shorten the retelling. Divide the children into small groups to copy the text and illustrate the large pages for a class book or wall story.

The Old Man & His Door by Gary Soto
a retelling

The old man, *el viejo*, is chasing his dog. The old woman, *la vieja*, tells him to bring *el puerco*, the pig, to the *comadre's* house. The old man never listens to his wife.

El viejo thought he was to take *la puerta*, the door. He took the door off the hinges and put it on his back.

The old man hid under *la puerta* so bees wouldn't sting him. Then he put honey from the beehive in his hat. *El viejo* put his hat on the door.

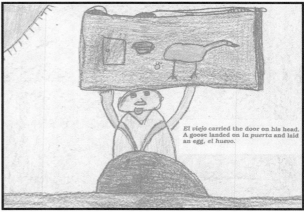

El viejo carried the door on his head. A goose landed on *la puerta* and laid an egg, *el huevo*.

THE BROWN DOOR

To develop a voice in writing, children need multiple opportunities to respond to literature. For example, their responses to the old man's ingenious ideas about his door could be as varied as their young imaginations—a new ending, an original story, a letter to a character or the author, a journal entry, or perhaps a story of what they would do if they had a brown door.

Encourage them to write independently with developmental spelling because children pay conscious attention to phonemes when they identify sounds in the words they are writing. As with all authors, they will be eager to share their creative ideas with others.

I use my door to play Knock! Knock! with my friend. Her name is Kerry.

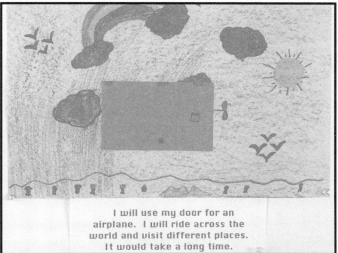

I will use my door for an airplane. I will ride across the world and visit different places. It would take a long time.

LINGUISTIC AWARENESS

Storybooks are a powerful tool for moving beyond mere tolerance to understanding those of other languages, races, and cultures. In her story *Whoever You Are,* Mem Fox portrays children all over the world laughing and crying, playing and learning. The book celebrates the richness of the bonds that unite children of all cultures. *Subway Sparrow* by Leyla Torres is the story of four strangers who do not speak the same language, yet work together to free a sparrow trapped on a subway train. In a colorful, pleasing format, Susan Kuklin's *How My Family Lives in America* shows loving families celebrating their heritages. It is a splendid photo essay of children from three cultures honoring the special days and family traditions their parents remember from childhood.

Bilingual or codeswitching texts, such as *The Old Man & His Door* and *Abuela* by Arthur Dorros, validate the first language of children and give them something positive to contribute. And in so doing, they broaden the linguistic awareness of all learners in the classroom.

Moon Rope Un Lazo a la luna, a Peruvian legend beautifully illustrated by Lois Ehlert, is an example of a story presented in a different bilingual format. The Spanish text and the English text are side by side. *In My Family/En Mi Familia* by Carmen Lomas Garza also incorporates parallel text.

Literature is a powerful teaching tool in helping children understand cultures and experiences different from their own. They will see the world in a new way.

EVERYDAY LEARNING ACTIVITIES

Positive parenting; developmental learning activities; and a warm, nurturing environment are major factors in a child's academic success and lifetime learning.

Few children today grow up in multigenerational family households. Because society is segregated in many ways, it is up to us to take the time and set the stage for children to know and love someone of an older generation. It is through frequent, reassuring interactions with the elderly that children are able to create positive attitudes about aging. Television and films often promote narrow, negative stereotypes of older people as cranky, tired, and slow. It is only when children experience making friends with elderly people that they are able to dispel the distorted perceptions.

There is much for children to like about the cheery, lovable old man in the story *The Old Man & His Door* by Gary Soto. Perhaps the old man will remind them of someone in the family or the neighborhood they can befriend. Look for more quality storybooks that offer a window into understanding the needs of the elderly. Read together the poignant *Somebody Loves You, Mr. Hatch* by Eileen Spinelli and the joyous *The Song and Dance Man* by Karen Ackerman. Then plan ways for children to be attentive friends to older people, perhaps by encouraging the young ones to draw a picture, make a card, sing a song, take a walk, have a picnic, or share a book. Intergenerational friendships benefit everyone as children and the elderly find pleasure in each other's company.

* In the story *The Old Man & His Door,* an old man used his unhinged door for many surprising things, and the door became very important. Talk about ways to make something special on a child's door. Measure the right size paper to cover the door and then lay it flat on a work surface. Let the child paint it or decorate it with fabric and colored paper, string, stickers, markers, or whatever she chooses. If children share a room, divide the paper into parts so each one has a space. When the paper is dry, hang it on the door. *(creativity)*

* The ages between three and five are thought to be the optimum years for developing creativity. Creative people are those who can imagine. Play "what if" games with children. Why not begin with a child's door? *What if the door opened into the jungle? A planet in space? A doctor's office? A mole tunnel under the ground? What if cars ran on water instead of gas? What if we walked on our heads instead of our feet?* Reverse roles and have the children make up "what if" games for you to imagine what will happen. Laugh, exaggerate, and have fun! *(creativity, problem solving)*

* Be a mirror partner as you stand and face a child. Whatever movement or posture she initiates, you imitate. You are a mirror reflection of her every movement. When it is your turn to lead, suggest a character for her to depict, such as an old man or a baby. Call out an action word like pounce or slither, or a descriptive word like droopy or graceful. Let her think of words for you to act out, too. *(body movement, vocabulary)*

* Children are fascinated with paper punches. Put out multiple colors of paper and let them punch holes to their messy hearts' content. Have them separate the dots into piles for each color. Line up ten paper dots and count out loud from one to ten and ten to one. Group the paper dots by twos and by fives and count out loud. Let the children paste patterns on paper or create designs. Then turn cleanup into a game. Attach masking tape or Scotch tape to the end of a plastic glass or a wooden block and have the children count how many dots they captured with the tape. *(math concepts)*

On Market Street

by Arnold Lobel

* Concept of giving
* Letter-sound association
* A class alphabet book
* Vocabulary
* Comparing/Contrasting

* Process writing
* Graphing/Classifying
* A family activity
* Theme topic: stores

SETTING THE STAGE

Instantly singable songs and the appealing rhyme and rhythm of finger plays will encourage children to be involved in story time.

"ABC Rock" by Greg and Steve, *We All Live Together, Vol. 1*
(A bright, singable tune with letter echoes)

"Sounds from A–Z" by Rosenshontz, *Share It*
(Clever sounds for each letter of the alphabet with an easy refrain)

ALPHABET LETTERS

Alphabet letters here and there,	*(point left and right)*
Twenty-six letters everywhere,	*(point all over)*
Mix them up and move them around,	*(roll hands)*
And you'll find words all over town.	*(hands open, palms up)*
Letters are short, and letters are tall.	*(hand low, hand high)*
And some have the silliest shape of all.	
But put them all together and you will see	*(roll hands)*
How helpful alphabet letters can be.	*(hands open, palms up)*

Mary Cornelius

JACK-IN-THE-BOX

Jack-in-the-box all shut up tight.	*(fingers wrapped around thumb)*
Not a breath of air, not a ray of light.	*(other hand covers fist)*
How tired you must be all down in a heap.	*(lift off)*
I'll open the lid and up you will leap.	*(thumb pops up)*

FIRST READING

Tell me everything you see on the interesting cover of this book. Do you wonder how one little boy can carry all those things? The name of the book is *On Market Street*. It is a Caldecott Honor Book because of the very beautiful pictures. The artist's name is Anita Lobel and the words were written by Arnold Lobel. Do you suppose they are in the same family? The story is about a little boy who went shopping on Market Street. He bought something for every letter of the alphabet.

Just inside the cover on the half-title page you will see the boy putting on his shoes. Are his clothes different from yours? What is on the floor by his chair? Perhaps that pouch will hold the coins the boy will need to buy things on Market Street. Listen to the poem that begins our story.

GETTING INVOLVED

Would you want the boy who stopped at all the stores on Market Street to be your friend? Tell me what kind of a boy you think he is. Were you surprised that he gave away everything he bought on Market Street?

Let's talk about who we would give the presents to if they were ours to give away. I would be excited to give all the books to my children because they never stop reading. And I would give the musical instruments to the hedgehogs in the storybook *The Happy Hedgehog Band* so they could make their tum-tum-te-tum music in the forest. But wait, we need to begin at the beginning. Let's start with the letter *A*. Who knows someone they would like to give the apples to? Tell us why you chose that person. I gave away the books, so tell me to whom would you give the clocks. We'll go through the whole alphabet, and you may have the fun of giving everything away. When we get to the very end, we'll put the pouch of pennies on the chair and curl up in bed with the sleepy white cat.

Variation: There are many ways to group the things the little boy bought on Market Street. How would you like to group them? How many categories shall we have? We will make a list of objects for each category. *(One day you might divide the purchases into things to eat, things to wear, things for play. Another day you might categorize by the stores where the objects could be bought.)*

A CLOSER LOOK

With each rereading of a story, children gain new understanding. Pause often for a spontaneous flow of oral language as the children share their feelings and observations. Extend the learning process with your own questions in repeated readings of the story.

✳ *This book is an extraordinary visual experience from beginning to end. Point out fascinating details and something humorous or special on each page. For example, on the letter* E *page, notice the rooster faces, the eggcup knees, the cooked eggs, and the decorated egg on a ribbon.*

✳ Let's read the poem again. Tell me who a *merchant* is. What is a *market? (vocabulary)*

✳ What do the words mean "to catch my eye"? *(comprehension)*

✳ What does it mean to "stroll the length of Market Street"? *(comprehension)*

✳ Tell me the stores the child is looking at as he stands on the cobblestone street. *(observation)*

✳ Now look at those stores in the last picture. How are they different? *(observation)*

✳ I loved the shoes the artist put on the feet of all the people. What did you like in the pictures? *(reflecting)*

✳ If the boy had kept one present for himself, which present do you think he would have kept? *(analyzing)*

✳ Which one would you want to keep? *(reflecting)*

✳ Would you like to go shopping on Market Street? *(reflecting)*

✳ What would you carry in the pouch? *(reasoning)*

✳ I wonder if the boy ever went back to Market Street. *(reflecting)*

STORY TIME EXTENSIONS

I Spy: An Alphabet in Art selected by Lucy Micklethwait

From Letter to Letter by Teri Sloat

The Guinea Pig ABC by Kate Duke

The Handmade Alphabet by Laura Rankin

Wildflower ABC: An Alphabet of Potato Prints by Diana Pomeroy

BALANCED LITERACY ACTIVITIES

POETRY

I HAD A NICKEL
I had a nickel and I walked around the block.
I walked right into a baker shop.
I took two doughnuts right out of the grease;
I handed the lady my five-cent piece.
She looked at the nickel and she looked at me,
And said, "This money's no good to me.
There's a hole in the nickel, and it goes right through."
Says I, "There's a hole in the doughnut, too."
Folklore

INVOLVEMENT

✱ The opening verse in *On Market Street* sets the stage and gives a purpose to all the pages that follow. The closing verse brings everything to a satisfying conclusion. It is the poetry that tells the heartwarming story. Emphasize something different in the words each time you read. Stop often for a cloze activity, perhaps pausing for the children to provide the action word in each sentence. Another time as you read, omit the nouns. The children will soon memorize the familiar words.

✱ Gather the actual objects Anita Lobel has drawn for each letter. Add small pictures for the few things you can't bring to class. Put all the objects together in the middle of your circle. As you read, call on a child to find the object that was purchased on Market Street for each alphabet letter.

✱ Write word cards to replace the objects. Display them on a pocket chart. The next time you "stop at all the stores" on Market Street, have the children match the word cards to the alphabet letters.

✱ Compare the detailed, visually rich illustrations of this story with the art styles of other alphabet books in your room such as the lively, bold pictures in *Chicka Chicka Boom Boom*.

INTEGRATION

I GAVE THEM ALL AWAY

Continue the activity you began in the Getting Involved section on page 158. Write on chart paper the following words:

> I strolled the length of Market Street
> to see what I might give away.
> And I gave . . .
> the _____ to _____
> because _____.

Structure writing, as well as process writing, allows children to create connections to their own experiences. And that is what gives meaning to their writing as evidenced by their answers: "I gave the eggs to a hen because she loves chicks"; "I gave the gloves to the homeless because they have cold hands"; "I gave the wigs to bald eagles because they have no hair."

A POUCH OF PENNIES

The child carried the coins he spent on Market Street in a little pouch. Fill a pouch with twenty-six pennies. Brainstorm with the children about spending the pouch of pennies in just one store—a toy store, a pet store, a food store, and so on. What could they buy for each letter of the alphabet? When the children have decided where they will go shopping, create a store-shaped caption book. On each page, print the words *A penny for* _____. Add a letter of the alphabet to each page before you give the pages to the children to illustrate. Choose a small group of children to draw a story cover, *A Pouch of Pennies;* a title page; and a final page, *We spent them all on Market Street!*

A penny for a hamster .

I STOPPED AT ALL THE STORES

Take an imaginary walk down a Market Street your children have created in the room. Name the kinds of stores you find there and the goods sold in each store. Divide the children into small groups, with each group deciding which store they will draw on a large section of white paper. Label the storefronts and tape the sections together into one long mural. Hang your mural on the wall, in the hall, or on a clothesline so everyone "can stroll the length of Market Street to see what they might buy."

F IS FOR FAMILY

Activities that involve a child's family build a bridge from home to school. To create your own class alphabet book, give each child an alphabet letter to take home with a note explaining that the activity is to be family project. Together, the family will decide what to draw for the child's letter and how to decorate the page, using scraps and odds and ends at home. (Of course you will arrange for any child to do his page at school, if necessary.) As the illustrated pages are brought back to school, mount them on pieces of colorful poster board. Tape the pages together to make an unusual accordion alphabet book that will stretch across your room.

A LETTER GRAPH

To have some fun with letter-sound association, make a letter card or create a letter box from a cutoff milk carton for each letter of the alphabet. Write an uppercase and a lowercase letter on each card or carton. Line them up around your room. Have the children bring from home two small objects and line them up in front of the appropriate letter on the floor. You have created a floor graph. Which letter has the most objects? The least? The same as another letter? How many more objects in *B* than *Z*?

Extension: Have each child draw pictures of his objects on small pieces of paper. Glue the children's pictures on an alphabet graph to hang in the room.

A SIMULATION: A CORNER STORE

Create a simulation of an old-time corner store in your classroom. Provide shelves, a counter, a cash register, play money, paper and pencils and markers, plastic fruit and vegetables, shopping baskets, food bins, paper bags, dress-up clothes, and perhaps a pouch of pennies. Have the children help supply the props as well as canned goods, empty food boxes, and little baskets. Decide what hours the store will be open. Add a sign-up sheet for store clerks to take turns at the cash register. Create a store sign or a banner to hang over your store.

Let the children decide what they want to write, individually or in groups, about their corner store. Writing is a natural way to learn language. Some may choose to make lists of things to buy or shoppers who came into the store. Others may write their own stories about buying presents for friends.

EVERYDAY LEARNING ACTIVITIES

Positive parenting; developmental learning activities; and a warm, nurturing environment are major factors in a child's academic success and lifetime learning.

On Market Street with words by Arnold Lobel and pictures by Anita Lobel is a magnificent example of the importance of quality art in children's books. Pictures invite a child into a book and create the excitement that makes him turn each page. Pictures give information that would take chapters to describe. Parents and caregivers can encourage a child to look, really look, until he is immersed in the illustrations. Every time he opens the book, he will see things he didn't notice before. Look for beautiful artwork. Know the names of some skillful, gifted illustrators of children's books.

* Encourage a child to be free to give answers and opinions without fear of correction. Play "Let's Window Shop" when you have extra time at the mall. Stand in front of any store window and ask a child what gift he would choose to buy for grandma. Whatever the choice, assure him that grandma would just love it! Then you pick out something for a friend. Just do one or two people per window and keep the game fun. You are trying to reinforce the fact that the child's ideas are good. You can do the same activity with catalogs or just pretending, to develop imagination. *(self-confidence)*

* When it is time to do some real shopping, have a child help you make a list. Circle the beginning letter of every item on the list and see whether she can name them. When you are in the store, find the right section for an item on your list and see whether the child can find it by recognizing the first letter. *(letter identification)*

* When a child is interested in learning to write his name, help him make letters out of clay or pipe cleaners, in sand or rice, or by tracing over your letters on a magic slate. Always have his name in front of him while he is learning, with one capital letter and the other letters lowercase. When the child is ready for paper, a green dot on the left side is a signal to begin here. Show the child how to make each letter, always starting at the top and coming down, always large and on paper that has no lines. Make a colorful card with the child's name on it. Let him take it to bed, put it on his cereal bowl, tape it on his door, or tie it on his teddy bear. Pride's the name of the game. *(name recognition)*

* Turn your home into an *On Market Street* shopping adventure. Give a child a pouch of twenty-six pennies "to see what she might buy." Every time she finds something for a letter of the alphabet, she gives a penny to the merchant—mom, dad, whomever! Another time, pretend to visit a pet store or the zoo. Buy an animal for each letter of the alphabet. *(letter-sound association)*

Peter Spier's Rain

by Peter Spier

* Cultural diversity
* Story structure
* Concepts of print
* Parts of speech

* Math/science concepts
* Wordless book
* Nonfiction
* Structure writing/Guided writing

SETTING THE STAGE

Instantly singable songs and the appealing rhyme and rhythm of finger plays will encourage children to be involved in story time.

"It's Raining, It's Pouring" by Sharon, Lois & Bram, *Mainly Mother Goose*

"Raindrops Keep Falling on My Head" recorded by B.J. Thomas, *B. J. Thomas' Greatest Hits*

MY STORYBOOK
I love my little storybook.
I read it every day.
I cannot read the words just yet,
But I know another way.

I look at all the pictures,
They tell me what to say.
So now I read to Mommy
'Cause that's the game we play!
Mary Cornelius

FIRST READING

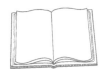

Wordless books have a valuable place in children's literature. The joyful process of reading pictures is the earliest stage of reading. Wordless books encourage children to notice the details of beautiful illustrations, make discoveries for themselves, and anticipate what is going to happen next. Because the plot is supplied through the illustrations, children concentrate on telling the story in their own words. You are just a skillful guide. The children are the real storytellers. They will feel a sense of accomplishment in their ability to read a complete book.

Peter Spier's Rain is an extraordinary example of an illustrator skillfully beginning a story before the title page. After encouraging the children to discuss the cover and the title, lead them through the marvelous storytelling details of the opening pages.

Our story about rain begins on the very first page inside the cover. Where do you think the children are playing? Tell me what animals you see. What can you name that is growing? Tell me about the little houses in the picture. How many places do you see water? I see shapes everywhere. Look at the swing set and the shed and the birdhouse. You name some more. What do you see that is made out of metal? Of wood? Of rubber? Of cloth? I see a number of garden tools. Can you find them? Would you like to be playing there, too?

Tell me what changes you see in the picture on the half-title page. I wonder why the little girl is holding out her hand. Tell me why you think the cat is running. I see a new little house by the birdbath. Tell me about it.

Now look at the changes on the title page. Why do you suppose mother is beckoning? Tell me about the little houses you see for insects or animals or even make-believe houses that you think of in your heads. (A hutch is a house for rabbits, a beehive is for bees, a rain barrel is a house for rain, a sunflower is a house for seeds, a cloud is for raindrops, a dog is a house for fleas!)

Do you think the story on these pages happened before the picture on the cover? What do you predict the children will do next?

GETTING INVOLVED

Let's think about all the things you like to do in the rain, like stomping or splashing or sliding. You tell me more words that describe what you could do. Now listen very quietly to my humming voice and see if you know the song I am humming. *(Hum the tune of "The Farmer in the Dell.")* This time you hum along with me. Now we're ready to sing some words: "We're stomping in the rain; We're stomping in the rain; Hi-ho the derry-o; We're stomping in the rain." *(Children stomp with you as the whole group sings.)* Every verse we will change to a new word you gave me *(such as clapping, marching, dancing, sailing, jumping, and so on)* until it is time to go inside out of the rain.

A CLOSER LOOK

With each rereading of a story, children gain new understanding. Pause often for a spontaneous flow of oral language as the children share their feelings and observations. Extend the learning process with your own questions in repeated readings of the story.

* *Point out some specific things you want the children to see, such as water reflections, drainpipes, footprints in the mud, animals hiding, a spiderweb shining with raindrops, a driving rain, scavenger raccoons and mice, and so on. Every page in this book is rich in visual detail.*

* Why do you suppose the author put his name in the story title, *Peter Spier's Rain*? *(reasoning)*

* What would you like to say to Peter Spier about his book? *(reflecting)*

* Have you ever gone for a walk in the rain? *(reflecting)*

* Do you think the children are very far from home? *(analyzing)*

* Tell me the part of their adventure you liked best. *(reflecting)*

* Tell me everything you can remember about the animals in the rain. *(observation)*

* Let's read the pictures again and look for all the things that happened to the umbrella. *(observation)*

* Would you agree that the umbrella was an important part of the story? *(evaluating)*

* In your opinion, were the children having fun in the rain? *(evaluating)*

* Did their fun end when they went inside their house? *(evaluating)*

* How did the artist show you when it was nighttime? Morning? *(observation)*

* If you could write words for the last picture, what would you say? *(reflecting)*

STORY TIME EXTENSIONS

Just You and Me by Sam McBratney

Cat and Mouse in the Rain by Tomek Bogacki

Thunder Cake by Patricia Polacco

Mushroom in the Rain by Mirra Ginsburg

Umbrella by Taro Yashima

BALANCED LITERACY ACTIVITIES

POETRY

COUNTRY RAIN
The road is full of saucers,
saucers full of rain,
some of them fluted,
some of them plain,
saucers brown as coffee,
saucers full of sky,
saucers full of splashes
as our feet flump by.
    Aileen Fisher

MUD
    by Polly Chase Boyden
    from *Read-Aloud Rhymes for
      the Very Young*
    by Jack Prelutsky

INVOLVEMENT

✳ Rain is so much a part of our everyday lives that children already know and enjoy many songs about rain. Every time you are ready to take another *picture walk* through *Peter Spier's Rain,* hum the melody of a familiar rain song. Encourage the children to join in as soon as they recognize the melody. B. J. Thomas uses children's voices in a catchy rendition of "Raindrops Keep Falling on My Head." Young children will enjoy "If All the Raindrops Were Lemon Drops" recorded on *Barney's Favorites.*

✳ Each illustration in *Peter Spier's Rain* is full of extraordinary storytelling details. Guide the children through many rereadings of the story by focusing on something different each time you read the pictures. For example, find all the things that caught the rain as it fell, such as the birdbath, the swimming pool, puddles, a wheelbarrow, the children's boots, and many more. Another time, find compound words in the illustrations. Drainpipe, raincoat, footprint, clothesline, woodpile, and doghouse are just a beginning.

✳ Decide which of the above activities you want to list on a chart. Each response is a springboard into a reading and writing experience. If the children decide to write the words of a song, have them make an illustrated big book of the text. Put the book and a tape of the children singing the song in a listening center.

INTEGRATION

RAIN, RAIN, RAIN

A wordless book always presents an opportunity for children to tell the story in their own words. Brainstorm together about all the things the rain fell on in the story until every child has an idea of something to draw. Give each child a page with the words *Rain on the* _____ printed at the top. Act as scribe and finish each child's sentence with the words he has illustrated. Create a cover for your caption book, *Peter Spier's Rain,* a retelling by . . . .

AND RAIN MAKES APPLESAUCE

Talk about the silly things that happened in the imaginative storybook *And Rain Makes Applesauce* by Julian Scheer. Ask the children to think of other silly things that could happen in their own story. Talking and laughing together as you share ideas will give everyone a chance to think of ideas to draw on their apple-shaped pages. Print the sentence each child dictates as you ask him to name letters and say the sounds he hears. Make some additional pages with the words *And rain makes applesauce* to add as every fourth page of the book. Mount the children's pages on red paper and bind them into a class big book for your reading center.

RAINCOATS, PLEASE

Have children bring various kinds of rainwear to class. Compare your collection to what the children wore in the story. Then dress up one child in all the articles of rain gear. Have him stretch out on the floor on a large piece of bulletin board paper. Trace around his body and cut it out for the children to paint. Center the figure on a bulletin board and label everything the child is wearing. Have each child decide what he wants to draw or paint from the rainy day adventure. Encourage the children to make their drawings large. Add their pictures to the rainy day scene, label them, and paint the stormy sky with a light blue paint wash. Your children have told *their* story of *Peter Spier's Rain*. The purpose of an art expression is to make meaning out of a story.

THE READING CORNER

* Poems paint pictures in the imagination. No two children will be feeling, seeing, or thinking the same things as you read to them the picturesque poem "Country Rain." Meaning will grow with each reading. Enjoy "Country Rain" as the perfect beginning to your extended story times.

* Fill your reading baskets with fascinating books about rain, mud, and irresistible puddles. With classical music playing, read to the children *Listen to the Rain* by Bill Martin, Jr. and John Archambault. They will love the lyrical sounds of "lightning-flashing, thunder-crashing, sounding, pounding, roaring rain." In contrast, read the cumulative tale of another land, *Bringing the Rain to Kapiti Plain: A Nandi Tale* by Verna Aardema. Some children may choose *Rain Talk,* Mary Serfozo's story of a little girl enjoying the sounds and pleasures of a rainy day; *Rain Song* by Lezlie Evans; or *Let's Look at Rain,* a colorful nonfiction book by Jacqueline Dineen.

* The rich language of the story *Mud* by Mary Lyn Ray begins with the marvelous story opener, "One night it happens." Winter melts into spring and the frozen earth turns into magnificent mud, "gooey, gloppy, mucky, magnificent mud." What child could resist it? Equally appealing is the lovely collage art of a child's squishy mud play in Kimberley Knutson's rhythmic *Muddigush.*

* *The Piggy in the Puddle* by Charlotte Pomerantz is full of tongue-twisting nonsense about a young pig "in the merry middle of a messy muddle." (Are you already smiling?) *Puddles* by Jonathan London and *The Puddle* by David McPhail are two more engaging read-alouds about little characters, rain, puddles, and mud. Perhaps now is the time to read again, and illustrate, the inviting *saucers* in *Country Rain.*

THE WRITING CORNER

* A story structure matrix is a visible tool to help children understand the literary elements of time, place, characters, events, and ending. Have the children choose two stories to discuss and compare the story elements. Children need to talk, and to listen to others, to make sense out of what they are learning about how stories unfold. Then have them write their summarizing phrases for each story on the matrix (see p. 117).

* After enjoying a story about mud, show the children a jar of mud and water and ask them if they think the two can mix. Without coming to a conclusion, simply put the jar in a writing center. As the children go to the center during the week, have them shake the jar and write and illustrate sentences about what they discovered.

EVERYDAY LEARNING ACTIVITIES

Positive parenting; developmental learning activities; and a warm, nurturing environment are major factors in a child's academic success and lifetime learning.

A child learns by watching, but mostly by doing. It is the firsthand, real-life experiences that create learning. Think about the word *water*. It is usually among a child's first words because the child actually experiences the word in so many ways: she drinks it, bathes in it, swims in it. That's a key to the way any child learns best, by actually experiencing something. It is the sensory experiences that are the most important of all. Take a ride in a truck, a boat, or a train. Show a child a waterfall, a pond, a river. Visit a petting zoo. Let her talk to a police officer and visit the fire station. Visit daddy or mommy's workplace. Go to a music store and have someone demonstrate the instruments. Take her fishing. A child is acquiring knowledge all the time through her five senses, and that knowledge becomes the basis for thinking skills.

✳ Let a child have her own wonderful adventure in the rain, just like the storybook *Peter Spier's Rain* by Peter Spier, if you are sure there is no danger of lightning. You could create your own rain by shooting a hose into the air in the yard. An old shower curtain can be turned into a quick slip and slide. *(sensory experience)*

✳ Water play is a natural tranquilizer. Squeezing soap bubbles out of a sponge or just playing in soapy water can calm an overstimulated child. Let a child hand wash some dishes, pouring water back and forth from cups to containers, or whip up a soapy froth with an eggbeater. *(sensory experience)*

✳ Every age loves the water. Provide a bucket of water and an old paintbrush or sponge. Let a child wash the car (you won't have to worry about soap drying), or "paint" the side of the house, a wood fence, tree trunks, sidewalks, rocks, the driveway, and so on. *(sensory experience)*

✳ Water does many fascinating things. It can turn to ice, melt, or create hot steam. Water can clean the dirt from your hands or turn dirt into mud. It can make seeds grow, turn soap into bubbles, cook food, or make popsicles. Try them all and see. *(science concepts)*

✳ Will they sink or float? Fill a pan full of water. Put it on a folded towel on the floor or in the bathtub or play outside with the pan. Collect some objects, such as a cork, a spoon, a pebble, a sponge, and a marble. Explain that you are doing an experiment to see what will sink and what will float. Ask the child to predict (a word that will fascinate) after you have tried a few objects. Use the same group of objects a number of days in a row. See if she can presort into sink or float piles. *(classifying)*

✳ More fun with a sponge . . . and water, of course. Add a small amount of liquid detergent to the water and let the child squeeze out some bubbles. Add a drop of red food coloring to one bowl of water and blue to another. Mix the colors and watch them turn purple. *(sensory experience)*

Peter's Chair

by Ezra Jack Keats

* Concept: you are special
* Phonemic awareness
* Identifying feelings
* Parts of speech
* Classifying

* Nonfiction
* Structure writing/Model writing/Guided writing
* A family activity

SETTING THE STAGE

Instantly singable songs and the appealing rhyme and rhythm of finger plays will encourage children to be involved in story time.

"I Wonder If I'm Growing Up" by Raffi, *Singable Songs for the Very Young*

"Sing a Happy Song" by Greg and Steve, *We All Live Together, Vol. 3*
(How to get your smile back when things go wrong)

THE LITTLE RED BOX

Oh, I wish I had a little red box	*(make shape with hands)*
To put my mommy in.	*(hands lift into box)*
I'd take her out and kiss, kiss, kiss	*(lift to mouth and kiss)*
And put her right back again.	*(place back in box)*

Oh, I wish I had a little red box	*(make shape with hands)*
To put my daddy in.	*(hands lift into box)*
I'd take him out and hug, hug, hug	*(wrap arms around self)*
And put him right back again.	*(place back in box)*

Repeat, changing to brother and jump, jump, jump
Repeat, changing to sister and tickle, tickle, tickle
Repeat, changing to baby and rock, rock, rock

GUESS WHAT I SEE

If I look in the mirror,	
Guess what I see?	*(fingers circle eyes)*
Someone who looks just like me!	*(point to self)*
And if you stand beside me,	
It is also true,	
I can see someone who looks just like you!	*(fingers circle eyes)*
	(point away)

FIRST READING

I wonder if you remember these stories by Ezra Jack Keats. (Hold up *Whistle for Willie* and *The Snowy Day*.) Do you recognize the little boy on the cover of this book? Tell me what else you see. Where do you think Peter is? Do you have an idea why Peter is looking at the chair? That little blue chair is so special that the name of this story is *Peter's Chair*. Read the title with me. Can you read the author's name, too?

Let's turn to the title page for a surprise. Look, there's Willie! Read that page with me, too. Now we are ready for the story about Peter, Willie, and the blue chair.

GETTING INVOLVED

Let's talk about Peter's shoes. Do you think they were an important part of the story? Tell me why you think Ezra Jack Keats named the story *Peter's Chair* instead of Peter's shoes.

Look at all the different kinds of shoes jumbled up in this pile. I want you to find a matching pair and tell me who you think would wear the shoes—an infant, a teenager, grandpa, a worker, a ballplayer, a dancer, whoever you think. If you study the shoes carefully, you'll see clues as to who might wear them.

Words that describe things are called adjectives. I am wondering how many adjectives you can think of to describe all these different shoes. You are right—they are scruffy, polished, holey, clunky, shiny, heavy, smelly—that's quite a list! I like your adjectives.

Now I want you to think of another kind of word. Think of something your shoes can do. Then act it out for us and we'll guess what your action word is such as climb a tree or kick a ball. You'll get ideas if you look at our lineup of different shoes. Who has an idea for an action word?

Before we put the shoes away, look at the shoes your friends are wearing. I wonder whose shoes look the most like Peter's shoes. Help me decide, and then we'll get *Peter's Chair* and see whether you are right.

A CLOSER LOOK

With each rereading of a story, children gain new understanding. Pause often for a spontaneous flow of oral language as the children share their feelings and observations. Extend the learning process with your own questions in repeated readings of the story.

✳   What do you want to tell me about the story? *(evaluating)*

✳   What do you think made the blocks come tumbling down? *(comprehension)*

✳   Why did the noise bother Peter's mother? *(comprehension)*

✳   I wonder if you ever have been told to be quiet because a baby was sleeping. *(reflecting)*

✳   Why did Peter's father paint the cradle, the high chair, and the crib the color pink? *(reasoning)*

✳   How did that make Peter feel? *(comprehension)*

✳   I wonder if you have ever felt that way. *(reflecting)*

✳   Tell me what Peter chose to take with him when he ran away. Why did he choose those things? *(reasoning)*

✳   Did Peter and Willie go very far? *(comprehension)*

✳   Why did Peter help his father paint the chair pink? *(analyzing)*

✳   Do you know someone like Peter? *(application)*

STORY TIME EXTENSIONS

Koala Lou by Mem Fox

I Love You the Purplest by Barbara M. Joosse

My Brother John by Kristine Church

Whose Mouse Are You? by Robert Kraus

William's Doll by Charlotte Zolotow

(The song "William's Doll" is recorded on Free to Be You and Me *by Marlo Thomas.)*

BALANCED LITERACY ACTIVITIES

POETRY

BROTHER

I had a little brother
And brought him to my mother
And I said I want another
Little brother for a change.
But she said don't be a bother
So I took him to my father
And I said this little bother
Of a brother's very strange.

But he said one little brother
Is exactly like another
And every little brother
Misbehaves a bit he said.
So I took the little bother
From my mother and my father
And put the little bother
Of a brother back to bed.

Mary Ann Hoberman

INVOLVEMENT

A SPECIAL CHAIR

Ezra Jack Keats didn't give us any particular reasons why Peter's chair was special, other than Peter wanted to save it from being painted pink like all his other baby things. Put a chair in the middle of the circle. Ask the children to think of descriptive words to tell you all about that chair. Then ask them to think of reasons why that chair was special to Peter.

Choose a child to sit in Peter's chair. Surround him with the other items from the story: blocks, a stuffed dog, a cradle and high chair (hopefully from a nearby housekeeping center), a cookie and a dog bone, a shopping bag, a picture of a baby, a picture of an alligator, a pair of shoes, and a paintbrush. As you read the story, go around the circle and have a child pick up an item to give to Peter. (Can you see the juggling act?) At the end of the story, let Peter decide which things he will share and which things he will keep.

INTEGRATION

WE ARE SPECIAL, TOO

Children never tire of a dress-up box. Have them bring dress-up items and fun accessories from home until your box is overflowing. Pair up the children and let them help each other dress. (Obviously, two at a time will be just right for this activity.) Then give each child a large piece of butcher block or bulletin board paper to draw his dressed-up friend. To add print, have each child dictate or write a sentence to add to the cutout drawing. Arrange the cutouts of the children on a large bulletin board titled We Are Special, Too. Reading and smiles guaranteed!

A TREASURE SHELF

Think of something special from your childhood such as an old quilt. Bring the quilt to class, hidden in a bag. Give descriptive words as clues to help the children guess what is in the bag. Then print a phrase such as *Miss Lane's patchy quilt* and put it with the quilt in a special place in your room. Have the children take turns bringing in things that are special to them. Encourage them to use descriptive words as clues as they play the same guessing game. Display all the objects in your special place, with a descriptive phrase in front of each treasure.

Variation: Perhaps the children will want to play the game "Twenty Questions" (see p. 5).

UNPACK YOUR PERSONALITY

Gather the children around you as you sit with a brightly decorated bag on your lap. As you slowly pull things out of the bag, explain that each item tells something special about you. You have included a book because reading is still an adventure for you. You put in a tennis ball because you are proud you are always learning something new. You included a little tree branch because you like to be outside to jog or hike. When you have emptied your bag, explain that you have just unpacked your personality, all the different things that make you who you are.

Every day pull a child's name from the bag. It will be her turn to take the bag home, fill it with her personality, and bring it back to class. Write a note to parents emphasizing it is the child's responsibility to choose the items for the bag. (It helps to keep two bags going so someone is always ready to share.) When a child has had a turn, have her draw a picture and write about all the things she brought when she unpacked her personality. Encourage the child to draw on her knowledge of letters, sounds, and words as she writes. Invented spelling develops phonemic awareness as children play with the sounds of language.

THE IMPORTANT THING ABOUT PETER

In the classic nonfiction book *The Important Book,* Margaret Wise Brown writes about a variety of topics. Although the author lists many facts about each topic, she begins and ends with the most important thing such as "The most important thing about rain is that it is wet."

Brainstorm with the children about all the things that made Peter special. Decide on the most important thing. For example, *The most important thing about Peter was that he shared.* Write the children's sentence at the beginning of your chart story. Then write a few more sentences that describe Peter. Model the writing process. Think out loud about the sounds of words so children hear and see the sound-letter connections. Emphasize one-to-one correspondence and punctuation. End your story with the same statement: *The most important thing about Peter was that he shared.*

THE IMPORTANT THING ABOUT ME

The last page of *The Important Book* is a message from Margaret Wise Brown to each child who reads her story: "The most important thing about you is that you are you!" Lead the children in a discussion about what makes each one of them special and different from anyone else in the room.

Give each child a piece of twelve-by-eighteen-inch white paper on which is printed, *The most important thing about me is* _____. After each child has drawn a big picture of himself, have him write developmentally or you act as scribe and complete the sentence with the words he dictates. Frame the pictures, just as Peter's baby picture was framed. Cut large rectangles from the center of brightly colored twelve-by-eighteen-inch construction paper, leaving a two-inch border all the way around for the frame. Display the pictures in your room as a gallery of very important little people.

A CELEBRATION

Have a baby day. Invite moms to bring their babies to class and share with the children about baby care, routines, and schedules. Ask the moms to talk about the skills their babies are learning right now and the importance of babies playing, listening to music and soft voices, and being held and loved. Most important, have the moms share what is special about each baby and each big brother or sister who is proudly watching in the room.

EVERYDAY LEARNING ACTIVITIES

Positive parenting; developmental learning activities; and a warm, nurturing environment are major factors in a child's academic success and lifetime learning.

The story *Peter's Chair* by Ezra Jack Keats may open the door for children to be honest about their own feelings: that someone else in the family seems more important right now. A child needs to be understood and to be able to say, "Today I feel like Peter!" Each child needs to hear that no one can ever take her place. Show children there is enough love to go around. Give some special little attention every day. It is natural for brothers and sisters to want your undivided attention. Siblings can be best friends, but it takes skillful parenting to make each child feel good about herself. Don't compare children. Comparing just says someone is "not measuring up." It causes resentment and destroys a child's self-esteem. Remember, no two children are alike and each one came with her own set of "blueprints." When they are getting along, praise, praise, praise them for taking care of each other. Read together *Koala Lou* by Mem Fox, *When the Teddy Bears Came* by Martin Waddell, and *I Love You the Purplest* by Barbara M. Joosse. They are reassuring stories of unconditional love.

✳ Play Peter's game of hiding. Remind a child to leave her shoes sticking out from under the curtains or the bed or the couch. Be sure to hide your shoes for her to find. List all the hiding places for some fun with words in print. *(creative play)*

✳ Get a plain, cardboard box so children can act out the song "Oh, I Wish I Had a Little Red Box." There are so many concepts you can teach with a box. You may be busy in the kitchen, but all you need is your voice to keep a child thinking. Is the box full or empty, heavy or light, rough or smooth, round or rectangular, old or new, big or small? Will it fit under your bed, on the chair, inside the cabinet? *(critical thinking)*

✳ Children need to be taught over and over that they are special and have very special first and last names. Encourage children to introduce themselves by using both first and last names. Let them print a name, including their own last name, to hang on every teddy bear, doll, or animal in the house. Gather up the cards from time to time and let the children read the names. Ask them to give Peter a last name—it will probably be their own! *(self-esteem)*

✳ Copying simple shapes prepares a child for the more exacting task of copying letters. Give her unlined paper, a green dot for a starting point, an example to look at, and lots of praise. *(fine motor)*

✳ Make each child in the family feel special by being the Child of the Week. Just rotate the weeks and mark the calendar. The Child of the Week makes all the little decisions that are so important to children, such as where to sit in the car or at the dinner table, which cereal to buy, which bedtime books to choose, which special friend to invite over. Add an unusual table setting at the Child of the Week's place at the table. It is one more way to make a child feel special. *(self-esteem)*

The Pig in the Pond

by Martin Waddell

SETTING THE STAGE

Instantly singable songs and the appealing rhyme and rhythm of finger plays will encourage children to be involved in story time.

"Splish Splash, I Was Takin' a Bath" recorded by Bobby Darin
(An upbeat, silly song to add motions to)

"Summersongs" recorded by John McCutcheon
(Celebrate summer with songs about swimming holes and camp outs)

I HAD A LITTLE PIG

I had a little pig	(hold in hands)
I fed him in a trough,	(draw rectangle with fingers)
He got so fat	(arms make circle)
His tail dropped off!	(behind back, swoop down)
So I got me a hammer	(pick up hammer)
And I got me a nail,	(pick up nail)
And I made my little pig	
A brand-new tail!	(hammering motion)

DICKORY, DICKORY, DARE

Dickory, dickory, dare	(slap knees)
The pig flew up in the air,	(arms fly over head)
The man in brown	
Soon brought him . . .	(reach up, pull down)
DOWN!	(touch floor)
Dickory, dickory, dare	(slap knees)

FIRST READING

Tell me what you see on the cover of our storybook. We know ducks love to swim, but can pigs swim? Why do you think a pig would jump into the water with a duck?

The title of our story is *The Pig in the Pond* by Martin Waddell and the illustrator is Jill Barton. She has made you smile already and you have seen only the cover! Let's look at the picture on the title page. Tell me some words that you think describe the pig and I will write a list of your words. When we have finished the story, we will add more descriptive words to your list.

Now tell me what you think the story will be about. *(Pause often as you read, using the cloze technique to draw children into the marvelous silliness. Also pause at appropriate places for children to predict what will happen next in this join-in-the-fun story.)*

GETTING INVOLVED

You be the voices of the animals as they talk throughout our story. What does a duck say? A goose? A pig? When I hold up one finger, you make the animal sound one time, just like the word I am pointing to on the page. When I hold up two fingers, or three, or four, you make the sound that many times. Let's practice.

Now show me how the pig turned around and around, stamped her foot, twirled her tail, and splashed into the pond. She splashed eight times, so I know we are sure to get wet! Show me how the animals "spread the word about, above and beyond." And here comes the most fun of all—Neligan is getting ready to jump. Take off your hat, next your pants and boots, now your shirt, and oh dear me—off comes the underwear. *Splash! Sploosh!* Sit down in the water! You are ready to help me read *The Pig in the Pond* again.

A CLOSER LOOK

With each rereading of a story, children gain new understanding. Pause often for a spontaneous flow of oral language as the children share their feelings and observations. Extend the learning process with your own questions in repeated readings of the story.

✳ Do you think the pig in the story was Neligan's pet? *(reflecting)*

✳ How did the ducks and geese invite the pig into the pond? *(interpretation)*

✳ Why were the ducks and geese splashed out of the pond? *(analyzing)*

✳ Did the farm animals hurry to see the pig in the pond? Do you think they were surprised? *(comprehension)*

✳ How did Neligan find out the pig was in the pond? *(comprehension)*

✳ Did you think the pig was going to get in trouble? *(reflecting)*

✳ I wonder if the pig went swimming every day. *(reflecting)*

✳ I wonder if Neligan and the animals joined him every day. *(reflecting)*

✳ Would you have chosen to jump into the water? *(reflecting)*

✳ Why did Neligan take off his hat and put it on the pig's head? *(analyzing)*

✳ Would you like to be on Neligan's farm? *(evaluating)*

✳ Would you like to have a pig as a pet? *(reflecting)*

STORY TIME EXTENSIONS

All Pigs Are Beautiful by Dick King-Smith

Toot and Puddle by Holly Hobbie

If You Give a Pig a Pancake by Laura Joffe Numeroff

The Great Pig Escape by Eileen Christelow

Pigs Aplenty, Pigs Galore! by David McPhail

BALANCED LITERACY ACTIVITIES

POETRY

MARY MIDDLING
Mary Middling had a pig,
Not very little and not very big,
Not very pink, not very green,
Not very dirty, not very clean,
Not very good, not very naughty,
Not very humble, not very haughty,
Not very thin, not very fat:
Now what would you give for a pig like that?
Rose Fyleman

THE PIGS
by Emilie Poulsson
from *Read-Aloud Rhymes
for the Very Young*
by Jack Prelutsky

FAMILIAR FRIENDS
by James S. Tippett
from *An Arkful of Animals*
by W. C. Houghton

INVOLVEMENT

DRAMATIZATION

What a delightful theater-in-the-round drama. A plastic pool, filled with foam blocks or Styrofoam popcorn, would make a perfect pond for splashing. Consider a different activity to dramatize each laugh-out-loud rereading:

* Brainstorm movements to accompany each animal sound as well as the phrases, "The pig's in the pond," "splash," and "splooosh." Movement helps children internalize meaning.

* Have the children make drama props in your art center, such as hats, headbands, ears, and noses. If the children would like character name cards around their necks for the drama, remember they gain confidence by being paired with another child.

* Perform the story as a choral reading, with the children divided into groups. Each group is assigned a different part of the story for a "lovely bit of joyful malarkey!"

* Add the sound of a rhythm instrument (or whatever you have) for each animal's voice and the splashing: a scraper for the duck, a party favor horn for the goose, a drum for the pig, a xylophone sweep for "splash," and all the instruments playing an extended sound for "splooosh." Can't you hear the fun?

* Sing this playful song to the tune of "The Farmer in the Dell." Begin softly, getting louder with each verse as the pond gets crowded.

  1. The ducks are in the pond ("quack!"). The ducks are in the pond ("quack!").
     The sun is shining brightly, so the ducks are in the pond!

  2. The geese are in the pond ("honk!"). The geese are in the pond ("honk!").
     The sun is shining brightly, so the geese are in the pond!
     SPLASH!! (shouted)

  3. The pig is in the pond ("oink!"). The pig is in the pond ("oink!").
     The ducks and geese got splashed right out. The pig is in the pond!

  4. They all went in the pond! ("whee!") They all went in the pond! ("whee!")
     The animals and farmer, too. They all went in the pond! SPLASH!!

INTEGRATION

A SIMULATION: THE FARM

With the pond as a focal point, create a simulation of a farm in your room. The pond could be a bunch of pillows, a quilt, a braided rug, or a plastic pool. Add a fenced-in pigsty with a papier-mâché pig and stuffed animals brought from home. Make a trough for pig food; add a play wheelbarrow and some tools. A child's wagon could be Neligan's cart. Make a barn and farmhouse out of huge cardboard cartons to complete the barnyard scene.

Keep paper, pencils, and rulers on the farm. Children could write messages, make signs, label rows of plants, chart the buckets of feed, and name the stalls in the barn. Have them write a schedule for chores and another for feeding the animals. Suggest they draw a map to the pond so all the animals can find their way.

Using the dialog from the story, have the children plan a drama of their own to perform for parents or other children. To get ready for the celebration, they will need to make lists of props for the play, costumes to make, invitations to write, songs to sing, and party food to prepare. Now that's a print-rich environment worthy of a pigsty! Enjoy the excitement of the literacy learning that always takes place when children make connections to real-life experiences.

THE PIG'S IN THE POND

Oral language development has a direct impact on learning to read. Children transfer their understanding of language to the written word. On chart paper, write the words from the story that were chanted by the disbelieving animals:

The _____'s in the pond. The _____'s in the pond.
The word spread about above and beyond.
At Neligan's farm, the _____'s in the pond.

Add sticky notes along the bottom of the chart, three each for Neligan, the pig, duck, goose, cow, goat, sheep, hen, dog, and cat.

Circle the children around the pond, each one wearing an animal name card. Start them clapping to a steady beat. A leader, standing by the chart, will take the three *pig* sticky notes from the bottom of the chart and put them in the blanks. Immediately, the children with *pig* name cards will step into the pond. With the leader pointing to each word on the chart, everyone in the circle will read the printed words together while the beat goes on. Continue the fun until all the animals and Neligan have joined the pig in the pond for the final "splash! splooosh!" You have made the purpose of reading words come alive.

THE PIG AND THE PLOT

Creative drama activities, especially acting out the sequence of events, set the stage for students to discover that stories have a plot structure. One of the simplest ways to diagram the events of a story is with a simple story matrix, identifying *B*—the beginning in which the characters and the problem are introduced; *M*—the middle in which a definitive action builds toward a climax; and *E*—the ending, which resolves the conflict. Decide on sentences to put in the story matrix for each child to illustrate individually.

Neligan's pig sat by the pond.

The pig splashed the ducks and the geese out of the pond.

Neligan and the animals joined the pig in the pond.

For a more complex story matrix, write on chart paper the headings *Setting, Characters, Events,* and *Ending*. Talk about the setting and the characters. Then, as the children discuss the story events, write them first on sentence strips. Place the sentences in order in a pocket chart. Ask the children what would happen to the story if you changed the order. Have a child put the strips in the wrong order and have the students act out the story. Involvement is a powerful teaching tool. Children will see for themselves the importance of plot structure. With the story events sequenced correctly, copy them on your matrix. Have the children draw the setting of the story, the ending in the pond, and the characters. The matrix is a record of the children's discoveries as they learn from Martin Waddell how stories unfold.

The Pig in the Pond

Setting

Events
1. The pig sat by the pond
2. The ducks and geese invited him in the water.
3. Neligan's pig jumped in
4. The animals rushed to the pond.
5. Neligan joined the pig in the pond!
6. All the farm animals jumped in too!

Ending

Characters

by Martin Waddell
Illustrated by Jill Barton

MARY MIDDLING

Just listening to the words of "Mary Middling" makes you smile. Rose Fyleman must have had a wonderful sense of humor, and perhaps a fancy for pigs. Ask the children what pictures come to mind while they are listening to the poem. Make a list of adjectives for Mary's pig and compare it with the list the children made for Neligan's pig when they first read the story. Put the charts side by side.

The rich language in "Mary Middling" begs to be illustrated. Write it as a poem chart with the children adding little pigs of every description, or have them illustrate one phrase per page to stretch around your room in a colorful, mounted wall mural. Poetry gives us the pleasure of looking at ordinary things through a magnifying glass.

NELIGAN'S WRITING SHOP

✳ I WONDER

An art expression is a visual interpretation of a story. Through art, children discover meaning and make connections to their own lives. The same is true with writing. After creating a mural of *The Pig in the Pond,* model a response of your own to the story such as "I wonder if Neligan had a wife to share the work" or "I wonder if the animals ever jumped into the pond in winter." Because children write with more energy when they make their own decisions, offer many choices—writing "I wonder" statements, a letter to a character, a new story ending, a poem. Children who write freely with invented spelling identify sounds in the words they write and develop phonemic awareness. Use individual editing conferences for spelling changes before surrounding the mural with the children's written responses. What a colorful invitation to "read the room."

✳ A FARM IS NOT A FARM . . .

Brainstorming with children focuses on the prior knowledge they bring to an experience. Ask them what they know about farm life. Find out what they would like to make a list of: A farm is not a farm without. . . ? Work jobs to be done? Feed for the animals? Tools? Crops to be planted? What do you hear on a farm? Smell? See? The children's writing could be individual or in cooperative groups with each group deciding how they will record, edit, illustrate, and present their list to the class.

MINI LANGUAGE LESSONS

✳ A child's command of letters and sounds is commensurate with the time spent in approximating writing. To facilitate that writing, create a word wall of high-frequency words such as the words Martin Waddell used most often in his story—was, went, water, on, in, didn't, don't, around, from, and out. Choose two or three from your list to add to your word wall on successive days. That list alone will offer multiple mini language lessons.

✴ To teach letter-sound association in meaningful context, write the words *was, went,* and *water.* Point to the two words, Word Wall, and ask the children how the words you have just written are similar. Ask them for the name of the letter *w,* then the sound the *w* makes. Lead the children on a word hunt around the room, looking for other words that begin like *was.* Write them all on a word web (there's that letter again!) with a large *W* in the middle.

✴ To develop phonemic awareness, brainstorm about a word family for the word *went* by covering the letter *w* (the onset) and pointing out *ent* (the rime). Demonstrate how the children's ability to read one word will lead to their writing other words in the same word family. Encourage them to reproduce the new words on a chalkboard, with rubber ABC stamps, or by writing the onset in one color and the rime in another. In later lessons, introduce the skill again using the words *pig* and *pond.*

✴ Using the literature and children's responses in the room, focus on one-to-one correspondence and left-to-right progression. Another time, teach the contractions *didn't* and *don't* from the words already on the word wall. When reading and writing skills are taught in context, they have meaning.

WE LOVE YOU, NELIGAN

Farmer Neligan is as irresistible as the pig. Because children make meaning by connecting to their own prior experiences, Neligan will take on the attributes of someone they know and love. Make a list of the adjectives they use to describe the farmer, another experience with the power of words. Now you have a third chart to join Mary Middling and The Pig.

A VENN DIAGRAM

Read to the children *Farmer Duck,* another language-rich story by Martin Waddell in which a slothful farmer makes a dear duck do all the chores. When the duck becomes "too sleepy and weepy" to continue, farmyard animals come to his rescue. Create a Venn diagram for the children to record their responses as they compare the farmers, the setting, and the characters in the two humorous stories *The Pig in the Pond* and *Farmer Duck.*

Variation: The Piggy in the Puddle by Charlotte Pomerantz is a catchy verse story about a young pig determined to play in the mud. The playful language and the surprising solution to "a messy muddle" are irresistible. *The Piggy in the Puddle* and *The Pig in the Pond* would also be an interesting combination for a Venn diagram.

AN AUTHOR STUDY

Martin Waddell is one of the most successful and best-loved children's writers of our day. His stories are rich with the patterning of language. What would the children like to know about him? His childhood? His more than eighty storybooks? Provide the resources for the children to do an author study that is sure to be fascinating.

Mr. Waddell's stories will serve as models to children who, in their own writing, are learning the importance of beginning and ending sentences. Ask the children why "There once was a duck who had the bad luck to live with a lazy old farmer" is a *hook* that draws the reader into *Farmer Duck.* Read Waddell's *The Happy Hedgehog Band* that begins, "Deep in the heart of Dickon Woods lived a happy hedgehog named Harry." How could a reader not turn to the next page?

EVERYDAY LEARNING ACTIVITIES

Positive parenting; developmental learning activities; and a warm, nurturing environment are major factors in a child's academic success and lifetime learning.

Martin Waddell's wonderful sense of silliness comes alive in the delightful artwork and repetitive text of *The Pig in the Pond*. As children chime in on the many words and animal sounds that are repeated throughout the story, they are creating patterns of learning in their brains. Research tells us a child's brain develops in patterns. Perhaps that is one rationale for a child's love of the predictable phrases of fairy tales that have endured for generations. Possibly that is why a child does not tire of repetitions as we do. The rhythmic patterns of stories like *The Pig in the Pond* are excellent memory builders because they put information into a child's long-term memory. Furthermore, that explains why routines, which are rehearsed and predictable, are so helpful to a child. The rituals create patterns, making it easy for a child's brain to know what is coming next, much like the favorite storybook she asks for over and over again.

✳ Make library visits a regular activity and decide ahead of time how many books a child may choose and how many you will choose. Look for more titles by Martin Waddell such as the favorites *Owl Babies* and *Can't You Sleep, Little Bear?* His stories are full of the repetitive phrases children enjoy. *(making choices)*

✳ Using a brown paper bag, small sponges, and pink paint, have children sponge paint the bag on both sides. When the paint is dry, let them attach ears, a nose, and a squiggly tail cut from colored paper. Glue on a pair of wiggly eyes. (Now there's a lesson on rhyming words—squiggly and wiggly!) Help the children plan a puppet show to retell *The Pig in the Pond*. They will love making their pigs turn around, stamp, twirl their tails, and pretend to splash in the pond. *(creativity)*

✳ Together, make blue Jell-O to be the *pond* in *The Pig in the Pond*. Use animal crackers to create your own math story problems. "One cow jumped in the pond. Along came three more. How many cows were in the pond?" "Three ducks were swimming in the pond. One flew away. How many ducks were left in the pond?" Be sure to reverse roles and let a child make up problems for you to solve. When you are finished, eat all the animal crackers in the pond and teach the concept of zero. *(math concepts)*

✳ Put water in a bucket, a plastic pool, the bathtub, or the kitchen sink. Collect an assortment of objects, such as small pieces of bark, buttons, paper clips, sponges, a cork, toy boats, shells, a block, and so on. Let the children help you gather things that will add to the learning. As they put one object at a time into the *pond*, ask them what is happening. Why do they think some objects float and some sink? *(science concepts)*

Rosie's Walk

by Pat Hutchins

* Story structure
* Cultural diversity
* Vocabulary
* Directionality phrases
* Predicting
* Structure/Process writing
* Nonfiction
* Theme topic: foxes

SETTING THE STAGE

Instantly singable songs and the appealing rhyme and rhythm of finger plays will encourage children to be involved in story time.

"Walk Outside" by Raffi, *One Light, One Sun*
(A bouncy, happy song about what a child finds on a walk)

"Walkin'" by Sharon, Lois & Bram, *Stay Tuned*

LITTLE BOY BLUE

Little boy blue,	*(beckon)*
Come blow your horn,	*(blow horn)*
The sheep's in the meadow,	*(point to right)*
The cow's in the corn!	*(point to left)*
Where is the boy who looks after the sheep?	*(raise arms questioningly)*
He's under the haystack fast asleep.	*(sleep)*

HERE IS THE BEEHIVE

Here is the beehive. Where are the bees?	*(left hand fisted)*
Hidden away where nobody sees.	*(cover with right hand)*
Watch and you'll see them come out of the hive,	*(uncover beehive)*
One, two, three, four, five.	*(fingers up)*
Bzzzzzzzz . . . all fly away!	*(fingers fly away)*

FIRST READING

Today we are going to read a funny story about Rosie the hen. The name of the book is *Rosie's Walk*. It was written and illustrated by Pat Hutchins and she did a very clever thing in her book. She used very few words because she wanted the pictures to tell the story and make you smile.

What do you see on the cover? Does that little house have a name? I wonder if Rosie knows she is being followed. Tell me what you think will happen. Let's turn to the title page for a bigger picture of where Rosie lives. If you look very closely, your eyes will find many different things on Rosie's farm. What do you see? Tell me how the colors make you feel.

Now let's read. Before I turn each page, tell me what you predict is going to happen. *(Prediction teaches children to use visual detail and gives them a sense of purpose in reading.)*

GETTING INVOLVED

It's time now to have some fun with the story. Let's pretend you are Rosie, out for a walk in the barnyard. Look around the room and see what we can use for the rake *on* the ground, the pond that Rosie walked *around,* and the haystack she climbed *over.* Next, we need to find something for the mill; the fence that Rosie walked *through;* and last, the beehive she walked *under.* Better not forget to find her henhouse. That's where the story begins and ends.

It looks like we have the barnyard all ready for *Rosie's Walk.* It is always fun to move to music, so let's put music on now. I'll choose a few children to move to the beat and follow Rosie. When you go *around* the pond, say the word *around.* When you go *over* the haystack, say the word *over.* When you get back to the henhouse, you may each choose someone to take your place following Rosie.

The children will have as much fun setting up the barnyard as acting out the directionality phrases. Some excellent musical accompaniment pieces might be "The Baby Elephant Walk" by Henry Mancini, the patriotic song "Stars and Stripes Forever," or the "March" from The Nutcracker Suite.

A CLOSER LOOK

With each rereading of a story, children gain new understanding. Pause often for a spontaneous flow of oral language as the children share their feelings and observations. Extend the learning process with your own questions in repeated readings of the story.

* Did the pictures make you feel Rosie's barnyard was a friendly place? *(reflection)*

* Tell me why we call a fox *sly?* Why is he crouching? *(interpretation)*

* Why didn't the fox see the rake when he pounced on Rosie? *(comprehension)*

* I wonder if Rosie knew she was being followed. Did the frogs know? The goat? The beaver? *(reflecting)*

* Did Rosie know the string was around her foot when she walked past the mill? *(interpretation)*

* What would happen if we changed the order of things in the story? *(application)*

* Tell me what you thought was the funniest thing that happened to the fox. *(reflecting)*

* In your opinion, did the artist tell the story through the faces of the fox and the hen? *(evaluating)*

* Did Rosie ever know she was in danger? *(comprehension)*

* Do you think the fox will come back to Rosie's henhouse? *(reflecting)*

STORY TIME EXTENSIONS

Flossie and the Fox by Patricia McKissack

Hattie and the Fox by Mem Fox

The Fox Went Out on a Chilly Night illustrated by Peter Spier

Up North in Winter by Deborah Hartley

Watch Where You Go by Sally Noll

BALANCED LITERACY ACTIVITIES

POETRY

A LITTLE TALK
The big brown hen and Mrs. Duck
Went walking out together;
They talked about all sorts of things—
The farmyard, and the weather.
But all I heard was:
"Cluck! Cluck! Cluck!"
And "Quack! Quack! Quack!"
from Mrs. Duck.

Anonymous

JUMP OR JIGGLE
Frogs jump
Caterpillars hump

Worms wiggle
Bugs jiggle

Rabbits hop
Horses clop

Snakes slide
Sea gulls glide

Mice creep
Deer leap

Puppies bounce
Kittens pounce

Lions stalk—
But—
I walk!

Evelyn Beyer

INVOLVEMENT

CHORAL READING

The humor and bold colors of *Rosie's Walk* will easily lead readers through the thirty-two words of the simple text. Even the youngest of children will be ready to join you in your rereadings of *Rosie's Walk*.

WE ARE WALKING

Using the same directionality course the children arranged in the Getting Involved section, consider having students perform the movements as a solo. Have the children circle around the outside of the barnyard scene, singing the following words to the tune of "Yankee Doodle":

> We are walking 'round and 'round, in a circle we go,
> Over, under, through, around, now *Justin* takes a solo!

At this point *Justin* goes through the directionality course alone, calling out the words as he performs the actions. The children can keep the beat going by clapping. When *Justin* is finished, he chooses a new soloist and the children circle around singing the song again.

THE FOX WENT OUT

Sing the traditional children's favorite "The Fox Went Out on a Chilly Night" after reading and talking about the fox's moonlight hunting trip. The song originated in colonial times, so certainly it has been enjoyed by many children. The musical notation is printed in the back of the storybook.

INTEGRATION

A WALL MURAL

Children can retell the story of Rosie and the fox with one big barnyard scene much like the title page of the book. Using colored chalk or small paint sponges, have the children create a simple ground and sky backdrop on large bulletin board paper. Let each child paint and cut out something from construction paper to add to the background, such as the henhouse, barn, trees, pond, haystack, and so on. Follow the sequence of the story when you add the children's objects to the mural. Add the story title and the author's name. Beginning on the left, label the mural with the story phrases *across the yard*, *around the pond*, and so on for independent, paired, or choral reading. An art expression sets the stage for meaningful reading and writing.

A CIRCLE STORY MAP

There are six major events in *Rosie's Walk,* which begins and ends at the henhouse. Because the children have already created the story setting and acted out the story events in their barnyard scene, they will understand the simple story matrix. Diagram the events on a large circle story map divided into six sections. Tell the story with pictures, beginning with a picture of Rosie's henhouse placed over the top of the circle. As you read *Rosie's Walk,* have a child place a simple child-drawn picture of the barnyard, the pond, the haystack, the mill, the fence, and the beehives in each section of the circle.

Print the *directionality phrases* on sentence strips for children to *match* to the pictures as they retell the story in independent or paired reading. Keep *Rosie's Walk*, the six pictures, and the six phrase cards available to the children, perhaps in a reading basket or in your dramatic play center, for repeated reading successes.

PREDATOR AND PREY

In your nonfiction books and children's nature magazines, point out animals that are considered to be predators and those that are prey. Ask the children what they think the words mean and which animals they would put in each group. Brainstorm ideas of a predator and prey to replace Rosie and the fox in an innovation of *Rosie's Walk.* Decide on two new animal characters such as a bird and worm, an octopus and fish, or a mouse and hawk. Discuss the *setting* and the *plot* for your story such as a mouse in the desert going over a rock, around a cactus, through a tumbleweed, across a snake's back, unaware that it is being followed by a hawk. Have the children dictate new directionality phrases and illustrate the pages individually or in pairs. The very last page could read *and got back in time for dinner.* Authoring a story motivates children to practice reading it again and again.

JUMP OR JIGGLE

Make the rich vocabulary and strong rhythm of "Jump or Jiggle" come alive by pantomiming the action words. Write the poem in a class accordion book. Have the children illustrate a cover, a title page (be sure to give credit to Evelyn Beyer), and thirteen pages with a different phrase, such as *frogs jump,* written at the top of each page. Encourage the children to depict the action of each animal as well as where the animal might be. Provide an additional *But I walk* page for the remaining children to illustrate and add every third page of the book. Can't you just see the action? Because the children have already memorized the text with oral repetition, they will delight in reading their book.

LET'S LOOK AT FOXES

In most children's literature, the fox is portrayed as a character feared by farmers and animals. Ask the children what they know about foxes and record their answers on a chart titled What We Think We Know about Foxes. Model for the children some things you wonder about foxes: "Is there anything good about them? Do they take care of their families?" Ask the children what questions they have and write their responses on a second chart, What We Want to Know about Foxes.

Provide an abundance of nonfiction picture books and encourage the children to study the pictures for answers to their questions. Read aloud Eve Bunting's *Red Fox Running,* a book of absolute beauty as a fox searches a breathtaking landscape for food. Look at the large photos of fox mothers and pups, habitats, prey, and predators in *Fox* by Caroline Arnold. Talk about *Tracks in the Wild* by Betsy Bowen. Have each child share a picture and a sentence about one thing she has learned and add them to your final chart, What We Have Learned about Foxes.

EVERYDAY LEARNING ACTIVITIES

Positive parenting; developmental learning activities; and a warm, nurturing environment are major factors in a child's academic success and lifetime learning.

The delightful hen in *Rosie's Walk* by Pat Hutchins was alone on her walk and made all her own choices. She was an independent little hen. One of the best ways adults can help young children is to give them opportunities to make choices, to make small decisions on their own, to begin to reason and to think for themselves. Giving choices is also a positive discipline tool. So often you can avoid a power play or a head-on collision in getting a child to do something by simply giving him a choice. With your help and with safe boundaries, a young child is able to make choices—a wonderful step toward independence. Start out by giving a child two well-thought-out options, such as "Would you like to have a friend over or do you want to play outside with your brother?" "Do you want me to read you a story now or when you are ready for bed?" Allowing a child to make decisions is teaching him early to be a problem solver and an independent person. Right after the child has made a choice, he needs immediate acceptance. Don't crush the self you are trying to encourage.

✳ Have fun with the *directionality* concepts in *Rosie's Walk*. Set up a simple path for children, saying the words with them as they go *around* a chair, *over* a pillow on the floor, *under* a table, and *through* an open-ended box. Add new words: next to, in front of, behind, beside, above, between, on the top, middle, and bottom. When children understand directional words with their bodies first, it is much easier for them to understand such words in print. *(perceptual motor)*

✳ Blocks and Legos are excellent, creative toys that allow a child to use her imagination. Blocks can be anything she decides in her mind they will be, such as the henhouse, silo, windmill, tractor, beehives, fence, or milk cans from *Rosie's Walk*. A child will discover new ways to stack, build, and balance blocks as she learns by trial and error. *(creative play)*

✳ The most important part of reading aloud is letting a child talk about the story. Ask her to tell you what she liked or didn't like about the pictures, the characters, the story. When she talks, the story has meaning in her mind. That is true of every storybook you read together. If a child enjoyed *Rosie's Walk*, look for more books by the popular children's author, Pat Hutchins. *(story meaning)*

✳ Walking on a *balance beam* is great for coordination, muscle control, and balance. Balance beams are everywhere; they are on landscaping timbers in front yards, concrete strips that mark off parking spaces in parking lots, cracks in sidewalks, low walls, a ladder flat on the ground, a yardstick put down on the floor, or even a strip of masking tape on the carpet. Begin with a *beam* that is on the ground so the child will be at ease as she practices. After she masters walking in a straight line, try walking sideways or even backward. *(gross motor coordination)*

The Runaway Bunny

by Margaret Wise Brown

TEACHING FOCUS

* Family relationships
* Identifying feelings
* Story structure
* Process writing

* Math/science concepts
* Matching pairs
* Nonfiction
* Theme topic: houses

SETTING THE STAGE

Instantly singable songs and the appealing rhyme and rhythm of finger plays will encourage children to be involved in story time.

"Baby Mine" recorded by Art Garfunkel, *Songs from a Parent to a Child*
(A sweet song reassuring children of their parents' love)

"A Bushel and a Peck" by Sharon, Lois & Bram, *In the Schoolyard*

LITTLE BUNNY

There was a little bunny who lived in the wood.	
He wiggled his ears as a good bunny should.	*(fingers over ears)*
He hopped by a squirrel.	*(jump fingers up arm)*
He wiggled by a tree.	*(wiggle hands)*
He hopped by a duck.	*(jump fingers up arm)*
And he wiggled by me.	*(point to self)*
He stared at the squirrel.	*(circles around eyes)*
He peeked round the tree.	*(peek through hands)*
He stared at the duck.	*(circles around eyes)*
But he winked at me!	*(wink)*

LITTLE ELEPHANTS

One, two, three, four, five,	*(count fingers)*
Five little elephants standing in a row.	
This little elephant stubbed his toe.	*(point to each finger)*
This little elephant said, "Oh, oh, oh,"	
This little elephant laughed and was glad,	
This little elephant so thoughtful and good,	
He ran for the doctor as fast as he could.	

FIRST READING

Do you remember the story *Goodnight Moon?* The same author, Margaret Wise Brown, wrote this story, too. It is called *The Runaway Bunny*. In fact, the illustrator hid one of the pictures from *The Runaway Bunny* on one of the pages in *Goodnight Moon*. Let me show you. *(Show the picture of the bunny fishing from* The Runaway Bunny *and also the page from* Goodnight Moon *where the same picture is hanging on the bedroom wall.)*

There is a surprise in *The Runaway Bunny* also. I'll turn the pages and you tell me when you see a picture from the storybook *Goodnight Moon* (*the cow jumping over the moon from* "Hey Diddle Diddle"). Finding the same picture in another book is like finding a secret message from the author. This story is about a little bunny who tells his mother how he will run away. She answers by telling him how she will catch him every time and bring him back because she loves him so much. Do you think that is the conversation they are having on the cover of the book?

GETTING INVOLVED

Let's talk about some of the new words we just heard in the story. There were always some clues to help us understand the words. When the bunny wanted to be a fish, he used the word *trout:* Tell me what you think that means. When the bunny talked about a garden, he said he would be a *crocus*. What's a crocus? When the bunny decided to join a circus, he used the words *trapeze* and *tightrope*. Did you find them in the circus picture? Now that we have learned the new words, let's stand up and pretend to be the mother rabbit. Every time the bunny runs away, we will bring him back.

When the bunny decides to:	We will:
. . . swim in the trout stream	. . . cast out our fishing lines
. . . be a rock	. . . climb the mountain to find him
. . . hide as a crocus	. . . be gardeners with hoes to find him
. . . fly as a bird	. . . be tall trees for him to fly to
. . . sail as a boat	. . . blow gently and bring him back
. . . swing on a trapeze	. . . walk the tightrope carefully
. . . run back home	. . . give him a big hug and climb into our hole in the ground.

A CLOSER LOOK

With each rereading of a story, children gain new understanding. Pause often for a spontaneous flow of oral language as the children share their feelings and observations. Extend the learning process with your own questions in repeated readings of the story.

✳ In your opinion, was "Once there was a little bunny who wanted to run away" a good story starter? *(evaluating)*

✳ Did the little bunny ever tell his mother *why* he was running away? Do you have any ideas? *(analyzing)*

✳ I wonder if you ever felt like the little bunny. *(reflecting)*

✳ Why is mother rabbit fishing with a carrot instead of a worm? *(association)*

✳ Tell me what equipment mother rabbit needed to be a mountain climber. *(observation)*

✳ I love the picture of the garden. Tell me which picture you liked. *(evaluating)*

✳ Would you agree that the illustrations in color were the important ones in *The Runaway Bunny*? *(evaluating)*

✳ Why is mother rabbit in the clouds? *(comprehension)*

✳ Why do you think the little bunny decided to stay where he was? *(analyzing)*

✳ Tell me how the picture of mother rabbit and little bunny in the rocking chair makes you feel. *(reflecting)*

✳ What would you like to say to the author, Margaret Wise Brown, about *The Runaway Bunny*? *(reflecting)*

STORY TIME EXTENSIONS

If You Were My Bunny by Kate McMullan

Guess How Much I Love You by Sam McBratney

The Diggers by Margaret Wise Brown *(reissue of a classic)*

Where Are You Going, Little Mouse? by Robert Kraus

Seven Little Rabbits by John Becker

BALANCED LITERACY ACTIVITIES

POETRY

A HOUSE
Everyone has a house,
  a house,
everyone has a house.
The bear has a cave,
the bird a nest,
the mole a hole,
but what is best
is a house like ours
  with windows and doors
  and rugs and floors.
Everyone has a house,
  a house,
everyone has a house.
Charlotte Zolotow

MOONSTRUCK
I'd like to see rabbits
under the moon,
dancing in winter,
dancing in June,
dancing around
while twilight lingers
and blinkey-eyed stars
look down through their fingers.
I'd like to see rabbits
under the moon,
but I always,
always
have to go to bed too soon.
Aileen Fisher

INVOLVEMENT

✱ After each rereading of *The Runaway Bunny,* celebrate the mother's love for the little bunny by singing Sharon, Lois & Bram's "Skinnamarink" and "A Bushel and a Peck" or Art Garfunkel's "Baby Mine," cheerful songs about love.

✱ After dramatizing all the ways the bunny will run away and how his mother will find him, have the children think of new things the bunny might become. How will the mother bunny find him and bring him back?

✱ Make pairs of word cards showing what the bunny will be and what the mother will become to find him, such as a fish and a fisherman, a crocus and a gardener, and so on. Include the new ideas the children have suggested. Draw picture clues next to the words. Give every child a word card to hang around his neck as he looks for the child who has the other card in his pair. The bunny with the fish picture will look for the mother bunny with the fisherman picture and so on. The children will sit in pairs, ready to stand and dramatize their parts as the story is read again.

✱ Turn all the word cards facedown on the floor. The children can play a memory game, turning the cards over one at a time, trying to make matches.

INTEGRATION

MOONSTRUCK

How did Aileen Fisher think of writing a poem about rabbits dancing? How did she think of the words "blinky-eyed stars look down through their fingers"? The appeal of poetry to children is found first in the beauty of the well-chosen words and then in their responses as they see and feel the word pictures. Surround the lovely poem "Moonstruck" with the children's oral language. Children create meaning when they make connections to their own lives. What child would not understand "but I always, always have to go to bed too soon"?

I WILL BE A CROCUS

The warm colors in the illustration of the runaway bunny in the garden are much like the bold, bright pictures of Lois Ehlert's beautiful story *Planting a Rainbow.* Her cheery book is also the story of a mother and a child as they plant flowers (including crocuses!) in the family garden every year.

Before your children create a rainbow flower garden that will brighten your room for days, talk about *The Reason for a Flower* by Ruth Heller and *The Tiny Seed* by Eric Carle. Have fun with the marvelous words and cumulative pattern of the lovely *Rose in My Garden* by Arnold and Anita Lobel. Don't miss the magnificent photographs of an amaryllis, from bulb to spectacular bloom, in *A Flower Grows* by Ken Robbins. And any child will be richer for learning the name of each gorgeous full-page flower in *Alison's Zinnia* by Anita Lobel.

Divide your children into small groups, each group deciding on the color they will use to create flowers for the garden—red, orange, yellow, green, blue, and purple. Offer each group a choice of art materials, such as bright tempera paint, construction paper, tissue paper, and water-based markers, to mix and match as they create the flowers for their part of your wall mural garden. Cluster the same colored flowers together as Lois Ehlert did in her vivid garden pictures. Let the children decide which art medium to use to make the runaway bunny and his mother and where to put them in your colorful rainbow garden (see p. 211, *The Tale of Peter Rabbit*).

A HOUSE

Listening to "A House" by Charlotte Zolotow will give children another delightful experience with poetry. Make a list of everything they discover about the poem—the repetition of the phrase "everyone has a house," the spacing of the text, the sounds they hear, the different words, and so on. Ask the children what is important about their own houses. Read entertaining books about animal houses such as the imaginative *A House Is a House for Me* by Mary Ann Hoberman. Enjoy the lovely illustrations of a crab's search for a perfect home in Megan McDonald's *Is This a House for Hermit Crab?*, Robert Kalan's *Moving Day*, and Eric Carle's *A House for Hermit Crab*. Give the children the opportunity to choose any of the following responses:

✴ Create an animal and its house from clay. Have the children decide how to group and label their animal houses, perhaps by habitats.

✴ Paint or draw an animal house and write a story about it.

✴ Draw, paint, or tear from construction paper the child's home, perhaps labeling the "windows and doors and rugs and floors."

✴ Print the text of the poem "A House" on a number of large pieces of paper. Create a wall mural for the children to illustrate and read.

✴ Create a Venn diagram of two of the stories to show the similarities and differences of the crabs, their adventures, and their houses.

✴ Write a poem, a letter to an author, a journal entry, a story. Children see themselves as authors when they make their own decisions about writing.

EVERYDAY LEARNING ACTIVITIES

Positive parenting; developmental learning activities; and a warm, nurturing environment are major factors in a child's academic success and lifetime learning.

In the story *The Runaway Bunny* by Margaret Wise Brown, a little bunny tells his mother all the ways he will run away. She reassuringly tells him all the ways she will find him and bring him back. It is a comforting story of warmth and security and love. Perhaps it carries the message that every child is looking for when he has been naughty or has threatened to run away. He wants to know, especially after he has been disciplined, that he is still loved. Of course he is! Love is a very real part of discipline. The two terms do not have to contradict each other. The only time they will is when an adult belittles a child and destroys his self-esteem by making statements such as, "You are bad," or "You never do anything right," or "You never learn! How many times do I have to tell you?" Harsh words condemn the child as a person and destroy his sense of being loved. In contrast, loving discipline conveys the message, "I love you too much to let you go too far. What you did was wrong, but I still love you as a person." Good discipline leaves the door open for a time of reattachment that says, "I love you." A child needs to hear the words over and over again. Touching a child when you tell him that you love him just reinforces the message. A child needs to know that there is nothing he can ever do or say that will cause you to stop loving him. He doesn't have to earn your love by being good. He has it by being born, just like the little bunny in *The Runaway Bunny.*

✳ A picnic is a simple family activity that is a real favorite with children. Give them the responsibility of planning your next picnic—a wonderful lesson in making choices. Let the children decide where it will be (even the backyard is an option). Write lists of what food you will have and who will come, including special guests they invite themselves. *(making decisions)*

✳ In the story *The Runaway Bunny,* the little bunny seemed to be a gentle, quiet bunny. Sometimes we call a gentle, quiet child a shy child, as though something is wrong. Every time we repeat the label in her presence, we cause her to become more shy. She will prove we are right because she believes us. If you feel a child is unusually shy, don't label her. Instead, appreciate the child's temperament. Build her confidence. Encourage her to look into your eyes when she is speaking. Teach her to give eye contact to others as well. The more you encourage a child, the more relaxed she will be. *(social development)*

✳ Give a child the opportunity to be a gardener like the mother rabbit in *The Runaway Bunny.* Show her how to prepare the soil and plant real seeds. Plant a wooden stick in the garden also. Give the child the responsibility of watering both the seeds and the stick. Chart your observations daily. *(observation)*

✳ Put three small, familiar objects such as a button, a marble, and a bottle cap in front of a child. Have her turn around while you hide one object in your hand and ask, "What do I have?" Make the game more difficult by increasing the number of objects you put out or by choosing unfamiliar objects. Name them and talk about them. You are increasing her vocabulary while having fun. Be sure to give the child some turns at choosing and hiding. Some day, make the items all edible and end the game with party time. *(concentration)*

Skip to My Lou

by Nadine Bernard Westcott

SETTING THE STAGE

Instantly singable songs and the appealing rhyme and rhythm of finger plays will encourage children to be involved in story time.

"Skip to My Lou" by Greg and Steve, *We All Live Together, Vol. 1*

"Grandpa's Farm" by Sharon, Lois & Bram. *Sing A–Z*

STEPPING OVER STEPPING STONES

Stepping over stepping stones,	*(walk in place)*
One, two, three,	*(clap three times)*
Stepping over stepping stones,	*(walk in place)*
Come with me.	*(beckon)*
The river's very fast,	*(roll hands)*
And the river's very wide,	*(arms out wide)*
And we'll step across on stepping stones,	*(walk in place)*
And reach the other side.	*(jump with two feet)*

FIVE FAT SAUSAGES

Five fat sausages frying in a pan,	*(hold up five fingers)*
All of a sudden one went 'BANG'	*(clap hands loudly)*
Four fat sausages frying in a pan,	*(hold up four fingers)*
All of a sudden one went 'BANG'	*(clap hands loudly)*
Three fat sausages frying in a pan,	*(hold up three fingers)*
All of a sudden one went 'BANG'	*(clap hands loudly)*
Two fat sausages frying in a pan,	*(hold up two fingers)*
All of a sudden one went 'BANG'	*(clap hands loudly)*
One fat sausage frying in a pan,	*(hold up one finger)*
All of a sudden it went 'BANG!'	*(clap hands loudly)*
and there were NO sausages left!	*(no fingers left)*

FIRST READING

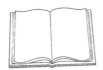

Does the cover of this book make you smile? Tell me a story about what you think is happening. There is a word in the title that tells us the animals and the little boy are skipping. The title of the story is *Skip to My Lou*. Some of the words of the story are from an old, old American folk song. Nadine Bernard Westcott knew all about that song when she wrote and illustrated this book. When you name the animals and the people in the picture on the title page, you have already found most of the characters in the story.

The next page shows us that Ms. Westcott dedicated the book to her mother and father. Why do you think she drew a picture of a kitchen table under those words? On the page next to the dedication page you can see the musical notes for the song. Look on the shelf above the song. The fun has started!

GETTING INVOLVED

Many years ago, a fiddler played the music of *Skip to My Lou* on his fiddle while children and old people clapped their hands and danced to the beat of the happy music. Let's pretend there is a fiddler sitting right here in the middle of our circle. We'll clap and sing the words to the chorus while he plays his fiddle: "Lou, Lou, skip to my Lou *(sing three times)*, Skip to my Lou, my darling." Then the children all got partners and skipped around the circle while they sang the words. Each one of you can get a partner and we'll skip and sing just as they did.

Maybe the children skipped too fast because the next verse tells us they lost their partners! The words are, "Lost my partner, what'll I do? *(sing three times)*, Skip to my Lou, my darling." Let's stand in our places in the circle and sing that verse, too.

I know the children started the singing game all over again because the next verse says, "I'll get another prettier than you *(sing three times)*, Skip to my Lou, my darling." Let's get new partners and skip around the circle one more time. Then we can sit down in our places and look at the story again.

A CLOSER LOOK

With each rereading of a story, children gain new understanding. Pause often for a spontaneous flow of oral language as the children share their feelings and observations. Extend the learning process with your own questions in repeated readings of the story.

Skip to My Lou is so rich in humor and visual detail that a few questions can't begin to capture the playfulness of the delightful text and illustrations. The children will want to study the pictures again and again.

* What do the words mean, "The farm's all in order"? *(comprehension)*

* How did the flies discover the sugarbowl? *(reasoning)*

* How did the cats discover the buttermilk? *(observation)*

* What's a *parlor?* How did the pigs get the pancakes? *(interpretation)*

* Did each cow have a different job to do in the kitchen? *(observation)*

* Tell me about the eyes looking out from behind the open door in the kitchen. *(reasoning)*

* What is a *pantry?* What did the roosters get into? *(comprehension)*

* How did the little boy and the dog end up in the bathtub? *(observation)*

* Tell me which room you think was the messiest. *(reflecting)*

* In your opinion, who was having the most fun? *(evaluating)*

* Why was the boy worried when he looked at the clock? *(comprehension)*

* Did the fun stop when the animals helped clean up? *(interpretation)*

* Did you think they were going to clean up in time? *(reflecting)*

* Where in the story did you think, "Oh, I just love that part"? *(reflecting)*

STORY TIME EXTENSIONS

She'll Be Comin' Round the Mountain by Tom Birdseye

The Happy Hedgehog Band by Martin Waddell

The Relatives Came by Cynthia Rylant

Miss Mary Mack adapted by Mary Ann Hoberman

There's a Hole in the Bucket by Nadine Bernard Westcott

BALANCED LITERACY ACTIVITIES

POETRY

JELLY ON THE PLATE

Jelly on the plate,
Jelly on the plate,
Wibble wobble, wibble wobble,
Jelly on the plate.

Paper on the floor,
Paper on the floor,
Pick it up, pick it up,
Paper on the floor.

Piggy in the house,
Piggy in the house,
Kick him out, kick him out,
Piggy in the house.

Traditional

INVOLVEMENT

✳ The foot-tapping, infectious melody of *Skip to My Lou* makes it impossible for children to stay quiet. No wonder it has been around for so long. For a different rereading, have the children hum the tune and read the pictures as you turn the pages. Another time, sing every word of the text. The children will spontaneously join in singing or clapping.

✳ Make name cards for the animal characters: the flies, cats, pigs, cows, roosters, and sheep. Add picture clues by drawing the faces of the animals on the word cards. Give each child a yarn-tied name card to put around his neck. Group the pigs together, the roosters together, and so on as the children sit in a circle. As you reread the story, have the children join in only on the words their animals say. For example, only the flies will say "Shoo fly shoo," only the cats will say "two by two," only the roosters will say, "Cock-a-doodle-do," and so on.

✳ Turn the name cards over and write the names of the animals without any picture clues. Spread them out in front of the children. Let each one point to an animal name he can read and put that word card around his neck for the dramatization.

✳ Have the children stand in a circle with one child in the middle. As you begin singing the chorus of the song, the child in the middle closes her eyes and twirls around with her arm extended. Whoever she is pointing to when you finish the chorus joins her in the middle. The two join hands and skip around the circle as the children sing the name of the child just chosen:

Abby, Abby, skip to my Abby,
Abby, Abby, skip to my Abby,
Abby, Abby, skip to my Abby,
Skip to my Abby, my darling!

Then Abby becomes the child in the middle, repeating the game and choosing a new child the same way. Everyone sings that child's name as the two skip around the circle.

✳ Put the word cards, a tape of the children singing, and a copy of *Skip to My Lou* in your listening center for a rollicking good time in independent reading.

INTEGRATION

SKIP, TRIP, FLIP, DRIP

Write on chart paper, using alternating lines of color, the now familiar words of the song, "Skip to My Lou." Ask the children to point out *anything* they know about the text—letters, sounds, words, punctuation. They are making discoveries, sharing knowledge, and learning from each other. Then read the text together.

Over the course of many sessions, there will be opportunities for mini language lessons. Have the children frame the high-frequency words *to* and *my* with their hands or slider frames, flashlights, or pointers. Add the words to the word-wall resource in your room. Demonstrate one-to-one correspondence and left-to-right progression. Teach about capital letters, commas, and exclamation points. Brainstorm about a word family for *skip* by covering the letters *sk* (the onset) and pointing to *ip* (the rime). Write a list of the words the children suggest and add to it daily. When children are engaged in a happy reading experience, they will learn.

QUARTER TO THREE

A book as rich in humor and visual detail as this one will surely spark the imaginations of children. Talk about what new chaos the boy might have found if no one had come home until three o'clock! Expect a lot of conversation as the children share ideas. Then in groups of four, have the children decide where their new animals will cause a disturbance, such as *fleas in the haystack, shoo fly shoo; birds in the popcorn, two by two;* and *goats in the closet, what'll I do!* Each group will illustrate their new phrases with the fourth page saying just the text, *Skip to my Lou, my darling!* Let the children decide on a background color for mounting their four pages. The different colors will become natural dividers as you bind the various stanzas into a class big book.

fleas in the haystack,   birds in the popcorn,   goats in the closet,   Skip to my Lou, my darling!

A CIRCLE STORY

The circle of winsome characters on the cover of *Skip to My Lou* is a reminder that the story is also a circle. Draw a large circle on chart paper and divide it into six sections. Place a small picture of the boy sitting on the front porch to identify the beginning and the ending point of the story. Starting at the top and moving clockwise, have the children draw a small picture of each event in the story—*the flies in the sugarbowl, cats in the buttermilk,* and so on. Write a phrase to add to each colorful segment. The children will be the storytellers as they *circle* their way through the story events.

OUR FAVORITE CHARACTERS

Have the children recall the mischievous characters as they appeared in sequence in the story. Write the name of each animal at the top of a six-column wall graph. Then give each child a small square of paper on which to draw her favorite character. Let her choose a background from a variety of colored squares and mount her picture.

Before you place the pictures on the graph, have the children estimate how many drawings will be tallied in each column. Record their estimates. With the children sitting in front of the graph, add each child's picture to the appropriate column.

Encourage the children to make observations of the columns as you talk about more than, less than, how many more, how many less, equal, and zero. Have the children dictate summarizing sentences. Write them on a chart, which the children can illustrate. They will read the graph and the sentences often because the silliness of the animal characters is so appealing.

EVERYDAY LEARNING ACTIVITIES

Positive parenting; developmental learning activities; and a warm, nurturing environment are major factors in a child's academic success and lifetime learning.

Evenings for today's busy families can be extra hectic when adults are oh, so tired and children are oh, so desirous of the spotlight. Stop a minute as you arrive home, or even if you have been there all day long. Gather everyone close—perhaps all on your lap at the same time, all talking at once, all needing hugs and attention. Give it, and you will find it will be so much easier to move on to the next thing on the schedule. Sometimes we let television take over because it keeps children quiet. Remember that television doesn't challenge a child's mind or her body, and it robs her of time spent with you. Sometimes only fifteen minutes together will change the whole mood of an evening. Use those minutes to sing silly songs or read a story. That's what reading is all about, sharing happy moments together. If you merely looked at the words to *Skip to My Lou* on the pages of the storybook, something would be missing. To convey the rhythm and the absurdity of the story, the words must be read aloud or sung. In just those few minutes of reading or singing together, you can create an infectious, happy mood in a home.

✳ *Skip to My Lou* by Nadine Bernard Westcott is an example of a book that will last a child through many years of learning. There is always something new to discover in the extraordinary illustrations. Each time you read the story, have the child point out new things he has discovered on the pages. He will be creating a lens for himself through which he will always view the book. *(visual discrimination)*

✳ The child and the animals in *Skip to My Lou* started to straighten up the house at quarter to two, getting everything done in fifteen minutes. Play a game of cleaning up a child's room or some part of the house before the timer goes off in fifteen minutes. Then celebrate! Working together is the best way to teach a young child responsibility. *(learning responsibility)*

✳ Make a child conscious of the many numbers in his world. Have him look for numbers inside the house, on the clock, on the telephone and the oven, on storybook pages and the television. Look for numbers outside such as speed limits and house numbers. *(numeral concepts)*

✳ Make up some directions in everyday activities that will help a child learn the concept of left and right. Ask her to wash her right arm first, dry her left leg first, open the car door with her right hand, and so on. Remember to be helpful. A child will work on left and right a long time before mastering the skill. *(left and right)*

✳ A child's first scribbles are the beginning of writing, followed by random letters that have no sound-symbol relationships in her mind. Eventually she will put letters on paper to represent the sounds she hears in words. That is the beginning of phoneme awareness, or the knowledge of phonics. Keep a writing box always available, full of colorful paper, pencils, crayons, erasers, perhaps a glue stick, a ruler, and scissors. Encourage and value a child's early efforts in writing, for through writing she will learn to read. *(process of writing)*

The Snowy Day

by Ezra Jack Keats

TEACHING FOCUS

* Phonemic awareness
* Cultural diversity
* Content writing/Process writing
* Math/science concepts

* Author recognition
* Comparing/Contrasting
* Nonfiction
* Theme topic: snow

SETTING THE STAGE

Instantly singable songs and the appealing rhyme and rhythm of finger plays will encourage children to be involved in story time.

"Good Morning, Mr. Weatherman" by Hap Palmer, *Patriotic and Morning Time Songs*

"The First Snowfall" by John McCutcheon, *Wintersongs*
(A beautiful recording)

THE SNOWMAN

Roll him and roll him until he is big.	*(follow action as rhyme*
Roll him until he is fat as a pig.	*indicates)*
He has two eyes and a hat on his head.	
He'll stand there all night,	
While we go to bed.	

SNOW MEN

Five little snow men	*(hold up five fingers)*
Standing in a row.	*(point to each one)*
Each with a hat	*(hand on head)*
And a big red bow.	*(pretend to tie bow)*
Five little snow men	*(hold up five fingers)*
Dressed for a show,	*(move hand from head to toe)*
Now they are ready,	
Where will they go?	*(palms up, questioning)*
Wait 'til the sun shines,	*(circle arms over head)*
Soon they will go	
Down through the fields	*(arms down to lap)*
With the melting snow.	*(curl up as you melt)*

FIRST READING

Look at the cover of our story today. Tell me what kind of a day it is. Those are the very words the author chose for the title of the story, *The Snowy Day*. Does the little boy look familiar? Do you know his name? The author, Ezra Jack Keats, wrote about Peter and his dog, Willie, in two other stories: *Whistle for Willie* and *Peter's Chair*. He not only wrote the books, he illustrated them as well. Mr. Keats received an honor called a Caldecott Award for the illustrations in *The Snowy Day*.

Let's look at the pictures of Peter on the cover, inside the cover, and on the title page. You will see all of them again somewhere in the story. Now we're ready to read about Peter and *The Snowy Day*.

By reading three books by the same author, children will feel they know Peter and will recognize the author's name. You want them to understand that Ezra Jack Keats' work was writing and illustrating books. Consider doing an author study of this beloved writer, who was known for his use of collage illustrations in the thirty-two children's stories he wrote.

GETTING INVOLVED

Let's share Peter's delightful adventure in the snow. First, better put on your warm snowsuit; next, pull on your rubber boots; then your hood and scarf; and last, your mittens. Now we are ready to join Peter outside. Pretend your feet are sinking into the crunchy snow. Point your toes out. Point your toes in. Smack that snow-covered tree with a stick. Uh-oh, brush the snow off your head! Now lie down in the snow and gently move your arms and legs to make a snow angel. Make a snowball and carefully put it in your pocket before you go inside. Now let your mother help you take off all that heavy clothing and get ready for bed. Oh dear, where is your snowball now? Climb into your warm bed, pull up the covers, and dream of more snow gently falling everywhere.

Another time, have a mitten match. Each child will match his mitten (real or paper) to one hanging on a clothesline or lined up on the floor. Sort the mittens by size or by color. Then make a mitten floor graph.

A CLOSER LOOK

With each rereading of a story, children gain new understanding. Pause often for a spontaneous flow of oral language as the children share their feelings and observations. Extend the learning process with your own questions in repeated readings of the story.

* What would you like to say to Ezra Jack Keats about the story *The Snowy Day? (reflecting)*

* Could the story have happened on a *summer* morning? *(reasoning)*

* Who do you think piled the snow "along the street to make a path for walking"? *(reasoning)*

* What made the third track in the snow when Peter dragged his feet? *(comprehension)*

* Tell me all the things you remember Peter doing in the snow with his feet. His hands. *(observation)*

* Have you ever had a good time doing something alone, like Peter? *(reflecting)*

* In your opinion, was Peter wise not to join the snowball fight? *(evaluating)*

* Tell me why you think Peter's snowman was smiling. *(reflecting)*

* Do you think the story would have been different if Peter's dog, Willie, had been with him? *(evaluating)*

* How could Peter have saved his snowball? *(reasoning)*

* Peter dreamed about the sun melting the snow. What happens to our dreams when we wake up? *(reasoning)*

* Where do you think Peter lived if his friend lived "across the hall"? *(analyzing)*

* Imagine you were the friend across the hall. What would you and Peter do together? *(reflecting)*

STORY TIME EXTENSIONS

In the Snow by Huy Voun Lee

First Snow by Kim Lewis

Snowballs by Lois Ehlert

The Mitten adapted by Jan Brett

Katy and the Big Snow by Virginia Burton

BALANCED LITERACY ACTIVITIES

POETRY

IT FELL IN THE CITY
It fell in the city,
It fell through the night,
And the black rooftops
All turned white.

Red fire hydrants
All turned white.
Blue police cars
All turned white.

Green garbage cans
All turned white.
Gray sidewalks
All turned white.

Yellow NO PARKING signs
All turned white
When it fell in the city
All through the night.
                    Eve Merriam

INVOLVEMENT

A CELEBRATION OF SNOW

✱ Music is a great accompaniment to body expression and pantomime. The lovely classical music "Snowflakes Are Dancing" by Claude Debussy invites children to move rhythmically. Use paper snowflakes suspended on strings for individual props as children respond to the dancing music. Another time, encourage them to move as Peter moved in *The Snowy Day*—walking, dragging his feet slowly, whirling, sliding down a hill, and making angels in the snow. Classical music stimulates learning and creativity as it surrounds children with the patterns of pleasant, soothing sound.

✱ The last sentence of *The Snowy Day* says, "After breakfast Peter called to his friend from across the hall, and they went out together into the deep, deep snow." Ask the children to think about where Peter lived, who his friend might be, and what new adventures they may have had together in the snow. The children will be creating new endings to the story and sharing ideas for journal writing. They also will be surrounding the text with oral language and making connections to their own lives.

✱ Enjoy a family's anticipation of the arrival of snow in Charlotte Zolotow's marvelous story *Something Is Going to Happen*. Let the children celebrate with the story characters by turning their bodies into a single snowflake, a blizzard, an icicle, a snowman, a snow-covered tree, or any way they would like to move to interpret the happiness of the story.

INTEGRATION

WHEN WINTER COMES

Explore the fascinating world of snow and how it protects plants and animals. *Snow Is Falling* is a clearly written and appealing nonfiction book by Franklyn M. Branley. *When Winter Comes*, a nonfiction resource book by Russell Freedman, describes how animals prepare for and survive the winter season in the woods. Jim Arnosky's picture book *I See Animals Hiding* shows how the whiteness of snow protects animals as they blend into the winter landscape. Have each child write one fact she has learned. As a group, decide what sentences to write on a class chart, What We Know about Snow.

Extension: *The Snowy Day* can introduce a weather theme, culminating with the children writing stories about Peter on The Rainy Day or The Windy Day. The above study could also lead to an interest in what happens to plants and animals on stormy, windy, or very hot days.

SNOWY RHYMES

The title of your class chart, What We Know about Snow, has already introduced rhyming words. Each day choose one high-frequency word from the story, such as *snow, day, night, see, this, that, made,* or *deep*. Write the word in the center of colorful chart paper and make a web of rhyming words around it. After a number of days, your charts will be lining the walls, inviting the children to read and rhyme.

IT FELL IN THE CITY

In Eve Merriam's poem "It Fell in The City," the simple text paints a lovely word picture of colors turning white in a silent snowfall. Print the poem on chart paper. Encourage the children to make observations about the repetition of phrases, the arrangement of the words, the sounds they hear, and the meaning of the poem. Have them suggest a way to identify the color words and the words "turned" and "white" every time they appear in the poem.

Decide how you can tell the story of snow falling in the city on a wall mural. With a variety of art mediums such as tempera paint, colored chalk, construction paper, fabric scraps, or water-based markers, let each child choose what he will make to add to the scene. Then have the children decide how to blanket the colorful city with snow.

IT FELL OUTSIDE THE CITY

Snow, a lovely wordless picture book by Isao Sasaki, is the story of a little train station almost buried by snow "outside the city." As the children talk about the story, make a list of all the things they noticed that were "all turned white" by snow. Using the pattern of Eve Merriam's poem, have the children write their own poem about snow falling everywhere outside the city. The first verse might read, *It fell outside the city, It fell through the night, On the little train station, All turned white.* Because the now familiar original poem and the list of snow-covered objects from *Snow* are visible on charts, the new poetry could be an individual, a small group, or a large group activity.

THE SNOWMAN PARTY

What child hasn't dreamed about a snowman as a friend? *The Snowman,* a charming wordless book by Raymond Briggs, *Midnight Snowman* by Caroline Feller Bauer (which begins with a teacher reading the story *The Snowy Day*), *Our Snowman* by M. B. Goffstein, and *The Snowman Who Went for a Walk* by Mira Lobe are all adventures with snowmen on wonderfully snowy nights.

Imagine what would happen if the snowmen came to life after the children went to bed. How would they move? Would they celebrate by having a party? Who would come to the party? Let the children create a wall mural using whatever art medium and sentences they choose to tell their story.

THE CLASS SNOWMAN

Put a large snowman outline on a bulletin board. Ask the children to estimate how many cotton balls it will take to cover each of the three circles in the snowman's body. Record their estimates. Have the children count out sets of ten cottonballs and tally the sets as they use them to fill each circle. Contrast the number of sets needed for the small, medium, and large circles. Compare the numbers with their estimates.

Then have the children add features, clothing, a name, and labels for all the parts of their snowman. Together, write a story on chart paper using the labels already placed on the snowman, such as *My name is Sparkles. I have a red hat, a carrot nose, stretchy suspenders, black boots,* and so on. Would Peter enjoy receiving a letter from the class snowman?

EVERYDAY LEARNING ACTIVITIES

Positive parenting; developmental learning activities; and a warm, nurturing environment are major factors in a child's academic success and lifetime learning.

In the book *The Snowy Day* by Ezra Jack Keats, Peter was curious about the snowball when he put it in his pocket. A child's curiosity is enormous! It is a powerful tool for learning. A child is programmed to learn about the world around her through her five senses. She needs to feel, to smell, to taste, to watch and listen, and to learn by doing. Encourage this wonderful curiosity. Ask a child questions that cause her to think and predict and problem solve. Accept all her answers, right or wrong, and praise her thinking so she will keep on trying. And when she asks you questions, take the time to answer. You really want a child to wonder about things and ask "why?" A curious child will never stop learning.

✱ Children have a natural curiosity about animals. How do they stay warm? Where do they sleep? How do they find food in the winter? Read the appealing nonfiction book *I See Animals Hiding* by Jim Arnosky. Enjoy *Up North in Winter* by Deborah Hartley, a folksy story of a fox too cold to move in a bitter winter chill. As a family, string Cheerios on pipe cleaners to put out for the birds. Spread peanut butter and bird seed on pinecones or bread. Watch from a window and tally the number of birds that come daily for a snack. *(science, math concepts)*

✱ For a summer activity, suggest that a child place an ice cube on a hot sidewalk. As she watches it melt, ask her to explain why she thinks that is happening. When all signs of the water are gone, explain the word evaporation . . . that the sun lifts tiny drops of water high into the air and they form rain clouds. When the clouds get heavy with water drops, it will rain. Almost everything we do with a child, inside and outside, can become an impromptu learning experience. *(logical thinking)*

✱ Children do not tire of repetition as we do. They will enjoy reading *The Snowy Day* again. Have a child draw or cut out her own smiling snowman and add cotton balls, a hat, pipe, buttons, scarf, nose, arms, and feet. Then encourage her to think of a short, simple story about her smiling snowman. Write down the story that she dictates. Read the story with her over and over as you move your finger under each word. Make an exaggerated swoop back to the left again every time you finish a line. The child will recognize that letters become words written down, one of the first steps in understanding print on a page. *(reading)*

✱ Whatever the season, encourage a child to observe and describe what her ears hear, how the sky and plants look, how the air smells, and how the wind and ground feel. *(sensory learning, language skills)*

✱ Classical music creates lifetime learning connections in a child's brain. Have music playing often throughout your child's day, while she builds, looks at storybooks, eats, and plays. *(sensory learning)*

The Tale of Peter Rabbit

by Beatrix Potter

* Story structure
* A class alphabet book
* Vocabulary
* Math/science concepts

* Oral storytelling
* A family activity
* Nonfiction
* Theme topic: gardens

SETTING THE STAGE

Instantly singable songs and the appealing rhyme and rhythm of finger plays will encourage children to be involved in story time.

"Little Rabbit Foo-Foo" by Sharon, Lois & Bram, *Mainly Mother Goose*
(Children love this song about a naughty bunny and the consequences of his actions)

"All I Really Need" by Raffi, *Baby Beluga*
(All I really need is a song in my heart and love in my family)

HERE IS MY BUNNY

Here is my bunny with ears so funny	*(make a fist, two fingers up)*
And here is his hole in the ground.	*(other fist makes a hole)*
When a noise he hears,	
He pricks up his ears,	*(wiggle two fingers)*
And hops in his hole with a bound.	*(pop fingers into hole)*

LITTLE PETER RABBIT

Little Peter Rabbit   *(follow action as rhyme indicates)*
had a fly upon his nose.
Little Peter Rabbit
had a fly upon his nose.
Little Peter Rabbit
had a fly upon his nose
And he flicked it till it flew away.

FIRST READING

Today's story is called *The Tale of Peter Rabbit*. Another way to say it would be *The Story of Peter Rabbit* because the word *tale* means a story. Peter is really a dear, friendly little rabbit, but he's standing all alone. Do you have any idea where he might be? He was a very curious rabbit and that got him into trouble. Do you know what the word *curious* means? I'm sorry to say Peter also was naughty and that got him into trouble, too.

Beatrix Potter is the lady who wrote the story about Peter, many years ago. She was lonely when she was growing up, so she made friends with all the little animals around her house. She wrote stories about them to cheer up a sick neighbor boy who lived up the lane. Beatrix Potter also drew the beautiful pictures. Now I'm curious to take a look!

The inflection and feeling in your voice will help the children understand the wonderful new words Beatrix Potter uses such as implored, exerted himself, trembling, and scuttered.

GETTING INVOLVED

Now it's your turn to be just a little bit naughty and get into mischief. You can be Peter Rabbit. Watch me and I'll show you just what to do, but we must be very quiet so cross old Mr. McGregor doesn't catch us in his garden. First, let's squeeze under the gate. *(Get down low, but stay in your place.)* We better rush all over the garden because Mr. McGregor discovered us and we forgot the way back to the gate. *(Run silently in place.)* Oh-oh, our jackets are caught in the gooseberry net and we better wriggle free. *(Wriggle from head to toe.)* There's the watering can in the toolshed. Jump in and hide. *(Make one jumping motion in place.)* Uh-oh, water! Better jump out without a sound! Let's start running *(run in place)* and not stop until we are safely home underneath the big fir tree.

Another time, have the children interpret the marvelous, descriptive words in the story—implored, exert, trembling, puzzled, lippity-lippity, and scuttered.

A CLOSER LOOK

With each rereading of a story, children gain new understanding. Pause often for a spontaneous flow of oral language as the children share their feelings and observations. Extend the learning process with your own questions in repeated readings of the story.

* The story says Peter Rabbit's father was put in a pie. What does that mean? *(comprehension)*

* Why do you think Mrs. Rabbit bought five currant buns? *(association)*

* Tell me why you think Peter Rabbit looked for some parsley? *(comprehension)*

* What is a gooseberry net? How did it trap Peter? *(reasoning)*

* In your opinion, was the watering can a good hiding place? *(evaluating)*

* How did Peter Rabbit know the cat was a real cat? *(reasoning)*

* What do you think cousin Benjamin Bunny told Peter Rabbit about cats? *(reasoning)*

* In your opinion, should Mr. McGregor have returned Peter Rabbit's jacket and shoes? *(evaluating)*

* I wonder if the camomile tea was medicine. *(reflecting)*

* Would the story have been different if Mr. McGregor had caught Peter Rabbit? *(analyzing)*

* Do you suppose Peter Rabbit ever visited Mr. McGregor's garden again? *(reflecting)*

* Do you know someone like Peter Rabbit? *(application)*

* If you could talk to the story characters, what would you say to Peter Rabbit? The sparrows? Mr. McGregor? Mrs. Rabbit? *(reflecting)*

* Have you read any other stories by Beatrix Potter? *(reflecting)*

STORY TIME EXTENSIONS

Rabbits and Raindrops by Jim Arnosky

Ten Little Rabbits by Virginia Grossman

Rabbit Seeds by Bijou LeTord

There's More . . . Much More by Sue Alexander

Two Bad Ants by Chris Van Allsburg

BALANCED LITERACY ACTIVITIES

POETRY

TOMMY
I put a seed into the ground
And said, "I'll watch it grow."
I watered it and cared for it
As well as I could know.
One day I walked in my back yard,
And oh, what did I see!
My seed had popped itself right out
Without consulting me.
Gwendolyn Brooks

THE TOAD AND THE RABBIT
by John Martin
from *Read-Aloud Rhymes for
the Very Young*
by Jack Prelutsky

INVOLVEMENT

✳ Beatrix Potter was a master at using beautiful language to convey the meaning of her text to children. Can you imagine what would happen to her wonderful word picture of the friendly sparrows, "who flew to Peter in great excitement and implored him to exert himself," if the story was using a controlled vocabulary? The inflection of your voice and the context of the words will give meaning to the rich vocabulary in *The Tale of Peter Rabbit*. Talk with the children about the many new words they have heard in the story—*mischief, frame, implored, exert, sieve, lippity-lippity, trembling, puzzled, scuttered, fortnight,* and *camomile.*

✳ Add to the children's understanding by dramatizing the story. Have them find places in the room for the fir tree, the baker, the gate to Mr. McGregor's garden, his toolshed, and the pond. Mark the places with signs. Make name cards with the story characters' names and pictures to hang around the children's necks. As you read the story again, the children can mime their parts with expression and movement.

✳ As an oral language experience, guide the children in a discussion of the parts of the story they thought were sad, funny, or suspenseful. Talk about the beginning, middle, and end of the story and give the children the opportunity to think of a new ending for *The Tale of Peter Rabbit.*

✳ Begin each day with another of Beatrix Potter's many stories about Peter Rabbit and his animal friends. Keep a collection in your library corner.

INTEGRATION

PETER RABBIT'S ABC BOOK

Print one letter of the alphabet on each line of a class chart. Let the children decide on characters or objects from the Peter Rabbit stories for each letter of the alphabet. Think of imaginary rabbit names for the difficult letters such as *Q, Y,* and *Z.* When the chart is complete, give each child a piece of paper with an uppercase and a lowercase letter printed on it. Write the name of the story character or object each child has drawn under his picture. Choose children to make a cover, *Peter Rabbit's ABC Book,* and a title page. Mount the pages on colorful construction paper and add your class book to your collection of Beatrix Potter stories.

A NEW ADVENTURE

Was *The Tale of Peter Rabbit* the only adventure in Peter's life? Ask the children if they think he often wandered away from his home "underneath the root of a very big fir tree." With the children grouped around you, begin another tale about Peter. For example, "One dark, stormy night little Peter Rabbit scuttered out of his home under the fir tree. He hurried lippity-lippity across the meadow to a large circus tent." Have the children continue the story with their own ideas. If the story plot begins to ramble, encourage them to think of a dramatic turning point that will lead to an ending. Oral storytelling is a form of authoring that provides valuable language experiences and helps children grasp story structure.

STORYBOOK GARDENS

The best of children's literature includes many stories about flower and vegetable gardens and the people who cared for them. *Linnea in Monet's Garden* by Christina Bjork is a lovely depiction of a child's visit to the great painter's home and beloved garden. In Barbara Cooney's *Miss Rumphius,* a dear lady scatters lupine flower seeds everywhere to make the world more beautiful.

The Giant Vegetable Garden by Nadine Bernard Westcott is a wonderfully absurd story about townsfolk who dream of prizes as big as the enormous vegetables they grow. The clever illustrations of *Tops and Bottoms* by Janet Stevens portray hard-working Hare and his magnificent vegetables. *Rabbit Seeds* by Bijou LeTord is the story of a little rabbit gardener who carefully tends his garden.

"Tommy" is the story of yet another gardener, told in poetic form. It is so childlike and yet so representative of all seeds planted everywhere. Ask the children what pictures they see in their heads when you read the words of the poem. What kind of seed do they think it was that "popped itself right out"? And now a question for you—What child could not envision himself planting a seed just like Tommy?

A SIMULATION: THE GARDEN

✳ Make a list on chart paper of everything the children will need to plant a garden in the room. Talk about the tools used by the gardeners in the stories. Look for more tools in *Who Uses This?*, a nonfiction picture book by Margaret Miller, and *Growing Vegetable Soup,* a story with bold and vibrant gardening pictures by Lois Ehlert. (See also the full-color Inquiry insert.) On a second chart, list the work jobs for which the children will be responsible. Decide together on the best place in the room to plant your garden.

✳ Because lima bean seeds germinate quickly with the stem, roots, and leaves easily visible, have the children plant their seeds in rich soil in clear plastic cups or baggies. Plant additional seeds nearby in a container filled with soil. The children will understand the growing process that is taking place under the soil before the leaves appear.

✳ Invite moms and dads to school to talk about their gardens; help plant additional seeds; and contribute gardening gloves, tools, and seedlings.

✳ Make simple graphs on which the children can record their daily observations about the growth of the seeds.

✳ Keep paper, pencil, and rulers in your garden. The children can make signs, label the rows of plants, and print schedules for watering. Suggest they draw and write the observations they would like to share with others. Perhaps the children will think of writing messages about the garden to Peter Rabbit or Tommy.

✳ From old clothing, have the children make a class scarecrow, with a stuffed paper-bag head and painted face, an old hat, and some straw. Prop it up on a broomstick. Add a watering can and a child-size wheelbarrow full of books about rabbits, seeds, and gardens to your inviting gardener's corner.

EVERYDAY LEARNING ACTIVITIES

Positive parenting; developmental learning activities; and a warm, nurturing environment are major factors in a child's academic success and lifetime learning.

In *The Tale of Peter Rabbit* by Beatrix Potter, mother rabbit quietly stated her limits to her children: "You may go into the fields or down the lane, but don't go into Mr. McGregor's garden." When Peter disobeyed and lost his clothes for the second time, mother rabbit quietly put him to bed.

You are probably doing your best teaching when your voice is softest. A quiet voice usually conveys kindness and love and understanding. A quiet voice says you are in control of yourself and the situation, and when an adult is speaking softly, children must quiet down to hear what is being said. In contrast, yelling is very poor discipline because it does not model correct behavior. The child is actually in control because he has caused *you* to lose your control. When speaking quietly, it is far easier to train a child to listen and do what you ask. Because your voice conveys a great deal of love and respect, you can expect the same in return. When a child is grown, how he remembers your voice will be the way he remembers you.

✳ Reading aloud to a child is the single most important way to plant within him the desire to learn to read himself. Even more important, a child will associate reading with something wonderful—your attention and your quiet voice. Make a list of each year's favorite read-aloud book titles for a child to keep. What a pleasant memory for a child. *(reading aloud)*

✳ As a child's vocabulary continues to grow, encourage him to see the connection between *opposite* words. Begin with obvious pairs such as big and little, and happy and sad. Encourage a child to find opposites for open, out, over, rough, tiny, sick, long, and broken. This is a good game to play if you are busy in the kitchen, riding in the car, or waiting somewhere away from home. Also, let the child give a word to you and you supply the opposite. *(language development)*

✳ Wrap a piece of tape on one end of a piece of yarn, stiffening it so it can act as a needle. Tie a small section of straw to the other end of the yarn. Help a child cut straws into one-inch sections. You have already taught three new words: stiffening, inch, and section. Stringing the straw pieces will develop small muscles. *(eye-hand coordination, language)*

✳ Using masking tape on the floor, make a "hopping path" for a child and Peter Rabbit. Have her hop forward along the tape, first on one foot, then the other. With toes parallel to the tape, have the child hop over and back again on one foot. With practice, add hopping backward; hopping with alternate feet; and, finally, hopping with eyes closed. *(gross motor skills)*

✳ Children's curiosity makes them born investigators. Keep available a magnet, a magnifying glass, a measuring tape, and a yardstick for impromptu discoveries. In their play, children find many things to look at, measure, and compare. The fun is in the spontaneous learning. *(science concepts)*

Ten, Nine, Eight

by Molly Bang

* Phonemic awareness
* Concepts of print
* Math/science concepts
* Parts of speech

* Sorting/Classifying
* Vocabulary
* A floor graph
* Family relationships

SETTING THE STAGE

Instantly singable songs and the appealing rhyme and rhythm of finger plays will encourage children to be involved in story time.

"Ten in the Bed" by Sharon, Lois & Bram, *Elephant Show Record*
(A very funny version with many surprises)

"Go to Sleep/Where's My Pajamas?" by Sharon, Lois & Bram, *Elephant Show Record*

ONE, TWO, BUCKLE MY SHOE
One, two, buckle my shoe;   *(follow actions as rhyme indicates)*
Three, four, knock at the door;
Five, six, pick up sticks;
Seven, eight, lay them straight;
Nine, ten, a big fat hen.

I HAVE TEN LITTLE FINGERS
I have ten little fingers and they all belong to me.   *(follow actions as rhyme indicates)*
I can make them do things, would you like to see?
I can shut them up tight. I can open them wide.
I can put them together . . . or make them hide!
I can make them jump high, I can make them jump low.
I can put them together, and hold them just so.

FIRST READING

Tell me a story about the little girl in yellow on the cover. Do you think you would like to play with her? There is only one other person in this story. Let's look at the title page. Who do you think that person is? Now let's look on the next page. Tell me what you think they are doing. Could they be counting the little girl's toes?

When you count, do you begin with the number ten or the number one? The little girl in our story always begins with the number ten because she likes to count backward. That's because she and her daddy have a special little routine every night when it is bedtime. The name of our story is *Ten, Nine, Eight* and it was written by Molly Bang. She received a Caldecott Honor Award for her illustrations in the book. I wonder which one will be your favorite.

GETTING INVOLVED

Fill a pretty basket full to overflowing with a wide assortment of objects. Include ten things usually associated with bedtime such as a toothbrush, soap, and a night-light. Also include some items that were a part of the story such as a Raggedy Ann doll, a toy horn, blocks, and shells. To complete the activity, mix in a number of objects that were not in the story illustrations and are probably not part of a child's bedtime routine.

Make the colorful basket the center of attention in your circle. Ask the children how you decided what to put in the basket. Write a list of their ideas. (At the end of the activity, come back to the list. Did it include your three groups?) Let the children each take from the basket one item to hold. Tell them they are going to help you sort the objects into three piles. If they are holding something they remember seeing in the story Ten, Nine, Eight, *they will put their object by the storybook. If they have something that reminds them of bedtime, they will put it by your teddy bear. And if their object belongs in neither pile, they will put it under your chair.*

Count the items in the three groups. Line them up in parallel rows, matching one to one, to make a floor graph. As you compare the sets, use the terms greater than, smaller than, most and least. To end the activity, put only the bedtime group in front of you. Remove one object at a time as you count down from ten to zero. Good night!

A CLOSER LOOK

With each rereading of a story, children gain new understanding. Pause often for a spontaneous flow of oral language as the children share their feelings and observations. Extend the learning process with your own questions in repeated readings of the story.

✳ How many of the nine soft friends are stuffed animals? Which would be the lightest to carry? The heaviest? *(reasoning)*

✳ Do you think the shoes are all the same size? What happened to the missing shoe? *(comprehension)*

✳ Why is the cat looking at the shells? *(reasoning)*

✳ What do you think the words *bedtime routine* mean? *(vocabulary)*

✳ In your opinion, did the daddy and the little girl in *Ten, Nine, Eight* have a bedtime routine? *(application)*

✳ Why do you think the author started with the number ten instead of the number one? *(reasoning)*

✳ Would it have changed the story if she had started with the number one? *(analyzing)*

✳ My favorite picture was on the title page. Did you have a favorite? *(reflecting)*

✳ Which stuffed animal would you take to bed? *(reflecting)*

✳ How did the story make you feel? Would you change anything? *(reflecting)*

STORY TIME EXTENSIONS

Muddle Cuddle by Laurel Dee Gugler

Splash! by Ann Jonas

Ten Old Pails by Nicholas Heller

big fat hen by Keith Baker

I Spy Two Eyes: Numbers in Art selected by Lucy Micklethwait

BALANCED LITERACY ACTIVITIES

POETRY

PRETENDING
When you are in bed and it's cold outside,
do you ever pretend that you have to hide?
Do you curl up your toes?
Do you wrinkle your nose?
Do you make yourself little so none of you shows?

Do you pull the sheet over the whole of your face
and pretend you are in some faraway place?
Mother thinks you are sleeping,
but she does not know
that all tucked in your bed, you have places to go.
Bobbi Katz

HUSHABYE MY DARLING
by Clyde Watson
from *Read-Aloud Rhymes
for the Very Young*
by Jack Prelutsky

INVOLVEMENT

* A loving book, warm pictures, bedtime, and music just go together. Don't overlook the Sharon, Lois & Bram songs mentioned on a preceding page. "Ten in the Bed" and "Go to Sleep/Where's My Pajamas," a lullaby that turns into a rollicking, hoedown-style hunt for bedtime items, are too much fun to miss.

* Include a variety of songs in your rereadings of *Ten, Nine, Eight*. The traditional song "Ten Little Indians" reinforces the emphasis on sets that is found in the story. The music to the familiar folk song "Roll Over! A Counting Song" is included in the storybook. If you are feeling really adventurous, sing the words of *Ten, Nine, Eight* to the tune of "This Old Man." Just keep turning the pages as you sing the melody. The text for the numbers ten through seven will make up the first verse, the numbers six through three will be the second verse, the numbers two and one and then singing the numbers ten through one backward will finish out the last verse. It is surprising how easily the words fit the tune. Make a tape of the children singing their favorite song and put it in a listening center.

* Most children know and enjoy the game "Doggie, Doggie, Where's Your Bone?" Adapt it to the story by putting a shoe under a chair and changing the words to "Ten, nine, eight; Where's your shoe? Somebody took it; I know who!"

INTEGRATION

FOCUSING ON WORDS

* The simple rhythm of *Ten, Nine, Eight* makes it a natural for rereadings. When focusing on language rather than number sets, have the children listen for rhyming words. Write each rhyming word pair on a sentence strip. Draw a boldly colored, jagged line down the middle of the strip to separate the words. Cut them apart. Let the children find the rhyming word pairs by matching the colored jagged edges.

* Another time, have the children listen for, and talk about, the descriptive words. Make a sentence strip book of adjectives. Print one phrase such as *small toes* on each sentence strip for the children to illustrate. Use the same color marker for all the adjectives. Choose a second color for all the nouns. Print the numerals in the top left corner just like in the storybook. Spread out the finished sentence strips for the children to sequence from ten to one. Add a child-illustrated cover and title page and you have a simple reproduction of *Ten, Nine, Eight*. Let each child take the class book home for a night, perhaps to read aloud at bedtime.

MY BEDTIME COUNTING BOOK

Young children are fascinated with the concept of homework. Why not give them the assignment of creating their own bedtime counting books? Prepare a small blank book for each child to take home with a brief note to parents. Each child will study her bedroom and decide what she would like to say good night to. Then she will draw a set of ten objects on the first page, nine on the second, and so on until she reaches the number one and says *Good night* on the last page. Parents can label the sets on each page. Have the children bring their *Ten, Nine, Eight* books to school to share before the counting books become a part of their bedtime routines.

A COUNTING SONG

In *Roll Over! A Counting Song*, Merle Peek has illustrated the old American folksong "Roll Over." Author Mordecai Gerstein uses amusing animals and adjectives in his delightful version of the same bedtime favorite.

After singing and dramatizing the words, have the children write a class innovation. Using watercolor paints, crayons, or a collage of colored scraps, have them make a quilt on a bed for each page. The faces of the children (or animals or teddy bears) will be just above the quilt. Print the words *Roll Over, Roll Over!* on the left side of each page. Under a folded flap on the right, print the words *And one fell out.* The number of children's faces above the quilt will decrease from ten to one on succeeding pages, with the last child saying *Good night!* on the last page.

Joyce Dunbar's *Ten Little Mice,* a beautifully illustrated story of mice leaving one by one to find a safe mouse hole, can be adapted to the same countdown innovation. Your children will also enjoy *Ten Little Animals,* a delightful story by Laura Jane Coats. She has used ten different animals and a rhyming text to expand the well-known favorite "Five little monkeys jumping on the bed; One fell off and bumped his head." In *One Bear All Alone,* Caroline Bucknall has combined cuddly teddy bears, bedtime, counting, and a rhyming text. Each book offers integrated learning at its best.

A SORTING TUB

Fill a colorful plastic tub with small objects. Have the children sort the objects, making a set for each numeral, such as ten Legos, nine buttons, eight crayons, and so on. Add laminated numeral cards, including zero, to the tub. Ask the children what they found in the tub to match to the zero. Were there any elephants? Then there were zero elephants! Any chocolate cakes? Then there were zero chocolate cakes. As the children take turns sorting the sets, they will be eager to tell you what they found in the tub for the set of zero.

EVERYDAY LEARNING ACTIVITIES

Positive parenting; developmental learning activities; and a warm, nurturing environment are major factors in a child's academic success and lifetime learning.

Try not to compare your days, your parenting, or your caregiving to others who appear never to have a bad day. Remember that children have different temperaments and parents have different frustration levels and problems. There are no perfect parents, caregivers, or children anywhere. Sometimes we just have to tell children that we are sorry we yelled or made a poor decision, but that doesn't mean we stopped loving them. Smile at the bad days and tell the world about the good ones, especially when the children can hear your words. It will be a message on their inner tape recorders that they will hear over and over. Mornings are always new beginnings.

✳ Draw simple stick figures of each part of a child's bedtime routine, such as brushing his teeth, taking a bath, getting a drink (one drink!), putting on his pajamas, and reading a book. Print the phrase at the bottom of each page. It is important that children see words written down. You could be really clever and take photos of the child or have him help cut pictures of a toothbrush, soap, pajamas, and so on out of magazines. Paste the pictures on paper or index cards. Put the child's name on the front and call it his very own bedtime book. Have the child sequence the pictures in just the order he wants to get ready for bed, with the understanding that when you have finished the last picture, it is time to say good night. It simply takes the power play out of getting into bed. The pictures say we are done! Why not make the last picture one of the child in bed with his favorite stuffed animal? *(sequencing)*

✳ Review all the positive and fun things that happened during the day, perhaps when a child is in bed and you are quietly talking. Begin with morning, then afternoon, then evening. Ask questions like, "Do you remember what you ate for breakfast?" or "What did we do after your lunch today?" This will encourage a child to think in sequence as well as end the day on a happy note. By always following the morning, afternoon, and evening pattern, your child will be practicing first, middle, and last. *(concept of time)*

✳ After reading the loving storybook *Ten, Nine, Eight* by Molly Bang, help a child make her own bedtime book. Staple the pages together, decide on your routine, and write the numerals and phrases on the pages such as:

10—brush teeth	6—a bedtime story	3—lights out
9—wash face and hands	5—a hug	2—count down 10–1
8—pajamas	4—a kiss	1—good night!
7—drink of water		

✳ Mix a small amount of food coloring and milk together. With a small paintbrush, paint a numeral on a slice of bread. Then toast and butter it for a nice surprise! Have a child count out a matching set of carrot curls or cereal to enjoy eating with the magic number toast. *(numerals and sets)*

✳ Give a child a large, mixed-up assortment of buttons, old keys, rocks, nails, nuts and bolts, crayons, Legos, whatever! Challenge her to think of ways to organize all the objects. Then have her think of containers such as muffin tins to hold the sorted items. *(classifying)*

The Three Billy Goats Gruff

by Paul Galdone

* Letter-sound relationships
* Story structure
* Choral reading
* Position words

* Model writing
* Process writing
* Math/science concepts
* Oral storytelling

SETTING THE STAGE

Instantly singable songs and the appealing rhyme and rhythm of finger plays will encourage children to be involved in story time.

"Once I Saw Three Goats" by Sharon, Lois & Bram, *Singin' and Swingin'*

"Bill Grogan's Goat" recorded on *Disney's Silly Songs*
(A funny song about a hungry goat and the trouble he gets himself into)

OVER THE HILLS

Over the hills and far away	*(bounce hands)*
We skip and run and laugh and play.	*(clap hands)*
Smell the flowers	*(sniff a flower)*
and fish the streams,	*(cast a fishing line)*
Lie in the sunshine	*(sleep, cheek resting on hand)*
and dream sweet dreams.	

THE ANT HILL

Once I saw an ant hill	
With no ants about.	*(closed fist)*
So I said, "Dear little ants,	
Won't you please come out?"	*(hands cupped to mouth)*
Then, as if they'd heard me call,	
One, two, three, four, five	*(bring fingers out)*
Came out—and that was all!	*(big shrug)*

FIRST READING

The name of our story today is . . . why don't I let you read it? What animal do you see on the cover? How many are there? You've already named two of the words in the title. Another word is Billy and the goats' last name is Gruff. Can you put those words together to make a title? Let's read it: *The Three Billy Goats Gruff.*

Tell me all the words that come to mind when you see a picture of a goat. Where do you think these three goats are? What do you predict is going to happen? This story has been a favorite for many, many years. In fact, your grandma and grandpa probably read this book when they were children. I imagine they said the words right out loud. You may join me with the TRIP, TRAP, TRIP, TRAP and the ugly troll's roars if you like. I wonder if *The Three Billy Goats Gruff* will be one of your favorite stories, too.

GETTING INVOLVED

I wonder if the author wanted us to change our voices when we read *The Three Billy Goats Gruff.* Why do you think he said the tiniest Billy Goat Gruff had a very small voice? Show me what you imagine his voice sounded like when he said, "Oh, it's only I." Do you think his hooves made a very small sound, too? Show me what the second goat's voice sounded like when he said, "Oh, it's only I." Were his hooves louder? I know you can't wait to sound like the voice of the third Billy Goat Gruff! Did his hooves make the loudest sound of all?

I think you are ready to tell the story yourselves. Look around the room and find something we can use for the bridge. Where do you think the meadow should be? Remember, you are all storytellers, so roar with the troll and make the bridge creak and groan when the goats cross over. Be sure to change your voices from little to big to biggest. I will nod to someone to be the youngest Billy Goat Gruff or the second or third to go over the bridge. When we get to the end of the story and say, "Snip, snap, snout, This tale's told out," you may lie down in the meadow to rest.

A CLOSER LOOK

With each rereading of a story, children gain new understanding. Pause often for a spontaneous flow of oral language as the children share their feelings and observations. Extend the learning process with your own questions in repeated readings of the story.

* What would you tell your grandma and grandpa about *The Three Billy Goats Gruff?* *(reflecting)*

* Tell me how you felt when you saw the ugly troll. *(reflecting)*

* Do you think the goats had a plan when they told the troll to wait for the next goat? *(analyzing)*

* Imagine you were the troll. Would you have waited for the third Billy Goat Gruff? *(reflecting)*

* Would you like to have the name Gruff for your last name? *(reflecting)*

* I used to think it was the goats that said, "TRIP, TRAP, TRIP, TRAP." Were you surprised it was the bridge talking? *(reflecting)*

* Why do you think the words "TRIP, TRAP, TRIP, TRAP" are printed with capital letters? *(reasoning)*

* Why are the troll's words printed with capital letters? *(reasoning)*

* Tell me why it was important to the goats to go up the hillside to the fine meadow. *(comprehension)*

* Would the story be different if we changed the order of the goats going across the bridge? *(application)*

* Where in the story did you think, "Oh, I just love that part"? *(reflecting)*

* What do you suppose happened to the ugly troll after it fell into the rushing river? *(reasoning)*

* Do you think the words "So snip, snap, snout, This tale's told out" were a good story ending? *(evaluating)*

STORY TIME EXTENSIONS

Goat's Trail by Brian Wildsmith

Anno's Counting Book by Mitsumasa Anno

Goldilocks and the Three Bears retold and illustrated by Jan Brett

Animal Numbers by Bert Kitchen

Over in the Meadow illustrated by Ezra Jack Keats

BALANCED LITERACY ACTIVITIES

POETRY

OVER IN A MEADOW
Over in a meadow, in the sand, in the sun,
Lived an old mother frog and her little froggie one.
"Croak!" said the mother; "I croak," said the one,
So they croaked and were glad in the sand, in the sun.

Over in a meadow, in a stream so blue,
Lived an old mother fish and her little fishies two.
"Swim!" said the mother; "We swim," said the two,
So they swam and were glad in the stream so blue.

Folk rhyme

INVOLVEMENT

DRAMATIZATION

✳ With the familiar, predictable pattern of *The Three Billy Goats Gruff,* choral reading will be spontaneous. The children are probably already joining you in the rhythmic repetition of "TRIP, TRAP, TRIP, TRAP" and the voice of the troll saying, "Who's that tramping over my bridge?" Add to the fun and keep children listening intently by dividing the children into five groups, one group to be the voice of the bridge saying "TRIP, TRAP," a group to respond for each of the three goats, and one group to be the angry voice of the troll.

✳ *The Three Billy Goats Gruff* presents an ideal setting for creative dramatics. The language will come to life as the children role-play the characters. Have the children find a place in your room for a meadow, a river, and a bridge made from blocks, boxes, or a table. Provide materials in your art center for children to create hats or headband goat ears and a wild hat or an ugly nose for the troll. Because children often gain confidence dramatizing parts in pairs, create two props for each character. Leave the props in your dramatic play center. Add paper and pencil to the center to encourage children to use written language in their play.

INTEGRATION

ON THE WAY TO THE MEADOW

To tell the story on your bulletin board, pencil sketch on white paper a simple outline of hills, a meadow, and a bridge for children to paint. Use the medium of tear art to make the troll, goats, flowers, trees, fish, and rocks to add to the scene. (You probably won't lack for volunteers to make the snaggle-tooth troll!) Have the children recall position words used in the story—*in the valley, up the hillside, over a river,* and so on. Print the phrases on sentence strips for the children to add to the mural. Be sure to keep pointers nearby for children to point to the print in paired or independent reading.

A RETELLING

The lovable story illustrations of the three goats make them appear to walk off the pages and into your room. Your children will be just waiting to tell a story about them. Perhaps they will think of first names for the goats and the unhappy troll before retelling the story in their own words. Guide the children through the retelling by asking a sequence of questions. Begin with, What happened at the beginning of the story? As the children answer, help them say the words in a short, clear sentence. Write the sentence on a story chart, modeling the writing process as the children watch. Continue in the same manner with the following questions: What happened at the end? What happened in the middle of the story? What important event(s) happened between the beginning and the middle? What happened between the middle and the end of the story? Model for the children how to edit their story, inserting and deleting words on the story chart until it is just right. Print one sentence of text on each page of a class book or wall story for the children to illustrate. In independent reading, child-authored stories are often chosen over the originals because of the simple, familiar text.

FLIP, FLOP, FLIP, FLOP

To write an innovation of *The Three Billy Goats Gruff,* brainstorm with the children about other animals that could be the main characters in the story. Talk about changing the setting and the characters, for example, three wandering seals could FLIP, FLOP, FLIP, FLOP over a bridge to an island on the other side. After allowing plenty of time for oral language (children

often talk in *paragraphs!*), help them develop the plot, one sentence at a time, as you record the story on a chart. After many rereadings, let the children decide how to reproduce the story.

THE LETTER G

Letter-sound relationships have meaning for children when they are taught in the context of familiar words. Write the word *goat* in the middle of a web. Ask the children for the name of the letter *g*, then the sound the letter makes. Talk about any of their names or words they see in print that begin with the letter *g*. As you add new words to the web, talk about the sound the letter makes. In the same manner, use the word *gruff* to teach the consonant combination of *gr*. Add new words as children discover them in their reading, writing, and listening experiences.

MESSAGES

Children love to receive messages, anywhere, anytime. Begin every day with a message on a message board for your class. Encourage them also to write messages, perhaps in their daily journal writing.

Dear Troll,
Let's be friends. We need a guard at the gate to the meadow. Will you please come?

The Three Billy Goats Gruff

Surprise your children one morning with an exciting message that there is a special-delivery letter for them in the office. You won't want to leave anyone behind as you pick up your letter—a scroll-like, ribbon-tied message from the three billy goats gruff to the troll. Read the letter slowly, waiting for the children to read as many words as they can. Then, as a class, write an answer from the surprised troll to his new friends, the three goats.

LETTERS FROM STORYBOOK CHARACTERS

Just as your children delighted in the letter from the billy goats to the troll, so will they enjoy the letters in some endearing storybooks. Read the letters about an imaginary whale written by a child to her teacher, *Dear Mr. Blueberry,* in a story by James Simon. A little girl writes letters to befriend a bear hiding under her stairs in Joanna Harrison's *Dear Bear.* In *The Gardener* by Sarah Stewart, a girl describes in her letters a cantankerous uncle whom she lovingly transforms. Read also the story of a special party invitation in *A Letter to Amy* by Ezra Jack Keats and the tall, tall tale of *The Long, Long Letter,* written by Elizabeth Spurr. Storybooks often give birth to children's imaginative ideas in writing. Perhaps they will spontaneously write a letter to someone special.

THREE BY THREE

Ask the children why they think the number three is the most often used number in folktales and nursery rhymes—three little kittens, three blind mice, three little pigs, and many more. Have fun with the number three in the context of stories and poetry in your shared reading. Introduce your children to the fascinating watercolor art of *Anno's Counting Book.* Anno, who says every child is a natural mathematician, has interwoven sets of numbers into a countryside scene that changes with the seasons. See how many sets of threes your children can discover in Anno's interesting picture. Have available more richly illustrated number books such as Bert Kitchen's *Animal Numbers* and the ingenious *From One to One Hundred* by Teri Sloat.

EVERYDAY LEARNING ACTIVITIES

Positive parenting; developmental learning activities; and a warm, nurturing environment are major factors in a child's academic success and lifetime learning.

Staying on task is a skill every child must develop for successful learning. Encourage a child to practice that skill at home by allowing her to do more and more things independently. Expect her to finish a job you give her to do. Require her to put toys away before bedtime. She will learn to stay on task if you begin with small jobs you know she can succeed in. Then build up to larger tasks. The more you praise a child, the harder she will try and the better she will feel about herself. By participating in family chores, a child will know she is a valuable member of the family. She will learn the esteem-building lesson that the family functions more smoothly when she does her part. It's nice to be counted on! Encourage her to also stay on task when eating, or playing, or looking at a book. Reading requires a child to attend to the end.

✳ The repeated patterns of words in *The Three Billy Goats Gruff* by Paul Galdone invite children to join in the fun of the story. Build a bridge out of blocks, pillows, chairs, or bodies. Talk about how the voices changed for each of the three goats going over the bridge. Ask what the troll's voice sounded like as he sat under the bridge. Add a sound effect like knocking every time you repeat the words "trip trap trip trap." Then have the children choose parts and have fun acting out the story. *(story participation)*

✳ Make an obstacle course using furniture. Children can jump over a pillow, crawl under a table, hop around a stool, walk backward to a chair, and so on. Play "Follow the Leader," with the children taking turns being the leader. (Include only those activities you normally allow.) *(perceptual motor)*

✳ Make cookies together. Place different sizes of dough on the cookie sheet. Talk about size when baking or eating the cookies. Group them according to big, bigger, biggest. *(comparative sizes)*

✳ Blow bubbles together. Talk about big, bigger, and biggest; first, second, and third; or small, middle, and large. Watch the bubbles float over and under things. Do bubbles move differently when a fan is on or when you blow them outside? *(comparative sizes)*

✳ Gather a collection of balls. Have children sort them according to weight and size. Ask them to predict how the balls will move down a simple ramp made of cardboard, books, or pieces of wood. Will some balls move faster than others? What makes the biggest difference, the ramp or the ball? *(comparisons)*

✳ Make a tape of you and a child reading together *The Three Billy Goats Gruff*. By pointing to the familiar, repetitious words on each page as she listens to the tape, the child will understand that print carries a message and that reading is fun. *(reading skills)*

✳ Encourage a child to retell *The Three Billy Goats Gruff* in her own words. She will learn to organize her thoughts, put things in proper order, and speak clearly. Even the troll would be proud! *(sequencing)*

To Market, To Market

by Anne Miranda

TEACHING FOCUS

* Cultural diversity
* Story structure
* Parts of speech
* Math/science concepts
* Phonemic awareness
* Mini language lessons
* Vocabulary
* Nonfiction

SETTING THE STAGE

Instantly singable songs and the appealing rhyme and rhythm of finger plays will encourage children to be involved in story time.

"Let's Go to Market" by Greg and Steve, *We All Live Together, Vol. 5*

"Mrs. Murphy's Chowder" by Nancy Cassidy, *KidsSongs 2*
(A silly lady puts wacky things into her chowder)

TO MARKET TO MARKET

To market, to market,	*(walk feet forward)*
to buy a fat pig,	*(arms round in front)*
Home again, home again, Jiggety jig.	*(walk feet backward)*
To market, to market,	*(walk forward)*
To buy a fat hog,	*(arms round in front)*
Home again, home again, Jiggety jog.	*(walk backward)*
To market, to market,	*(walk forward)*
To buy a plum bun,	*(hands cupped)*
Home again, home again,	*(walk backward)*
Market is done.	*(sit down)*

MAKING SOUP

Chop, chop, chippety chop!	*(clap hands to beat)*
Cut off the bottom and cut off the top.	*(clap low, clap high)*
What we have left we'll put in the pot.	*(gather up and dump)*
Chop, chop, chippety chop!	*(clap hands to beat)*

FIRST READING

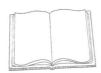

I love this book! The lady in the story is hilarious and she makes me chuckle right out loud. Tell me what makes you smile when you look at the cover. Do you think you would like to be in the store when this funny lady goes shopping? In the story, she turns a simple visit to the supermarket into utter chaos. What do you think is going to happen?

The name of the story is *To Market, To Market*. The illustrator, Janet Stevens, is a Caldecott Honor artist. Ms. Stevens has done something clever in her pictures. Did you notice that part of the picture on the cover is black and white, almost like a collage of black and white photographs? Why do you suppose the artist did that? Tell me what becomes important in the picture. Now look at the picture of the parking lot on the dedication page—black and white again, with just one spot of color. Where do your eyes go in the picture?

Now let's look at the shopping lady on the title page. What do you notice? Do you think those fat purple shoes will be important in the story? Notice where they are on the very next page, the copyright page, and the next page and the next! Those shoes seem to have a life of their own in the story.

GETTING INVOLVED

Look who just came into our room pushing a shopping cart. It's the zany shopping lady! She's wearing that silly hat with the red flower, and the wild flowered dress and the blue coat. Look at the purple glasses and the big black purse. Sure enough, there are the purple shoes! Is it the same lady who went shopping at the supermarket? Why do you think she is carrying the storybook *To Market, To Market*? Now this is exciting! She is going to read the story to us herself.

A CLOSER LOOK

With each rereading of a story, children gain new understanding. Pause often for a spontaneous flow of oral language as the children share their feelings and observations. Extend the learning process with your own questions in repeated readings of the story.

✳ Do you think the author knew the Mother Goose rhyme "To Market, To Market"? *(reasoning)*

✳ In your opinion, was the color purple important in the story? *(evaluating)*

✳ Do you suppose that is why the artist used purple letters in the title? *(reflecting)*

✳ Tell me why you think the purple shoes always appear in the top left corner of the page. *(analyzing)*

✳ Why are the words "THIS IS THE LAST STRAW!" in capital letters? *(analyzing)*

✳ What do you think the woman's voice sounded like when she said those words? *(reflecting)*

✳ I noticed more words in the story written in the same bright red capital letters. Why do you think they were capitals? *(reasoning)*

✳ Why did the lady go shopping wearing just one purple shoe? *(comprehension)*

✳ Would your mother do that? *(reflecting)*

✳ I love the picture of the lady dancing and singing with the duck on her head. Which picture did you like? *(evaluating)*

✳ In your opinion, what was the funniest part of the story? *(evaluating)*

✳ Would you agree that making hot soup for lunch was a good idea? *(evaluating)*

✳ If you could write words for the last picture, what would you write? *(reflecting)*

STORY TIME EXTENSIONS

Market Day by Eve Bunting

Uno, Dos, Tres: One, Two, Three by Pat Mora

The Market Lady and the Mango Tree by Pete and Mary Watson

A Fairy Went A-Marketing by Rose Fyleman

The Seven Silly Eaters by Mary Ann Hoberman

BALANCED LITERACY ACTIVITIES

POETRY

SUPERMARKET, SUPERMARKET

Supermarket, supermarket,
shelves piled high
with brand-new products
for you to buy:

Vegetable soapflakes,
filtertip milk,
frozen chicken wings ready to fly,

shreddable edible paper towels,
banana detergent,
deodorant pie.

Eve Merriam

LITTLE SEEDS

Little seeds we sow in spring,
growing while the robins sing,
give us carrots, peas and beans,
tomatoes, pumpkins, squash and greens.

And we pick them,
one and all,
through the summer,
through the fall.

Winter comes, then spring, and then
little seeds we sow again.

Else Holmelund Minarik

INVOLVEMENT

EVERY CHILD IS A STORYTELLER

Anne Miranda's story is probably one of the most entertaining read-alouds your children will experience all year. You can spend no better time responding to *To Market, To Market* than just laughing and talking together. Every rereading will be more fun than the last if the children can *talk* about the zany lady and her unruly animals. Conversations allow children to think out loud about stories and to make connections to their own lives. They undoubtedly will have stories to tell about shopping carts and funny ladies, perhaps even purple shoes!

JOINING IN

Pause often for a cloze activity as you read, letting the children fill in a rhyming word or phrase. Another time, let the children respond antiphonally. One group will say with you the beginning phrase, "To market, to market, to buy a red HEN." The other group will join in on "Uh-oh! That pig left the pen." Continue the antiphonal reading to the end of the story. Participation causes children to internalize book language.

SHOPPING WITH THE LADY

Children have a natural ability for drama because they are pretenders. Have the children make and stuff construction paper animals and grocery items. Put in the center of the circle a child-size wagon or shopping cart just waiting to be filled. As you narrate the story, pause each time you say the words "To market, to market." A child will pick up an animal and put it in the shopping cart until all the animals are in. Now it's time to take them out. Beginning with the words, "The PIG's in the kitchen," a child will take out an animal and put it somewhere in the room. The cart will be empty just in time to make room for POTATOES and some ripe red TOMATOES. Then home again, home again with the vegetables and into the pot for soup!

INTEGRATION

A SENSE OF STORY

Dramatizing the sequence of events in *To Market, To Market* is a natural starting point in helping children develop a sense of story. Children learn that stories have a beginning, which presents the characters and sometimes the problem; a middle, which is a turning point incident in the story; and an ending, which resolves the problem. The beginning, middle, and ending of *To*

Market, To Market are easy to recognize. Ask the children to identify the setting where the action takes place. Then list on chart paper the chaotic characters of the story and the important descriptive words. Let the children decide how to create a colorful mural of the story characters; the setting; and the beginning, middle, and end of the story plot.

PLUMP GOOSE ON THE LOOSE

* *Noun and Adjective Matching:* Part of the appeal of Anne Miranda's story is her wonderful use of language. To show the importance of her descriptive words, read a few paragraphs of the story, omitting the adjectives. Then using one color, print on separate short sentence strips the names of the animals. Using a second color, print the descriptive words on separate strips. Place all the words randomly in the pockets of a pocket chart. Have the children match the adjectives and nouns as they appear in the story.

* *Rhyming Word Pairs:* Using a third color, print on sentence strips the words that rhyme with each animal's name. Place them also in the pocket chart for the children to match and rhyme, such as PIG and jig, HEN and pen, GOOSE and loose. You are presenting on one chart the skills of word recognition, parts of speech, and rhyming sounds.

* *An Adjective Mobile:* Have the children brainstorm more words to describe each animal. Place the name of an animal on the top of a coat hanger and suspend on a piece of ribbon the additional adjectives.

* *Word Families:* In another mini language lesson, choose a single word such as HEN. Say the sound of *H* (the onset or initial consonant sound) and the sound of *en* (the rime or ending sound). Write *en* on a chart and have the children make a list of words that rhyme with HEN. Hearing and seeing words that rhyme helps children learn phonemes, the small segments of sound that make up language. Follow the same pattern of identifying sounds with the words COW and GOOSE.

OBSERVATION JOURNALS

Every math and science center needs available and inviting writing tools. On a number of consecutive days, put in the science center something the lady in the story purchased at the market. Let the children study it under a magnifying glass or a microscope and measure it with a measuring tape. Have each child sketch the object in his observation journal and write a description of what he has observed.

Let the children take turns being reporters. Incorporate their journal observations into your daily news time.

By recording what they have learned in observation journals, children practice note taking, observation, and process writing skills. As a class, discuss what the children have learned through discovery and journaling. Compile class observations by having each child write about and illustrate one fact from his journal. Edit the writing because the facts will be displayed for others to read. Mount the pictures and facts on colorful backgrounds and exhibit them in your science area. Reading and writing take place all day in all subject areas when words have meaning.

A SHOPPING LIST

"I'm hungry, I'm cranky—now what will I do? To market, to market, to buy . . ." As the children name the items the funny lady shopped for, write them on a list. Then using buddy drawing, have the children copy the words and draw the items on a long Shopping List. Model for them the skills of making their drawings large, filling the space, stroking in one direction, and boldly outlining with markers.

GROWING VEGETABLE SOUP

The gentle poem "Little Seeds" is a perfect accompaniment to the bold, vividly illustrated *Growing Vegetable Soup* by Lois Ehlert. (Turn to the full-color Inquiry insert to see children's magnificent illustrations of the poem "Little Seeds.") In both the poem and the story, children plant seeds and "watch over them and weed until the vegetables are ready for us to pick." There are many lists to write from the storybook—tools for work; names of the seeds and sprouts; how to care for the plants; vegetables ready to pick; and finally, the preparations needed to "cook them into vegetable soup!"

Make plans for cooking your own soup in the classroom. From your Shopping List, have each child choose a vegetable to bring from home, ready to chop and put in the cooking pot. Don't forget the rice and spices. Will the children invite to lunch the zany lady who came into the room pushing the shopping cart? Perhaps she will be included when you tally the results to the question, *Did you like the soup?*

TO MARKET TO MARKET TO BUY . . .

Have the children pretend they accompanied the lady on her hilarious shopping trip. What one item in the store would they want to buy? Make another list, this time recording their choices. With large pieces of paper and watercolor paint, let each child paint the food she wants to buy. Then work together to make a bulletin board. On large paper, outline, measure, and draw the lines and wheels of a shopping cart to put everything in. Cover the metal lines of the cart with silver tape. Label the children's food before you pile it all in the impressive shopping cart. Now, where can you add those purple shoes to your attractive bulletin board? A classroom is always made more inviting when children's art says, "This is a happy place!"

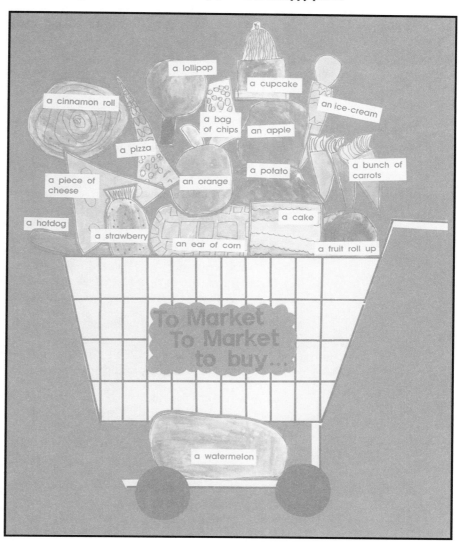

MARKETS OF MANY LANDS

Market! by Ted Lewin is a beautifully illustrated book of international marketplaces from Morocco to the New York waterfront. People come to market to sell what they grow, catch, or make in their villages. An African village market is the setting of *The Market Lady and the Mango Tree* by Pete and Mary Watson. In Pat Mora's *Uno, Dos, Tres: One, Two, Three,* two sisters shop for Mama's birthday presents in a colorful Mexican market. In *Saturday Sancocho* by Leyla Torres, clever Mama Ana trades her eggs at the marketplace for ingredients to make sancochos. Making a Venn diagram of any of the books about other cultures would be a fascinating study.

EVERYDAY LEARNING ACTIVITIES

Positive parenting; developmental learning activities; and a warm, nurturing environment are major factors in a child's academic success and lifetime learning.

Lighten up! You desperately need a sense of humor with little ones. A child has a tremendous amount of energy and persistence. She probably can outlast you on everything! Be careful about turning little things into challenges. Try defusing a potential power play with a funny face or goofy words or a nonsensical song. A child will giggle with delight at your silliness. The laughter will refresh both of you as it swings wide the door of cooperation.

Choose your battles. You do not have to win them all. Good discipline does not mean keeping a child totally subservient. If you hold the reins too tightly, she simply cannot grow up. Some choices are absolutely essential to her gaining independence. It really will not matter down the road if she demanded a blue cup every day for a month or insisted that you stop singing in the car when a tape was playing. Refuse to let everyday battles take on absurd proportions. When you ask for a behavior, it is up to *you* to follow through and be sure the child obeys. However, when you use humor and laughter to dispel tension, you will be better able to teach the important lessons.

* *To Market, To Market* by Anne Miranda is an example of an inviting storybook that a child can read by herself. You want her to gain the skill of telling a story in her imagination as she looks at the pictures. If the child reads the story aloud, let her record it on a tape recorder. Then provide a large sheet of paper and let the child illustrate her own story as you play back the tape. *(storytelling)*

* Writing is a natural way for a young child to learn language. Pretend to be the silly lady in *To Market, To Market* and write a grocery list as the child watches. Let her help you check things off when you shop. Write other lists—a plan for the day, jobs to be done, things to buy, children to invite to a party, reminder notes. Read lists often with children. You are teaching them that print is an important part of our daily lives. *(words in print)*

* Music feeds a child's brain. The roadways of learning that classical music create in the brain are the same pathways of learning a child will use for critical thinking skills. Play classical music, such as selections from Mozart, Beethoven, and Vivaldi, while your child is building, reading, painting, eating, playing. *(brain development)*

* Building blocks are the ultimate creative toys. Ask a child to tell you something about what she has built. Write a sentence or two, date it, hang the words on the blocks, and take a picture of the child sitting by her creation. That's one for the photo album. All construction play is the foundation of math and spatial skills, a reason to be sure girls are as involved in planning, building, and measuring as boys. *(math skills)*

* Rather than putting everything precious out of reach and out of sight, hold a delicate object for a child to study. Talk about why the item is valuable and breakable. Let the child draw it, talk about it, or create an image of it with clay or play dough. You are teaching a child to be perceptive. To see art everywhere in life, plan visits to an art gallery, a concert, a ballet, a puppet presentation, a children's theater. Most important, talk about the experiences afterward. *(artful experiences)*

Tough Boris

by Mem Fox

* Identifying feelings
* Letter-sound relationships
* Mini language skills
* Math/science skills
* Parts of speech
* Model writing/Process writing
* Vocabulary
* A family activity

SETTING THE STAGE

Instantly singable songs and the appealing rhyme and rhythm of finger plays will encourage children to be involved in story time.

"Pirate Song," recorded by Bill Harly, *Big, Big World*
(A vigorous song about a pirate's life, full of humor and gusto!)

"Percival the Parrot" by Hap Palmer, *Sally the Swinging Snake*
(Great tune and rhythm with children moving front/back/side/up/down/circle around)

A PIRATE

A pirate looked out from the top of a tree	*(hand above eyes)*
I think I see an island said he	
I must have a ship	*(outline ship in air)*
I must have a crew	*(point to children)*
To sail to the island in the sea.	*(hands glide ahead)*

A pirate climbed down from the top of a tree	*(hands climb down)*
There's treasure on the island said he	*(digging motion)*
I must have a ship	*(outline ship in air)*
I must have a crew	*(point to children)*
To sail to the island in the sea.	*(hands glide ahead)*

THE SEA

Behold the wonders of the mighty deep	*(arms stretch wide)*
Where crabs and lobsters learn to creep,	*(fingers creep)*
And where fishes learn to swim	*(palms together, wiggle)*
and clumsy sailors tumble in.	*(hands tumbling motion)*
(Repeat, changing to pirates, children)	

FIRST READING

Does the cover of this book make you want to look inside? Tell me all the words that come to your mind when you see a pirate. What do you predict will happen in the story? It seems to me there is always a parrot and a map in a pirate story. Why would that be? The author, Mem Fox, has written a delightful story about a pirate named Tough Boris. Kathryn Brown, the illustrator, has told so much of the story in her wonderful pictures that the author didn't need to write many words.

Let's read the pictures of *Tough Boris*. The mysterious tale begins on the title page. The pirates have left their ship and are rowing toward land. What is Tough Boris holding in his hand? On the dedication page, you can see someone is watching from the top of a cliff. Who do you think the boy is? What is the black case he is holding beside him? As we turn the pages, look at each page carefully for story clues. Be watchful for the boy and the black case for they tell a story too. Then we are going to begin again and look for the parrot in every picture. He squawks and talks to Tough Boris through the whole story because he sees things the pirates don't see. You can discover a lot about a story by reading the illustrations.

GETTING INVOLVED

Do you wonder who buried the treasure and drew the map the pirates found? I noticed the map had a colorful border around it, so someone must have taken a lot of time to draw it. What did you notice? Do you think the pirates could have found the treasure without the map?

Now it's your turn to be pirates. I have hidden some treasure here in our room for you to find. Pretend to climb down the rope ladder on the side of your pirate ship. Careful now as you step into the dinghy and row the little boat to land. When you climb out, be sure to put your shovel and pickax on your shoulder. Pirates always carried them. Walk about slowly and stealthily (what do you think that means?). Pretend to dig with your shovel any place in the sand where you think the treasure might be hidden. Count as you dig five holes in five different places in our room. Then come sit down and tell us what you found.

Not one pirate found the treasure I hid. We need to look at my map! Here, the arrows point straight ahead to the bookcase. Now which way do we go? Yes, turn right to the easel. Now the arrows point to the right again, to the art center. Where do we go now? The map tells us to turn left and go to the teacher's desk. Look, there is a big *X* on the bottom drawer. I think we found it! Sure enough, pirate gold—the kind we can eat right now while we listen to *Tough Boris* one more time.

A CLOSER LOOK

With each rereading of a story, children gain new understanding. Pause often for a spontaneous flow of oral language as the children share their feelings and observations. Extend the learning process with your own questions in repeated readings of the story.

* Do you wonder where Tough Boris got the treasure map? *(reflecting)*
* Would you agree that the little boy and his black case are an important part of the story? What about the parrot? *(evaluating)*
* Do you think the author wanted us to decide how the pirates got the boy's violin case? *(analyzing)*
* In your opinion, was the boy foolish to stow away on a pirate ship? *(evaluating)*
* Why is the boy climbing up the net while the pirates are fighting over the case? What is a *crow's nest? (comprehension)*
* Was Tough Boris puzzled when he opened the case and saw the violin? *(evaluating)*
* Where is the boy hiding while the pirates search the ship for the violin? *(comprehension)*
* Why do you think the pirates liked the boy's music? *(analyzing)*
* Tell me why you think the boy gave the violin case to Tough Boris. *(evaluating)*
* Do you think the boy was crying when the violin case went into the sea? *(reflecting)*
* I wonder what the boy is thinking when he is standing alone on the sand. *(reflecting)*
* What would you say to the boy? To Tough Boris? *(reflecting)*
* Did the story *Tough Boris* make you change your mind about pirates? *(reflecting)*

STORY TIME EXTENSIONS

Pirates: Robbers of the High Seas by Gail Gibbons
Edward and the Pirates by David McPhail
I Wish I Had a Pirate Suit by Pamela Allen
Maggie and the Pirates by Ezra Jack Keats
Sometimes I Feel Like a Mouse: A Book About Feelings by Jeanne Modesitt

BALANCED LITERACY ACTIVITIES

POETRY

PIRATES
Pirates are nasty
And pirates are mean.
Pirates are smelly
'Cause pirates aren't clean.

Pirates are scary
And pirates are rough.
Pirates aren't gentle
'Cause pirates are tough.

Do pirates have a heart?
Do pirates sometimes cry?
Yes, they have feelings
Just like you and I.
Louise Stuart

THE SAD STORY OF A LITTLE BOY THAT CRIED
Anonymous
from *For Laughing Out Loud*
by Jack Prelutsky

SOMETIMES
by Jack Prelutsky
from *Rainy Rainy Saturday*
by Jack Prelutsky

INVOLVEMENT

✳ *Tough Boris* so brilliantly weaves text and illustrations together that few words are needed to tell the story. Yet those few words are a predictable reading pattern. Divide the children into two groups for antiphonal reading, one group reading with you the initial phrase such as "He was tough" and the second group reading with you the response such as "All pirates are tough." In another reading, add classical music as a background and ask the children if it added to the story. Choral reading lets children explore the *voice* of a story.

✳ Enjoy an upbeat, lighthearted response to *Tough Boris* by singing the following words to the tune of "My Bonnie Lies over the Ocean." Children can keep the rhythm by alternating clapping hands and slapping thighs.

A pirate sails 'round on the ocean.	Pirates fight! Pirates steal!
A pirate sails 'round on the sea.	Pirates sail 'round on the sea, the sea.
A pirate makes his home on the ocean.	Pirates fight! Pirates steal!
A pirate's much tougher than me!	A pirate's much tougher than me!

The children could add additional verses by changing the words in the last line of the chorus to much *scarier,* much *meaner,* and so on.

INTEGRATION

STORYTELLING IN ART

A retelling is an invitation to children to bring to a story *their* thoughts and language. Oral language and art expressions reveal the meaning children have given to the written word. Guide a discussion of what happened in the story at the beginning, the end, the middle, and the events in between. Then take dictation as the children tell in their own words the sequence of events. Model the writing process for them so children hear and see the sound-letter connections. Ask the children where to put capital letters, commas, and periods. Challenge them to move sentences around to retell the story plot accurately and to take out sentences that are not needed. Write the corrected text of the retelling in short sections for the children to illustrate.

Children cannot be rushed into good art; they need unhurried periods of time to create their pictures. Play classical music as the children work because music stimulates learning and creativity. Encourage your artists to make their drawings large and fill the page, adding details to tell the story. Have them outline their figures with black marker before painting the illustrations. Mount the pages of the children's retelling and make a stand-up accordion book to read together often. An art-rich environment is as enjoyable and full of learning as a print-rich environment.

3. *They brought the treasure box and the violin case aboard their ship. The pirates had to pull and drag the treasure box over the rail.*
4. *The pirates did not notice, but Peter snuck on the ship to get his violin back. He climbed up the net and jumped into the crow's nest.*
5. *Three mean and massive pirates were wrestling over the violin case but Tough Boris got it. He opened the case and found Peter's violin. Peter felt sad and scared because he thought Tough Boris would break his violin.*
6. *That night, when most of the pirates were asleep, Peter peeked into Boris's window. Tough Boris was holding the violin and wondering who it belonged to.*

GREEDY AND FEARLESS

Mem Fox used six strong words to describe the pirates. One at a time, as the children watch, write the six adjectives across the top of a chart. As you write, ask them to listen for the beginning, middle, and ending sounds that make up the words. Then talk about the meaning of each adjective. The thoughts that children bring to the words will be unique and varied because of their prior experiences. Write their responses on the chart under each adjective. Have the children create a colorful character web for Tough Boris by surrounding him with their descriptive words. With each rereading of the lists of adjectives, story meaning will grow.

Variation: Write the adjective *tough* on a word card and put it in the first pocket of a pocket chart. In the pocket underneath, place the sentence card *All pirates are tough*. Continue with the other five adjectives and sentences that follow in the story. You have created a retelling, a word study, and an independent reading experience.

OUR FAVORITE CHARACTERS

As the children talk about each of the story characters, they will be sharing discoveries and learning from one another. Ask them to decide on a favorite character and to have a reason for their choice. You are encouraging them to respond individually to *Tough Boris*. Arrange their responses on an unusual graph that will undoubtedly stretch far beyond one bulletin board.

Tally the children's choices for their favorite character. Draw or use computer art to create a circle graph that shows the percentage of the circle given to each story character. Also make a bar graph with vertical numerals representing the choices for favorite characters on the left and the names of the story characters listed horizontally on the bottom. You are teaching percentages and forms of graphing with eye-appealing visual pictures.

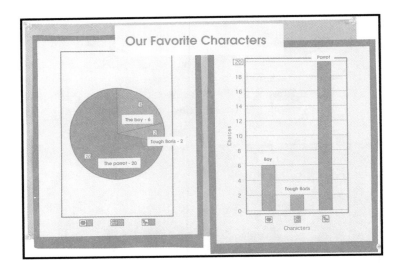

A PIRATE MAP

Look again at the map on the first page of the storybook and ask the children what they see. Talk about the border, the title box, the land and water, the compass, and the *X* for the location of the treasure. Use resource books such as *Pirates: Robbers of the High Seas* by Gail Gibbons to find other pictures of maps. Then, thinking as pirates would think and using colored pencils for detailed drawings, have the children make their own imaginative maps. Next, they are ready to create the treasure.

A TREASURE TROVE

Children will be fascinated with the colorful illustrations of treasure chests and the daily life of "robbers of the sea" in the historical nonfiction book *Pirate* by Richard Platt. Have the children bring from home small boxes they can transform into mysterious treasure chests. Ask families to help find brightly colored fabric, foil, an old lock, brads, anything with which the children can decorate the *outside* of the chest. Together, have them hunt for treasure to hide *inside* the chest, perhaps old jewels, coins, letters, or maps. Imagination is a treasure in itself! Ask also for cotton, colored tissue paper, or velvety fabric to line the inside of the chest.

In the classroom, let each child paint or embellish his chest with his own pirate ideas—drawings of ships, maps, swords and daggers, flags and sails. Seal each chest with a clear, water-based sealant spray and display your treasure trove of chests for all to admire.

MY STORY

Art expressions encourage reading and writing. Let the children decide what they would like to write about. Writing has a purpose when children write from their own experiences and have an audience waiting to hear their stories. Teaching children the concept of audience early on benefits their writing development. Young writers learn to invest in their work and improve their craft when they understand that writing is something to be read and listened to.

PIRATES SOMETIMES CRY

Poetry speaks to a child's imagination. Read the poem "Pirates" by Louise Stuart and give the children time to think and feel and talk about what they have heard. No two children will have the same verbal response to the word images. Talk about how the feelings of pirates are like their own feelings. Poetry lets children safely respond with emotion while they are together in a group. Give them the opportunity to *feel* through art expressions as well, providing a choice of media such as crayon-resist paint wash. Display the illustrated poem in your permanent, yearlong poetry corner. It will surely cheer a child who is having a sad day.

I CRY, TOO

The storybook and the poem will open the door to many discussions about feelings. Let your children move to the text of *Sometimes I Feel Like a Mouse: A Book About Feelings* by Jeanne Modesitt. In the story, a child roars, snuggles, cries, and moves like a variety of animals as he expresses his feelings. Read also *My Many Colored Days* by Dr. Seuss. Each day is described in terms of color and emotions with childlike charm. Children will want to read the rhyming text themselves. Read also Jack Prelutsky's poem "Sometimes." It begins with the poignant words, "Sometimes I simply have to cry, I don't know why, I don't know why."

Children comprehend the meaning of a story when they make connections to their own lives. That is why oral language must surround the language of literature. Encourage the children to talk about times when they feel sad. Rich group conversations extend everyone's understanding and teach children to listen to each other. Let them express their feelings in a colored chalk art response, perhaps while listening to "It's Alright to Cry" sung by Rosy Grier (*Free to Be You and Me* by Marlo Thomas and Friends). Art, as well as music, is a language of feelings.

I WONDER

It is aesthetic reading and writing that captures learners and brings them back to a story. Turn to the last picture in the story of the boy standing alone on the sand. Model for the children your own thoughts: "I wonder if the boy had a family. I wonder if he ever saw the pirates again." Have the children talk about and write their own "I wonder" statements and stories.

The children's questions about pirates may lead to research, which can be organized under the topic headings What We Think We Know about Pirates, What We Want to Know about Pirates, and What We Have Learned about Pirates. (For a model of children's inquiry and research, see the full-color Inquiry insert.)

EVERYDAY LEARNING ACTIVITIES

Positive parenting; developmental learning activities; and a warm, nurturing environment are major factors in a child's academic success and lifetime learning.

Tough Boris was a mean, greedy old pirate—tough as nails, massive, and fearless. Yet when his parrot died, he cried. Author Mem Fox concludes her poignant story with the words "All pirates cry. And so do I." Children's poet, Jack Prelutsky, writes about not knowing why he is feeling sad, yet he simply has to cry. Children want so much to be understood, whether they are sad, angry, or happy. Not only must *we* understand, we must help a *child* understand the feelings that come unbidden into her mind. Identify and validate a child's feelings for her, even before she has language. When you reflect feelings back to her, you are helping her get in touch with the person inside. One of the most demanding jobs of a parent or caregiver is to contain, not erase, the emotions of a child. In so doing, you never ask a child to deny her feelings. To be emotionally healthy, the child must hear repeatedly that her feelings are important. A child who is allowed her own feelings and thoughts will not become dependent on someone else to do her thinking and feeling for her.

✳ Talking about storybooks is as important as reading aloud. Encourage a child to talk about her own feelings as well as those of Tough Boris, the boy, and the pirates. *Sometimes I Feel Like a Mouse: A Book About Feelings* by Jeanne Modesitt and *My Many Colored Days* by Dr. Seuss will also open the door for a child to discuss feelings. *(identifying feelings)*

✳ When you return from an outing of any kind, draw a simple map for a child. Arrows and *X*s could show where you started, went to the right or left or straight ahead, and came home. You are introducing a child to the visual concept of directions on paper and giving her the skills to make her own maps. Bury a secret treasure in the yard and make a colorful map for children to follow to find the treasure, just like Tough Boris. *(spatial skills)*

✳ Dressing up allows children safely to be someone else, to try on other roles for size. Nothing will appeal to children more than dressing up as pirates. Check your dress-up box for scarves that can become bandannas, neck pieces, and sashes. Make capes from pieces of fabric or towels. Add yarn-tied eye patches and cardboard daggers and swords. A child who can *tell* a story in words and in play is preparing for *reading* a story on paper. *(storytelling)*

✳ Make a simple counting book by folding and stapling together a few pages of plain paper. Put one number, an illustration, and the words on each page—1 pirate, 2 parrots, 3 treasure chests, and so on. On separate pieces of paper, have the child make pirate flags to cut out and glue on the pages as lift-up flaps, perhaps over the numerals. *(math concepts)*

✳ Using a brown paper bag and small sponges for each paint color, have a child paint a large Tough Boris face. When the paint is dry, cut through both thicknesses of the paper bag. Staple the edges together, leaving an opening to stuff with tissue paper. Add a craft stick for a handle. A child could choose to make a boy, a parrot, or a pirate ship. Any art is acceptable because the process is more important than the product. Never say to a child, "I can't draw." That implies there is a right and a wrong way to make something. There is never a wrong way to be creative. *(creativity)*

The Very Hungry Caterpillar

by Eric Carle

TEACHING FOCUS

* Letter-sound relationships
* Days of the week
* Nutrition
* A floor graph
* Vocabulary
* Nonfiction
* Math/science concepts
* Structure writing

SETTING THE STAGE

Instantly singable songs and the appealing rhyme and rhythm of finger plays will encourage children to be involved in story time.

"Today Is Monday"—*traditional*
(A catchy, cumulative song featuring a different food for each day of the week. The music notation is included in the storybook *Today Is Monday* by Eric Carle)

"Little Ara Bella Miller" by Sharon, Lois & Bram, *Mainly Mother Goose*

SLEEPY CATERPILLARS
Let's go to sleep the little caterpillars said
As they tucked themselves into their beds.
They will awaken by and by
And each will be a lovely butterfly!

(wiggle fingers)
(fold into hand)
(open hands slowly)
(fly fingers)

THE CATERPILLAR
A caterpillar crawled to the top of a tree.
"I think I'll take a nap," said he.
So—under a leaf he began to creep
To spin a cocoon;
Then he fell asleep.
All winter he slept in his cocoon bed,
Till Spring came along one day and said,
"Wake up, wake up, little sleepyhead.
Wake up, it's time to get out of bed."
So—he opened his eyes that sunshiny day.
Lo! He was a butterfly—and flew away!

(walk fingers up one arm)

(two fingers under other palm)

(hands under cheek)
(wrap hand over the fingers)

(both hands open)

(blink eyes)
(flying motion with arms)

FIRST READING

The name of the story is *The Very Hungry Caterpillar*. It is the only book I know of that has little round holes in it! Eric Carle drew the colorful pictures and he also wrote the words. The story is about a little caterpillar and a very special home he built for himself. But I don't want to spoil the surprise. Let's read!

The compelling sequence and color-splashed pictures will encourage the children to join in on the repetitive phrase, "But he was still hungry."

GETTING INVOLVED

Are you ready for a really big word? It is *metamorphosis*. Say that slowly with me. Metamorphosis means all the changes that happened to the caterpillar from the day of his birth until he became a beautiful butterfly.

We can act out the word metamorphosis. Pretend you are all tiny caterpillars. First, *pop* out of your tiny eggs. Now *stretch* out on your leaves and *rub* your tummies because you are hungry. *Nibble* through one apple, then two pears *(name all the foods in sequence)*. Oh dear, now you all have stomachaches. Better nibble some green leaves and then build cocoons all around yourselves. *Lie* very still and sleep awhile. Now it's time to *chew* a little hole to get out. Look at you! You are beautiful butterflies! *Fly* away and find green leaves to land on. *(Model every action as you lead the children through the body movements.)*

A CLOSER LOOK

With each rereading of a story, children gain new understanding. Pause often for a spontaneous flow of oral language as the children share their feelings and observations. Extend the learning process with your own questions in repeated readings of the story.

* What would you like to say about the story *The Very Hungry Caterpillar? (evaluating)*

* Would you agree that "In the light of the moon a little egg lay on a leaf" was a good beginning to the story? *(evaluating)*

* Did the caterpillar eat more or less fruit each day? *(comprehension)*

* Tell me how the pages changed when the caterpillar ate through the fruit. *(observation)*

* What would happen to the story if we changed the order of the food the caterpillar ate? *(application)*

* Do you think the caterpillar made wise choices of food to eat on Saturday? *(reasoning)*

* Have you ever had a stomachache from eating too much? *(reflecting)*

* Do you know someone like the hungry caterpillar? *(application)*

* Tell me why you think eating a leaf made the caterpillar feel better. *(reasoning)*

* I wonder why it is important for a caterpillar to eat a lot before it builds a cocoon around itself. *(reasoning)*

* Is two weeks a long time? *(comprehension)*

* Tell me what you know about butterfly wings. *(reflecting)*

* What do you think is going to happen all over again? *(analyzing)*

STORY TIME EXTENSIONS

Seven Blind Mice by Ed Young

One Potato: A Counting Book of Potato Prints by Diana Pomeroy

Counting Wildflowers by Bruce McMillan

Frogs Jump by Alan Brooks

The Biggest House in the World by Leo Lionni

BALANCED LITERACY ACTIVITIES

POETRY

LITTLE ARA BELLA MILLER
Little Ara Bella Miller
Had a fuzzy caterpillar.
First it crawled upon her mother,
Then upon her baby brother.
   They said to
   Ara Bella Miller,
   "Put away
   Your caterpillar!"
            Anonymous

FUZZY WUZZY, CREEPY CRAWLY
by Lilian Schulz
from *Real-Aloud Rhymes for the Very Young*
by Jack Prelutsky

ONLY MY OPINION
by Monica Shannon
from *Read-Aloud Rhymes for the Very Young*
by Jack Prelutsky

INVOLVEMENT

A FLANNEL BOARD STORY

✳ Put all your little artists to work making the thirty-two objects in *The Very Hungry Caterpillar,* including the moon, two leaves, the egg, the sun, a small and a large caterpillar, a cocoon, and a butterfly. Provide tagboard, fabric scraps, tissue paper, markers, and a very important paper punch. Back each item with a piece of felt. Spread out the 32 objects in front of the flannel board. As you read the story again, pause often to give time for the children to choose the appropriate object and place it in sequence on the flannel board. The emphasis of the activity will be sequencing the story objects in a left-to-right progression. In the following activity, the emphasis will be matching the food to the days of the week.

✳ Write name cards for the days of the week, modeling for the children the writing process as you think out loud about letters and sounds. Spread out the word cards and story objects from the above activity. Begin with the sentence, "One Sunday morning the warm sun came up and—pop!—out of the egg came a tiny and very hungry caterpillar." Ask a child to find the word card for Sunday and then put next to it the sun, egg, and tiny caterpillar. The children can continue matching the food to each day of the week, working from left to right on the flannel board or on the floor. Remind them to look often at *The Very Hungry Caterpillar,* especially when sequencing Saturday's feast.

Variation: Place small pieces of magnetic tape on the backs of the story objects and word cards to do the activities on a magnetic board.

KALOMP, KALOMP, KALOMP!

For a visual enactment of the story that will absolutely delight your children, gather large pieces of multicolored felt and a green sock. Make from the sock a caterpillar hand puppet long enough to stretch up your arm. Add a red felt mouth, squiggly eyes, and pipe cleaner antennae. From the appropriate colors of felt, cut one red apple, two yellow pears, three purple plums, and so on, ending with the brown cocoon. In the center of each felt object, cut a round hole large enough for the puppet's head to fit through. Make also from felt a multicolored butterfly.

Before beginning the story, put the sequenced pieces of felt in a pile on your lap and prop the book open on an easel stand. Your hands are then free to work the puppet and props. When the caterpillar eats through one apple, pick up the red felt apple and push the puppet through the hole, "Kalomp, kalomp, kalomp! But he was still hungry!" When he eats through two pears, pick up the yellow felt pears one by one. "Kalomp, kalomp, kalomp! But he was still hungry!" Continue to push the felt pieces up your arm until the caterpillar has munched through the green leaf. Then wrap him up in the brown felt cocoon until the moment he nibbles his way out as a beautiful butterfly. Every child in the room will want to "kalomp" the caterpillar through the holes!

INTEGRATION

FEED THE HUNGRY CATERPILLAR

Using a large piece of bulletin board paper, have the children paint a huge caterpillar with twelve body segments. Be sure to put his smiling face on the left. Add to the learning by researching how many feet and eyespots a caterpillar has. Print the story title and the author's name on your bulletin board.

On tagboard, print sets of word cards for the days of the week, the months of the year, and number words, again verbalizing about letter-sound relationships as you write. The children can independently choose a set of cards to read and sequence on the body segments of the very hungry caterpillar.

MY HUNGRY CATERPILLAR

Give each child a piece of white construction paper with the same sentence printed on the bottom, *My hungry caterpillar* _____. After brainstorming about all the things busy little caterpillars do, have each child choose one action word to finish his sentence. Encourage him to depict the hunching or inching or chewing or slithering as he illustrates his sentence. Tear art of sponge paint would make wonderfully bright caterpillars, dressed up with yarn "spines" or pipe cleaner antennae. Have a small group of children create a cover and a title page for a class caption book. Books that children write themselves are the most popular ones in the room.

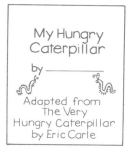   

NUTRITION

Using real food or the felt-backed pieces from *The Very Hungry Caterpillar* (see p. 244), have the children sort the food the caterpillar ate into healthful and not healthful groups. Using a floor graph with two columns, graph the healthful and not healthful food. Discover which has more, which has less, how many more, how many less. The children can also make a picture graph to hang up by drawing the food items on small squares of paper and charting them in two columns on a large piece of bulletin board paper. Brainstorm additional categories for graphing—hot or cold, finger food or silverware food, smooth or rough texture. Encourage the children to think of ways to group food, such as by color, shape, taste, or food section in the supermarket.

LEARNING THROUGH INQUIRY

Children never tire of talking about caterpillars. Introduce fascinating nonfiction books, such as *Look . . . A Butterfly* by David Cutts, *Butterfly Story* by Anca Hariton, *Backyard Insects* by Millicent E. Selsam, and *From Egg to Butterfly* by Marlene Reidel.

Over a period of time, lead the children through the KWHL steps of research. (See the full-color Inquiry insert.) First ask the children what they know about the creepy crawlers. Record their answers on a chart, What We Think We Know about Caterpillars. Next ask them what questions they have, modeling for them one of your own questions: Is the hard shell around a caterpillar called a pupa, a cocoon, or a chrysalis? Record the children's questions on a chart titled, What We Want to Know. Ask also how they can find answers to their inquiries, making a third class chart, How We Will Find Out. After involving the children in research, discussions, and individual and group responses, record on the last chart, What We Have Learned.

EVERYDAY LEARNING ACTIVITIES

Positive parenting; developmental learning activities; and a warm, nurturing environment are major factors in a child's academic success and lifetime learning.

In the story *The Very Hungry Caterpillar* by Eric Carle, the caterpillar's home was a very special place for him, a safe and protected place where he could grow and change. To children also, home is a haven and a safety zone. Our children need to hear us say, "This home is special and different from any other. You are safe here and we will take care of you. You don't have to be like anyone else. You can make mistakes and no one will laugh at you. You are always loved. When you walk in that door you are safe because our home is a very special place."

✻ On trips to the grocery store, take a list of all the food the very hungry caterpillar ate. Have children look for the foods and cross them off the list. Children need to see words written down in a way that has meaning for them. *(words in print)*

✻ Make up your own counting songs. Children will love them. Sing and practice counting in everyday activities—putting on shoes and socks, setting the table, putting away toys. Count cracks in the sidewalk and cars on the street. *(counting sets)*

✻ Sketch four simple pictures on index cards: an egg, a caterpillar, a chrysalis, and a butterfly. Write the words on the bottom. Have a child sequence them, beginning on the left. *(sequencing)*

✻ Write the days of the week on the top of seven index cards. On each card, have children draw what the very hungry caterpillar ate that day. Write the numeral that matches each set. Let the children choose what they want on Saturday's card. Put a ring through "caterpillar" holes in the upper left corner of the cards and make your own book for the children to read. *(days of week and sets)*

✻ Every day choose a different way to *classify* food: hot or cold, healthful or not healthful, finger food or silverware food, smooth or rough texture. You could also *group* by colors, fruits, vegetables, dairy products, or desserts. Remember, a child enjoys sensory learning, so let her touch, taste, and smell as she groups. *(classification)*

✻ Let a child draw, color, and cut out a paper butterfly. Eric Carle made his from a tissue-paper collage. Make a bracelet by stapling together the ends of a narrow strip of colored paper. Then staple the butterfly's body to the bracelet. The paper circle will slip over the child's hand and the butterfly will *fly* as she waves her hand and moves to music. *(fine motor skills, body movement)*

✻ Find foods in the pantry or in the store to match every color in the beautiful butterfly. Print a color word at the top of a page. Repeat the color word as you write the foods the children have discovered, such as red apples, red Jell-O, red jam. *(words in print)*

Where the Wild Things Are

by Maurice Sendak

* Letter-sound relationships
* Phonemic awareness
* Parts of speech
* Mini language lessons
* Vocabulary
* Structure writing/Process writing
* Concepts of print
* Story structure

SETTING THE STAGE

Instantly singable songs and the appealing rhyme and rhythm of finger plays will encourage children to be involved in story time.

"When Things Don't Go Your Way" by Hap Palmer, *Backwards Land*

"Monster's Holiday," recorded by Bonnie Phipps, *Monster's Holiday*
(The delightful accompaniment of folk instruments makes the song great fun)

WILD THINGS

I have five terrible wild things.	*(hold up one hand)*
I dreamed them in my head.	*(point to head)*
And if they try to scare me	*(two hands up, scary)*
I'll dream that they are dead!	*(fist closed)*
They'll run with me.	*(wiggle five fingers)*
They'll jump with me.	*(jump five fingers)*
But when I'm done with them,	*(five fingers still)*
I'll say 'good bye'	*(wave with left hand)*
and they will fly	*(fingers fly away)*
out of my life again!	*(hand behind back)*

Mary Cornelius

THREE GHOSTESSES

Three little ghostesses,	*(three fingers up)*
Sitting on postesses,	*(sitting motion)*
Eating buttered toastesses.	*(fingers to mouth)*
Greasing their fistesses,	*(rub hands together)*
Up to their wristesses,	*(touch wrists)*
Oh, what beastesses	*(shake finger)*
To make such feastesses!	*(palms up)*

FIRST READING

Does the cover of this book make you want to read the story? Tell me what you see. What words would you use to describe the character sitting there with his eyes closed? The title of the story is *Where the Wild Things Are,* so the author called it a wild thing. Do you think the wild thing is friendly?

Many years ago, when Maurice Sendak wrote and illustrated the story, some people were concerned that little children would be frightened by the pictures. But they were wrong. Children loved the pictures and were not frightened at all. In fact, Mr. Sendak received a very important award for his wonderful make-believe wild things. I'll show you the words—Winner of the Caldecott Medal for the Most Distinguished Picture Book of the Year. What do you think the word *distinguished* means? In the story, a little boy named Max has an adventure with the wild things and they become his friends.

GETTING INVOLVED

I love the words "the ocean tumbled by." I wonder how the author thought of them. Let's talk about some of the new words we heard in *Where the Wild Things Are*. The story said Max made *mischief*. Tell me what that word means. Next it said the vines were hanging from the *ceiling*. Where would that be? Our story said an ocean tumbled by with a *private* boat for Max. Do you think that means a boat just for him? We know the wild things *gnashed* their teeth. Was that something good? What did Max mean when he wanted the wild *rumpus* to start? Did the illustrations tell you what a rumpus is?

I'll say all the new words one more time. You pretend to be Max and act out the meaning of the words. When we are finished, you can tiptoe with Max to his very own room where he found his supper waiting.

A CLOSER LOOK

With each rereading of a story, children gain new understanding. Pause often for a spontaneous flow of oral language as the children share their feelings and observations. Extend the learning process with your own questions in repeated readings of the story.

* Tell me how you were feeling as I read *Where the Wild Things Are.* *(reflecting)*

* Would you agree that "The night Max wore his wolf suit and made mischief" was a great story starter? *(evaluating)*

* Have you ever made mischief? *(reflecting)*

* Were the changes in Max's bedroom happening in his imagination? *(comprehension)*

* Would you have sailed with Max on the boat? *(reflecting)*

* How do you think Mr. Sendak thought of the words "he sailed in and out of weeks and almost over a year"? *(analyzing)*

* Do you think Max was frightened when he saw the wild things? *(analyzing)*

* I wonder if the wild things had families. What do you think? *(reflecting)*

* In your opinion, why did the wild things make Max their king? *(evaluating)*

* Tell me how Max punished the wild things just like his mother had punished him. *(application)*

* Do you have a favorite wild thing? *(reflecting)*

* Why do you think Max's supper was waiting for him? *(reasoning)*

* I wonder if Max ever saw the wild things again. What do you wonder about? *(reflecting)*

STORY TIME EXTENSIONS

Toad by Ruth Brown

The Dark at the Top of the Stairs by Sam McBratney

There's an Alligator Under My Bed by Mercer Mayer

There's a Nightmare in My Closet by Mercer Mayer

One Hungry Monster: A Counting Book in Rhyme by Susan O'Keefe

BALANCED LITERACY ACTIVITIES

POETRY

SOMETHING IS THERE
Something is there
  there on the stair
    coming down
      coming down
        stepping with care
        Coming down
          coming down
          slinkety-sly.

Something is coming and wants to get by.
Lilian Moore

IN A DARK WOOD
In a dark, dark wood
  there was a dark, dark house,
And in that dark, dark house
  there was a dark, dark room,
And in that dark, dark room
  there was a dark, dark cupboard,
And in that dark, dark cupboard
  there was a dark, dark shelf,
And on that dark, dark shelf
  there was a dark, dark box,
And in that dark, dark box
  there was . . .
    A MONSTER!
Author unknown

INVOLVEMENT

✳ Children will delight in many rereadings of *Where the Wild Things Are*. To help them interpret and verbalize the story, choose a new focus each time you read. Discuss feelings, imagination, problem solving, predicting, or the meaning of the wonderful vocabulary.

✳ *Where the Wild Things Are* offers an ideal setting for creative dramatics. To make the language come to life, have the children pantomime the movement of all the story characters. Another time, have them add sound effects.

✳ Create wild thing paper-bag hand puppets, paper-plate face masks, or stick puppets. Have Max, the king, lead a wild thing parade, ending with his marvelous magic trick as you return to the forest.

✳ Involve the children in making simple literacy props, such as headband wolf ears for Max, headband monster horns, yarn hair and tails, a cardboard box boat, and paper tree branches. The children will be able to retell the story through dramatic play. Even in the wild rumpus, it appears the wild things were silent.

INTEGRATION

CLAY WILD THINGS

Modeling clay is an excellent medium for creative expression. Give each child a clump of clay to create his own wild thing. Encourage verbal interaction among the children as they describe their wild things taking shape. Give each child a sentence strip beginning with his name such as *Riley's wild thing* _____. Finish each child's sentence as he dictates. Display the clay wild things and sentences in a prominent place for independent reading. The purpose of structure writing is to create easily read, predictable text.

IN MY IMAGINATION

Let the children share ideas about the endless things we can do in our imaginations. It is the talk that surrounds literature that leads to meaningful writing. Give each child a large piece of drawing paper with one sentence printed on the bottom: *In my imagination, I can* _____. After they have drawn pictures, have the children finish the sentence with developmental spelling. Edit the sentences before you mount the pages to make an accordion book titled *In My Imagination*.

A TREEFUL OF WILD THINGS

Involve the children in a discussion of why children, animals, and wild things like to climb trees. Then have the children paint a large tree on bulletin board paper. Let them create their own wild things from construction paper and a variety of materials. Add a conversation bubble coming from each wild thing's mouth, *"I like to* _____*."* Hang the creatures on the tree.

STRATEGIES AND SKILLS

Authentic literature responses provide a natural setting for the teaching of reading and writing strategies and skills. They offer meaningful encounters with print.

✳ Use the words in the title *Where the Wild Things Are* to teach letter-sound awareness. Focus on the letter *w* and its corresponding sound in the word *wild,* and the consonant combination *wh* in the word *where.*

✳ List words that rhyme with the word *thing.* Remove the onset *th* and keep the rime *ing.* Add new onsets to develop phonemic awareness.

✳ Choose three high-frequency words such as *where, are,* and *thing* to add to the word wall in your room.

✳ Present the concept of possessives by copying onto a sentence chart the children's original sentences about their clay wild things. *(Riley's wild thing has claws.)*

✳ Use the conversation bubbles coming from the mouths of the creatures on the tree to teach quotation marks.

✳ In different lessons, brainstorm all the ways the children can finish each sentence.

   My wild thing _____.
      (You are teaching action words.)
   My wild thing is a _____ monster.
      (You are teaching describing words.)
   My wild thing says, "_____."
      (You are teaching quotation marks.)

✳ Because the story begins and ends in Max's bedroom, *Where the Wild Things Are* can be retold on a *circle story map.*

A FOREST OF WILD THINGS

As a celebration of learning, have the children create on bulletin board paper a simple forest scene. Have each child use small paint sponges or colored chalk to make his own wild thing character. Under each wild thing, place a sentence the child has written, patterned after the sentences in the Strategies and Skills section. Have the children paint a large figure of Max as king. Surround his figure with all the words the children can think of to describe the leader of the wild things. Add the book title and the author's name to your wall mural. The individuality and variety of wild things will tell a wonderful story to be read again and again.

I WONDER

Model for the children how to think and wonder about a story: "I wonder what would have happened if a wild thing had sailed home in Max's boat" or "I wonder if Max ever wore his wolf suit again." Encourage the children to wonder, too. Perhaps what they are wondering about will become a new adventure with Max, a journal entry, or a letter to Mr. Sendak. Children understand the different purposes for writing when they are able to make choices. And now I am wondering, what will they choose to write?

EVERYDAY LEARNING ACTIVITIES

Positive parenting; developmental learning activities; and a warm, nurturing environment are major factors in a child's academic success and lifetime learning.

In the story *Where the Wild Things Are* by Maurice Sendak, little Max got angry when his mother disciplined him. It is natural for a child to respond in anger to discipline. However, it is the job of a parent or caregiver to contain the emotions of a young child. A child out of control needs an adult who is calm and in control, offering the security of consistent limits that say, "You're safe. I won't let you go too far." That doesn't mean asking a child to deny his feelings. Instead, label his feelings for him and say in a calm, matter-of-fact voice, "You are angry because . . . but the rule in this house is there will be no hitting." You can take so much emotion out of upsets when you have simple, unbendable rules. Are you wondering about a good starting point? Why not begin with, "The rule in our house is, I will speak to you only one time when I ask you to do something." Then follow through. Parents and caregivers who repeat their requests and get louder and louder until they finally yell, just train their children not to respond until they hear someone yelling. There is so much less anger in a situation when adults stay in control and quietly prevent a power play. Remember, "The rule in this house is . . ."

❋ Help a child create her own wild thing using a paper plate for a face and scrap items such as bits of yarn, rubberbands, bottle caps, string, twist tabs, buttons, markers, and so on. Give her a large paper bag for storing her wild thing. Since she created it, she gets to control her wild thing and send it away whenever she wants. *(dramatic play)*

❋ Encourage a child to "sail away" in a cardboard box or a plastic laundry basket. Ask her questions about *where* she is going, *what* she will be seeing, and *who* will be traveling with her. If you encourage a child to use her imagination now, she will be far less apprehensive later about right or wrong answers. Build both her confidence and her language ability by praising all her answers and entering into the fun yourself. *(dramatic play)*

❋ Ask a child to make up a story about a magazine picture or perhaps just one page in an imaginative story like *Where the Wild Things Are*. Listen carefully. Perhaps you will *hear* her own feelings as she talks. Ask just the right questions to encourage her storytelling. A child who cannot tell a story will have great difficulty reading and writing a story later on. *(oral storytelling)*

❋ Help a child make his very own good night book. Simply fold some pieces of plain, white paper and staple them together along the fold. On the bottom of each page write the words, *Good night* _____. Fill in the blanks with whatever words he chooses and have him draw or cut out a picture to go with each page. The child will love reading his own book every night as he says good night to the people and things that are special to him. *(words in print)*

❋ Make a masking tape ladder on the floor. Let children jump, two feet together, over the rungs. Next, have them hop on one foot from bottom to top and hop on the other foot from top to bottom. Demonstrate how to walk heel to toe along the sides of the ladder as though it were a balance beam. Suggest the children think of more things to do on the ladder. The development of gross motor skills precedes the development of fine motor skills. *(motor coordination)*

Whistle for Willie

by Ezra Jack Keats

* Cultural diversity
* Process writing
* Letter-sound relationships
* Phonemic awareness

* Mini language skills
* Concepts of print
* Math/science concepts
* Nonfiction

SETTING THE STAGE

Instantly singable songs and the appealing rhyme and rhythm of finger plays will encourage children to be involved in story time.

"Whistle While You Work," recorded on the Disney soundtrack to *Snow White*
(Always a favorite; pucker up and join in the whistling)

"I'm in the Mood" by Raffi, *Rise and Shine*
(An upbeat song about whistling, singing, and clapping)

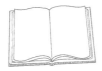

FIVE LITTLE PUPPIES

Five little puppies were playing in the sun;	*(left hand up)*
This one saw a rabbit and he began to run.	*(bend thumb)*
This one saw a butterfly and he began to race;	*(bend second finger)*
This one saw a pussy cat and he began to chase;	*(bend third finger)*
This one tried to catch his tail	
And he went round and round.	*(bend fourth finger)*
This one was so quiet; he never made a sound.	*(bend little finger)*

MY LOOSE TOOTH

I had a loose tooth,	*(follow action as rhyme indicates)*
A wiggly, jiggly loose tooth.	
I had a loose tooth, hanging by a thread.	
So I pulled my loose tooth,	
This wiggly, jiggly loose tooth,	
And put it 'neath my pillow,	
And then I went to bed!	

FIRST READING

What is the boy doing on the cover of our story? Look at his pucker! Can you make your lips pucker like his? Now slowly say the word "whistle." Did you hear a whistling sound? The word *whistle* is the first word in the title of the story. Tell me who you think the boy is whistling for. The dog's name is also in the title and it begins with a *W*, too. Can you guess his name? Let's read the title and the author's name together.

The first book Mr. Keats wrote about Peter and Willie was called *The Snowy Day*. Children enjoyed that book so much he decided to write another story about the little boy and his dog. In this story, *Whistle for Willie*, Peter wished he could whistle. Have you ever wished you could do something other children can do? Let's read the title page together.

The uninterrupted initial reading of Whistle for Willie *will immerse the children in the rich text and illustrations of the story as they anticipate the delightful ending.*

GETTING INVOLVED

Let's move to the music that's playing. I'll lead you through all the things Peter did in the story. Whirl around on the sidewalk . . . whirl *to the left*, whirl *to the right*, whirl *faster and faster*, now *slower and slower*. Careful! You feel just like Peter did when he stopped whirling. Do you remember what Peter did next? Climb *inside* the empty carton and try to whistle. Now climb out and draw a long line on the sidewalk with your chalk. Go *around* the girls jumping rope and *around* the barber pole and right up to your front door. Pucker up again! Can you whistle yet? Time to put an old hat on your head and practice in front of the mirror. Now walk like Peter did *along* a crack in the sidewalk. Can you run away from your shadow? Jump *high*, jump *low*, jump *to the left*, jump *to the right*. Oh, Oh, here comes Willie! Scramble *under* the carton. Pucker up! Blow *up*, blow *down*, blow *to the left*, blow *to the right*. You did it! I hear your whistles and so does Willie. Here he comes! Give him a great big hug and carry him home to your mom and dad. Now whistle your way to the grocery store and whistle your way home again with the groceries.

Another time, have the children pretend to blow up three balloons and act out the rhyme "Here is a big balloon, here is a bigger balloon, here is the biggest balloon you can see. Can you help me count them? One, two, three." Direct the children to blow one balloon to the left, one to the right, and one straight up in the air, blowing hard until all the balloons disappear.

A CLOSER LOOK

With each rereading of a story, children gain new understanding. Pause often for a spontaneous flow of oral language as the children share their feelings and observations. Extend the learning process with your own questions in repeated readings of the story.

* Tell me what you liked about the story *Whistle for Willie. (evaluating)*

* Would you like to have a dog like Willie? Does he make you smile? *(reflecting)*

* Why did Peter want to learn to whistle? *(comprehension)*

* Do you already know how to whistle? *(reflecting)*

* Why did everything turn down and up and up and down when Willie stopped whirling? *(comprehension)*

* Did the red, yellow, and green lights really pop off of the street light? *(comprehension)*

* Tell me what happened to Peter's chalk when he came to the girls' jump rope and the barber pole. *(reasoning)*

* Why do you think Peter pretended to be his father? *(comprehension)*

* Is it possible to run away from your shadow? *(analyzing)*

* In your opinion, how did Peter learn to whistle? *(evaluating)*

* I wonder what new thing you have learned that makes you feel proud. *(reflecting)*

STORY TIME EXTENSIONS

Whistling Dixie by Marcia Vaughan

At the Crossroads by Rachel Isadora

Hue Boy by Rita Phillips Mitchell

Shadows and Reflections by Tana Hoban

Bear Shadow by Frank Asch

BALANCED LITERACY ACTIVITIES

POETRY

HIDE-AND-SEEK SHADOW
I walked with my shadow,
I ran with my shadow,
I danced with my shadow,
I did.
Then a cloud came over
And the sun went under
And my shadow stopped playing
And hid.
Margaret Hillert

WHISTLING
by Jack Prelutsky
from *Read-Aloud Rhymes for
the Very Young*
by Jack Prelutsky

COULD IT HAVE BEEN A SHADOW?
by Monica Shannon
from *The Random House Book
of Poetry for Children*
by Jack Prelutsky

INVOLVEMENT

WHISTLING A TUNE

✱ Play instrumental music with a varying beat to encourage the children to freely explore moving as Peter did, whirling, walking, running, and jumping off their shadows. Keep the music playing softly as the children sit down. Begin reading *Whistle for Willie*. Stop at just the right point to let the children interact with the text by moving as Peter did. Then begin reading again, following that pattern until Peter whistles his way to the store. The children will have choreographed their own musical version of the story.

✱ Surprisingly, beanbags are another way to encourage children to move as Peter did in the story. The Kimbo recording *Bean Bag Fun* presents an assortment of fun beanbag games that suggest ways of moving. The song "Tom Tom Bean Bag" directs children to move to the right and to the left. Another song, "Musical Bean Bags," presents a selection of fast and slow tempos. It is through movement and music that children create story meaning.

INTEGRATION

WHISTLE JUST FOR FUN

Begin a discussion of all the reasons why people whistle by telling a story about when you heard someone whistling. When an adult tells a story, it sets the stage for children to be storytellers. Begin writing on chart paper all the reasons why people whistle.

When each child has an idea, give her drawing paper with the caption written on the bottom, *Whistle for* _____. Have each child draw a picture of her own face and add whistling lips cut or torn from red construction paper. Finish each child's sentence as she dictates. Every fourth page print "WHISTLE JUST FOR FUN!" Have a small group of children decorate the cover and title page with red whistling lips. Mount the pages on red construction paper and bind them into a class book for your reading center.

SILLY WILLIES

Children look for the little daschund, Willie, in Ezra Jack Keats' stories. With brown paint and skinny potato halves, let each child potato print Willie's long body. Have them change to very small potatoes or brown and black markers to add Willie's pointed face, dark eyes, floppy ears, short legs, and thin tail. Surround the Silly Willie pictures on your wall with book covers from *The Snowy Day, Whistle for Willie,* and *Peter's Chair.*

AUTHOR'S CHAIR

Keep available in your writing center blank books so children can draw and write their own stories about Peter and Willie. Writing with phonetic spelling helps children pay conscious attention to the sounds that make up words. Put a sign-up sheet by the Author's Chair for children to take turns sharing their stories with the class. Children see themselves as writers when they choose to write for their own purposes and for an audience.

WHAT PETER CAN DO

As you read the story again, ask the children to listen for all the things Peter can do. List their answers on a class chart. Write the same sentences on sentence strips for children to match to the chart or sequence in a pocket chart.

Use the relevant text of What Peter Can Do to teach skills and strategies. Point out concepts of print in your short, frequent sessions, with time given for application in authentic reading and writing. Present also in ongoing lessons a variety of phonemic awareness and structural analysis skills. Teach the initial consonant sound of *w* in *wear, walk,* and *Willie.* Introduce the consonant combination *cr* in the word *crack.* Teach the long vowel sound in the word *line,* noting the silent *e.* Talk about the short vowel sound in the words *can, crack,* and *hat.* Build rhyming word families for the words *can, walk,* and *hug* by changing the initial consonant sound, the onset, and keeping the ending sound, the rime. Clap to the beats heard in the two syllable words *Willie, whistle, father,* and *along.* Children learn skills in context because then they have meaning.

HIDE-AND-SEEK SHADOW

As a child like Peter, Margaret Hillert must have played many times with her shadow. The rich images of her poem "Hide-and-Seek Shadow" will bring to children's minds their own experiences with shadows. And that is how children make sense out of poetry—by making connections to their own lives. Let them bring their thoughts and feelings to the poem. Talk about the phrases "the sun went under" and "my shadow stopped playing and hid." After you have read the poem many times, print the text on chart paper using alternating lines of color. Have the children draw little illustrations around the words *shadow, cloud,* and *sun.* Place the poem on a mural or in your permanent I Can Read poetry corner.

DANCING SHADOWS

Enjoy reading *Bear Shadow* by Frank Asch and *Shadows and Reflections* by Tana Hoban. Point out in the illustrations where shadows fall. Go outside on a sunny day and be observant of the shadows made by buildings and trees. Let the children discover what happens to their shadows when they stand in a shaded place.

Create your own mural of "Hide-and-Seek Shadow." As the children paint or draw a background scene, talk about where to place dark shadows. To help children draw pictures of themselves in motion, have them strike poses for each other as if their bodies were running or dancing. Then model how to tear from black construction paper free-form shadows for the children to attach to their figures. They will be walking, running, and dancing with their hide-and-seek shadows right across your mural.

EVERYDAY LEARNING ACTIVITIES

Positive parenting; developmental learning activities; and a warm, nurturing environment are major factors in a child's academic success and lifetime learning.

In *Whistle for Willie* by Ezra Jack Keats, it took Willie a while to be able to do what the older children could already do. In a child's imagination, he can do anything and become anyone he wants to be. Young children love the play world of fantasy and imagination where they can pretend to be big and powerful. Most children love a dress-up box of old shoes and hats and clothes. Every day they will think up something new to do or be, and thinking is a real part of creativity and imagination. It is so easy to increase a child's language skills when he is role-playing by asking where he is going, what tools he will need, and who he will see along the way. The development of imagination also allows a child to play more by himself. Some children take comfort in imaginary friends who are always loyal, always loving, and always ready to play.

✳ Expand a child's imaginary play to include the whole family. Collect props for a prop box to role-play whatever the child or the family is interested in—a camping trip, a shoe store, a restaurant, a beauty salon (now who wouldn't smile at daddy with curlers in his hair?). It doesn't require many props to act out a heartwarming story like *Whistle for Willie*. *(dramatic play)*

✳ Look for everyday shapes and objects to sort according to size. In the kitchen, gather all kinds of spoons together and have children sort them. Place like sizes in piles. Use measuring spoons, soup spoons, teaspoons, serving spoons, mixing spoons, and wooden spoons. Count the piles and compare sets. Teach *greater than* and *less than*. Another day, line up the spoons from smallest to largest. Teach *left and right; in the middle; next to; between; first, second,* and *third. (sorting, directionality)*

✳ Be ready to play the "Spoon Game" more than once! Have a child count out ten spoons for you to hide anywhere in the house. The spoons should be partly visible. Set the timer on the stove and see how many spoons a child can find before the timer goes off. Each spoon could count for two points, teaching a child to count by twos. Then have each spoon count five points and count by fives. Beat the clock or beat the score! *(visual perception)*

✳ To help a child learn left-to-right progression, point out that we always read the left page of a storybook first, the right page next. (In writing, we always start at the left side of the page. Put a green dot for "go" in the left corner.) A fun way to reinforce this idea is to begin reading a well-loved storybook upside down. The child will delight in correcting you! Then, with the book held the proper way, point to and read the right page before you read the left page. The child will recognize the mixed-up story and love the silliness. *(directionality)*

✳ Tape the voices of your family all taking parts reading a favorite story like *Whistle for Willie*. Play the tape in the car or as part of a bedtime routine. Use the familiar voices as a "security blanket" when someone in the family has to be away for a while. *(family relationships)*

Who Took the Farmer's Hat?

by Joan L. Nodset

SETTING THE STAGE

Instantly singable songs and the appealing rhyme and rhythm of finger plays will encourage children to be involved in story time.

"Down on Grandpa's Farm" by Raffi, *One Light, One Sun*

"Grandmother's Farm" by Hap Palmer, *Witches' Brew*

THE FARMER'S TREE

Here is the tree with leaves so green.	*(make tree with arms)*
Here are the apples that hang between.	*(clench fists)*
When the wind blows the apples fall.	*(fists fall)*
Here is a basket to gather them all.	*(hands make basket)*

MY BOOK

This is my book; it will open wide	*(hands open like book)*
To show the pictures that are inside.	
This is my ball, so big and round,	*(fingertips touching, make circle)*
To toss in the air	*(hands toss high)*
Or roll on the ground.	*(rolling motion down low)*
Here's my umbrella to keep me dry	*(hands touching over head)*
When the raindrops fall	*(fingers wiggle down)*
From the cloudy sky.	
This is my kitten; just hear her purr	
When I'm gently stroking her	*(one hand strokes other)*
Soft, warm fur.	

FIRST READING

The cover of this book makes me smile. I have never seen a hat walking along in the grass by itself. Or is the hat walking by itself? Tell me what you think. Do you have any idea who would wear a big hat like that? The answer is in the title, *Who Took the Farmer's Hat?* The title of the story is asking you a question. Who do *you* think took the farmer's hat? What do *you* predict will happen in the story? Tell me if you see any clues on the title page. Let's read and see if you guessed who took the farmer's hat.

Children love the predictable pattern in Who Took the Farmer's Hat? *Encourage them to join in every time the farmer asks, "Did you see my old brown hat?"*

GETTING INVOLVED

Have any of you ever played the game "Doggie, Doggie, Where's Your Bone?" Today we are going to play a game just like that, only we are going to change the words and say, "Farmer, farmer, where's your hat? Somebody took it just like that!" I need a farmer to sit in the chair and I'm going to put a little hat under the chair. Now close your eyes and I'll choose a squirrel to come take the hat and hide it behind his tail. Shhh, move ever so quietly, squirrel. Don't let the farmer hear you. Everyone else say the words with me, "Farmer, farmer, where's your hat? Somebody took it just like that!" *(Use the animals in sequence as they appeared in the story.)*

A CLOSER LOOK

With each rereading of a story, children gain new understanding. Pause often for a spontaneous flow of oral language as the children share their feelings and observations. Extend the learning process with your own questions in repeated readings of the story.

* Did you guess who took the farmer's hat? *(reflecting)*
* Has the wind ever run away with something of yours? *(reflecting)*
* Would you agree that "The farmer had a hat, an old brown hat" was a good story starter? *(evaluating)*
* Tell me why you think none of the animals recognized the farmer's old brown hat. *(reasoning)*
* What did the squirrel think the farmer's hat was? The mouse? The fly? The duck? *(comprehension)*
* What would happen if we changed the order of the animals the farmer talked to? *(application)*
* Do you think the words *round* and *brown* were important? *(analyzing)*
* If you were on the farm, where would you tell the farmer to look for his hat? *(reasoning)*
* There was only one egg when the farmer looked in the nest, but there were four baby birds. What happened? *(reasoning)*
* Imagine you were the farmer. What would you have said to Bird? *(reflecting)*
* Which hat did you like better, the old one or the new one? *(evaluating)*
* I wonder if the wind ever blew away the new hat. *(reflecting)*
* In your opinion, was "And how Bird likes that old brown nest!" a happy ending to the story? *(evaluating)*
* Did *Who Took the Farmer's Hat?* make you think of another story? *(reflecting)*

STORY TIME EXTENSIONS

The Hat by Jan Brett
The Purple Hat by Tracey Campbell Pearson
Mike's Kite by Elizabeth MacDonald
It's Too Noisy! by Joanna Cole
Mother Halverson's New Cat by Jim Aylesworth

BALANCED LITERACY ACTIVITIES

POETRY

THE MARE
Look at the mare of Farmer Giles!
She's brushing her hooves on the mat;

Look at the mare of Farmer Giles!
She's knocked on the door, rat-a-tat!

With a clack of her hoof and a wave of her head
She's tucked herself up in the four-post bed,

And she's wearing the Farmer's hat!
Herbert Asquith

THE SPRING WIND
by Charlotte Zolotow
from *Read-Aloud Rhymes for the Very Young*
by Jack Prelutsky

WIND TAKES THE WORLD
by Eve Merriam
from *You Be Good & I'll Be Night*
by Eve Merriam

INVOLVEMENT

THE FARMER LOST HIS HAT

Play the music to the song "The Farmer in the Dell." First have the children walk to the rhythm, then clap to the rhythm. Next, have the children clap and sing as they play the familiar game "The Farmer in the Dell."

Brainstorm with the children about ways they could adapt the words of the song to the story *Who Took the Farmer's Hat?* Their variation might be something like this, beginning with a farmer in the middle of the circle and adding one child with every verse:

The farmer lost his hat, The farmer lost his hat,
Heigh-ho, the derry-o, The farmer lost his hat.

The farmer asked the Squirrel, The farmer asked the Squirrel,
Heigh-ho, the derry-o, The farmer asked the Squirrel.
(Add verses for the Mouse, the Fly, the Goat, the Duck, and the Bird.)

The Bird found the hat; the Bird found the hat,
Heigh-ho, the derry-o, The Bird found the hat.
(Sing the Bird stands alone for the final verse.)

THE FARMER AND HIS FRIENDS

Involve the children in a discussion of what they should include in a farmyard scene to tell the story of *Who Took the Farmer's Hat?* Pencil in a simple outline on a large piece of bulletin board paper to guide them as they paint. Then have the children paint the story characters, the farmer, and his hat on strong doubled paper. After they have cut out and stuffed the characters, staple them to the bulletin board for a colorful, three-dimensional mural. Label everything the children have painted and add the author's name and the story title. Across the bottom print the words *The farmer had a hat, an old brown hat. Oh, how he liked that old brown hat!* You have added another fun experience with *words in print* to your room.

INTEGRATION

DID YOU SEE MY OLD BROWN HAT?

Bring an old brown hat to class. Talk about all the things that Squirrel, Mouse, Fly, Goat, Duck, and Bird imagined the farmer's hat to be. As you twist and turn the hat into different shapes and positions, ask the children to describe what the hat looks like to them and where they might have found it.

Have each child tear a hat out of brown construction paper and paste it on a piece of white paper on which the words *Did you see my old brown hat?* are printed on the top and the words *"No," said* _____ *. "I saw a* _____ *."* are printed on the bottom. Using crayons, markers, or scraps of paper, encourage the children to turn their hats into something imaginary. Give each child the opportunity to read his sentences and talk about his picture. Have the children illustrate a cover, a title page, and a surprise ending to your new class book, *Did You See My Old Brown Hat?* Structure writing is a first step in writing to learn and learning to write.

HATS OF MANY LANDS

In *The Purple Hat* by Tracey Campbell Pearson, everyone in town joins a lively search for Annie's beloved purple chapeau. The story is a perfect beginning to exploring the topic of hats. *Martin's Hats* by Joan W. Blos is the story of a boy who dashes, hat by hat, through a grand round of adventures. In the joyful, childlike story *Happy Birthday, Moon* by Frank Asch, Bear wants to buy a hat for the moon. The favorite *Whose Hat?* by Margaret Miller is an inviting look at the hats professionals wear.

Storybooks also present a fascinating window into other cultures. In a lovely Scandinavian farm setting in Jan Brett's *The Hat,* a hedgehog crawls into a woolen stocking cap and can't shake it from his head. In Patricia Polacco's *Chicken Sunday,* the rich folk art of the Ukraine showcases the story of a lovely hat, a gramma, and African-American children. Family stories and memories are shared in *Aunt Flossie's Hats and Crab Cakes Later* by Elizabeth Fitzgerald Howard. *Hats Hats Hats* by Ann Morris presents a photographic look at hats from all over the world as well as the reasons for wearing them.

HAT DAY

Send home notes in the shape of little hats, announcing Hat Day. The children may wear any kind of hat to class. As each child models her hat, decide together what makes the hat unique. Give the children the opportunity to write about their own hats, someone else's hat, a storybook hat, or something totally unrelated. Children need to make choices if they are going to see themselves as authors.

A SIMULATION: THE HAT SHOPPE

Provide an endless assortment of supplies for the children to create their own original hats, such as paper plates, bowls and cups, feathers, felt and fabric pieces, pipe cleaners and straws, cotton, buttons, sparkles, ribbon and yarn, strawberry baskets and meat trays, crepe and tissue paper, and so on. Surely you will want to show off just a little! Draw a parade route and mark the rooms and people you want to visit. Enjoy a class hat parade, with you and the children wearing your original hats. Tally the compliments you received while parading.

After returning to your room, have each child decide on a price tag for his hat. Staple the hats to your Hat Shoppe bulletin board, complete with price tags, names, and sentences. Create a hat store in front of your bulletin board. Provide play money, a cash register, paper and pencils to write store hours, open and closed signs, receipts, a tally of sales, and a sign-up sheet for clerks and customers. Sale's on!

HAT MATH

Graph the hats using a three-column floor graph. Let the children decide on the criteria such as Fun Hats, Fancy Hats, and Work Hats. *Estimate* the circumference of each hat. Then measure it with yarn. Hang the pieces of yarn vertically on the chart. Compare the lengths and arrange them from shortest to longest. Estimate how many cotton balls will fill the center of the smallest and largest hats. Then fill the hats. Count the cotton balls into sets of ten and compare the numbers.

EVERYDAY LEARNING ACTIVITIES

Positive parenting; developmental learning activities; and a warm, nurturing environment are major factors in a child's academic success and lifetime learning.

When the wind swept away the farmer's hat in the story *Who Took The Farmer's Hat?* by Joan Nodset, the farmer asked each of his animal friends the very same question, "Did you see my old brown hat?" Each animal answered by telling the farmer what it had actually seen: "the old brown pot" or "the old brown boat." The animals were sharing the information they had gathered just by looking with their eyes. That's the way children learn, too. That knowledge becomes the basis for their thinking skills. This week concentrate on all that a child can learn through seeing. With a little guidance, a child can be taught to really look and see. Everything she notices visually will be getting her ready for the complex skill of reading where she must notice the many differences in letters and words. Look out the window together and name everything you can see, both far and near. Compare what you can see at night, from the same window, with what you can see in the daytime. Sit in a favorite chair together and name everything you can see in the room. At night, in the dark, try to remember everything you saw in the daytime. Look out of the window of the car or pretend you are looking out the window of a moving train. Whether in the park or in the schoolyard or in a store, encourage a child to observe everything and to talk about what she sees. So much can be learned through the fun, casual experiences of everyday living.

✳ Eye-hand coordination is essential to a child's fine motor development. The fingers are one of the last areas of the body to develop. Give a child many, many opportunities to cut and paste. Teach her to paste around the outside of things, which is a *tracking* skill in itself. Just putting a blob of paste in the middle of something doesn't give much practice in developing the skill. Give her paper or old catalogs to simply cut, cut, cut, which is another tracking skill. *(eye-hand coordination)*

✳ Another effective activity to strengthen finger muscles and develop coordination is to give a child spring-type clothespins. Have her pinch them open and put them around the top of a container like a coffee can. Give her some objects to pick up with the snapping motion of the clothespin and then drop inside the container. Fat, uncooked beans are a good starter. When the game is over, everything can go inside the coffee can for a fast cleanup, waiting for the next time. *(fine motor skills)*

✳ The grocery store is an excellent place to reinforce many learning concepts. Look at a can of beans. What shape is the lid? Hold a pineapple. Does it feel rough or smooth? What size container of milk should we buy? Show me the largest box of laundry powder. Find a fruit that is yellow. Point to a box that is a square. Directions keep a child occupied while she learns to really look and see. *(visual perception)*

✳ Read again the story *Who Took the Farmer's Hat?* Talk about the kinds of hats people wear. Find out what hat is your child's favorite as well as the favorite hats of others in the family. Then have a child make a book about hats and draw a picture on each page. Fold some pieces of drawing paper and staple them together on the fold. On the bottom of the first page print the words *I have a hat*. On the second page, write *Mommy has a hat,* and so on. The last page could be, *The farmer has a hat, too*. *(words in print)*

Bibliography

A Is for Aloha by Stephanie Feeney, 1980 University Press of Hawaii, 35

A You're Adorable illustrated by Martha Alexander, 1994 Candlewick, 9

Aardvarks, Disembark! by Ann Jonas, 1990 Greenwillow, 141

Abuela by Arthur Dorros, 1991 Dutton, 151

Africa Calling Nighttime Falling by Daniel Alderman, 1996 Whispering Coyote, 85

African Animals' ABC by Philippa-Alys Browne, 1995 Sierra Club Books, 35

After the Flood by Arthur Geisert, 1994 Houghton, 139

Alaska's Three Bears by Shannon Cartwright, 1992 Paws Four, 17

Alexander and the Terrible, Horrible, No Good, Very Bad Day by Judith Viorst, 1972 Atheneum, 71

Alison's Zinnia by Anita Lobel, 1990 Greenwillow, 193

All Aboard ABC by Doug Magee and Robert Newman, 1990 Dutton, 47

All Pigs Are Beautiful by Dick King-Smith, 1993 Candlewick, 177

Alphabet Puzzle by Jill Downie, 1988 Lothrop, 33

Amos & Boris by William Steig, 1971 Farrar, 121, 123

And Rain Makes Applesauce by Julian Scheer, 1985 Holiday, 166

Animal Numbers by Bert Kitchen, 1987 Dial, 221, 223

Animal Orchestra, A Counting Book by Scott Gustafson, 1995 Greenwich, 47

Animals in Winter by Susanne Riha, 1989 Carolrhoda, 17

Anno's Counting Book by Mitsumasa Anno, 1975 Crowell, 221, 223

Ask Mr. Bear by Marjorie Flack, 1932 Macmillan, 1

At the Crossroads by Rachel Isadora, 1991 Greenwillow, 255

Aunt Flossie's Hats and Crab Cakes Later by Elizabeth Fitzgerald Howard, 1991 Clarion, 263

Babushka's Mother Goose by Patricia Polacco, 1995 Philomel, 39, 40

Backyard Insects by Millicent E. Selsam, 1991 Turtleback, 245

Barnyard Banter by Denise Fleming, 1994 Holt, 57

Bear Shadow by Frank Asch, 1984 Prentice Hall, 255, 257

Bear's Toothache, The by David McPhail, 1972 Little, 3

Bears Out There by Joanne Ryder, 1995 Atheneum, 17

Bedtime for Francis by Russell Hoban, 1960 Harper, 7

Bee Tree by Patricia Polacco, 1993 Philomel, 69

Benjamin's Barn by Reeve Lindbergh, 1990 Dial, 57

big fat hen by Keith Baker, 1994 Harcourt, 47, 215

Biggest House in the World, The by Leo Lionni, 1968 Pantheon, 243

Birth of a Whale, The by John Archambault, 1996 Silver, insert

Blueberries for Sal by Robert McCloskey, 1948 Penguin, 13, 106

Bringing the Rain to Kapiti Plain: A Nandi Tale by Verna Aardema, 1981 Dial, 167

Brown Bear, Brown Bear, What Do You See? by Bill Martin, Jr., 1971 Holt, 19, 32

Busy Beavers by Lydia Dabcovich, 1988 Dutton, 76

Butterfly Story by Anca Hariton, 1995 Dutton, 245

Can't You Sleep, Little Bear? by Martin Waddell, 1988 Candlewick, 9, 182

Caps for Sale by Esphyr Slobodkina, 1940 Addison Wesley, 25

Cat and Mouse in the Rain by Tomek Bogacki, 1997 Farrar, 165

Chameleons by Claudia Schneiper, 1989 Carolrhoda, 76

Change of Plans, A by Alan Benjamin and Steven Kellogg, 1982 Four Winds, 41

Chicka Chicka Boom Boom by Bill Martin, Jr. and John Archambault, 1989 Simon, 31

Chicken Sunday by Patricia Polacco, 1992 Philomel, 122, 127, 263

Chickens Aren't the Only Ones by Ruth Heller, 1993 Grosset, 59

Chrysanthemum by Kevin Henkes, 1991 Greenwillow, 95

Color by Ruth Heller, 1995 Putnam, 21

Come a Tide by George Ella Lyon, 1990 Orchard, 139

Completed Hickory Dickory Dock, The by Jim Aylesworth, 1990 Atheneum, 39

Cookie's Week by Cindy Ward, 1989 Putnam, 121

Counting Wildflowers by Bruce McMillan, 1986 Lothrop, 243

Country Crossing by Jim Aylesworth, 1991 Atheneum, 45

Dark at the Top of the Stairs, The by Sam McBratney, 1996 Candlewick, 249

Martin's Hats by Joan W. Blos, 1984 Morrow, 263

May I Bring a Friend? by Beatrice Schenk de Regniers, 1964 Alladan, 119

Midnight Farm, The by Reeve Lindbergh, 1987 Dial, 133

Midnight Snowman by Caroline Feller Bauer, 1987 Atheneum, 205

Mike's Kite by Elizabeth MacDonald, 1990 Kendall, 11, 261

Miss Mary Mack adapted by Mary Ann Hoberman, 1998 Little, 148, 197

Miss Rumphius by Barbara Cooney, 1982 Viking, 127, 210

Mitten, The adapted by Jan Brett, 1989 Putnam, 147, 203

Mole's Hill by Lois Ehlert, 1994 Harcourt, 101, 103

Monkey and the Crocodile, The by Paul Galdone, 1969 Seabury, 27

Monkey Do! by Allan Ahlberg, 1998 Candlewick, 27

Moon Rope/Un lazo a la luna by Lois Ehlert, 1992 Harcourt, 151

Mother Goose and the Sly Fox by Chris Conover, 1989 Farrar, 39

Mother Halverson's New Cat by Jim Aylesworth, 1989 Atheneum, 261

Mouse Mess by Linnea Riley, 1997 Blue Sky Press, 89

Mouse Paint by Ellen Stoll Walsh, 1989 Harcourt, 21

Mouse Told His Mother, A by Bethany Roberts, 1997 Little, 133

Mouse's Tale, A by Pamela Johnson, 1991 Harcourt, 95

Moving Day by Robert Kalan, 1996 Greenwillow, 107, 193

Mr. Gumpy's Outing by John Burningham, 1970 Holt, 139

Mr. McGill Goes to Town by Jim Aylesworth, 1991 Atheneum, 103

Mr. Rabbit and the Lovely Present by Charlotte Zolotow, 1962 Harper, 125

Mrs. Huggins and Her Hen Hannah by Lydia Dabcovich, 1985 Dutton, 101, 103

Mrs. Katz and Tush by Patricia Polacco, 1992 Bantam, 121

Mud by Mary Lyn Ray, 1996 Harcourt, 167

Muddigush by Kimberley Knutson, 1992 Macmillan, 167

Muddle Cuddle by Laurel Dee Gugler, 1997 Annick, 215

Mushroom in the Rain by Mirra Ginsburg, 1974 Macmillian, 165

My Brother John by Kristine Church, 1990 Tambourine, 171

My Friend Whale by Simon James, 1991 Bantam, insert

My Many Colored Days by Dr. Seuss, 1996 Knopf, 239, 240

My Son John by Jim Aylesworth, 1994 Holt, 40

Napping House, The by Audrey Wood, 1984 Harcourt, 131

Night Noises by Mem Fox, 1989 Harcourt, 9

Noah's Ark by Peter Spier, 1977 Doubleday, 137

Nora's Surprise by Satomi Ichikawa, 1994 Philomel, 121

Oh, A-Hunting We Will Go by John Langstaff, 1974 Macmillan, 143

Old Black Fly by Jim Aylesworth, 1992 Holt, 33, 34

Old Man & His Door, The by Gary Soto, 1996 Putnam, 149

On Market Street by Arnold Lobel, 1981 Greenwillow, 157

One Bear All Alone by Caroline Bucknall, 1985 Dial, 217

One Duck Stuck by Phyllis Root, 1998 Candlewick, 107

One Fine Day by Nonny Hogrogian, 1971 Simon, 51

One Hungry Monster: A Counting Book in Rhyme by Susan O'Keefe, 1992 Little, 249

One of Each by Mary Ann Hoberman, 1997 Little, 39, 91, 95

One Potato: A Counting Book of Potato Prints by Diana Pomeroy, 1996 Harcourt, 243

Otters Under Water by Jim Arnosky, 1992 Putnam, 75

Our Snowman by M. B. Goffstein, 1986 Harper, 205

Over in the Meadow illustrated by Ezra Jack Keats, 1971 Scholastic, 221

Owl Babies by Martin Waddell, 1992 Candlewick, 182

Owl Moon by Jane Yolen, 1987 Philomel, 63

Papa, please get the moon for me by Eric Carle, 1986 Simon, 63

Patchwork Quilt, The by Valerie Flournoy, 1985 Dial, 11

Peace at Last by Jill Murphy, 1980 Dial, 133

Peck Slither and Slide by Suse MacDonald, 1997 Harcourt, 5

Peter Spier's Rain by Peter Spier, 1982 Doubleday, 163

Peter's Chair by Ezra Jack Keats, 1967 Harper, 169, 202, 256

Picnic by Emily Arnold McCully, 1984 Harper, 41

Pig in the Pond, The by Martin Waddell, 1992 Candlewick, 175

Piggy in the Puddle, The by Charlotte Pomerantz, 1974 Macmillan, 167

Pigs Aplenty, Pigs Galore! by David McPhail, 1993 Dutton, 177

Pirate by Richard Platt, 1994 Dorling Kindersley, 238

Pirates—Robbers of the High Seas by Gail Gibbons, 1993 Little, 235, 238

Planting a Rainbow by Lois Ehlert, 1988 Harcourt Brace, 192

Polar Bear, Polar Bear, What Do You Hear? by Bill Martin, Jr. 1991 Holt, 21

Positively Mother Goose by Diane Loomans, 1991 Starseed, 39

Pretend You're a Cat by Jean Marzollo, 1990 Dial, 139

Puddle, The by David McPhail, 1998 Farrar, 167

Puddles by Jonathan London, 1997 Viking, 167

Purple Hat, The by Tracey Campbell Pearson, 1997 Farrar, 263

Quilt, The by Ann Jonas, 1984 Greenwillow, 11

Quilt Story, The by Tony Johnston, 1985 Putnam, 11

Rabbit Seeds by Bijou LeTord, 1984 Four Winds, 209, 211

Rabbits and Raindrops by Jim Arnosky, 1997 Putnam, 209

Rain Song by Lezlie Evans, 1995 Houghton, 167

Rain Talk by Mary Serfozo, 1990 McElderry, 167

Random House Book of Poetry for Young Children by Jack Prelutsky, 1983 Random

Reason for a Flower, The by Ruth Heller, 1983 Scholastic, 193

Read-Aloud Rhymes for the Very Young by Jack Prelutsky, 1986 Knopf

Rebel by John Schoenherr, 1995 Philomel, 76

Red Fox Running by Eve Bunting, 1993 Clarion, 187

Relatives Came, The by Cynthia Rylant, 1985 Bradbury, 197

Roll Over! A Counting Song by Merle Peek, 1981 Houghton, 216

Rose in My Garden by Arnold and Anita Lobel, 1984 Greenwillow, 193

Rosie's Walk by Pat Hutchins, 1968 Macmillan, 183

Rough-Face Girl, The by Rafe Martin, 1992 Putnam, 117

Runaway Bunny, The by Margaret Wise Brown, 1942 Harper, 62, 189

Running the Road to ABC by Denizé Lauture, 1996 Simon, 33, 35

Saturday Sancochos by Leyla Torres, 1995 Simon, 231

School by Emily Arnold McCully, 1990 Harper, 142

School Picnic, The by Jan Steffy, 1987 Good Books, 41

Seasons and Someone, The by Virginia Kroll, 1994 Harcourt, 113, 115

Secret Place by Eve Bunting, 1996 Clarion, 107

Seven Blind Mice by Ed Young, 1992 Philomel, 243

Seven Little Rabbits by John Becker, 1992 Turtleback, 191

Seven Silly Eaters, The by Mary Ann Hoberman, 1997 Browndeer, 228

Shadows and Reflections by Tana Hoban, 1990 Greenwillow, 255, 257

She'll Be Comin' Round the Mountain by Tom Birdseye, 1994 Holiday, 197

Shrinking Mouse by Pat Hutchins, 1997 Greenwillow, 89

Skip Across the Ocean: Nursery Rhymes from Around the World by Floella Benjamin, 1995 Orchard, 84

Skip to My Lou by Nadine Bernard Westcott, 1989 Little, 196

Sleep, Baby, Sleep: Lullabies and Night Poems by Michael Hague, 1994 Morrow, 85

Sleep, Sleep, Sleep: A Lullaby for Little Ones Around the World Nancy Van Laan, 1995 Little, 85

Sleepytime Book, The by Jan Wahl, 1992 Tambourine, 9

Snow by Isao Sasaki, 1980 Viking, 205

Snow Is Falling by Franklyn M. Branley, 1986 Turtleback, 204

Snowballs by Lois Ehlert, 1995 Harcourt, 203

Snowman, The by Raymond Briggs, 1986 Random, 142, 205

Snowman Who Went for a Walk, The by Mira Lobe, 1984 Morrow, 205

Somebody Loves You, Mr. Hatch by Eileen Spinelli, 1991 Bradbury, 127, 156

Something Is Going to Happen by Charlotte Zolotow, 1988 Harper, 204

Sometimes I Feel Like a Mouse: A Book About Feelings by Jeanne Modesitt, 1992 Scholastic, 235, 239, 240

Song and Dance Man, The by Karen Ackerman, 1988 Knopf, 156

Songs Are Thoughts: Poems of the Inuit by Neil Philip, 1995 Orchard, 113

Sootface: An Ojibwa Cinderella Story by Robert D. San Souci, 1994 Doubleday, 117

South African Night, A by Rachel Isadora, 1998 Greenwillow, 85

Splash! by Ann Jonas, 1995 Greenwillow, 215

Storm by W. Nikola-Lisa, 1993 Atheneum, 11

Story of Ping, The by Marjorie Flack, 1933 Viking, 75

Subway Sparrow by Leyla Torres, 1993 Farrar, 151, 155

Tale of Peter Rabbit, The by Beatrix Potter, 1893 London, 1986 Scholastic, 193, 207

Tamarindo Puppy, The by Charlotte Pomerantz, 1980 Greenwillow, 154

Ten Little Animals by Laura Jane Coats, 1990 Macmillian, 217

Ten Little Mice by Joyce Dunbar, 1990 Harcourt, 217

Ten Little Rabbits by Virginia Grossman, 1991 Chronicle, 209

Ten, Nine, Eight by Molly Bang, 1983 Penguin, 213

Ten Old Pails by Nicholas Heller, 1994 Greenwillow, 215

There's a COW in the Road! by Reeve Lindbergh, 1993 Dial, 21

There's a Hole in the Bucket by Nadine Bernard Westcott, 1990 Harper, 197

There's a Nightmare in My Closet by Mercer Mayer, 1984 Dial, 249

There's an Alligator Under My Bed by Mercer Mayer, 1987 Dial, 249

There's More . . . Much More by Sue Alexander, 1987 Harcourt, 209

They Put on Masks by Byrd Baylor, 1974 Scribner, 114

Thomas' Snowsuit by Robert Munsch, 1985 Annick, 69, 72

Three Billy Goats Gruff, The by Paul Galdone, 1973 Clarion, 219

Three Hat Day, A by Laura Geringer, 1985 Harper, 29

Three Jovial Huntsmen by Susan Jeffers, 1973 Bradbury, 145

Thunder Cake by Patricia Polacco, 1990 Philomel, 165

Time for Bed by Mem Fox, 1993 Harcourt, 12, 63

Time To . . . by Bruce McMillan, 1989 Lothrop, 69

Time to Sleep by Denise Fleming, 1997 Holt, 133

Tiny Seed, The by Eric Carle, 1987 Scholastic, 193

To Market, To Market by Anne Miranda, 1997 Harcourt, 225

Toad by Ruth Brown, 1996 Dutton, 249

Today Is Monday by Eric Carle, 1993 Philomel, 242

Tomorrow's Alphabet by George Shannon, 1996 Greenwillow, 33

Toot and Puddle by Holly Hobbie, 1997 Little, 177

Tops and Bottoms by Janet Stevens, 1995 Harcourt, 101, 103, 211

Tough Boris by Mem Fox, 1994 Harcourt, 233

Tracks in the Wild by Betsy Bowen, 1993 Little, 187

Train, The by David McPhail, 1977 Little, 45

Train Song by Diane Siebert, 1990 HarperCollins, 46

Trains by Gail Gibbons, 1987 Holiday, 48

Trains by Seymour Reit, 1990 Golden Books, 47

Trains by Anne Rockwell, 1988 Dutton, 48

Turnaround Wind, The by Arnold Lobel, 1988 Harper, 11

Two Bad Ants by Chris Van Allsburg, 1988 Houghton, 209

Umbrella by Taro Yashima, 1958 Viking, 165

Uno, Dos, Tres: One, Two, Three by Pat Mora, 1996 Clarion, 153, 228, 232

Up North in Winter by Deborah Hartley, 1986 Puffin Unicorn, 185, 206

Very Hungry Caterpillar, The by Eric Carle, 1969 Collins World, 20, 241

Wait Till the Moon Is Full by Margaret Wise Brown, 1948 Harper, 63

Watch Out! Big Bro's Coming! by Jez Alborough, 1998 Candlewick, 95

Watch Where You Go by Sally Noll, 1990 Greenwillow, 185

We Had a Picnic This Sunday Past by Jacqueline Woodson, 1998 Hyperion, 41

We're Going on a Bear Hunt by Michael Rosen, 1989 McElderry, 46, 97

We're Making Breakfast for Mother by Shirley Neitzel, 1997 Greenwillow, 3

Wednesday Surprise, The by Eve Bunting, 1989 Clarion, 3

Whales' Song, The by Dyland Sheldon, 1991 Dial, insert

Whales, The by Cynthia Rylant, 1996 Blue Sky, insert

What Do You Do at a Petting Zoo? by Hana Machotka, 1990 Morrow Junior, 23

What do you do with a kangaroo? by Mercer Mayer, 1973 Scholastic, 27

What Neat Feet by Hana Machotka, 1991 Morrow, 21

What's in Fox's Sack? by Paul Galdone, 1982 Clarion, 51

When the Teddy Bears Came by Martin Waddell, 1994 Candlewick, 174

When the Woods Hum by Joanne Ryder, 1991 Morrow Junior, 69

When We Went to the Zoo by Jan Ormerod, 1991 Lothrop, 23

When Winter Comes by Russell Freedman, 1981 Dutton, 204

Where Are You Going, Little Mouse? by Robert Kraus, 1986 Greenwillow, 191

Where the Wild Things Are by Maurice Sendak, 1963 HarperCollins, 126, 247

Whistle for Willie by Ezra Jack Keats, 1964 Viking, 202, 253

Whistling Dixie by Marcia Vaughan, 1995 HarperCollins, 255

Who Sank the Boat? by Pamela Allen, 1982 Coward McCann, 89

Who Took the Farmer's Hat? by Joan L. Nodset, 1963 Harper, 259

Who Uses This? by Margaret Miller, 1990 Greenwillow, 211

Whoever You Are by Mem Fox, 1997 Harcourt, 155

Whose Hat? by Margaret Miller, 1988 Greenwillow, 28, 263

Whose Mouse Are You? by Robert Kraus, 1970 Macmillian, 171

Why Noah Chose the Dove by Isaac Bashevis Singer, 1987 Farrar, 139

Wildflower ABC: An Alphabet of Potato Prints by Diana Pomeroy, Harcourt, 159

Wildlife 1–2–3: A Nature Counting Book, The by Jan Thornhill, 1989 Simon, 109

William's Doll by Charlotte Zolotow, 1972 Harper, 171

Wind Blew, The by Pat Hutchins, 1974 Macmillan, 11

Windy Day, The by G. Brian Karas, 1998 Simon, 11

Wolf Is Coming!, The by Elizabeth MacDonald, 1997 Dutton, 51, 53

Wolf Plays Alone by Dominic Catalano, 1992 Philomel, 145

Young Mouse and Elephant—An East African Folktale by Pamela J. Farris, 1996 Houghton, 89

Index

POETRY

Permissions

References: Jerome C. Harste, *Introducing the Center for Inquiry: Where Learners are Welcome and Come in All Sizes*, Talking Points Winter 1995 (*a quote at the end of the Inquiry Insert*). Ogle, D., *K-W-L: A Teaching model that develops active reading of expository text*, The Reading Teacher 39, 564–570 (*reference to KWHL model in Inquiry Insert*). *Your Baby and Child*, Penelope Leach, 1990, p427 (*a quote in Have You Seen My Duckling?*) Knopf. *The Very Hungry Caterpillar* puppet activity: *Librarians, Seminole County Public Library, Fern Park, Florida.*